T5-DGI-454

Expert Systems
Techniques, Tools and Applications

Edited by
Philip Klahr and Donald A. Waterman
The Rand Corporation

Addison-Wesley Publishing Company

Reading, Massachusetts ▪ Menlo Park, California ▪ Don Mills, Ontario ▪ Wokingham, England ▪ Amstersdam ▪ Sydney ▪ Singapore ▪ Tokyo ▪ Madrid ▪ Bogotá ▪ Santiago ▪ San Juan

Library of Congress Cataloging-in-Publication Data

Klahr, Philip Date
Expert systems.

Includes index.
1. Expert systems (Computer science) I. Waterman, D. A. (Donald Arthur) Date II. Title.
QA76.76.E95K48 1986 006.3'3 85-28595
ISBN 0-201-14186-8

A Rand Corporation Research Study

BCDEFGHIJ-HA-8987

Contributors

Monti D. Callero
The Rand Corporation
Santa Monica, California

Stephanie J. Cammarata
The Rand Corporation
Santa Monica, California

Edison M. Cesar
The Rand Corporation
Santa Monica, California

John W. Ellis, Jr.
The Rand Corporation
Santa Monica, California

William S. Faught
Intellicorp
Mountain View, California

William D. Giarla
The Rand Corporation
Santa Monica, California

Frederick Hayes-Roth
Teknowledge Inc.
Palo Alto, California

Brian M. Jenkins
The Rand Corporation
Santa Monica, California

James R. Kipps
The Rand Corporation
Santa Monica, California

Philip Klahr
The Rand Corporation
Santa Monica, California

David J. McArthur
The Rand Corporation
Santa Monica, California

David Jack Mostow
Rutgers University
New Brunswick, New Jersey

Sanjai Narain
The Rand Corporation
Santa Monica, California

Mark A. Peterson
The Rand Corporation
Santa Monica, California

J. Ross Quinlan
The New South Wales
Institute of Technology,
New South Wales, Australia

Stanley J. Rosenschein
SRI International
Menlo Park, California

Henry A. Sowizral
Schlumberger CAS
Palo Alto, California

Randall Steeb
The Rand Corporation
Santa Monica, California

Scott R. Turner
UCLA
Los Angeles, California

Donald A. Waterman
The Rand Corporation
Santa Monica, California

Robert B. Wesson
Knowledge Engineering Inc.
Austin, Texas

Contents

SECTION THREE

Applications 93

SECTION FOUR

Techniques 269

SECTION ONE

Introduction

This volume collects the most recent papers on artificial intelligence (AI) and expert systems written at The Rand Corporation. Rand's leadership in the field of AI started with the seminal work of Newell, Shaw, and Simon some thirty years ago and continues with recent work in expert systems and knowledge-based simulation. The first chapter in this volume provides a brief historical perspective of Rand's AI activity from its early days in the 1950s to its current efforts. Special attention is given to Rand's research during the past decade.

Chapter 1

Artificial Intelligence: A Rand Perspective

Philip Klahr and Donald A. Waterman

1.1 The Early Years: The Beginnings of Artificial Intelligence

The Rand Corporation played a major role in the early development of artificial intelligence (AI). Of the twenty chapters in the first published book on AI, the 1963 *Computers and Thought* anthology of Feigenbaum and Feldman, six had been previously published as Rand research reports [4,25,80,81,88,114]. Much of this early work in AI was the result of the collaboration of two Rand employees, Allen Newell and Cliff Shaw, and a Rand consultant, Herbert Simon of the Carnegie Institute of Technology (later to become Carnegie-Mellon University).

Beginning in the mid-1950s, Newell, Shaw, and Simon's research on the Logic Theory Machine, their chess playing program, and the General Problem Solver (GPS) defined much of the AI-related research during the first decade of AI. Their work encompassed research areas that are still prominent subfields of artificial intelligence: symbolic processing, heuristic search, problem solving, planning, learning, theorem proving, knowledge representation, and cognitive modeling. At Rand they left a legacy of publications that gave AI many of its building blocks and much of its momentum [71-91,102-104].

This chapter originally appeared as P-7172, The Rand Corporation, January 1986.

It is important to note that this surge of AI activity at Rand did not take place in isolation. It occurred at a time and place where a host of fundamental notions about computer science and technology were being generated. In the 1950s Rand was involved in designing and building one of the first stored-program digital computers, the JOHNNIAC[1] [35]; George Dantzig and his associates were inventing linear programming [15]; Les Ford and Ray Fulkerson were developing techniques for network flow analysis [31]; Richard Bellman was developing his ideas on dynamic programming [6]; Herman Kahn was advancing techniques for Monte Carlo simulation [48]; Lloyd Shapley was revolutionizing game theory [100]; Stephen Kleene was advancing our understanding of finite automata [58]; Alfred Tarski was helping to define a theory of computation [111]; and James Culbertson [13,14] and Alton Householder [45,46] were investigating the relationship between neural nets, learning, and automata.[2]

Within this milieu, Newell, Shaw, and Simon were developing methods and directions for AI research. Perhaps equally important was their development of appropriate computational tools for AI programming. Using the notion of linked-list structures to represent symbolic information, Newell and his associates developed the first symbol-manipulating and list-processing languages, a series of IPL (Information Processing Language) languages that culminated in IPL-V [77,92]. In their 1963 paper [9], Dan Bobrow and Bert Raphael (both of MIT at the time, but also Rand consultants) included IPL-V as one of the earliest and most highly developed list-processing languages.

Because of Rand's unique computing environment and its close ties to the Carnegie Institute of Technology, several Carnegie graduate students were attracted to Rand and several Ph.D. dissertations emerged, including those of Fred Tonge [114,115] and Ed Feigenbaum [24,25]. During the early 1960s, Feigenbaum, in collaboration with Simon, continued to publish Rand reports [26-30,105] describing his experiments with his verbal learning program EPAM. Even after completing his work at Carnegie, Feigenbaum remained a Rand consultant and was highly influential in Rand's research on expert systems and expert systems languages that emerged in the early 1970s. Newell and Simon also were Rand consultants during the 1960s and 1970s. One of their

[1] The JOHNNIAC, named after John von Neumann, a Rand consultant in the late 1940s and early 1950s, was in operation from 1953 to 1966. It was used extensively by Newell, Shaw, and Simon in their work on information processing.

[2] Much of the credit for creating this intellectually stimulating environment belongs to John Davis Williams, who led Rand's Mathematics Department in the 1950s, and also to the United States Air Force for its generous sponsorship of a broad range of research activities.

associates, Don Waterman, joined Rand in the mid-1970s and brought much of their influence on the use of production systems to Rand's first work on expert systems.

But AI also had its share of controversy, at Rand as elsewhere. Given its quick rise to popularity and its ambitious claims [106], AI soon had its critics, and one of the most prominent, Hubert Dreyfus, published his famous critique of AI [20] while he was consulting at Rand. In addition, the early promise of automatic machine translation of text from one language to another (the emphasis at Rand was on translation from Russian to English) produced only modest systems, and the goal of fully automated machine translation was abandoned in the early 1960s.

The research in machine translation did, however, serve to elucidate the difficult problems of automated language understanding and translation. As a result, work in this area turned more toward fundamental and generic issues of linguistic theory, and Rand engaged in over a decade of activity in computational linguistics. By 1967, Rand researchers had produced a wealth of literature (over 140 articles) on linguistic theory and research methods, computational techniques, the English and Russian languages, automatic content analysis, information retrieval, and psycholinguistics [44]. In addition, David Hays produced one of the earliest textbooks on computational linguistics [43].

During the 1960s, Rand provided a center in which natural-language researchers from all over the world could meet, communicate, and collaborate. Special seminar programs and summer symposia (e.g., [59]) provided ample opportunities for researchers to exchange ideas and test theories. Work at Rand during this period included a number of developments: Martin Kay and his associates were working on the MIND system, which focused on research in morphology [52], semantic networks [53,99], and parsing [49-51]; Jane Robinson was developing new syntactic analyzers [94]; Roger Levien and Bill Maron were developing the Relational Data File for information retrieval and question answering [63-65]; Larry Kuhns was developing a sophisticated query language for database inference [60,61]; and, in a somewhat different area, work was beginning on a new theory of "fuzzy sets" [7].

1.2 Human-Oriented Environments

Since its early involvement with the JOHNNIAC in 1953, Rand has continually worked on the development of human-oriented interfaces. Although much of this work has been outside the AI framework, the research has provided interactive computing environments that have made AI systems easier to design, implement, debug, and understand. Today, computational environments appropriate for AI systems comprise a prominent subfield of AI research.

Major milestones in Rand's work on human-oriented environments are JOSS, the Rand Tablet, Videographics, GRAIL, and BIOMOD. Cliff Shaw's JOSS [101], one of the world's first true interactive computing systems, executed interpretively, had execution tracing facilities, could be used to solve mathematical problems with considerable precision, and had a clean, easy-to-learn syntax. These characteristics influenced a number of later programming systems and environments. JOSS has remained a key computing resource at Rand for over 20 years and is still used today.

The Rand Tablet [16] was the first example of a two-dimensional writing surface for computer communication. A capacitative coupling between a stylus and a grid of wires embedded in the tablet provided sufficient accuracy to allow recognition of hand-printed characters approximately ¼-inch high. Entire interactive computing systems, including GRAIL and BIOMOD, were based on use of the Rand Tablet—in fact, the entire GRAIL system was programmed with the Tablet as the sole input device.

The Rand Video Graphic System [116] was one of the first interactive graphics systems to use raster-scan technology. High-resolution video displays were driven from a rotating magnetic disk. At a time when the cost of providing individual self-contained systems was prohibitive, this rapid-response system gave many users simultaneous access to precision computer graphics.

The GRAIL system [21] and its successor BIOMOD [34] pioneered the use of graphic displays and tablets as input-output devices for programming and modeling. GRAIL allowed the direct execution of programs defined by a combination of flowcharts and coding forms, in which each box on a top-level flowchart could itself be defined in terms of another flowchart or (at the lowest level) a coding form. BIOMOD applied these interactive concepts to a major biomedical modeling system, in which transfer equations and other forms of equations describing a dynamic system could be input directly on a displayed form. The results of a simulation defined by these equations could then be viewed graphically in terms of time-history plots of any of the variables (or combinations of them). More than 15 years ago these systems used a sophisticated real-time recognition algorithm for characters hand-printed on a tablet [33]. In addition to these prototype/demonstration systems, a number of studies were conducted, principally by Barry Boehm, on the effects on user productivity of improvements in the speed and dependability of response time of interactive computer systems [96].

In 1972, several people involved in Rand's human-machine interface work, including Keith Uncapher, Tom Ellis, Bob Anderson, and Bob Balzer (who was just beginning to develop some of his ideas on program specification [5]), left Rand to form the University of Southern California's Information Sciences Institute. Anderson returned to Rand the following year and started Rand's work in an area that was to become known as "expert systems."

Rand work on interactive systems in the late 1970s centered on developing UNIX-based tools, such as the Rand Editor [8] and the MH electronic message handler [10], and on research in interactive maps for dynamically displaying geographic information [3]. Map displays continued to play a prominent role in Rand research in the 1980s, particularly the color graphic displays used to depict geographic simulations dynamically.

1.3 Expert Systems

In the early 1970s, Bob Anderson and his associates began directing their attention toward providing aids for inexperienced computer users. The objective was to enable these users to exploit the power of computers, and even to program them, without having to become computer sophisticates. At the same time, Rand researchers were becoming increasingly interested in intelligent terminals and the possibility that such terminals might eventually be developed into powerful individualized computer workstations.

One of the initial goals of these researchers was to develop a simple, English-like language for computer users who were not programmers. Such a language, combined with intelligent terminals, could bring computers to a wide range of potential users by providing an easy-to-use interactive environment in which to work.

The Rand effort was influenced by the work of Ed Feigenbaum (who retained a continuing link to Rand as a consultant) and his associates at Stanford in the early 1970s, particularly in their use of rule-based models in the development of a system that became known as MYCIN. Anderson and his associates were particularly impressed with MYCIN's explanation facilities and its very readable English-like output. MYCIN's input, however, lacked this English-like quality because it had to be programmed in LISP, a high-level language that was much too sophisticated for novice computer users. Therefore, Rand set out to build a language that allowed simple, English-like input as well as output.

That effort resulted in the RITA (Rand Intelligent Terminal Agent) language [1,2].[3] RITA was designed by Rand researchers as a language for developing intelligent interfaces to computer systems. RITA's unique English-like syntax could be read fairly easily by nonprogrammers, and its control mechanism gave RITA programs easy access to the local operating system. The language was used for developing not only interface programs, but also expert systems, an application area to which RITA was not especially well suited. The problems that arose from attempts to develop expert systems in RITA (e.g., slow execution speed and the limited expressiveness of the syntax) led eventually to the development of the ROSIE language.

RITA was used with some success as a tool for heuristic modeling in studies of international terrorism [121]. This work, described in Chapter 4, combined the talents of computer scientists and social scientists in the design of an expert system to aid terrorism researchers in their analysis of terrorist activities. The project precisely defined the basic concepts needed for a model of terrorism and used these concepts in implementing the expert system.

The success of RITA at Rand, combined with a growing interest in rule-based systems in the AI community, led two Rand researchers, Don Waterman and Rick Hayes-Roth, to organize a workshop in 1977 on rule-based systems. The papers presented at the workshop were later published in a book that essentially defined this emerging technology [119].

When Phil Klahr and Stan Rosenschein joined Rand's AI staff in 1978, rule-based systems became a major focus of Rand's AI research. Six Rand researchers specializing in rule-based systems gathered for an intensive two-day workshop to design the next-generation rule-based language. Although RITA had proven to be quite useful, the workshop participants wanted to develop a more sophisticated, more general-purpose, and even more English-like language specifically designed for building expert systems. The result was the first design of ROSIE (Rule-Oriented System for Implementing Expertise) [117]. Rand has since produced several versions of ROSIE, each intended to extend and improve the language [22,39,107]. The most recent version is described in Chapter 2.

ROSIE has been used in the development of several expert systems in a variety of application domains. In one application, described in

[3] Most of Rand's work on expert systems, including RITA, ROSIE, and TATR, was supported by the Defense Advanced Research Projects Agency (DARPA) within its Information Processing Techniques Office.

Chapter 5, Rand researchers developed the Legal Decisionmaking System (LDS), a prototype expert system to assist attorneys and claims adjusters in settling product liability cases [122].[4] This system enabled researchers to explore the feasibility of applying knowledge-engineering techniques to the legal area. The work on legal reasoning, which initially focused on product liability in general, was later narrowed to the analysis and settlement of asbestos cases.

A second noteworthy application of ROSIE was in the area of military planning. As described in Chapter 6, a prototype expert system called TATR was developed to help targeteers select and prioritize airfields and target elements on those airfields [11]. The resulting program contained approximately 400 ROSIE rules.

Another military application of ROSIE was also underway at Rand during the early 1980s. RSAC, the Rand Strategy Assessment Center [18], was designed to provide military strategists with a war-gaming facility.[5] It combines a set of automated programs, or agents, with human teams to model superpower decisionmaking in conflict situations. RSAC used ROSIE to develop and implement the rule-based Scenario Agent, a policy-level model of nonsuperpower behavior [19,95]. The Scenario Agent reacts to a current hypothetical military situation by determining if there is a threat to a nonsuperpower and, if so, specifying actions to take (sending messages, granting overflight rights, changing alignments, etc.). ROSIE also influenced RSAC's development of RAND-ABEL, a C preprocessor that facilitates the encoding of rules and decision tables in a C-based environment [97,98]. RSAC also incorporates other AI techniques, such as scripts and goal-directed search, in its operational framework [109].

As expert systems research grew at Rand and in the AI community, Rick Hayes-Roth, Don Waterman, and Doug Lenat (of Stanford University at the time, but also a Rand consultant) organized a workshop in 1980 on rule-based systems and their application to the development of expert systems. This workshop produced the first comprehensive book on building expert systems [42], which includes a detailed comparison of expert–system-building languages [120]. Expert systems quickly became a prominent subfield of AI research and has provided a new set of tools for application in government and industry. Research in expert systems continues to be a primary focus of Rand's AI research activity.

[4] LDS was funded by Rand's Institute for Civil Justice.

[5] RSAC has been supported by the Director of Net Assessment, Office of the Secretary of Defense.

1.4 Knowledge-Based Simulation

Simulation has become a powerful mechanism for helping humans understand complex phenomena. Results produced by simulations have had substantial impact on a broad range of decisions in the military, government, and industry. Unfortunately, most simulations lack the utility needed for practical applications. Simulations are costly to build, poorly organized, inadequately understood by users, difficult to modify, and poor in performance. Since the early 1960s, Rand has explored and developed techniques to make simulations more useful, understandable, modifiable, credible, and efficient.

Much of Rand's research in simulation methodology in the 1960s revolved around the development of the SIMSCRIPT language [66] and its successor, SIMSCRIPT II [54]. More recently, a research group headed by Phil Klahr has focused on applying artificial intelligence and expert-systems technology to simulation.[6] The goal has been to develop a research environment that helps users build and refine simulations with which to analyze and evaluate various outcomes. The primary result of this work has been ROSS, (Rand Object-oriented Simulation System), an English-like, object-oriented simulation language [67,68]. ROSS, described in Chapter 3, provides a programming environment in which users can conveniently design, test, and modify large knowledge-based simulations of complex mechanisms.

Simulations written in ROSS are expert systems: they embody a human expert's knowledge of the objects that comprise the simulation domain. To build a ROSS simulation, it is necessary to specify the domain objects, their attributes, and their behavioral rules. ROSS has been used to design and build several military simulation systems, including a strategic air battle simulation called SWIRL (discussed briefly in Chapter 3, more thoroughly in [57]) and a tactical ground-based combat simulation called TWIRL [55]. The TWIRL system, described in Chapter 7, simulates a ground combat engagement between two opposing military forces. It includes troop deployment, artillery firing, air interdiction, and electronic communication and jamming. TWIRL was developed to experiment further with the ROSS language and to provide a prototype simulation that could be used to explore issues in electronic combat.

[6] Rand's research on knowledge-based simulation, including work on ROSS, SWIRL, and TWIRL, has been supported by Rand's Project AIR FORCE.

Computerized simulation can be a notoriously expensive tool, consuming huge amounts of computer time on powerful machines. Worse, a simulation may require many runs to adequately sample and explore the simulated system's behavior. However, the speed of almost all simulations can be dramatically increased by exploiting their inherent concurrency. In 1981, Henry Sowizral and Dave Jefferson (then at USC, but a full-time Rand consultant that summer), began investigating the use of parallel processing in simulations. Their effort resulted in the design of a parallel-processing computer architecture called Time Warp, which uses distributed simulation to significantly improve performance.[7] The Time Warp mechanism [47] accelerates a simulation's execution by removing the common restriction that simulated objects must always be synchronized in time.

1.5 Techniques for Expert Systems Development

To be effective, expert systems must contain a substantial amount of domain expertise organized for efficient search. In the late 1970s, Rand began to address issues of acquiring and effectively using such expertise. Research was conducted in a number of areas, such as acquiring knowledge by example, iteratively refining and expanding that knowledge, devising efficient knowledge representations and structures for AI-based systems, and effectively using uncertain and inconsistent knowledge. During this same time period, work in opportunistic planning made extensive use of research in knowledge representation and organizational techniques to develop a cognitive model of planning [37,38].[8]

Rand's exemplary programming project focused on acquiring knowledge by example. The result of this work was the Exemplary Programming (EP) system [23,118], described in Chapter 8, which generates personalized computer programs from examples.[9] These programs can act as interfaces to complex computer systems or as intelligent assistants, freeing users from repeating detailed interactions with

[7] Time Warp research has been supported by Rand's Project AIR FORCE, the System Development Foundation, and Rand corporate funds.

[8] This work was funded by the Office of Naval Research.

[9] EP was supported by the Defense Advanced Research Projects Agency and Rand corporate funds.

applications programs. Writing such programs often cannot be justified because of the large number of programs needed, their personalized nature, and their fast-changing specifications. However, the EP methodology provides quick, easy, and inexpensive methods for creating individualized software of this type.

The acquisition, expansion, and refinement of knowledge was the focus of a Rand project on machine-aided knowledge acquisition [40,41,69]. This project, described in Chapter 9, addressed the transfer of expertise from humans to machines, as well as the functions of planning, debugging, knowledge refinement, and autonomous machine learning. The relative advantages of humans and machines in the building of knowledge-based systems were also considered, along with issues of representing and structuring knowledge efficiently [62].[10]

A primary focus of Rand's research program has been the development of AI technology and its use in problem domains of practical importance. An important concern is the use of uncertain and inconsistent knowledge in expert systems. To study the effectiveness of inference methods under uncertainty, Ross Quinlan developed the INFERNO system [93].[11] This work, described in Chapter 10, documents the methods that today's expert systems use to grapple with inexact but valuable knowledge and suggests a new approach that avoids some of the problems.

Since 1979, Rand has conducted research in the area of distributed artificial intelligence [12,108,110,113,123].[12] Rand researchers have concentrated on developing and testing cooperative behaviors for air fleet control. Their work, described in Chapter 11, involves a network of cooperating expert systems and focuses on cooperative behaviors for plan generation, communication management, role negotiation, and data fusion.

The chapters in this book discuss much, but not all, of Rand's work in AI and expert systems over the last decade. This chapter and the technical chapters that follow give references and pointers to other relevant material. Nevertheless, the work presented here does highlight the major themes of Rand's continuing research on AI and expert systems.

[10] These efforts were supported by a grant from the National Science Foundation.

[11] INFERNO was supported by Rand corporate funds.

[12] Rand's research on distributed problem solving has been supported by the Information Processing Techniques Office of the Defense Advanced Research Projects Agency.

References

1. Anderson, R. H., M. Gallegos, J. J. Gillogly, R. Greenberg, and R. Villanueva, *RITA Reference Manual*, Rand Report R-1808-ARPA, September 1977.
2. Anderson, R. H., and J. J. Gillogly, *Rand Intelligent Terminal Agent (RITA): Design Philosophy*, Rand Report R-1809-ARPA, February 1976.
3. Anderson, R. H., and N. Z. Shapiro, *Design Considerations for a Computer-based Interactive Map Display System*, Rand Report R-2382-ARPA, February 1979.
4. Armer, P., *Attitudes Toward Intelligent Machines*, Rand Paper P-2114-1, May 1962. Also in *Symposium on Bionics*, 1960. Reprinted in *Computers and Thought* (E. A. Feigenbaum and J. Feldman, eds.), McGraw-Hill, New York, 1963, 389–405.
5. Balzer, R. M., *On the Future of Computer Program Specification and Organization*, Rand Report R-622-ARPA, August 1971.
6. Bellman, R. E., *An Introduction to the Theory of Dynamic Programming*, Rand Report R-245, June 1953. Expanded to *Dynamic Programming*, Rand Report R-295, July 1956 (also published by Princeton University Press, 1957).
7. Bellman, R. E., R. E. Kalaba, and L. A. Zadeh, *Abstraction and Pattern Classification*, Rand Memorandum RM-4307-PR, October 1964.
8. Bilofsky, W., *The CRT Text Editor NED—Introduction and Reference Manual*, Rand Report R-2176-ARPA, December 1977.
9. Bobrow, D. G., and B. Raphael, *A Comparison of List-Processing Computer Languages*, Rand Memorandum RM-3842-PR, October 1963. Also in *Communications of the ACM*, 7, 1964, 231-240. Reprinted in *Programming Systems and Languages* (S. Rosen, ed.), McGraw-Hill, New York, 1967, 490-511.
10. Borden, B. S., R. S. Gaines, and N. Z. Shapiro, *The MH Message Handling System: User's Manual*, Rand Report R-2367-AF, November 1979.
11. Callero, M., D. A. Waterman, and J. R. Kipps, *TATR: A Prototype Expert System for Tactical Air Targeting*, Rand Report R-3096-ARPA, August 1984.
12. Cammarata, S., D. McArthur, and R. Steeb, *Strategies of Cooperation in Distributed Problem Solving*, Rand Note N-2031-ARPA, October 1983. Also in *Proceedings of the Eighth Interna-*

tional Joint Conference on Artificial Intelligence, Karlsruhe, West Germany, 1983, 767-770.

13. Culbertson, J. T., *Hypothetical Robots and the Problem of Neuroeconomy*, Rand Paper P-296, April 1952.
14. Culbertson, J. T., *Sense Data in Robots and Organisms*, Rand Paper P-378, May 1953.
15. Dantzig, G. B., *Linear Programming and Extensions*, Rand Report R-366-PR, August 1963. Published by Princeton University Press, 1963. Also see his (and his associates') reports in the series on "Notes on Linear Programming" published at Rand, 1954-1958.
16. Davis, M. R., and T. O. Ellis, *The RAND Tablet: A Man-Machine Graphical Communication Device*, Rand Memorandum RM-4122-ARPA, August 1964. Also in *Proceedings of the Fall Joint Computer Conference*, 26-1, 1964, 325–331.
17. Davis, M., S. Rosenschein, and N. Shapiro, *Prospects and Problems for a General Modeling Methodology*, Rand Note N-1801-RC, June 1982.
18. Davis, P. K., and J. A. Winnefeld, *The Rand Strategy Assessment Center*, Rand Report R-2945-DNA, March 1983.
19. Dewar, J. A., W. Schwabe, and T. L. McNaugher, *Scenario Agent: A Rule-Based Model of Political Behavior for use in Strategic Analysis*, Rand Note N-1781-DNA, January 1982.
20. Dreyfus, H. L., *Alchemy and Artificial Intelligence*, Rand Paper P-3244, December 1965.
21. Ellis, T. O., J. F. Heafner, and W. L. Sibley, *The GRAIL Project: An Experiment in Man-Machine Communications*, Rand Memorandum RM-5999-ARPA, September 1969. See also *The GRAIL Language and Operations*, RM-6001-ARPA, September 1969.
22. Fain, J., D. Gorlin, F. Hayes-Roth, S. Rosenschein, H. Sowizral, and D. Waterman, *The ROSIE Language Reference Manual*, Rand Note N-1647-ARPA, December 1981.
23. Faught, W. S., D. A. Waterman, P. Klahr, S. J. Rosenschein, D. M. Gorlin, and S. J. Tepper, *EP-2: An Exemplary Programming System*, Rand Report R-2411-ARPA, February 1980. A shortened version appears in *Proceedings of the ACM National Conference*, Detroit, 1979, 135–142.
24. Feigenbaum, E. A., *An Information Processing Theory of Verbal Learning*, Rand Paper P-1817, October 1959.

25. Feigenbaum, E. A., *The Simulation of Verbal Learning Behavior*, Rand Paper P-2235, March 1961. Also in *Proceedings of the Western Joint Computer Conference*, 19, 1961, 121-132. Reprinted in *Computers and Thought* (E. A. Feigenbaum and J. Feldman, eds.), McGraw-Hill, New York, 1963, 297–309.

26. Feigenbaum, E. A., *Computer Simulation of Human Behavior*, Rand Paper P-2905, May 1964.

27. Feigenbaum, E. A., and H. A. Simon, *Forgetting in an Association Memory*, Rand Paper P-2311, May 1961. Also in *Proceedings of the ACM National Conference*, 16, 1961, 2C2–2C5.

28. Feigenbaum, E. A., and H. A. Simon, *Performance of a Reading Task by an Elementary Perceiving and Memorizing Program*, Rand Paper P-2358, July 1961. Also in *Behavioral Science*, 8, 1963, 72-76.

29. Feigenbaum, E. A., and H. A. Simon, *A Theory of the Serial Position Effect*, Rand Paper P-2375, July 1961. Also in *British Journal of Psychology*, 53, 1962, 307–320.

30. Feigenbaum, E. A., and H. A. Simon, *Generalization of an Elementary Perceiving and Memorizing Machine*, Rand Paper P-2555, March 1962. Also in *Information Processing 1962, Proceedings of IFIP Congress* (C. M. Popplewell, ed.), North Holland, Amsterdam, 1963.

31. Ford, L. R., Jr., and D. R. Fulkerson, *Flows in Networks*, Rand Report R-375-PR, August 1962. Published by Princeton University Press, 1962. Also see their reports in the series "Notes on Linear Programming" published at Rand, 1954–1958.

32. Goldin, S. E., and P. Klahr, "Learning and Abstraction in Simulation," *Proceedings of the Seventh International Joint Conference on Artificial Intelligence*, Vancouver, 1981, 212–215.

33. Groner, G. F., *Real-Time Recognition of Handprinted Text*, Rand Memorandum RM-5016-ARPA, October 1966. Also in *Proceedings of the Fall Joint Computer Conference*, 1966, 591–601.

34. Groner, G. F., R. L. Clark, R. A. Berman, and E. C. DeLand, *BIOMOD: An Interactive Computer Graphics System for Modeling*, Rand Report R-617-NIH, July 1971.

35. Gruenberger, F. J., *The History of the JOHNNIAC*, Rand Memorandum RM-5654-PR, October 1968.

36. Halliday, M. A. K., *Some Aspects of the Thematic Organization of the English Clause*, Rand Memorandum RM-5224-PR, January 1967.

37. Hayes-Roth, B., and F. Hayes-Roth, *Cognitive Processes in Planning*, Rand Report R-2366-ONR, December 1978. A revised version appears as "A Cognitive Model of Planning," *Cognitive Science*, 3, 1979, 275–310.

38. Hayes-Roth, B., F. Hayes-Roth, S. J. Rosenschein, and S. Cammarata, *Modeling Planning as Incremental, Opportunistic Process*, Rand Note N-1178-ONR, June 1979. Also in *Proceedings of the Sixth International Joint Conference on Artificial Intelligence*, Tokyo, 1979, 375–383.

39. Hayes-Roth, F., D. Gorlin, S. Rosenschein, H. Sowizral, and D. Waterman, *Rationale and Motivation for Rosie*, Rand Note N-1648-ARPA, November 1981.

40. Hayes-Roth, F., P. Klahr, and D. J. Mostow, *Knowledge Acquisition, Knowledge Programming, and Knowledge Refinement*, Rand Report R-2540-NSF, May 1980.

41. Hayes-Roth, F., P. Klahr, and D. J. Mostow, *Advice-Taking and Knowledge Refinement: An Iterative View of Skill Acquisition*, Rand Paper P-6517, July 1980. Also in *Cognitive Skills and Their Acquisition* (J. Anderson, ed.), Lawrence Erlbaum Associates, Hillsdale, N. J., 1981, 231–253.

42. Hayes-Roth, F., D. A. Waterman, and D. B. Lenat (eds.), *Building Expert Systems*, Addison-Wesley, Reading, Mass., 1983.

43. Hays, D. G., *Introduction to Computational Linguistics*, American Elsevier, New York, 1967.

44. Hays, D. G., B. Henisz-Dostert, and M. L. Rapp, *Annotated Bibliography of Rand Publications in Computational Linguistics*, Rand Memorandum RM-3894-3, June 1967.

45. Householder, A. S., *Neural Nets for 'Toad T1'*, Rand Memorandum RM-671, August 1951.

46. Householder, A. S., *Some Notes for Simple Pavlovian Learning*, Rand Memorandum RM-678, September 1951.

47. Jefferson, D., and H. Sowizral, *Fast Concurrent Simulation Using the Time Warp Mechanism, Part I: Local Control*, Rand Note N-1906-AF, December 1982.

48. Kahn, H., *Use of Different Monte Carlo Sampling Techniques*, Rand Paper P-766, November 1955.

49. Kaplan, R. M., *The MIND System: A Grammar-Rule Language*, Rand Memorandum RM-6265/1-PR, April 1970.

50. Kaplan, R. M., *Augmented Transition Networks as Psychological*

Models of Sentence Comprehension, Rand Paper P-4742, November 1971. Also in *Artificial Intelligence*, 3, 1972, 77–100.

51. Kay, M., *Experiments with a Powerful Parser*, Rand Memorandum RM-5452-PR, October 1967.
52. Kay, M., and G. R. Martins, *The MIND System: The Morphological-Analysis Program*, Rand Memorandum RM-6265/2-PR, April 1970.
53. Kay, M., and S. Y. W. Su, *The MIND System: The Structure of the Semantic File*, Rand Memorandum RM-6265/3-PR, June 1970.
54. Kiviat, P. J., R. Villanueva, and H. M. Markowitz, *The SIMSCRIPT II Programming Language*, Rand Report R-460-PR, October 1968. Published by Prentice-Hall, Englewood Cliffs, N. J., 1969.
55. Klahr, P., J. Ellis, W. Giarla, S. Narain, E. Cesar, and S. Turner, *TWIRL: Tactical Warfare in the ROSS Language*, Rand Report R-3158-AF, October 1984.
56. Klahr, P., and W. S. Faught, "Knowledge-Based Simulation," *Proceedings of the First Annual National Conference on Artificial Intelligence*, Palo Alto, 1980, 181–183.
57. Klahr, P., D. McArthur, S. Narain, and E. Best, *SWIRL: Simulating Warfare in the ROSS Language*, Rand Note N-1885-AF, September 1982. A shortened version appears as "SWIRL: An Object-Oriented Air Battle Simulator," *Proceedings of the Second National Conference on Artificial Intelligence*, Pittsburgh, 1982, 331–334.
58. Kleene, S. C., *Representation of Events in Nerve Nets and Finite Automata*, Rand Memorandum RM-704, December 1951. Also in *Annals of Mathematics Studies, 34* (C. E. Shannon and J. McCarthy, eds.), Princeton, 1956, 3–41.
59. Kochen, M., D. M. MacKay, M. E. Maron, M. Scriven, and L. Uhr, *Computers and Comprehension*, Rand Memorandum RM-4065-PR, April 1964.
60. Kuhns, J. L., *Answering Questions by Computer: A Logical Study*, Rand Memorandum RM-5428-PR, December 1967.
61. Kuhns, J. L., *Interrogating a Relational Data File: Remarks on the Admissibility of Input Queries*, Rand Report R-511-PR, November 1970.
62. Lenat, D. B., F. Hayes-Roth, and P. Klahr, *Cognitive Economy*, Rand Note N-1185-NSF, June 1979. A shortened version appears as "Cognitive Economy in Artificial Intelligence Sys-

tems," *Proceedings of the Sixth International Joint Conference on Artificial Intelligence*, Tokyo, 1979, 531–536.

63. Levien, R. E., *Relational Data File: Experience with a System for Propositional Data Storage and Inference Execution*, Rand Memorandum RM-5947-PR, April 1969.

64. Levien, R. E., and M. E. Maron, *Relational Data File: A Tool for Mechanized Inference Execution and Data Retrieval*, Rand Memorandum RM-4793-PR, December 1965.

65. Levien, R. E., and M. E. Maron, *A Computer System for Inference Execution and Data Retrieval*, Rand Memorandum RM-5085-PR, September 1966. Also in *Communications of the ACM*, 10, 1967, 715–721.

66. Markowitz, H. M., J. C. Hausner, and H. W. Karr, *SIMSCRIPT: A Simulation Programming Language*, Rand Memorandum RM-3310-PR, November 1962. Published by Prentice-Hall, Englewood Cliffs, N. J., 1963.

67. McArthur, D., and P. Klahr, *The ROSS Language Manual*, Rand Note N-1854-AF, September 1982 (updated September 1985).

68. McArthur, D., P. Klahr, and S. Narain, *ROSS: An Object-Oriented Language for Constructing Simulations*, Rand Report R-3160-AF, December 1984.

69. Mostow, D. J., and F. Hayes-Roth, *Machine-aided Heuristic Programming: A Paradigm for Knowledge Engineering*, Rand Note N-1007-NSF, February 1979. A shortened version appears as "Operationalizing Heuristics: Some AI Methods for Assisting AI Programming," *Proceedings of the Sixth International Joint Conference on Artificial Intelligence*, Tokyo, 1979, 601–609.

70. Narain, S., D. McArthur, and P. Klahr, "Large-Scale System Development in Several Lisp Environments," *Proceedings of the Eighth International Joint Conference on Artificial Intelligence*, Karlsruhe, West Germany, 1983, 859–861.

71. Newell, A., *The Chess Machine: An Example of Dealing with a Complex Task by Adaptation*, Rand Paper P-620, December 1954. Also in *Proceedings of the Western Joint Computer Conference*, 7, 1955, 101–108.

72. Newell, A., *On Programming a Highly Parallel Machine to be an Intelligent Technician*, Rand Paper P-1946, April 1960. Also in *Proceedings of the Western Joint Computer Conference*, 17, 1960, 267–282.

73. Newell, A., *New Areas of Application of Computers*, Rand Paper P-2142, November 1960. Also in *Datamation*, January 1961.

74. Newell, A., *Some Problems of Basic Organization in Problem-Solving Programs,* Rand Memorandum RM-3283-PR, December 1962. Also in *Proceedings of the Second Conference on Self-Organizing Systems* (M. C. Yovits, G. T. Jacobi, and G. D. Goldstein, eds.), Spartan Books, Washington, D.C., 1962, 393–423.

75. Newell, A., *Learning, Generality and Problem-Solving,* Rand Memorandum RM-3285-1-PR, February 1963. Also in *Information Processing 1962, Proceedings of IFIP Congress* (C. M. Popplewell, ed.), North Holland, Amsterdam, 1963, 407–412.

76. Newell, A., *A Guide to the General Problem-Solver Program GPS-2-2,* Rand Memorandum RM-3337-PR, February 1963.

77. Newell, A. (ed.), *IPL-V Programmers' Reference Manual,* Rand Memorandum RM-3739-RC, June 1963.

78. Newell, A., and J. C. Shaw, *Programming the Logic Theory Machine,* Rand Paper P-954, February 1957. Also in *Proceedings of the Western Joint Computer Conference,* 11, 1957, 230–240.

79. Newell, A., J. C. Shaw, and H. A. Simon, *Problem Solving in Humans and Computers,* Rand Paper P-987, December 1956.

80. Newell, A., J. C. Shaw, and H. A. Simon, *Empirical Explorations of the Logic Theory Machine: A Case Study in Heuristics,* Rand Paper P-951, March 1957. Also in *Proceedings of the Western Joint Computer Conference,* 11, 1957, 218-230. Reprinted in *Computers and Thought* (E. A. Feigenbaum and J. Feldman, eds.), McGraw-Hill, New York, 1963, 109–133.

81. Newell, A., J. C. Shaw, and H. A. Simon, *Chess-Playing Programs and the Problem of Complexity,* Rand Paper P-1319, September 1958. Also in *IBM Journal of Research and Development,* 2, 1958, 320–335. Reprinted in *Computers and Thought* (E. A. Feigenbaum and J. Feldman, eds.), McGraw-Hill, New York, 1963, 39–70.

82. Newell, A., J. C. Shaw, and H. A. Simon, *The Processes of Creative Thinking,* Rand Paper P-1320, January 1959. Also in *Contemporary Approaches to Creative Thinking* (H. E. Gruber, G. Terrell, and M. Wertheimer, eds.), Atherton Press, New York, 1962, 63–119.

83. Newell, A., J. C. Shaw, and H. A. Simon, *Report on a General Problem-Solving Program,* Rand Paper P-1584, February 1959. Also in *Proceedings of the International Conference on Information Processing,* UNESCO, Paris, 1959, 256–264.

84. Newell, A., J. C. Shaw, and H. A. Simon, *A Variety of Intelligent Learning in a General Problem Solver,* Rand Paper P-1742,

July 1959. Also in *Self-Organizing Systems* (M. C. Yovits and S. Cameron, eds.), Pergamon Press, New York, 1960, 153–189.

85. Newell, A., and H. A. Simon, *Current Developments in Complex Information Processing*, Rand Paper P-850, May 1956.

86. Newell, A., and H. A. Simon, *The Logic Theory Machine: A Complex Information Processing System*, Rand Paper P-868, July 1956. Also in *IRE Transactions on Information Theory*, IT-2, 1956, 61–79.

87. Newell, A., and H. A. Simon, *The Simulation of Human Thought*, Rand Paper P-1734, June 1959. Also in *Current Trends in Psychological Theory*, University of Pittsburgh Press, 1961, 152–179.

88. Newell, A., and H. A. Simon, *GPS: A Program That Stimulates Human Thought*, Rand Paper P-2257, April 1961. Also in *Lernende Automaten* (H. Billing, ed.), R. Oldenbourg KG, Munich, 1961, 109-124. Reprinted in *Computers and Thought* (E. A. Feigenbaum and J. Feldman, eds.), McGraw-Hill, New York, 1963, 279–293.

89. Newell, A., and H. A. Simon, *Computer Simulation of Human Thinking*, Rand Paper P-2276, April 1961. Also in *Science*, 134, December 22, 1961, 2011–2017.

90. Newell, A., and H. A. Simon, *Computer Simulation of Human Thinking and Problem Solving*, Rand Paper P-2312, May 1961. Also in *IRE Transactions on Information Theory*, IT-8, 1962, 94-133. Reprinted in *Computers and Automation*, 10, April 1961, and in *Datamation*, June/July 1961.

91. Newell, A., H. A. Simon, and J. C. Shaw, *Elements of a Theory of Human Problem Solving*, Rand Paper P-971, March 1957. Also in *Psychological Review*, 65, 1958, 151–166.

92. Newell, A., and F. M. Tonge, *An Introduction to Information Processing Language V*, Rand Paper P-1929, March 1960. Also in *Communications of the ACM*, 3, 1960, 205-211. Reprinted in *Programming Systems and Languages* (S. Rosen, ed.), McGraw-Hill, New York, 1967, 362–374.

93. Quinlan, J. R., *INFERNO: A Cautious Approach to Uncertain Inference*, Rand Note N-1898-RC, September 1982. Also in *The Computer Journal*, 26, 1983, 255-269.

94. Robinson, J. J., and S. Marks, *PARSE: A System for Automatic Syntactic Analysis of English Text—Parts I & II*, Rand Memorandum RM-4654-PR, September 1965.

95. Schwabe, W., and L. M. Jamison, *A Rule-Based Policy-Level*

Model of Nonsuperpower Behavior in Strategic Conflicts, Rand Report R-2962-DNA, December 1982.

96. Sevin, M. J., B. W. Boehm, and R. A. Watson, *A Study of User Behavior in Problemsolving with an Interactive Computer*, Rand Report R-513-NASA, April 1971.
97. Shapiro, N. Z., H. E. Hall, R. H. Anderson, and M. Lacasse, *The RAND-ABEL Programming Language: History, Rationale, and Design*, Rand Report R-3274-NA, August 1985.
98. Shapiro, N. Z., H. E. Hall, R. H. Anderson, and M. Lacasse, *The RAND-ABEL Programming Language: Reference Manual*, Rand Note N-2367-NA, October 1985.
99. Shapiro, S. C., *The MIND System: A Data Structure for Semantic Information Processing*, Rand Report R-837-PR, August 1971.
100. Shapley, L. S., *Notes on the n-person Game*, The Rand Corporation, 1951–1960.
101. Shaw, J. C., *JOSS: A Designer's View of an Experimental On-Line Computing System*, Rand Paper P-2922, August 1964. Also in *Proceedings of the Fall Joint Computer Conference*, 26-1, 1964, 455-464.
102. Shaw, J. C., A. Newell, H. A. Simon, and T. O. Ellis, *A Command Structure for Complex Information Processing*, Rand Paper P-1277, August 1958. Also in *Proceedings of the Western Joint Computer Conference*, 13, 1958, 119–128.
103. Simon, H. A., *Modeling Human Mental Processes*, Rand Paper P-2221, February 1961. Also in *Proceedings of the Western Joint Computer Conference*, 19, 1961, 111–120.
104. Simon, H. A., *The Heuristic Compiler*, Rand Memorandum RM-3588-PR, May 1963. Also in *Representation and Meaning* (H. A. Simon and L. Siklossy, eds.), Prentice-Hall, Englewood Cliffs, N. J., 1972, 9–43.
105. Simon, H. A., and E. A. Feigenbaum, *Studies in Information Processing Theory: Similarity and Familiarity in Verbal Learning*, Rand Memorandum RM-3979-PR, February 1964.
106. Simon, H. A., and A. Newell, "Heuristic Problem Solving: The Next Advance in Operations Research," *Operations Research*, 6, Jan–Feb, 1958, 1–10.
107. Sowizral, H. A., and J. R. Kipps, *ROSIE: A Programming Environment for Expert Systems*, Rand Report R-3246-ARPA, July 1985.
108. Steeb, R., S. Cammarata, F. A. Hayes-Roth, P. W. Thorn-

dyke, and R. B. Wesson, *Distributed Intelligence for Air Fleet Control*, Rand Report R-2728-ARPA, October 1981.

109. Steeb, R., and J. Gillogly, *Design for an Advanced Red Agent for the Rand Strategy Assessment Center*, Rand Report R-2977-DNA, May 1983.

110. Steeb, R., D. McArthur, S. Cammarata, S. Narain, and W. Giarla, *Distributed Problem Solving for Air Fleet Control: Framework and Implementation*, Rand Note N-2139-ARPA, April 1984.

111. Tarski, A., *A Decision Method for Elementary Algebra and Geometry*, Rand Report R-109, May 1951.

112. Thorndyke, P. W., *Heuristics for Human Knowledge Acquisition from Maps*, Rand Note N-1193-ONR, July 1979. Also in *Proceedings of the Sixth International Joint Conference on Artificial Intelligence*, Tokyo, 1979, 880–883.

113. Thorndyke, P., D. McArthur, and S. Cammarata, *Autopilot: A Distributed Planner for Air Fleet Control*, Rand Note N-1731-ARPA, July 1981. Also in *Proceedings of the Seventh International Joint Conference on Artificial Intelligence*, Vancouver, 1981, 171–177.

114. Tonge, F. M., *Summary of a Heuristic Line Balancing Procedure*, Rand Paper P-1799, September 1959. Also in *Management Science*, 7, 1960, 21-42. Reprinted in *Computers and Thought* (E. A. Feigenbaum and J. Feldman, eds.), McGraw-Hill, New York, 1963, 168–190.

115. Tonge, F. M., *A Heuristic Program for Assembly-Line Balancing*, Rand Paper P-1993, May 1960. Published by Prentice-Hall, Englewood Cliffs, N. J., 1961.

116. Uncapher, K., *The Rand Video Graphic System—An Approach to a General User-Computer Graphic Communication System*, Rand Report R-753-ARPA, April 1971.

117. Waterman, D. A., R. H. Anderson, F. Hayes-Roth, P. Klahr, G. Martins, and S. J. Rosenschein, *Design of a Rule-Oriented System for Implementing Expertise*, Rand Note N-1158-1-ARPA, May 1979.

118. Waterman, D. A., W. S. Faught, P. Klahr, S. J. Rosenschein, and R. Wesson, *Design Issues for Exemplary Programming*, Rand Note N-1484-RC, April 1980. Also in *Automatic Program Construction Techniques* (A. W. Biermann, G. Guiho, and Y. Kodratoff, eds.), MacMillan, New York, 1984, 433–460.

119. Waterman, D. A., and F. Hayes-Roth (eds.), *Pattern-Directed Inference Systems*, Academic Press, New York, 1978.

120. Waterman, D. A., and F. Hayes-Roth, *An Investigation of Tools for Building Expert Systems*, Rand Report R-2818-NSF, June 1982. Also in *Building Expert Systems* (F. Hayes-Roth, D. A. Waterman and D. B. Lenat, eds.), Addison-Wesley, Reading, Mass., 1983, 169–215.

121. Waterman, D. A., and B. Jenkins, *Heuristic Modeling Using Rule-Based Computer Systems*, Rand Paper P-5811, March 1977. Also in *Terrorism: Threat, Reality, Response* (R. H. Kupperman and D. M. Trent, eds.), Hoover Institution Press, Stanford, California, 1979, 285-324.

122. Waterman, D. A., and M. A. Peterson, *Models of Legal Decisionmaking*, Rand Report R-2717-ICJ, 1981. A shortened version appears as "Rule-Based Models of Legal Expertise," *Proceedings of the First Annual National Conference on Artificial Intelligence*, Palo Alto, 1980, 272–275.

123. Wesson, R., F. Hayes-Roth, J. Burge, C. Stasz, and C. Sunshine, *Network Structures for Distributed Situation Assessment*, Rand Report R-2560-ARPA, August 1980. Also in *IEEE Journal of Systems, Man, and Cybernetics*, January 1981.

SECTION TWO

Tools

The papers in this section describe Rand's current work in the area of knowledge-engineering tools, including tools for both expert-system development and knowledge-based simulation.

Chapter 2 describes the design and use of ROSIE, a knowledge-engineering language specifically designed for building expert systems. ROSIE evolved from the RITA language, developed earlier at Rand. ROSIE allows the programmer to describe complex relationships simply and to manipulate them symbolically and deductively. In addition, ROSIE supports network communications and patterned reading and writing to remote systems. It also provides for interactive, compiled, and interpreted computing, with a variety of debugging and programming tools.

Two things make ROSIE particularly noteworthy. First, ROSIE's syntax lets users write executable code that reads very much like English prose. The result is a "readable" language in which complex ideas can be easily expressed. This feature was incorporated in ROSIE to ease the problems associated with mapping domain expertise into formal rules. And second, ROSIE integrates two powerful programming paradigms—rule-based modeling and procedure-oriented computation. By combining these methods, the programmer can define procedures, called *rulesets*, each containing rules that may call other rulesets. Thus ROSIE programs can be organized in much the same way as LISP programs—as sets of nested, recursive subroutines or functions.

Chapter 3 provides an overview of the ROSS language. ROSS is one of the first languages to apply artificial intelligence and expert-systems techniques to the area of simulation. Although only a few research projects attempt to apply AI to simulation, it is clear that simulation can benefit substantially from AI methods. At the same time, simulation can provide an excellent environment for developing new AI techniques. Issues such as knowledge representation, explanation, knowledge acquisition, inference, and human-oriented interfaces are of great concern in simulation. At Rand, knowledge-based simulation has been a main research activity for several years, much of which is an outgrowth of the ROSS work.

ROSS is an object-oriented programming language. It enforces a *message-passing* style of programming in which the system to be modeled is represented as a set of *objects* and their associated *behaviors* (rules for object interaction). Objects communicate by sending messages that cause appropriate behavioral rules to execute. This style of programming is especially suited to simulation since the mechanism or process to be simulated often has a decomposition that maps naturally onto objects, and the real-world interactions between the objects can easily be modeled by object behaviors and object message transmissions.

In addition to describing some of the basic ROSS commands and features, the authors discuss the software, including a sophisticated screen-oriented editor and a color graphics package, that interfaces directly with ROSS. Facilities for browsing among objects and their behaviors are described, along with examples of browsing and editing that use SWIRL, the first large simulation written in ROSS.

Chapter 2

ROSIE: A Programming Environment for Expert Systems

Henry A. Sowizral and James R. Kipps

2.1 Introduction

2.1.1 ■ What Is ROSIE?

ROSIE (Rule-Oriented System for Implementing Expertise) is a programming environment for artificial intelligence (AI) applications. It provides particular support for designing *expert systems,* systems that embody knowledge of a domain and operate with that knowledge.

ROSIE uses a near-English syntax to represent facts and rules. A person unfamiliar with programming languages can read and understand a ROSIE program almost as if it were in English. The design of the ROSIE language rests on the assumption that a restricted subset of English can capture and encode knowledge sufficiently well for a practitioner in the subject area (domain) to read and understand it, and at the same time retain a sufficiently formal structure for mechanical

This chapter originally appeared as R-3246-ARPA, The Rand Corporation, July 1985.

interpretation by the computer. Such a language greatly facilitates communication between the knowledge engineer who must accurately capture relevant expertise and the domain expert whose expertise determines the final system.

An English-like programming language need not capture all of the subtlety and richness of English. Experts in a field tend to develop a shorthand, or jargon, for commonly held concepts or beliefs, which permits them to communicate with one another rapidly and effectively. Jargon also serves as a rather formal notation for expressing domain concepts, and ROSIE allows a notation close to the normal jargon of experts to be used for this purpose. For example, the following rule shows how the language of lawyers maps onto ROSIE[1]:

```
[RULE1:   RESPONSIBILITY FOR USE OF PRODUCT]
     IF   the use of the product (at the time of the plaintiff's loss)²
              is foreseeable,
          and that use is reasonable-and-proper
            or that use is an emergency
            or (there is a description by the defendant of that use
              and that description is improper)
            or there is no description by the defendant of that use,
[THEN]³   assert the defendant is responsible for the product's use.
```

The basic ROSIE rule form, *IF conditions, actions*, represents *prescriptive* expertise, which states what to do in various circumstances, rather than merely stating facts. We refer to facts as *descriptive* knowledge.

2.1.2. ■ What Are Rule-Based Expert Systems?

ROSIE was designed for building systems that reason symbolically. Many such systems incorporate and act on knowledge or expertise that is normally associated with human experts. Human experts know facts, or assertions, about their area of expertise (e.g, medicine, geol-

[1] Modeling legal decision making, a major application of ROSIE, is described in Waterman and Peterson (1981).

[2] Parentheses are used in ROSIE rules to eliminate possible surface-level ambiguities, such as determining which description is modified by a prepositional phrase. This particular set of parentheses specifies that *of the plaintiff's loss* modifies *time* and not *use* (as would be the case were the parentheses excluded). The parenthesized clause following the second *or* serves to group the two enclosed sentences as a singular logical unit.

[3] Square brackets enclose comments in ROSIE.

ogy, the bond market), and they know rules of inference that allow them to reason within that domain. The rules of inference are not guaranteed to produce the desired answer. They are not formal algorithms, but *heuristics*—rules of thumb or appropriate guides to reasoning. We call systems based on an expert's knowledge of a domain *expert systems*.

Rule-based systems provide an appropriate methodology for implementing expert systems. Rules are a natural formalism for capturing expertise, and they have the flexibility required for incremental development. As a problem—or the programmer's perception of it—changes, a rule-based system can be modified or extended gracefully, whereas traditional structured programs often must undergo drastic restructuring to accommodate new models or situations. For example, if the legislature were to pass a number of new laws that affect *the responsibility for the product's use*, we could extend our rule-based legal reasoning system by inserting the new laws as rules and possibly removing old rules or reestablishing precedence among the rules.

Rule-based expert systems[4] contain three main components:

1. A *database* of facts or assertions about some subject matter;
2. A *set of rules* of the form *IF conditions, action* (or *assertion*); and
3. A *monitor* (sometimes called an *inference engine*) that executes a set of rules, given a database. A monitor determines which rules can fire, resolves the conflict if more than one rule can fire, and then executes the chosen rule.

ROSIE supports all three components of a rule-based expert system. Assertions and denials modify a *database* of facts. *Rulesets* group rules into meaningful chunks. The user labels a ruleset with a particular word: either a noun, a comparative verb, or an imperative verb. Each ruleset also has an associated *monitor*. ROSIE provides three different kinds of monitors for controlling the execution of rules within a ruleset: sequential, cyclical, and random monitors. With planned future developments, ROSIE will allow an expert system developer or knowledge engineer to tailor-make monitors. This freedom will give the knowledge engineer tremendous flexibility to create customized control strategies, including monitors that perform forward chaining (deducing consequences from the facts in the database) or backward chaining (goal-directed invocation of rulesets that attempt to prove a

[4] We distinguish *rule-based* expert systems from those based on the predicate calculus or systems of intercommunicating objects. Although a ROSIE user can construct various types of expert systems, to simplify the present discussion we restrict our attention to rule-based systems.

goal by either further invocation of rulesets or directly finding the fact in the database), or mixed initiative strategies that combine both forward and backward chaining.

2.1.3 ■ ROSIE Philosophy and Architecture

ROSIE is a general-purpose tool for writing expert systems. It can support essentially any control strategy and data organization. A well-organized expert system written in ROSIE can represent logic and data in a highly readable form. Such readable code greatly facilitates interaction between the domain expert and the expert system developer.

We chose readability over writability as a major feature of the ROSIE language. The two concepts are by no means equivalent. In fact, as ROSIE moves closer to English, its readability may actually make the language more difficult to write. Negative interference with English (the inability to remember whether a construct is valid ROSIE or valid English) can make writing ROSIE programs difficult. Understanding these trade-offs is an important aspect of the ROSIE research project.

ROSIE provides rich, expressive power for creating and manipulating a database of concepts. It supports

- Adjectives, prepositional phrases, and relative clauses inside descriptions to generate sets of elements;
- Class structures and concepts of set membership and inclusion;
- Both transitive and intransitive verb phrases; and
- String pattern matching, the definition of rulesets and predicates, and other important capabilities.

Recent features include the capacity for a database to be shared by multiple ROSIE programs, the definition of demons (programs that awaken to perform some actions when an event occurs, such as searching the database for a specific proposition), and the introduction of meta-structures to provide ROSIE programs with a self-referential capability (the ability to describe, access, modify, and use linguistic structures).

A particular ROSIE expert system, also referred to as a performance program, consists primarily of the ruleset memory and the active database. The ruleset memory stores the performance program's rules of inference, the *prescriptive* knowledge that provides the system with the intelligence it needs to solve particular problems. The active knowledge base stores the program's *descriptive* knowledge, the facts that specify the particular problem requiring solution and the intermediate conclusions reached by the performance program. In addition, a performance program may use multiple databases, although only one database can be active at any time.

At a minimum, a performance program uses the ruleset memory and the active database. More elaborate programs also incorporate one or more inactive databases. Multiple databases can serve a variety of purposes. For example, they can represent alternative viewpoints concerning a problem. Thus one database might represent the viewpoint of one corporation or superpower, and the other databases might represent other corporations or political regimes. The performance program can switch from database to database, analyze each perspective, and assess the various viewpoints. Alternatively, a knowledge engineer might want to segment knowledge along a functional, structural, or procedural line. For example, a generalized diagnostic system could use the active database to drive its deductive component. One database might hold general diagnostic knowledge, and other databases might contain symptomatic and diagnostic information relevant to a particular subsystem. With the general database active, the system could determine which system subcomponent failed. The system could then activate the relevant subsystem database and continue the diagnosis in a more constrained environment.

2.1.4 ■ Examples

Examples provide a good introduction to ROSIE. Our first example is an expert system fragment that plans a camping trip. The expert system's user provides the weather conditions, the length of stay, and other parameters that describe the outing. The expert system uses this information to choose the equipment, food, and clothing the camper should bring along on the trip. The expert system consists of two parts:

1. The invariant camping knowledge, captured as facts, and
2. The pragmatics of choosing equipment, food, and clothing, captured in rulesets.

We start with some of the facts. The following assertions build a (partial) database of facts:

```
Assert t-shirt is a light layer and
    flannel shirt is a second layer and
    light sweater is a cool third layer and
    heavy sweater is a warm third layer and
    down-jacket is a coat.
```

```
Assert each of the light layer, the second layer, the warm third
     layer and the coat is a piece of clothing (in a layered
     top for winter).
Assert 'Layered clothing is effective against the cold' is a winter
     reason for (any piece of clothing (in a layered top for winter)).
Assert 'Cold nights' is a summer reason for the cool third layer.
```

This set of assertions establishes some important knowledge about camping. Campers know that multiple layers of light or medium-weight clothing provide more protection against the cold than a few pieces of heavy or thick clothing can. Campers also know that layered clothing allows them to regulate heat loss by adding or removing clothing. The assertions establish some of this information. They also include justification for some of the equipment. The first assertion defines the concept of layered clothing and associates a particular piece of clothing with each layer. The second assertion identifies the layer of clothing that a camper should use in winter. The third assertion provides the expert system with a justification for using layered clothing in winter. The fourth assertion provides a rationale for including a light sweater in the clothing list for summer.

This set of assertions also illustrates ROSIE's linguistic constructs. The first assertion shows how ROSIE can group related assertions into one rule, using the *and* conjunction. The second assertion introduces the *each of* iterator. An *each of* iterator causes its surrounding action (in this case, *assert*) to repeat once for each of its terms—an assert using the light layer, another using the second layer, and so on. The third and fourth assertions show some of the complexity that ROSIE can represent.

The second part of the expert system defines the reasoning used to select equipment, food, and clothing for the trip. We capture this knowledge with ROSIE's rulesets. A procedural ruleset illustrates how we define the imperative verb *choose-warm-clothes*:

```
To choose-warm-clothes:
[1]  Let the clothing-list be <>.
[2]  For each piece of clothing (in a layered top for winter), add that piece
     to 'the clothing-list'.
[3]  Assert the winter reason for (any piece of clothing (in a layered top for
     winter)) is preferred.
[4]  Add (a warm pair of pants) to 'the clothing-list'.
[5]  Add (a heavy pair of socks) to 'the clothing-list'.
[6]  Add (the hiking footwear) to 'the clothing-list'.
[7]  Assert the winter-spring reason for the hiking footwear is preferred.
[8]  For each winter accessory, add that accessory to 'the clothing-list'.
```

```
[9]  If the weather will be turning rainy, add (the rain-gear) to 'the clothing-
     list'.
End.
```

A top-level procedure, *produce a checklist*, invokes the *choose-warm-clothing* ruleset as well as other rulesets to create our camping checklist:

```
To produce a checklist:
[1]  Gather constraints.
[2]  Select the month:
        <'NOV', 'DEC', 'JAN', 'FEB'>
          let the season be winter and choose-warm-clothes;
        <'SEP', 'OCT', 'MAR', 'APR'>
          let the season be fall-spring and choose-moderate-clothes;
        Default:
          let the season be summer and choose-cool-clothes.
[3]  Choose-food.
[4]  Choose-equipment.
[5]  Print-checklist.
End.
```

First, *produce a checklist* calls *gather constraints*, a ruleset to determine the type of camping trip and the conditions of the trip. Then, depending on the time of year and anticipated weather conditions, it chooses appropriate clothing, food, and equipment. Finally, it displays the choices and, if necessary, justifies them.

These examples illustrate ROSIE's readability. Later sections of this chapter describe some of ROSIE's major linguistic structures and provide examples of their use. More substantial examples of systems written in ROSIE can be found in Callero et al. (1984), Fain et al. (1982), and Waterman and Peterson (1981).

2.1.5 ■ Historical Perspective

ROSIE has been an ongoing research effort at Rand since 1979. As the language has grown and evolved, we have worked at improving its expressive power without sacrificing its readability, at regularizing its grammar without sacrificing its expressiveness, and at extending its semantics without introducing new complexities.

The historic precursor to ROSIE was the Rand Intelligent Terminal Agent, RITA (Anderson and Gillogly, 1976; Anderson et al., 1977). Influenced by the success of early rule-oriented styles of knowledge representation and the appeal that their English-like explanation facilities had for users, RITA was a first attempt at making rule-based programming languages easier to use and understand. Production rules in

RITA were defined using an English-like syntax with a restricted set of options. RITA's database consisted of object/attribute/value triples. Its monitors allowed either pattern-directed control (forward chaining) or goal-directed control (backward chaining). Although its syntactic and expressive power was limited, RITA showed that a stylized form of English could describe procedural knowledge in rule-based languages.

The preliminary ROSIE design (Waterman et al., 1979) was proposed as a logical extension of RITA. The proposal outlined the deficiencies in RITA and described how they might be overcome. RITA was developed in the C programming language on a PDP 11/45 minicomputer. This limited environment severely restricted RITA's design. To circumvent the problem of RITA's inability to scope rules, ROSIE introduced the concept of *rulesets*.

ROSIE was initially developed using Interlisp on a DECSYSTEM-20. The implementers of early versions of ROSIE adopted several of RITA's best features, such as its input–output (I/O) pattern matcher. They also extended RITA's expressiveness and semantics. By 1981, the ROSIE design was relatively stable, and we began developing in-house applications. We also distributed copies of ROSIE (Version 1.0) to sites outside of Rand.

The first released version of ROSIE included direct support for many special-purpose operations. These were hardwired into ROSIE's grammar, as they are in other programming languages, because they did not fit into ROSIE's general linguistic structure. Some operations required special arguments, and others performed actions that were considered expedient in a programming language.[5] As the number of special-action verbs began multiplying, the grammar grew increasingly complex, and the need to simplify (or orthogonalize) became apparent. Examples of orthogonalization are the removal of the distinction between system-defined and user-defined operations, and the introduction of new data elements (i.e, *patterns*) to eliminate the need for special arguments.

The ROSIE system eventually outgrew the capacity of the DECSYSTEM-20, and in 1982, the development moved to VAX-Interlisp on a VAX 11/780 and Interlisp-D on the Xerox SIP 1100 (Dolphin). In 1983, we distributed ROSIE (Version 2.3) and began simplifying the language, expanding its functionality, and improving its performance. Two parallel efforts since that time have been the porting of ROSIE to

[5] These operations included large-grained database operations (*dump, activate, clear, deactivate,* etc.), I/O operations (*open, close, send, read,* etc.), utility operations (*dir, type, delete, copy, parse, build, load,* etc.), and other miscellaneous operations.

Portable Standard Lisp (PSL) and the development of a ROSIE compiler in C. We have also examined the needs of ROSIE users and added several new concepts, including *meta-elements, shared databases,* and *demons.*

We are currently examining ways of turning ROSIE into its own meta-language and optimizing the resulting code. Future releases of ROSIE will retain the strong features of the current ROSIE while extending the language's expressiveness and power.

2.2 The ROSIE Language

We have pursued several different objectives in designing the ROSIE environment. Our primary goal has been to create a language that encourages writing very readable code. To achieve this, we adopted two design criteria: minimality and completeness. These criteria embody two ordinarily competing qualities. Minimality argues against redundancy and verbosity, whereas completeness requires broad coverage of English-language structures. The net result is a language that serves as a general programming language for a very large range of tasks. It does not, however, make any particular kind of programming task trivial (contrary to what might be expected from a language designed specifically for a narrow class of problem-solving tasks).

We have used natural English as our guide when possible. Of course, English has many features that resist translation into precise computational interpretations. Nevertheless, we have given reasonable and relatively natural interpretations to a large number of complex linguistic constructs such as prepositional phrases, relative clauses, and sequences of adjectives. ROSIE recognizes and treats specially many English function words, such as articles, quantifiers, prepositions, and auxiliary verbs. ROSIE cannot distinguish content words, such as nouns and adverbs, however, because it does not understand their meaning. ROSIE has only a superficial knowledge of English, so the user has responsibility for ensuring the appropriate application of the surface language to support the desired semantic interpretations.

In our attempt to achieve maximal readability, we have replaced some anachronistic forms of programming diction. Most important, we replaced "If *condition* then *action* else *alternate-action*" with "If *condition, action,* otherwise *alternate-action.*" Those familiar with computer languages, and rule-based programming languages in particular, may initially find this design choice problematic. However, this return to proper English conforms to the principal design heuristic behind ROSIE: Let English be your model.

We divide our discussion of the ROSIE language into two areas. First, we describe ROSIE's fundamental structures—its lowest-level representations for knowledge. Second, we describe ROSIE's linguistic structures—the expressive qualities of the language.

2.2.1 ■ Fundamental Representational Structures

A knowledge engineer uses ROSIE's fundamental structures to represent a domain expert's knowledge. These structures combine with one another to form more complex structures. Ultimately, they are stored in databases and rulesets. As mentioned earlier, databases store descriptive knowledge, and rulesets store prescriptive or procedural knowledge. ROSIE represents descriptive knowledge as a set of primitive propositions in a database. The propositions might include the initial conditions of the problem, intermediate inferences drawn in the course of the expert system's computation, and final conclusions. ROSIE represents prescriptive knowledge by means of rulesets that consist of a monitor and a set of rules. The prescriptive knowledge describes how to solve a problem, given some facts. Each ROSIE-based expert system consists of one or more databases and one or more rulesets.

ROSIE uses its fundamental structures to store both types of knowledge. Though a ROSIE programmer creates both descriptive and prescriptive structures when programming, the program can manipulate only descriptive structures. ROSIE performance programs cannot yet access, modify, or generate new prescriptive information (i.e., rules).

ROSIE's fundamental structures include *basic elements, basic relational forms, meta-elements (propositions, intentional descriptions, intentional actions), databases, shared databases, rulesets, demons,* and *monitors.*

Basic Elements

ROSIE's elements define its space of concepts. These elements—ROSIE's data types—include *names, strings, numbers, tuples, class elements,* and *patterns.*

The *name* element allows ROSIE programs to represent literal names consisting of one or more words, for example, *John, Ship #3,* and *Tom Jones.* Multiword names provide a knowledge engineer with considerable flexibility in naming objects and concepts.

The *string* is a sequence of characters delimited by quotation marks (i.e., double quotes). Strings distinguish between upper- and lower-case characters and allow a greater range of expression than ROSIE's other elements. ROSIE provides operators, such as substring and concatenation, for manipulating strings.

ROSIE supports three types of *number* elements: simple numbers, unit constants, and labeled constants. A simple number is the familiar data type found in most programming languages—an integer or floating point number, such as *10* or *2.718,* with no units or labels. Unit constants and labeled constants, on the other hand, are more complex and are unique to ROSIE. A unit constant is a number followed by some composite units of measure, which can be combined under multiplication, division, or exponentiation. ROSIE carries the units along in computation and correctly manipulates them. For example,

```
Display 88 KM/HR * .625 M/KM.
    55.0 M/HR
Display 9.8 M/KG*SEC ↑ 2 * 5 KG.
    49 M/SEC ↑ 2
```

A labeled constant is a number prefixed by an arbitrary number of tokens, called a label. For example,

```
probability .4
time frame 19
```

are both labeled constants. Units and labels improve the expressiveness and readability of numeric computations. This capacity enhances the representational power of numbers, making their occurrence in ROSIE code meaningful.

The *tuple* combines a list of elements into a single structure. Any member of the ordered tuple can be of any element type including another tuple. For example,

```
<Raoul Wright, "Are you sure?", 2.4 children/family>
<matrix, <2, 3, 1>, <1, 3, 4>, <3, 3, 5>>
```

The *class element* specifies an entire set of elements. It is specified by a ROSIE description indicating which elements belong to the class. For example,

```
any number
any man whose father is ugly
any child where that child does wear sneakers
```

The *pattern* was formerly a special ROSIE construct available only for input–output (I/O) and matching operations. But in an effort to simplify and clarify the language, we promoted patterns to full element status. They remain the key construct underlying I/O and string manipulation. In addition, a user may now assert them and thereby put them into the database or pass them as arguments to rulesets.

TABLE 2.1 Examples of ROSIE Patterns.

<table>
<tr><th>Pattern</th><th>Matching String</th></tr>
<tr><td>{anything, "Fred", anything, end}</td><td>I know Freddy Smith
Freddy can't come
Fred</td></tr>
<tr><td>{something, "Tina", anything, "k"}</td><td>My Tinak
Tiny Tina can blink</td></tr>
<tr><td>{3 or more letters,
{":"|";"|","}, 1 blank,
1 or more numbers, return}</td><td>file: 1245<carriage-return>
los angeles, 90025<carriage-return></td></tr>
</table>

A pattern is a sequence of subpatterns enclosed in braces and separated by commas. Each subpattern in turn represents a restriction on the successive portions of the text string. The pattern either generates a string or matches against a string. For example, the subpattern *3 blanks* represents a sequence of three blank characters, and the subpattern *one or more numbers* represents a sequence of one or more numeric digits. To help illustrate the underlying concepts some samples of patterns are shown in Table 2.1.[6]

Besides the standard types of elements, more unusual elements, such as propositions, intentional descriptions, and intentional actions, which we call *meta-elements,* are also supported. Meta-elements extend the kinds of knowledge that can be expressed, represented, and manipulated. Though meta-elements are elements, and thus descriptive in nature, they capture intents rather than fixed quantities. Before we can discuss propositions, the first of the three meta-elements, we must introduce ROSIE's basic relational forms.

Basic Relational Forms

ROSIE relies on five basic relational forms to denote *class membership, predication, predicate complements, transitive verbs,* and *intransitive verbs.* The basic forms and an example of each follow:

element *is a* class-noun
    Australia II is a vessel

element *is* adjective
    Australia II is seaworthy

[6] The first pattern uses the keyword *anything,* which matches zero or more characters. The second pattern uses the keyword *something,* which matches one or more characters.

element *is* predicate-complement element
  Australia II is slightly underpowered

element *does* verb
  Australia II does float

element *does* verb element
  Martin does sail Australia II

We may also negate each relational form (for example, *Australia II is not seaworthy*), and we may include tense (for example, *Australia II was seaworthy*). Tense information creates a separate and distinct relational form; for example, *is a man* is independent of *was a man*. The "*is a* class-noun," "*is* adjective," and "*does* verb" relational forms all specify unary relationships. The "*is* predicate-complement element" and "*does* verb element" relational forms specify binary relationships.

We can extend the number of elements in a relationship by appending prepositional phrases, as in

```
Australia II is moored in Newport for the race
Australia II is rapidly drifting toward shore
Australia II does not have favor with Mr. Connors
```

The primitive relational forms provide the core for *propositions*.

Propositions

A proposition captures a basic relation as an element. ROSIE delimits a proposition by enclosing it in single quotation marks. For example,

```
'John Smith was late for work'
'Martin Scheider did punish Bill Mark in class'
'7 is a prime'
```

Since ROSIE permits a performance program to access, manipulate, and relate elements, propositions permit a knowledge engineer to operate with basic relations. For example, we can use the proposition *'Warren is interested in T-bills'* as an element in an assertion about a bank's belief system:

```
Midbank does believe 'Warren is interested in T-bills'
```

With this assertion in a database, a performance program can now access and manipulate this belief in a variety of ways. For example,

```
If the bank does believe any thing,
      consider that thing as unreliable.
Assert every proposition that Midbank does believe
```

The proposition provides a powerful capability to extend the range of problems ROSIE can handle. We demonstrate another aspect of the power that propositions provide by writing in ROSIE an inference engine that uses propositions to represent rules in a database. Rules 4 and 7, taken from an animal classification system, exemplify this:

```
[RULE 4]  Let the consequent of a new rule be 'animal is a bird'
            and assert each of 'animal does fly'
              and 'animal does lay eggs'
            is an antecedent of that rule.
[RULE 7]  Let the consequent of a new rule be 'animal is an ungulate'
            and assert each of 'animal is a mammal'
              and 'animal does have hoofs'
            is an antecedent of that rule.
```

The two assertions[7] not only encode the animal classification knowledge, but they also construct a meta-language that we can exploit in writing inference engines. Specifically, they provide a language that permits us to access the antecedent and the consequent of a rule independently.

Our illustrative inference engine provides a mixed-initiative inference capability. In this type of inference engine, we separate knowledge into facts and goals. We have a solution when we can infer the goals from the facts. The inference engine can use the rules in the database to chain forward from facts and backward from goals. It identifies all the rules that can fire in either the forward or backward direction, then discriminates among them to choose the next rule to apply. If it prefers one rule over all the others, it applies that rule; otherwise it stops. The top-level loop of our inference engine is

```
To infer:
Execute cyclically.
[1]  Discriminate among every rule that is capable of firing.
[2]  If there is a preferred rule, apply that rule.
End.
```

The *infer* ruleset uses a number of subsidiary rulesets. One, a predicate named *is capable of firing*, decides if a rule can fire by checking its antecedents against the fact space and the rule's consequents against the goal space. If all the rule's antecedents match the fact space or all of its consequents match the goal space, the rule can fire. The ruleset's code follows:

```
To decide a candidaterule is capable of firing:
[1]  If every antecedent of the candidaterule is a fact, assert the candidate-
     rule is chaining forward and conclude true.
```

[7] The *let* construct provides a variant method for asserting information into ROSIE's database.

```
[2] If every consequent of the candidaterule is a hypothesis, assert the can-
    didaterule is chaining backward and conclude true.
[3] Conclude false.
End.
```

After *infer* identifies all the rules that can fire, it selects the rule that is most preferred.[8] The *infer* ruleset presents the candidate rules for firing to *discriminate* one at a time. Thus, *discriminate* must decide between only the current most-preferred rule and the newest rule under consideration. The code for *discriminate* is

```
To discriminate among a newrule:
[1] If there is a preferred rule, if the newrule is preferable to that rule, deny
    that rule is preferred and assert the newrule is preferred, otherwise as-
    sert the newrule is preferred.
End.
```

Intentional Descriptions

An *intentional description* is an implicit reference to a class of elements. ROSIE descriptions (discussed later) are normally used in conjunction with a determiner or quantifier to immediately access one, some, or every member of a class of elements. Intentional descriptions provide a mechanism by which this access process can be suspended. In a sense, intentional descriptions act as pointers to element sets, serving a function similar to that of call-by-name in ALGOL.

Intentional descriptions take the form of a description prefixed by a determiner and delimited with single quotes, such as,

```
'the equipment list'
'a command'
```

Intentional descriptions permit knowledge engineers to represent and relate indefinite elements (e.g., *a plan, a target, a counter*) and generic concepts (e.g., *the product's use, the blue side, the clothing list*).[9] The explicit elements referenced by an intentional description may or may not exist (i.e., the set of elements described may be null).

[8] In our case, we choose forward chaining over backward chaining and lower-numbered rules over those with larger rule numbers. However, by changing the *is preferable to* predicate, *infer* can use another criterion for choosing a rule.

[9] ROSIE's indefinite article was an early attempt to provide such a facility. An indefinite description (e.g., *a truck*), when used for the first time, would add the relation *TRUCK #1 is a truck* to the database. Thereafter, *the truck* would evaluate to *TRUCK #1*. Although this technique proved adequate for many cases, attempting to represent multiple indefinite trucks led to difficulties. Although multiple instances could be asserted in the database, it was not possible to control how the different indefinite relations were used.

The set elements referenced by an intentional description can be accessed via the phrase *instance of*. Thus, *the instance of 'the clothing list'* might produce the tuple <*PARKA, HAT, T-SHIRT*>, while *every instance of 'a target at any airfield'* might produce *RUNWAY, MUNITIONS SOFT, POL SOFT,* and *MUNITIONS ASSEMBLY AREA.*

The call-by-name facility in ROSIE permits rulesets to affect global relationships specified by an intentional description. As an illustration, consider providing a generic facility to add elements to an existing set. The ROSIE rule

```
If the weather will be turning rainy,
    add (the rain-gear) to 'the clothing list'.
```

uses the intentional description *'the clothing list'* as an implicit reference to a tuple of elements. The *add* routine

```
To add an item to a list:
[1] Let the instance of the list be the concatenation of (the instance of the
    list) with <the item>.
End.
```

then accesses the explicit instance of that tuple and modifies it to include a new item.

Intentional Actions

The last meta-element, the *intentional action,* enables a knowledge engineer to represent an unexecuted action in the database and then perform that action at a later time. Intentional actions provide the raw material necessary to build systems that make plans and then execute those plans. Intentional actions also provide the raw material for building rudimentary simulations.

An intentional action suspends the invocation of an imperative verb. A possible invocation of the imperative verb *move* is

```
Move USS Nimitz from Le Havre to New York.
```

However, if this statement is used as an intentional action (i.e., is delimited by single quotes, as in *'Move USS Nimitz from Le Havre to New York'*), the intended maneuver is suspended, and the knowledge engineer can use it in a relationship. The knowledge engineer could, for example, store it in the database by using the following:

```
Assert 'Move USS Nimitz from Le Havre to New York' is an action for time
    100.
```

Later the performance program could evaluate the intentional action by using the action

```
Evaluate every action for time 100.
```

The meta-elements—proposition, intentional description, and intentional action—represent three of ROSIE's linguistic structures. Given a proposition, a ROSIE program can assert it into the database, remove it from the database, or test for its presence in the database. The intentional description stores an unevaluated description or access operator. That description can represent an indefinite concept or a particular relationship in the database. A ruleset can use intentional descriptions to change or retrieve the elements associated with a particular relationship in the database and to direct other rulesets to the same relationship. The intentional action stores an unevaluated imperative. Access to unevaluated actions permits ROSIE programs to plan, capture intended actions, and then later perform those actions.

Databases

ROSIE uses its database to store facts about the world and intermediate computational results. These facts and intermediate results must be *propositions,* which are stored using a three-valued logic system. ROSIE may store a proposition in the database as true or as false, or the database may not contain that proposition at all (which ROSIE interprets as indeterminate). The three-valued logic provides ROSIE with an *open-world assumption,* which implies that ROSIE may not have complete information about a particular situation and will not infer truth or falsity from the absence of a relevant proposition.

The user adds to the database by asserting new propositions or by defining particular values for named elements:

```
Assert Australia II is a vessel.
Let the vessel be Australia II.
Assert Australia II is not a loser.
```

ROSIE provides only limited support for handling contradictions. If the user asserts *Australia II is a vessel* and then asserts *Australia II is not a vessel,* a simple contradiction occurs. Only the latter of the two assertions will appear in the database. ROSIE stores propositions as a basic relationship with an attached truth value—a proposition is either provably true, provably false, or it does not exist in the database.

Asserting the negation of a proposition only changes its truth value. The user must deny the proposition to remove it from the database:

```
Deny Australia II is a vessel.
```

Conditionals allow users to check a database for the truth or falsity of a proposition:

```
If Australia II is a vessel, ...
```

The database plays a central role in ROSIE. Every assertion results in a database store command, and most conditions require testing the database. By modularizing the database in the design of ROSIE, we have laid the groundwork for independent system improvements. In particular, advances in database technology may ultimately feed into future implementations of ROSIE systems.

Most expert systems written in ROSIE contain more than a single database. The standard database in ROSIE is named Global. For complex applications, the user may activate other databases and operate on propositions stored within them. Users with very large databases may be able to modularize them and separately dump, restore, and activate each portion as needed. Multiple databases may also function to maintain separate contexts, or worlds, for hypothetical reasoning.

Special system rulesets have been written to simplify testing, adding, and removing propositions to designated databases. The following example illustrates some of these concepts:

```
Add 'US inflation rate is too high' to European viewpoint.
Add 'European opinion is unnecessarily negative about US economy' to US
    viewpoint.
If 'US inflation rate is too high' is true in European viewpoint and the US's
    inflation rate > 12 percent, remove 'European opinion is unnecessarily
    negative about US economy' from US viewpoint.
```

This example refers implicitly to the Global database and explicitly to the *US viewpoint* and *European viewpoint* databases.

Shared Databases

Distributed expert systems, also called distributed heuristic agents (Sowizral, 1983), consist of multiple expert systems that consult with one another to solve a common problem. ROSIE provides support for building such systems with a mechanism called *shared databases.*[10]

A shared database acts like a normal database: It stores relationships; it allows a program to make assertions, denials, and conditional tests; and it may be active or inactive. But beyond these expected activities, a shared database links the heuristic agents that share it. Like the blackboard model of HEARSAY-II (Erman and Lesser, 1975), a shared database provides a common, consistent, but changing scratchpad for use by multiple agents. Unlike the blackboard model, agents can concurrently access and modify a shared database, and, also unlike the blackboard model, only those objects sharing a particular database have access to it.

[10] The shared-database facility exists for only the Xerox SIP 1100 version of ROSIE, not the VAX-Interlisp version.

ROSIE ensures that each agent sharing a database has exactly the same information as any other agent sharing that database. A change made to a shared database by one agent is visible to all the other sharing agents. ROSIE does not ensure that each agent has identical information at all times, but rather that each agent's shared database experiences the same changes in exactly the same order that the other agents experience. All agents do not see a particular change at the same time, nor is the elapsed time between any two changes at one agent necessarily equal to the elapsed time between the same two changes at some other agent. Nevertheless, all the agents receive the same set of stimuli in the same order and in roughly the same time frame, so it is quite easy for a knowledge engineer to write deadlock-free code.

The shared-database facility hides the many vagaries of distributed programming from the knowledge engineers. They can develop distributed heuristic agents without worrying about concurrency issues such as the arbitration of concurrent updates to the shared database, ensuring reliable communications, and global consistency. The shared-database facility provides knowledge engineers with an effective mechanism for writing distributed heuristic agents, and, when used in conjunction with the demon facility (described in a later section), for constructing fairly intricate control structures with little difficulty.

Description. A shared database has a name that identifies it globally. An agent can turn a database into a shared database by executing

```
SHARE DATA IN database-name.
```

The database may or may not contain information. If no shared database with that name exists in the system, then the contents of the database become the initial contents for the shared database. If the system already contains a shared database with that name, however, this agent simply joins that community and receives a copy of that shared database. In the process, the agent loses whatever it had in its database at the time it invoked the "share data in" action.

An agent can stop sharing a database by executing

```
LOCALIZE DATA IN database-name.
```

After this action executes, the specified database no longer shares its contents with other agents in the system. It retains all the information it contained at the time the agent localized it, and any changes to it will not affect the shared database with the same name; likewise, changes to the shared database will not affect the now-local database.

The remaining shared-knowledge-base operations are identical to the operations permitted on a normal database. A knowledge engineer can assert sentences, deny sentences, and test sentences against the knowledge base. The assertion or denial of a sentence completes immediately; however, because a modification is sequenced globally, the change caused by it may not appear until some time in the future. Tests against the database return a value immediately.

An agent can have more than one shared database. An agent can share one of its databases with one set of agents, another database with another set of agents, and so on. In a sense, agents can belong to multiple committees that interact with one another using a semipublic forum. At one extreme, all agents can share one common database. At the other, two agents can interact privately by sharing a database between just themselves.

Architectures for Interacting Heuristic Agents. We have written several systems of distributed heuristic agents using shared knowledge bases. Among those systems are an intelligent secretary, a concurrent search and rescue scenario, and an adaptive route-planning system. The shared-database facility proved more than adequate for communicating among agents. Shared databases provide large latitude for decomposing and organizing complex problems into concurrent, cooperating tasks.

Information fusion presents one problem area for which ROSIE's shared-database facility can provide a possible architecture. For example, several data-concentrator expert systems could analyze the raw data that come into the system, identify items of interest, and report these findings to the integrator expert system through the shared database. The data concentrator reduces the volume of information to a manageable level. The integrator sees only the interesting information, but from a much broader perspective. The integrator may perform the required computation by itself, or it may also serve as a concentrator for a higher-level integrator.

Committee problem solving provides another area of interest for using multiple heuristic agents and ROSIE's shared-database facility. The database acts as the committee meeting room. The various agents place approaches, comments, and solutions in the shared database. This common knowledge then drives their individual attempts to solve the problem before them.

Yet another use for ROSIE's shared databases is to permit a knowledge engineer to connect existing expert systems into a conglomerate system. For example, we might have several expert systems that solve problems only in their narrow specialty. Instead of combining them into one monolithic expert system, we can coordinate their concurrent execution with a fourth expert system. That new expert system would then interact with the end user, translate the information the user provides into a form suitable for use by the expert systems, and translate the requests presented by those expert systems into queries for the end user.

Rulesets

One of the many features that distinguish ROSIE from other rule-based languages is its facility for rule subroutining. A ROSIE user can control the applicability and context of rules by organizing them into logical units called *rulesets*. ROSIE provides the user with three different kinds of rulesets for modularizing a program: *procedure*, *generator*, and *predicate* rulesets. Each serves a different function; each is invoked differently; each returns differently.

An example of a procedural ruleset is

```
To move a vessel from a source to a destination:
[1] Deny the vessel is docked at the source.
[2] Assert the vessel is docked at the destination.
End.
```

This ruleset essentially updates the database when it is invoked by a statement such as

```
Move USS Nimitz from Le Havre to Auckland.
```

Generator rulesets produce either a single value or all the members of some class. References to generators within ROSIE rules cannot be distinguished from references to the database elements. Thus, someone who reads ROSIE code is unaware of what produces a particular element or set of elements. An example of a generator ruleset is

```
To generate a vessel:
[1] Produce every moveable object at every port.
[2] Produce every moveable object under sail.
[3] Produce every steamship.
End.
```

This ruleset would be invoked by a statement such as

```
Display every vessel.
```

Predicate rulesets provide a means for determining the truth or falsity of any ROSIE primitive sentence through direct computation. When ROSIE tests a proposition against the database and the result is indeterminate, it invisibly invokes the corresponding predicate ruleset, if such a ruleset exists. The predicate ruleset can conclude true or false, or it can simply return and thus imply an indeterminate value. An example predicate ruleset is

```
To decide a vessel is seaworthy:
[1]  If the vessel does float, conclude true.
[2]  If the vessel does leak, conclude false.
End.
```

This ruleset would be invoked by a statement such as

```
If Australia II is seaworthy,
     move Australia II from Sydney to Newport.
```

Each ruleset type corresponds to a particular word class: generators correspond to nouns, procedures to imperative verbs, and predicates to comparative verbs. Rulesets allow domain words to be defined operationally in whatever fashion the knowledge engineer chooses, and only as precisely as necessary.

ROSIE users may also define system rulesets, which permit programmers to include Interlisp code in their ROSIE system. System rulesets may not call ROSIE rulesets, so they serve mainly to provide access to system parameters such as time of day, date, or other important information that ROSIE does not provide directly.

Demons

The word *demon* has come to have a specialized meaning in programming: It refers to a program (or ruleset) that lies dormant until a particular condition occurs, then is activated and takes some action. The ROSIE system samples changes to the database at key stages in the execution of a program. When a test or change occurs that meets a demon's condition for awakening, that demon becomes active. Demons can be used, for example, for tracing and debugging during program development, and for checking database consistency as the database undergoes changes.

The demon facility in ROSIE lets a knowledge engineer selectively capture control during the course of a performance program's execution. Demons cannot take control of a computation haphazardly; they get invoked at precise points. In ROSIE, they are invoked before

1. A proposition is asserted, denied, or tested against the database;
2. The database starts generating any elements from a description;
3. Each element gets produced by a generator matching a description; and
4. An imperative verb is invoked.

These points in the ROSIE operating cycle define four classes of demons.

A demon can decide whether or not the operation it preempted should occur. It can exit by using a *return* statement and thus prevent the completion of an operation, or it can exit by using *continue*, which causes the preempted operation to be completed.

Demons do not capture all assertions, denials, and so forth. Rather, they capture all assertions, denials, or operations that match their defining forms. Thus a knowledge engineer may selectively intercept the assertion of an *is a man* relation or the testing of an *a person1 does love a person2* relation. A knowledge engineer can exercise precise control over the relations in the database and thus ensure its consistency. For example, the following demon checks the age of any person we want to define as a man:

```
Before asserting a person is a man:
[1]  If the person's age is greater than or equal to 21, continue.
End.
```

If the person is 21 years of age or older, it permits the redefinition; otherwise it does not. A demon must explicitly *continue* for the preempted operation to be completed; otherwise, the demon returns and impedes the interrupted operation.

Using Demons for Communication Between Distributed Agents. Demons simplify the communication control structure of distributed heuristic agents. Without demons, a distributed agent must continually poll the shared database to discover any new information. With demons, an agent can respond to changes in the database as they happen.

Distributed agents use shared databases for communicating among one another. Agents *send* new information by asserting or denying propositions in the shared database. They *receive* information by testing for propositions or by generating elements from the shared knowledge base. To write an effective agent without using demons, a knowledge engineer must know what information to look for and when to look for it. An agent's standard structure usually consists of an infinite loop that checks for the presence of the anticipated information in the shared database and, when the agent discovers one of the possibilities, performs the appropriate actions—a process similar to hardware polling.

Demons significantly alter an agent's communication control structure. No longer must an agent check its shared database for new information. The knowledge engineer can write a *before asserting* or *before denying* demon for each of the possible communications. Then, when the information of interest appears in the shared database, the demon processes it directly. This changes an agent's computational structure from a *polling-driven* computation to an *interrupt-driven* computation.

The demon facility permits agents to capture attempts to assert, deny, or test propositions, to start generating elements, to produce elements, and to invoke verbs. However, in a shared database, only global asserts and denies will cause demons to execute. The other operations (testing propositions, beginning to generate elements, and producing elements) work only with an agent's local copy of the shared database. Thus, the demons that do not capture modifications execute only for the agent performing such operations.

A shared database can provide the necessary medium for communication without ever storing any information. This activity could result in a cluttered database, but demons can act as *sentries* that guard the database's contents. By *returning* rather than *continuing,* a demon can capture the communication, perform the required computation, and prevent the modification from entering the local database.

Using Demons to Emulate Frames. The demon facility allows ROSIE programmers to write frame-based performance programs. A frame is an abstract specification for a class of entities; it allows programmers to write systems from a behavioral perspective. Each entity, or instance of a frame, consists of a name, attributes, and the associated values of those attributes. Each attribute may also have three routines associated with it. The routines are invoked as a side effect of performing some operation on an attribute's value. The *if-added* routine is invoked when a value is added to the attribute; the *if-removed* routine is invoked when a value is removed from an attribute; and the *if-needed* routine is invoked when an attribute is queried for a value. In this paradigm, computations occur as side effects initiated by the manipulation of an attribute.

We can use the demon facility to manage frames. For each new frame type we can write two demons, one to capture control at the time of the frame's creation and the other to capture control at its destruction. The two demons also create and destroy the frame's associated attributes. For each manipulation of a frame, we must write a demon to capture the intended action and correctly update the affected frames.

Managing a meeting calendar provides a good example of the use of frames. Two different kinds of frames are needed, one to represent a meeting and another to represent a person. Attributes of a meeting include its participants, its starting time, its anticipated duration, its location, and its topic. To use the demon facility in defining a meeting frame with these attributes, we could write

```
Before asserting a meeting is a meeting:
[1] Assert <> is a participants of the meeting and assert NOTHING is a
    topic of the meeting and assert <> is a start of the meeting and assert
```

```
          <> is a duration of the meeting and assert <> is a location of the
          meeting
      [2] Continue.
      End.
```

(The corresponding *denying a meeting is a meeting* demon would be defined similarly.)

We can now create meetings with ROSIE's *create* verb. For example,

```
      Create a meeting
          and let "Setting priorities" be the topic of that meeting
          and let 8am be the start of that meeting
          and let 1 hour be the duration of that meeting
          and let room 247 be the location of that meeting.
```

When this action executes, *create* first generates a new name element from the description's class noun (*meeting* in this case) and a number. For example, assume that the new name element is *MEETING #34*. After generating a new name element, *create* automatically asserts that *MEETING #34 is a meeting*. The assertion causes the *before asserting a meeting is a meeting* demon to execute. It then asserts *<> is a participants of MEETING #34, NOTHING is a topic of MEETING #34, <> is a start of MEETING #34*, and so on. Finally, the demon continues by allowing *MEETING #34 is a meeting* to be added to the database. Now our original *create* statement continues executing with *let "Setting priorities" be the topic of that meeting*. Because of ROSIE's ability to handle anaphora, *that meeting* evaluates to *MEETING #34*, and because of the demon, *the topic of MEETING #34* already exists, so the use of the definite description is permitted.

The "person" frame operates similarly. It consists of two fields, the person's name and the person's meetings. The demon is defined by

```
      Before asserting a person is a person:
      [1] Assert no name is a name of the person and assert <> is a meetings
          of the person.
      [2] Continue.
      End.
```

With a frame for meeting and another for person, we can now write routines for manipulating these frames. The two activities we want to illustrate are adding a person to a meeting and removing a person from a meeting. We define a demon that captures the assertion that a person will attend a meeting by

```
      Before asserting a name will attend a meeting:
      Private subject.
      [1] If the name is a name of any person, let the subject be that person,
```

```
        otherwise, create a person and let that person's name be the name and
        let the subject be that person.
    [2] Add the meeting to 'the subject's meetings'.
    [3] Add the subject to 'the meeting's participants'.
    End.
```

This demon first uses the person's name to locate that person's frame. It then updates that person's list of meetings and updates the meeting's list of participants. Rather than continuing and letting a fact such as *JOHN will attend MEETING #34* enter the database, the demon returns, ensuring that unnecessary information does not clutter up the database. Similarly, we can write a demon that captures the assertion that a person will not attend a meeting:

```
Before asserting a name will not attend a meeting:
Private subject.
[1] If the name is a name of any person, let the subject be that person,
    otherwise, send {"I know of no person named ", the name, ".", CR} and
    return.
[2] Remove the meeting from 'the subject's meetings'.
[3] Remove the subject from 'the meeting's participants'.
End.
```

Monitors

With each ruleset, ROSIE associates a *monitor* or control program that specifies the execution order for all the rules in the ruleset. Currently, ROSIE supports three different monitors called *sequential*, *cyclic*, and *random*. These monitors execute a ruleset's rules in standard ways. The sequential monitor executes each rule in sequence and, after executing the last rule, causes the ruleset to return. The cyclic monitor also executes the rules in the ruleset in sequence; however, rather than returning when it executes the last rule, it reexecutes the first rule, and so on. The random monitor repeatedly executes the rules in the ruleset by randomly choosing the next rule to execute. Future versions of ROSIE will permit knowledge engineers to write their own monitors.

2.2.2 ■ Linguistic Structures

Our main goal in developing ROSIE is to provide an understandable programming language. We have used English to guide this development because it is the language of choice for most domain experts. Ideally, ROSIE should mimic English exactly. However, this extreme position presents two problems. First, an expressive and broadly based language such as English allows users to express concepts that might not map directly onto fundamental representational structures (of ROSIE or any other programming language). Second, users often need programming idioms (e.g., variables, *for* loops) that are awkward to express in English.

ROSIE allows programmers to specify complex sentences, but it cannot store such sentences directly in the database. Instead, it decomposes a complex sentence into its fundamental structures. ROSIE's complex linguistic forms extend the limited expressive capabilities of its basic representational forms and give the language an appearance much like that of English.

It is difficult to describe ROSIE's linguistic structure because the language is self-recursive. That is, some linguistic constructs rely on other linguistic constructs that rely on the former constructs. In the following discussion, we first present *terms,* which resemble noun phrases. Terms refer to specific things (i.e., ROSIE elements). A term may be either an explicit element (e.g., *Ronald Reagan*) or a description that refers to an element (e.g., *The United States President*). ROSIE's *descriptions* present a difficulty with recursion because a description can be modified by prepositional phrases (embedded terms) or relative clauses (embedded verb phrases). Next we consider ROSIE's *verb phrases,* both relational and comparative forms. This leads into a discussion of *sentences* and *conditions*. Finally, we discuss ROSIE's higher-level linguistic constructs, *rules* and *actions*.

Terms

ROSIE *terms* act as noun phrases. Terms permit ROSIE programmers to access, manipulate, and store elements. A term always generates one or more values, which are always elements. When a term evaluates, it becomes the element it generates. For example, when the term *the mayor of Los Angeles* evaluates, it becomes the element *TOM BRADLEY*. Thus, *Assert the mayor of Los Angeles is happy* would assert the proposition *'TOM BRADLEY is happy'* in the database.

Four kinds of terms exist:

1. *Element terms,* which consist of the elements and element constructors;
2. *Expressions,* which allow a user to compute a numeric quantity;
3. *Description-based terms,* which compute values by searching the database and optionally invoking rulesets; and
4. Linguistic forms that refer to elements, including possessive and anaphoric forms.

The element term includes all the elements and the special linguistic forms that create new elements. The number *probability .7* is not only an element but also a number term. Similarly, names, strings, tuples, patterns, propositions, class elements, intentional descriptions, and intentional actions also serve as both elements and terms. The terms that create new elements look much like actual elements; however, they permit the inclusion of embedded terms. The proposition constructor illustrates this point well: When ROSIE encounters a proposition term, it evaluates all embedded terms until only elements remain (since proposition elements can contain only a single primitive relational form and elements). For example, the proposition terms

```
'John Smith was late for work'
'The teacher did punish the student in class'
'3 + 4 is a prime'
```

could evaluate to

```
'JOHN SMITH was late for WORK'[11]
'MARTHA did punish JAMES in CLASS'
'7 is a prime'
```

Expressions also serve as terms. Expressions include the standard arithmetic infix operators as well as unary negation. ROSIE, with its built-in rulesets, also provides transcendental functions and other unary arithmetic operators. Typical expression terms include *3 + 4* or *the liquid's volume * the liquid's density*.

Every description-based term consists of a quantifier (*some, every*) or a determiner (*a, an, the*), followed by a description. For example, *every big burly man that does eat quiche* uses the quantifier *every* and implicitly iterates the enclosing action once for each element it generates. Thus, had the programmer used this term in the action *Display every big burly man that does eat quiche*, when ROSIE evaluated the statement it would execute it once for each element that satisfies the description *big burly man that does eat quiche*.

Descriptions

ROSIE would be quite stilted if it permitted only simple linguistic forms such as elements. A richer, more English-like flavor results from the use of *descriptions*, which represent elements much as variables represent values. A description consists of any number of adjectives, fol-

[11] When ROSIE evaluates a term, it generates an element. ROSIE prints all elements in uppercase.

lowed by a class-noun, followed by any number of prepositional phrases and possibly some relative clauses[12]

The sleek red vessel
Every vessel that does start on time

When descriptions and the basic relational forms are mixed, the resulting sentences can express complex concepts that are both readable and understandable. For example,

The vessel that does not start on time
    is not likely to win
Every eligible vessel that is moored in Newport
    is likely to race

Descriptions identify a base class (e.g., *vessel*) along with restrictions that narrow that class to the concept of interest (e.g., *seaworthy vessel that is docked in Newport*). In ROSIE, a description is always preceded by either a quantifier or a determiner. This is followed by the description itself, which consists of any number of adjectives, the base class noun with its prepositional attachments, and any number of relative clauses. Thus, a description designates a set of elements generated by the base class noun and constrained by the modifiers.

Since descriptions are used extensively to retrieve and add knowledge, it is important to understand how ROSIE interprets them. ROSIE interprets each modifier of the base class noun independently. The ROSIE assertion

Assert John is a big burly man who does eat quiche.

causes the addition of four propositions to the database:

JOHN is a man.
JOHN is big.
JOHN is burly.
JOHN does eat QUICHE.

ROSIE's interpretations of descriptions can lead to potential pitfalls. For example, with the additional assertion

Assert John is a small fry.

the database would contain

JOHN is a man.
JOHN is a fry.
JOHN is big.

[12] The examples include determiners and quantifiers to make reading the descriptions easier.

JOHN is small.
JOHN is burly.
JOHN does eat QUICHE.

This database would generate the same element, *JOHN*, when asked *Display every small man* and *Display every big man*.

We also use descriptions to retrieve information from the database. For example, the two actions *Display every seaworthy vessel* and *Display every vessel that is seaworthy* both generate the same elements. Each action first generates the set of all elements that are *is a vessel*. Next, ROSIE prunes this set by checking that each element also *is seaworthy*.

Thus, adjectives and class nouns are closely related but have different semantics. The "*is a* class-noun" relation establishes membership in a set, as in

Fudge is a sweet

The "*is* adjective" form modifies or predicates the element, as in

Fudge is sweet

In the first phrase, we establish *fudge* as a *sweet*. In the latter phrase, we establish that *sweet* describes or modifies *fudge*. ROSIE treats these two uses of sweet entirely separately. Asserting either of these propositions does not affect the other, and ROSIE cannot infer one from the other automatically without the user first establishing some additional relationships (e.g., that any sweet is sweet).

Prepositional phrases in English add specifics to a description. They play a significant role in ROSIE, becoming an integral part of the database relation by specializing the class definition. For example, the three phrases

a spot in the sun
a spot on the sun
a spot

have distinct meanings. ROSIE differentiates among descriptions with dissimilar prepositional phrases even when the class name is the same in all of them.

Relative clauses also add specifics to an English description, and they perform the same function in ROSIE. But unlike prepositional phrases, ROSIE's relative clauses restrict the set of elements generated by a description rather than become part of the database relation. ROSIE provides a number of distinct relative clause forms. The following are examples of descriptions with relative clauses and the relationships they represent.

Description:
A company which is bankrupt
An employee of ITT who does play tennis and who did retire

Relationships represented:
<element> is a company
<element> is bankrupt
<element> is an employee of ITT
<element> does play tennis
<element> did retire

Verb Phrases

Verb phrases provide the mechanism for constructing ROSIE sentences. Together with terms, ROSIE's verb phrases can perform a variety of functions. They can, for example, form basic relationships, compare elements, test propositions against the database, and determine the cardinality of a set of elements.

ROSIE permits five basic verb phrases, each capturing a specific class of English usage, and each mapping onto one of the five relational forms. The first basic verb phrase is *class membership,* using the *is, was,* and *will* verbs in conjunction with the indefinite article *a* or *an*. These verb phrases can include *be* and the negative *not*. Examples are

John Smythe is a doctor
Bill Walsh will not be a witness
Martha Jones was an individual with glasses

The second basic verb phrase is *predication*. This is similar to the class membership form, but it replaces the indefinite article with a relation-name and can also add prepositional elements. Examples are

Tom is happy
Rena was not alone at the time
Carol will be late (at the sound of the bell)

The *predicate complement,* the third kind of verb phrase, creates binary relations between the subject of the sentence and the term following the predicate complement. Examples are

Martin is nuclear powered
The play was not really exciting
US Steel will be running rapidly toward Bethlehem

The fourth type of basic verb phrase is the *intransitive verb,* as in

Spot did eat
Raoul does eat with a fork
Billy will not eat without a fuss

The final verb phrase type is the *transitive verb,* as in

Every student does study biology at school
Susan will cook a steak for dinner
Jill did not divide by 2

In addition to the basic verb forms, a few built-in *comparative verb forms* allow comparison of numbers and other elements. Element equality is tested by the equality sentence form, which can be written tersely with the = character or in expanded natural English as *is equal to*:

```
<term1> is equal to <term2>
<term1> = <term2>

<term1> is not equal to <term2>
<term1> ~ = <term2>
```

When number elements are tested for equality, they are equal only if both have the same units or labels and represent the same numeric value. Numbers that have different units or labels are not equal regardless of their numeric values. For example, these sentences will all test true:

```
33.2 = 33.2
40 miles/hour = 40 miles/hour
82 miles = 82.0 miles
17 apples ~ = 17
17 apples ~ = 17 oranges
```

ROSIE includes relational forms for comparing number elements (e.g., *greater than, not greater than, greater than or equal to, not greater than or equal to,* and so on for the *less than* comparisons. Comparisons can be made only between numbers with the same units or labels. All other comparisons are illegal and will generate errors. Comparative verb forms are *not* basic verb forms, and therefore they cannot be used in propositions or asserted into the database.

The remaining legal verb forms make a variety of tests that may or may not involve the database. Some are supplied for convenience; others fundamentally expand ROSIE's capabilities. Like verb forms, these forms are NOT basic sentences and therefore cannot be used in propositions or asserted into the database. They include sentences such as

```
'John is a student' is provably true
'John is not a student' is provably false
'John is not exemplary' is provably true
'John is exemplary' is provably false
```

These verb forms allow ROSIE to test proposition elements against the database. A proposition is *provably true* if it is found in the database, and it is *provably false* if its negation is found. If neither the positive nor the negative of the proposition exists in the database, the test *is not provably true* and the test *is not provably false* will both test true.

Verb forms that test the cardinality of a class of elements take the form

```
If there is a file for the employee, print that file.
If there is no file for the employee, request data.
If there is just one enemy ship, attack that ship.
If there is more than one enemy ship, surrender.
```

Sentences

The largest syntactical unit a programmer can add to a database is the *primitive sentence*. However, ROSIE permits the expression of more complex sentences. To add these to a database, ROSIE first decomposes the complex sentence into a set of primitive sentences. As we shall see, conditions, actions, rules, and rulesets all incorporate sentences to effect their results. The constructs discussed previously (e.g., terms, descriptions, verb phrases, etc.) are the building blocks of ROSIE sentences.

ROSIE's primitive sentences are those that define a single relationship. They are constructed with the legal relational forms, with terms in place of elements. The following are examples of primitive sentences:

```
John is a man
The student did not fail the exam
John does support the Republican candidate
Every boy does like some girl
John's father will not succeed in business
Any friendly ship was attacked before 1300 hours
```

There are also sentences that test the element generated by the term against the constraints of the description. All relationships must test true for the test to succeed. The *not* option negates the result of the test. If the tested sentence is a primitive sentence, it tests true only when a sentence in the database matches it exactly or when a predicate matching the sentence concludes true. For example,

```
If John is an exemplary student of math, display John.
If John is not an exemplary student who did pass the final
     and who did pass the midterm, disqualify John.
```

Other typical sentences are formed with the verb phrases described previously.

Conditions

Conditions are sentences that occur within the context of a test such as *if*, *while*, or *until*. Boolean combinations of sentences can be formed with the words *and* and *or*. The negation of a sentence is formed by inserting the word *not* in its appropriate location within the verb phrase of the sentence. The Boolean connectives *and* and *or* are given ordinary precedence during parsing, so that *and* groups conditions with higher precedence. To aid readability when several conditions participate in some test, the conditions can be separated by commas or grouped within parentheses.

Two example conditionals are

```
While John is happy and Mary is sad, ...
If the value > 0 or the sum is equal to 5, ...
```

Rules and Actions

Rules constitute the principal syntactic category of ROSIE. A ROSIE rule begins with the keyword *If* followed by a condition and the rule's associated actions. ROSIE permits degenerate rules that consist only of actions. Degenerate rules are equivalent to *If "true", actions.*

Actions are ROSIE's workhorses. They act upon ROSIE's database; they interact with the user; and they control the system's inferencing. There are several important types of actions, including

1. Actions that determine which propositions are affirmed in the database;
2. Actions that define conditional behaviors;
3. Actions that control iterations;
4. Actions for input and output;
5. Actions to invoke and terminate rulesets; and
6. Actions for file management.

We describe each of these in turn.

1. The database contains affirmed propositions, which can be positive or negative, depending on the verb form used. Because ROSIE supports three possible truth values (true, false, and indeterminate), the user must employ a variety of actions to manipulate the different types of data that can arise. The primary way in which the user affects the database is by asserting sentences. The *assert* action takes as its argument one or more sentences separated by *and*. Each of these is interpreted as one or more primitive sentences, and each is affirmed. When a primitive sentence is affirmed, its negation is denied. The effect of

the deny action is to delete the primitive sentence from the database if it exists.

2. ROSIE supports several actions that define conditional behaviors and conditional looping. These include the *if, unless, while,* and *until* constructs.

3. ROSIE supports a variety of types of iterative actions. The most significant of these is the *for each* action. This action takes a quantified description and an action as its arguments. ROSIE performs the action for the corresponding set of database elements that match the description. The *for each* action can be augmented with optional *until* and *while* conditions that restrict the iteration of the *for each* in the expected ways. The *for each* iteration terminates as soon as the *until* condition is satisfied or the *while* condition is no longer true. The user may also elide the *for each* and retain the *while* or *until* iterator.

4. ROSIE supports very flexible communications with other systems. The basic output action is *send,* and the basic input action is *read*. Send and read can address files, that is, data structures on the local machine. The key construct underlying the I/O and string-manipulation facilities in ROSIE is the *pattern*. A pattern is a description of a string, which can be as simple as a string constant or as complex as a regular expression defining the strings of interest.

5. Programs implicitly invoke predicate and generator rulesets. Each ruleset type uses distinct actions to exit. Procedural rulesets exit using the *return* action. Generator rulesets use either the *produce* or *return* actions to exit. Predicate rulesets use either the *conclude* or *return* actions to exit.

6. An entire package of other actions has been provided for interacting with files. The parse action reads a file of ROSIE source code, checks it for syntactic errors, produces an executable parsed version of the original file, and also produces a text version of the original file that may be edited. When the user *loads* the parsed version of the file, ROSIE immediately executes any rules in the file and indicates which rulesets have been defined. It also establishes the conditions necessary for interactive editing of rulesets.

ROSIE also provides many facilities to edit, maintain, and manipulate files, and it supports other constructs, including flow control actions. These are covered in detail in *The ROSIE Language Reference Manual* (Fain et al., 1981).

2.3 Initial Evaluation of ROSIE

2.3.1 ■ Major ROSIE Applications

The ROSIE environment has been used for major system development work by Rand projects and by external groups. Three examples illustrate the diversity of these applications: the development of a model of legal decision making (Waterman and Peterson, 1981); the design of the TATR tactical air target recommender (Callero et al., 1984); and the design of an experimental workstation (Adept) to aid combat intelligence analysts and combat operations decision makers (Beebe et al., 1984).

The legal decision making expert system demonstrated the appropriateness of using rule-based techniques to encode formal rules of law together with informal rules of procedure and strategy. The project explored a number of techniques for encoding legal knowledge. The final system took a restricted product-liability situation, examined it, and calculated a final dollar figure that represented the amount of money a plaintiff could recover in court.

The TATR system was designed to help Air Force tactical air targeteers plan strikes against enemy airfields. The system makes two major interacting choices: It chooses which airfields to strike and which targets to strike on those airfields. The planning system examines its options, evaluates the options against a set of metrics, and chooses the set that maximizes the effect on the enemy.

The Adept Workstation, developed by TRW Defense Systems, is an ambitious effort to help military analysts assess enemy activities, using near-real-time intelligence analysis. Much of the processing of diverse intelligence information involves the use of expert heuristic knowledge. The objectives of the project were to verify the functional design of the workstation for situation assessment and to demonstrate the feasibility of applying artificial intelligence techniques to this domain. The project included an explicit working demonstration system consisting of about 200 rules programmed in a combination of ROSIE and Lisp.

2.3.2 ■ Advantages of ROSIE

ROSIE has been in use for major system development approximately four years. Sufficient experience in its use has been gathered to allow an initial assessment of its advantages and disadvantages.

We believe major advantages have been demonstrated in all of ROSIE's applications. For example, results of an explicit evaluation phase for the Adept Workstation are summarized by Beebe et al. (1984) as follows:[13]

> ... the capabilities and potential of the AI software implementation was most appreciated. "Most encouraging was the thought patterns in the ... software." ... it has "the greatest potential for modification and enhancement." ... The analysts strongly approved having the code, that is the ROSIE rule base, in English-like form. This "is important if the analyst is to trust the automated system."

The primary advantages of ROSIE are its readability, flexibility, and expressiveness.

Readability. A knowledge engineer can write an application in ROSIE so that a specialist in that application area can read it and understand it. However, a knowledge engineer can also write obscure code in ROSIE—just as can be done in other programming languages and in natural languages. Whether a reader can understand the final system depends greatly on the overall structure of the program and its knowledge base. If the expert system's architecture matches the problem, the program almost always allows graceful expansion of the system. Often, a domain specialist can make straightforward additions or modifications directly, using existing ROSIE code as a template and modifying the language within that template. On the other hand, if a knowledge engineer writes the expert system with little thought to an appropriate underlying structure, the richness of ROSIE permits writing a diversity of structures that even the most psychic readers would find difficult to understand, modify, or expand.

Readability remains an important concern. Any tool or methodology that improves communication between a computer-trained knowledge engineer and the domain expert with whom that knowledge engineer must interact eases the construction of the expert system. Problems of the interface between the knowledge engineer and the domain expert present a very difficult barrier. If the domain expert cannot verify or understand the translation of his or her expertise, communication problems are exacerbated. It is clearly advantageous to have a medium that can serve as a common ground for the knowledge engineer and the domain expert to discuss ideas and their representation.

[13] The quotations within this excerpt are taken from questionnaires filled out by analysts evaluating the Adept Workstation.

Flexibility. Complex models are usually written as traditional computer programs, using deeply nested logic and specially tailored data structures. These models tend to be difficult to change, particularly when changes affect the fundamental structure of the program or data. In contrast, ROSIE—like other rule-based languages tailored for the production of expert systems—allows, and even encourages, the development of highly modular programs that retain considerable flexibility even as they expand.

ROSIE programs are primarily constructed from a set of conditional rules. ROSIE encourages structuring these programs with named rulesets that cluster rules into operations, generators, or predicates, which chunk important prescriptive knowledge into single units. However, ROSIE programs are predominantly flat structures composed of rules and assertions of facts. As such, they permit the graceful introduction of additional rules (or whole rulesets) and assertions. The resulting flexibility in the program's structure permits additions or even repackaging of rules into new rulesets that can dramatically modify program behavior without major reprogramming.

Expressiveness. ROSIE is a rich, complex language. It includes a wide variety of linguistic forms and permits the expression of complex concepts. We believe the English-like expressive power of ROSIE goes sufficiently beyond that of traditional programming languages to allow new modes of expression that can make the difference between success and failure in developing a complex model.

2.3.3 ■ Disadvantages of ROSIE

In its present form, ROSIE is not without disadvantages. We believe there are two primary areas that need improvement:

1. *Efficiency.* ROSIE as currently implemented in Interlisp executes too slowly to permit effective development and testing of complex models.
2. *Writability.* It is difficult to rewrite some English-language concepts in ROSIE.

Limited Efficiency. ROSIE was developed without concern for size or speed. Our objective was to ease the development of complex models. Yet models developed with ROSIE quickly grow to such a size that development, debugging, and testing involve frustrating delays. Some of the inefficiency is due to the implementation of ROSIE within Interlisp, which is already a complex system; some is due to the inherent complexity of ROSIE; and some is due to inefficiencies in implementation.

Currently, we are rewriting ROSIE from Interlisp into Portable Standard Lisp (PSL). This will not only circumvent Interlisp's size and complexity, it will also increase the availability of the ROSIE language, since PSL runs on a wide variety of machines. We are also improving the implementation and searching for ways to improve overall execution speed.

Limited Writability. Although knowledge engineers can express many and varied concepts in ROSIE, they may have trouble in finding appropriate linguistic forms for some concepts. ROSIE's expressiveness and its resulting complexity cause this difficulty. Its proximity to English causes negative interference—a knowledge engineer may try to express a concept in correct English phrasing, only to find that ROSIE does not support that phrasing. Mapping a correct English phrase into correct ROSIE structure may be difficult.

A language is *writable* if a user can learn it easily and can then easily write code that is relatively error-free, both syntactically and semantically. Restricting a language's syntax to a small, orthogonal and intuitive set of constructs can go a long way toward making a language writable. Such restrictions tend to make a language's rules of composition easier to remember and apply. We are in the process of orthogonalizing the language and are finding minimal but expressive constructs that have already helped make ROSIE more writable.

2.3.4 ■ Future Directions

ROSIE is still in the process of being extended and enhanced. Planned future changes to ROSIE fall into four categories: (1) expressiveness; (2) support for specialized structures; (3) meta-linguistics, meta-structures, and meta-control; and (4) knowledge-based optimization.

Expressiveness. ROSIE's broad expressive power permits the direct representation of a wide range of syntactic constructs. It does not, however, cover all of English. Some linguistic forms, such as passive sentential forms, that ROSIE cannot support can be restated in other ways that are acceptable to ROSIE. Other linguistic forms, primarily modals expressing what *could* be the case, or what *should* happen, are presently quite difficult to map into ROSIE. It is very difficult to express thoughts like *John should sue Mary* or *Susan might like windsurfing*. Extending ROSIE's linguistic constructs remains a large part of our research effort and will require careful study to identify graceful ways of extending the language.

Support for Specialized Structures. The primary goal of the ROSIE language research project is the development of a computer language that is directly readable by experts in a discipline. These experts not only use specialized jargon, they also structure their information in specialized ways. For example, information might be succinctly and readably presented in tabular form, such as a decision table (Shapiro et al., 1985). Also, experts often describe situations in terms of a set of objects, each having certain attributes with associated values or attached procedures (McArthur et al., 1984). Decision tables and objects seem sufficiently important to warrant their direct inclusion in ROSIE.

Meta-linguistics, Meta-structures, and Meta-control. Meta-linguistics will enable us to improve the expressiveness of ROSIE substantially without increasing ambiguity. Meta-linguistic constructs permit self-reference: that is, they allow a language to refer to itself. Phrases such as *the antecedent in the third rule* or *the description that references the theory of strict liability* can permit a knowledge engineer to write code that examines and manipulates procedural knowledge. Meta-linguistics and the supporting meta-structures will provide the support necessary to construct programs that reason self-reflexively, that can explain their actions, that can modify themselves, and that can learn.

Meta-linguistics and meta-structures will permit ROSIE users to tailor the language themselves. A full meta-language will allow users to write new monitors and thus control inferencing on a per-ruleset basis. For example, the sequential monitor might be rewritten as

```
To execute a set-of-rules in sequential order:
[1]  loop: if the set-of-rules is empty, return.
[2]  evaluate the first rule in the set-of-rules.
[3]  let the set-of-rules be the tail of the set-of-rules.
[4]  goto loop.
End.
```

Knowledge-Based Optimization. As ROSIE has evolved into a stable and mature programming environment, performance has become a critical issue. ROSIE is too slow for many applications, and as we expand it to include meta-linguistic capabilities, it will slow down even more. To correct this weakness, we are developing methods to optimize not only ROSIE's internal code but also the code that ROSIE generates when it compiles a ROSIE program into Lisp. We are applying some of these techniques in our rewriting of ROSIE into PSL. One such technique, symbolic evaluation, allows us to expand function calls that have at least one constant argument into an equivalent call on a new function. The new function does not need the constant argument since it assumes that value. This process of symbolic evaluation generates code that executes more rapidly, but may, at times, require more memory. With judicious application of the technology, however, we can increase the running speed of many routines without suffering any cost in memory.

Symbolic evaluation alone cannot achieve the necessary speed improvements, but symbolic evaluation together with other techniques that use the program's knowledge can. One such technique could analyze a ruleset together with all the other rulesets that use it or that it uses. In the process, the optimizer constructs a database of global information concerning each ruleset that can be used in applying optimization rules.

2.4 Conclusions

ROSIE is a powerful expert system programming language. Its combination of English-like syntactic structure and intuitive semantics makes it a powerful prototyping and development environment for knowledge engineers and domain experts, both of whom can use it to communicate with one another and with the computer.

ROSIE has shown that syntactic parsing techniques can go a long way toward humanizing programming languages. Syntactic resolution of word usage seems sufficient for encoding the prescriptive knowledge of a domain. Admittedly, domain semantics—the meaning ascribed to words within a domain—are very important to understanding ideas within that domain, but a knowledge engineer needs only to define them as completely as needed.

ROSIE's major drawback—its slow execution speed—remains a constraint on broader use. We are attacking this problem directly, and we expect that future versions of ROSIE will not only be expressive, readable, and writable, but will also support development and execution of expert systems in reasonable time frames.

Acknowledgments

We would like to thank the people involved with the current version of ROSIE, especially Larry Baer, Jill Fain, Bruce Florman, and Jed Marti. We would also like to thank Bob Anderson and Marietta Gillogly for their help in developing this report. Jim Dewar and Geneva Henry provided insightful and cogent reviews. Their suggestions substantially improved the report. We would especially like to thank Philip Klahr for repeatedly reading and commenting on earlier drafts. We alone take responsibility for any errors or inaccuracies that remain.

References

1. Anderson, R. H., M. Gallegos, J. J. Gillogly, R. B. Greenberg, and R. Villanueva, *RITA Reference Manual*, The Rand Corporation, R-1808-ARPA, September 1977.
2. Anderson, R. H., and J. J. Gillogly, *Rand Intelligent Terminal Agent (RITA): Design Philosophy*, The Rand Corporation, R-1809-ARPA, February 1976.
3. Beebe, H. M., H. S. Goodman, G. L. Henry, and D. S. Snell, "The Adept Workstation: A Knowledge Based System for Combat Intelligence Analysis," *Proceedings of the 7th MIT/ONR Workshop on C3 Systems*, MIT, Cambridge, Massachusetts, 1984.
4. Callero, M., D. A. Waterman, and J. R. Kipps, *TATR: A Prototype Expert System for Tactical Air Targeting*, The Rand Corporation, R-3096-ARPA, August 1984.
5. Erman, L. D., and V. R. Lesser, "A Multi-Level Organization for Problem Solving Using Many Diverse Cooperating Sources of Knowledge," *Proceedings of the Fourth International Joint Conference on Artificial Intelligence*, Tbilisi, USSR, 1975.
6. Fain, J., D. Gorlin, F. Hayes-Roth, S. Rosenschein, H. Sowizral, and D. Waterman, *The ROSIE Language Reference Manual*, The Rand Corporation, N-1647-ARPA, December 1981.
7. Fain, J., F. Hayes-Roth, H. Sowizral, and D. Waterman, *Programming in ROSIE: An Introduction by Means of Examples*, The Rand Corporation, N-1646-ARPA, February 1982.
8. Hayes-Roth, F., D. Gorlin, S. Rosenschein, H. Sowizral, and D. Waterman, *Rationale and Motivation for ROSIE*, The Rand Corporation, N-1648-ARPA, November 1981.
9. McArthur, D., P. Klahr, and S. Narain, *ROSS: An Object-Oriented Language for Constructing Simulations*, The Rand Corporation, R-3160-AF, December 1984.
10. Quinlan, J. R., *INFERNO: A Cautious Approach to Uncertain Inference*, The Rand Corporation, N-1898-RC, September 1982.
11. Schwabe, W., and L. M. Jamison, *A Rule-Based Policy-Level*

Model of Nonsuperpower Behavior in Strategic Conflicts, The Rand Corporation, R-2962-DNA, December 1982.

12. Shapiro, N., H. E. Hall, R. H. Anderson, and M. LaCasse, *The RAND-ABEL Programming Language: History, Rationale and Design,* The Rand Corporation, R-3274-NA, August 1985.
13. Sowizral, H. A., "Experiences with Distributed Heuristic Agents in ROSIE," *Proceedings of the IEEE Conference on Systems, Man, and Cybernetics,* Bombay, India, 1983.
14. Waterman, D. A., R. H. Anderson, F. Hayes-Roth, P. Klahr, G. Martins, and S. J. Rosenschein, *Design of a Rule-Oriented System for Implementing Expertise,* The Rand Corporation, N-1158-1-ARPA, May 1979.
15. Waterman, D. A., and M. A. Peterson, *Models of Legal Decisionmaking,* The Rand Corporation, R-2717-ICJ, 1981.

Chapter 3

ROSS: An Object-oriented Language for Constructing Simulations

David J. McArthur, Philip Klahr, and Sanjai Narain

3.1 Introduction

This chapter presents an overview of ROSS (Rand Object-oriented Simulation System), an object-oriented simulation language. ROSS is one of the first languages that attempts to marry artificial intelligence methods with simulation technology. We have found that the marriage benefits both parties. Simulation is a powerful inference and design tool that has been largely overlooked by artificial intelligence (AI) researchers; however, many human experts rely heavily on qualitative simulation to understand and fix complex systems. We believe that incorporating simulations as components would increase the power of many expert systems. Simulation is potentially a powerful tool for modeling, understanding, and designing complex systems, but present-day simulators do not have the features to allow simulation to fulfill its potential. This report discusses these shortcomings and shows how ROSS uses AI techniques to create a simulation environment that overcomes many of the limitations. The report is not a manual providing detailed

This chapter originally appeared as R-3160-AF, The Rand Corporation, December 1984.

discussions of the commands or rationale of the ROSS language. Those discussions are provided in McArthur and Klahr (1982), and equally detailed discussions of specific simulations written in ROSS can be found in Klahr et al. (1982a, 1982b) and Klahr et al. (1984). The language and its applications are described here only to the degree necessary to provide a general overview.

3.1.1 ■ Simulation as a Reasoning and Design Tool

It is often useful to be able to understand a dynamic system without manipulating it in the real world. Some real-world systems perform too slowly (e.g., economic systems), some have dangerous consequences (e.g., nuclear reactors), and some are awkward or impossible to manipulate directly (e.g., the solar system). In such cases, it is desirable to be able to draw conclusions about the behavior of the system by reasoning with a model of the system, rather than by observing the system itself.

Model-based reasoning has many uses. Most basically, it can be used to understand and predict the performance of the system. When the system is one that can be modified by the user, model-based reasoning can also be used for intervention and design. In some systems, only limited changes are possible (e.g., a medical treatment modifies bodily processes in a constrained way), but in others, the user has full control over structural properties (e.g., the design of a computer). For systems that can be modified, conclusions drawn by reasoning about system behavior can be used as a basis for making coherent structural changes. These changes then lead to an examination of the behavior of the new system and to more rounds of changes. A successful *design cycle* ideally converges on a system that exemplifies some predetermined behavioral properties.

Unfortunately, the intuitive methods currently used to model systems are inaccurate and incomplete, and mathematical (analytic) methods, though accurate, may be of limited value because of the difficulty of formally modeling all the complexities of many dynamic systems. Simulation represents a useful tool for reasoning about the possible behaviors of dynamic systems that potentially avoids the imprecision of intuition, while providing greater expressive power than mathematics.[1]

[1] We do not claim that simulation is the *only* means of modeling a system and drawing useful conclusions about its behavior, or even that it is necessarily the best means. Simulation is just one of many modeling tools. Moreover, simulations do not enable users to answer several important kinds of questions about the system being modeled. For a more detailed discussion of the inherent limitations of state-transition simulations, see Davis et al. (1982).

3.1.2 ■ Shortcomings of Existing Simulation Techniques

While simulation technology is potentially a powerful tool for modeling, understanding, and designing systems, large-scale simulators do not provide the features necessary to allow simulation to fulfill its potential. Four major shortcomings of present simulations and simulators are described in this section.

Inability to Verify the Completeness and Accuracy of Models

A large-scale simulator typically contains many types of knowledge that collectively comprise a model of a real-world system. Some types are explicitly represented and understandable (e.g., an object's properties, such as location, velocity, or altitude). Other types of knowledge, such as how objects behave, how they interact with other objects, and how they make decisions, may be impossible to understand. Users may have to search through volumes of manuals for behavioral descriptions that are buried in incomprehensible code. Even if the information can be located and understood, the user cannot be sure that the system actually performs as specified. Much can get lost in the translation to computer code. Furthermore, knowledge is typically not well structured. Embedded assumptions are hidden, scattered, and fragmented throughout the program. The initial structure of the first version of a simulation is often lost as more complexity is added or modifications are made. As a result, there is no assurance that the simulation embeds an accurate or complete model of the dynamic system. The user cannot have confidence in either the predictions or the design advice the simulation might suggest.

Inability to Modify Models and Construct Alternative Models

Models embedded in simulations cannot be easily modified; for many of the same reasons, they cannot be verified for accuracy. If the key behaviors of simulation objects are hidden in masses of code—or worse, distributed across the code—users will not be able to alter them in a coherent fashion. The simulation may thus inhibit rather than promote the easy changes required to provide a good environment in which to investigate alternatives.

Incomprehensibility of Results

A simulation that is intelligible, and thus can be verified to represent an accurate model, can confidently be expected to produce data that describe the behavior of the modeled dynamic system. However, if the data are not presented effectively, it can be almost impossible to see the most important behavioral properties of the system. For example, large military simulations can generate hundreds of pages of numeric output for each simulation run. Determining the main global features of the simulation's performance from such output is a slow process at best; at worst, important trends may be overlooked entirely.

Long Run Times

Even simulations that are intelligible and supply the support required to try out a wide range of alternatives are not useful if they are too slow. Certainly, simulations that have reached a final "production" state must execute rapidly. The analyst expects to simulate complex processes in minutes, not hours. On a more subtle level, it is frequently necessary to try out many parameter settings or investigate many alternative models to draw any reliable inferences from a simulation. Such multiple experiments are prohibitive if each run takes more than a few minutes. Unfortunately, many simulations run even slower than real time. (Our approach to speed is discussed in Jefferson and Sowizral (1982), and the speeds of several different implementations of a ROSS simulation called SWIRL are discussed in Narain et al. (1983).)

3.2 Overview of the ROSS Language

The ROSS language (McArthur and Klahr, 1982) was designed at Rand to overcome some of the shortcomings of existing simulations and to provide a superior environment in which to model, understand, and design dynamic systems. ROSS relies heavily on recently developed AI techniques and expert-systems technology (Hayes-Roth et al., 1983).

ROSS is an *English-like, object-oriented language*. Several examples of its English-like flavor are given later in this chapter. More detailed examples are presented in Klahr et al. (1984) and especially in Klahr et al. (1982b), which discusses virtually all the code of the SWIRL simulation. The English-like nature of the code makes it readable and makes the models embedded in it intelligible to users who may not be programming experts. ROSS's object-oriented nature, which is shared by the SMALLTALK (Goldberg and Robson, 1983), PLASMA (Hewitt, 1977), FLAVORS (Weinreb and Moon, 1981), and DIRECTOR (Kahn, 1979) languages, imposes a style of programming that is highly suited to simulation.

Because ROSS is interactive (it is implemented in Lisp), a ROSS simulation can be interrupted while it is running, the state can be queried or the code modified, and the simulation can then be resumed. With compiled simulation languages, such as SIMSCRIPT (Kiviat et al., 1968), the user must specify a simulation and let it run to completion before making any modifications. Thus, alternate designs can be explored in ROSS substantially more quickly and easily. ROSS's interactive nature also makes the debugging of simulations much simpler and faster. Over the course of constructing large simulations, this can mean substantial savings in development costs.

To make simulation results more comprehensible, ROSS provides a tracing facility that produces textual simulation output. In addition, ROSS is directly linked to a movie generator and graphics facility, so that visual representations can be generated as the simulation is running. This visual presentation is invaluable in discerning global trends in simulation performance.

ROSS has been operational for several years and has been implemented in a wide variety of Lisps (Narain et al., 1983), including Maclisp, Interlisp-20, Vax-Interlisp, Interlisp-D, Franzlisp, and Zetalisp. An earlier ROSS simulation, called SWIRL (Strategic Warfare In the ROSS Language), for example, provides a prototype of a design tool for military strategists in the domain of air battles (Klahr et al., 1982a, 1982b). SWIRL embeds knowledge about offensive and defensive battle strategies and tactics. It accepts from the user a simulation environment representing offensive and defensive forces, and it uses the specifications in its knowledge base to produce a simulation of an air battle. SWIRL also uses a graphical interface to let the user observe the progress of the air battle in time. Exploiting ROSS's ability to modify simulation objects and their behaviors easily, SWIRL encourages the user to explore a wide variety of alternatives and to discover increasingly effective options in offensive and defensive strategies. In the following section, we elaborate on the main features of ROSS that are used in SWIRL.

3.2.1 ■ The Structure of Object-oriented Simulation Models: Objects, Messages, and Behaviors

Object-oriented simulation languages enforce a style of programming that parallels the way we intuitively think of the processes in the dynamic system we are modeling. Many systems are naturally described in terms of separate components. For example, a car engine includes a carburetor, a transmission, and so on. Furthermore, the behavior of the system typically arises as objects interact by transmitting forces or information to one another or by coming into physical proximity. In ROSS, such systems are modeled in a very natural way with *objects* created to model each of the components of the dynamic system, and with the interactions between them modeled as *message passing*.

In ROSS, messages are sent from one object to another using the following kind of form:[2]

(1) (**ask** fighter-base1 send fighter2 guided by gci3 to penetrator4).

The general syntax for message transmissions is:

(2) (**ask** *<object>* *<message>*)

where *<object>* is the name of any ROSS object or actor, and *<message>* is any sequence of Lisp atoms defining a legal ROSS message. In (1), the object named *fighter-base1* receives the message *send fighter2 guided by gci3 to penetrator4*.

When an object receives a message, it must have a way of responding. The user therefore must define a *behavior* whose *pattern* matches the message and whose *actions* represent the appropriate response. In this case, the behavior might be:

```
(3)  (ask fighter-base when receiving
              (send >fighter guided by >gci to >penetrator)
        (ask !myself schedule after
               !(ask myself recall your scramble-delay) seconds
               tell !fighter chase !penetrator guided by !gci)
        (ask !myself add !fighter to your list of fighters-scrambled)
        (ask !myself remove !fighter from your list of
               fighters-available)).
```

More generally, behaviors, like all computations in an object-oriented language, are defined by message transmissions of the form:

(4) (**ask** *<object>* **when receiving** *<message-template>* *<body>*)

where *<object>* is the name of any ROSS object or actor, *<message-template>* is any sequence of Lisp atoms defining a legal ROSS message, possibly including variables, and *<body>* is any arbitrary ROSS or Lisp code.

Just as ROSS objects are meant to model components of a real-world system, behaviors model the repertoire of ways that particular kinds of objects can respond to different inputs, information, or forces in the real world. Note that behaviors are attached to specific objects; they are not global functions. This captures the notion that different kinds of real-world entities have different behavioral capabilities.

[2] Reserved ROSS keywords are shown in boldface.

When the message in (1) is sent, fighter-base1 will *pattern-match* that message (i.e., *send fighter2 guided by gci3 to penetrator4*) against the message templates of all the behaviors it knows until it finds the appropriate one, in this case *send >fighter guided by >gci to >penetrator*. This template matches the message because all the words in it either are identical to analogous items in the message or are *variables*. Variables are indicated by the prefixes > or +, and they match any word in the incoming message. Thus, *>fighter* matches *fighter2*, and the variable *fighter* will be bound to *fighter2* during the execution of the behavior associated with this template. (Similarly, *gci* will be bound to *gci3*, and *penetrator* will be bound to *penetrator4*.) Pattern variables such as *fighter* are prefixed by ! in the behavior body. This prefix forces the variable to be evaluated; in other words, its value is used, not its name (ROSS is a nonevaluating form of Lisp[3]). The behavior body itself embeds message transmissions, either to the object that received the current message (the object is always the value of the variable *myself*) or to any other object. Thus, a single message transmission can trigger an arbitrarily complex chain of subsequent transmissions.

3.2.2 ■ Object Hierarchies and Inheritance

Another important semantic concept in ROSS is that of object hierarchies and inheritance. In item (1) shown previously, a message was sent to an object called *fighter-base1*, while in (3), the user defined a behavior for an object called *fighter-base*. How can *fighter-base1* use a behavior that was defined for *fighter-base*? The answer is that although *fighter-base1* was not given this behavior directly, it can *inherit* it. To understand how inheritance works in ROSS, we need to understand how objects are created.

Objects can be created by forms such as

(5) (**ask** fighter-base **create instance** fighter-base1).

This message causes *fighter-base1* to be created as an instance of *fighter-base*. Semantically, *fighter-base* should be interpreted as denoting the class of all fighter-bases, while *fighter-base1* denotes a particular element of that class. This fundamental distinction between *generic* and *instance* objects is very useful in modeling real-world systems, which have dif-

[3] Lisps come in two basic types: evaluating and nonevaluating. An evaluating (or EVAL) version evaluates arguments to function calls before giving them to the function; a nonevaluating (or EVALQUOTE) version does not. For example, the EVALQUOTE form *list(a b)* and the EVAL form *(list 'a 'b)* give the same result, namely a list of two elements, *a* and *b*.

ferent kinds of components, each instance of which has the same or similar properties. For example, all dogs (at least all healthy, normal dogs) have four legs, and most dogs bark when they see the mailman. A good modeling language should provide a way to make these quantified statements and infer their truth for any particular dog. By allowing the creation of generic objects, ROSS provides a means of making quantified statements; by allowing inheritance, ROSS enables these statements to be instantiated for individuals.

The procedure of inheritance that models this instantiation is very simple. When an object (e.g., *fighter-base1*) has been created as an instance of a class (e.g., *fighter-base*), and the instance receives a message, it finds a behavior that matches the message by first looking at behaviors that have been explicitly attached to it. If it fails, it will consult the behaviors of the class objects of which it is an instance.

Simple inheritance has been generalized in two ways in ROSS. First, class objects may be subclasses of other objects, just as instances are members of classes. To create a subclass, one might say

(6) (**ask** fighter-base **create generic** prop-fighter-base)

(7) (**ask** fighter-base **create generic** jet-fighter-base).

This would indicate that there are two different kinds of fighter-bases, those that handle jets and those that do not. The importance of subclassing is that it allows users to express quantified statements of arbitrarily limited scope. There may be some things that all fighter-bases can do, some that only jet bases can do, and some that only prop bases can do.

Complex subclassing in ROSS can induce a class-inclusion *object hierarchy*. An example of the object hierarchy used in SWIRL is shown in Fig. 3.1. When an instance of a generic object in this hierarchy receives a message, it does an inheritance search up from its location in the leaves of the hierarchy to find an ancestral object that has a behavior matching the message it has received. Thus when matching an incoming message, *fighter-base1* will search, in order, object behaviors for *fighter-base1*, *fighter-base*, *fixed-object*, and *simulator*.

The object hierarchy in Fig. 3.1 is not strictly a tree. *AWACS* (a type of airborne radar) is a subclass of both *moving-object* and *radar*. This *multiple inheritance* is the second way simple inheritance has been generalized in ROSS. Multiple inheritance was not a feature of earlier object-oriented languages, but it has proven highly useful in our ROSS simulations. Its value derives from the fact that it is often useful to view an object from multiple perspectives, or as being described in several ways. From one perspective, an AWACS can be viewed as having the properties of an aircraft (a moving object); from another perspective, it can be viewed as a detector of electronic signals (a radar).

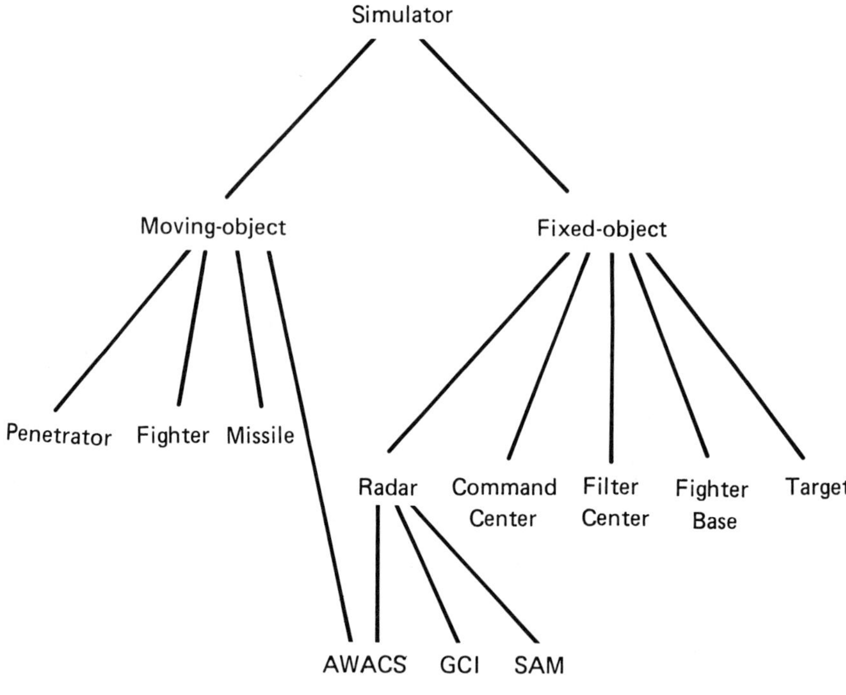

FIGURE 3.1 SWIRL Hierarchy of Basic Objects.

Finally, although we have been talking primarily about the inheritance of behaviors, ROSS objects also possess attributes, and they too can be inherited. The behaviors of ROSS objects model the dynamic actions and reactions of real-world entities (i.e., how they respond to a variety of inputs); the attributes of ROSS objects model the static features or properties of such objects (which may, however, dynamically change during a simulation). For example, we might have created the class object *fighter-base* as follows:

```
(8)  (ask fixed-object create generic fighter-base with
       position            (0 0)      ;position
       status              active     ;active or destroyed
       filter-center       nil        ;each base has one
       fighters-available  nil        ;list of free fighters
       fighters-scrambled  nil        ;occupied fighters
       fighters-destroyed  nil        ;its fighters lost
       scramble-delay      10         ;time to scramble once told
       alert-delay         10         ;delay to alert
       alert-duration      1800       ;how long to remain alert
       range               400.0)     ;how far its fighters can go
```

Now, when *fighter-base1* wants to find out its alert-duration, it uses the message transmission

(9) (**ask** fighter-base1 **recall your** alert-duration)

to find the value associated with *fighter-base*, effectively making the inference that since all fighter-bases have an alert-duration of 1800 seconds, it must have an alert-duration of 1800 seconds. Some of the attributes of *fighter-base* are to be interpreted as defaults rather than as required values. For example, although all fighter-bases have an alert-duration of 1800 seconds, the position of a particular fighter-base can be inferred to be (0 0) only if no other information about that base is available; that is, if the base does not have a position explicitly associated with it. Also note that some attributes are known to exist but are not given any default values. These attributes have a *nil* initial value. When *fighter-base* is asked to create instances of itself, values for these attributes must be specified.

ROSS provides commands to create and manipulate the attributes of objects. For example, the message

(10) (**ask** fighter-base1 **set your** status **to** destroyed)

will set the *status* attribute of *fighter-base1* to be *destroyed*. (If the particular attribute does not exist for the object, it is created.) The following message shows an example of modifying an inherited attribute:

(11) (**ask** fighter-base1 **increment your** alert-duration **by** 100).

If *fighter-base1* did not have a value for the attribute *alert-duration*, it would inherit the value of 1800 seconds from the *fighter-base* class to which it belongs, add 100 to it, and incorporate the result, 1900, as the value of its *alert-duration* attribute (without affecting any attributes of *fighter-base*). Attributes can be created and manipulated dynamically within a simulation or by a user at any time.

3.2.3 ■ Getting Simulations Started: Planning and the Clock

We have described computation in ROSS, but not simulation. A simulation language must provide a way of modeling events that occur over time. ROSS provides two such facilities. First, ROSS allows any object to plan an event to happen at any future time, using commands of the form

(12) (**ask** fighter-base1 **plan after** 20 **seconds**
tell fighter1 chase penetrator2 guided by gci3).

Once *fighter-base1* has issued this command, ROSS will ensure that the message embedded in the plan is sent to *fighter1*, not immediately, but after 20 seconds. (Of course, "20 seconds" refers to *simulated* real time, not real time or CPU time.) Operationally, this means that all messages planned to be sent 19 seconds or less in the future are guaranteed to be sent before this message, and all planned for 21 seconds will be sent after it.

To execute planned events, ROSS provides a clock. The clock is a primitive ROSS object (called *nclock*) that advances simulation time when given commands such as

(13) (**ask** nclock **tick**).

A "tick" is a variable number of seconds, determined by the *ticksize* attribute of *nclock*. When the clock ticks, it not only advances simulated real time by a given interval of time, it also sends each of the messages (in time order) that have been planned for the current time interval. For example, if (12) and then (13) were issued at time 120 with a clock ticksize of 25 seconds, the simulated real time would first advance to 140 seconds (the time of the next message to be sent in the current time interval), the message embedded in (12) (i.e., *tell fighter1 chase penetrator2 guided by gci3*) would be transmitted; and finally, the clock would advance to 145 and end the current tick.

The user can control the size of a tick by giving commands such as

(14) (**ask** nclock **set your** ticksize **to** 20).

Because users can decide how many ticks to execute at a time and can specify the size of a tick, they have complete control over the "grain" of the simulation. At one extreme, they can let a simulation run to completion without interruption; at the other, they can stop it after a very short duration, examine the state of any of the simulation objects in detail, and then resume running.

3.2.4 ■ Advantages and Disadvantages of Object-oriented Languages for Simulation

The main advantage of object-oriented languages for simulation is that they immediately suggest a way to view the dynamic system to be modeled. Our experience with SWIRL (Klahr et al., 1982a, 1982b) and TWIRL (Klahr et al., 1984) indicates that an object-oriented style of computation is especially suited to simulation in domains that may be thought of as consisting of autonomous *intentionally* interacting components. In such domains, the programmer can discern a natural mapping of their constituent components onto objects and of their intentional interactions, such as communication, onto message transmissions. Indeed, experts in many domains may find the object-oriented metaphor a natural one around which to organize and express their knowledge (Klahr and Faught, 1980).

However, in developing simulations in ROSS, we have discovered some events, or interactions between real-world objects, that are not as easily modeled as we might like them to be. These events are often side effects of deliberate actions (e.g., a penetrator appearing as a blip on a radar screen is a side effect of the penetrator flying its course and entering a radar range). Such events are important, since they may trigger other actions (e.g., a radar detecting a penetrator and notifying a filter center). However, these *nonintentional* events do not correspond to real-world message transmissions (e.g., a penetrator does not notify a radar that it has entered the radar range). An important issue in the development of SWIRL has been the problem of capturing these nonintentional events in an object-oriented framework (i.e., via message transmissions). This problem and its various possible solutions are discussed in Klahr et al. (1982b).

3.2.5 ■ English-like Code in ROSS

While the style of programming enforced by ROSS's object-oriented nature is the most important factor contributing to the modifiability of ROSS models, the highly readable character of the code is also important. Two features make ROSS code English-like. First, because behavior invocation uses pattern matching, the user can choose to define arbitrarily verbose behavior templates. Thus, in (3) the user employed the template

```
(15)  (send >fighter guided by >gci to >penetrator)
```

rather than the less English-like and less comprehensible

```
(16)  (send >f guided-by >g >p)
```

even though either is quite acceptable as a ROSS command. If one were to implement behaviors in Lisp as functions, the resulting function calls would about as unintelligible as the code in (16):

```
(17)  (send-guided-by-to fighter gci penetrator).
```

ROSS allows for even greater readability through its *abbreviations package*. This package was used in the development of SWIRL and TWIRL to generate code that would be comprehensible to strategic and tactical warfare experts who were programming novices. For example, after specifying the following abbreviations:

```
(18)  (abbreviate '(ask !myself) 'you)
      (abbreviate '(ask !myself recall your) 'your)
      (abbreviate '(!) 'the)
```

we could rewrite (3) as

```
(19)  (ask fighter-base when receiving
          (send >fighter guided by >gci to >penetrator)
      (~you schedule after !(~your scramble-delay) seconds
          tell ~the fighter chase ~the penetrator guided by ~the gci)
      (~you add the ~fighter to your list of fighters-scrambled)
      (~you remove ~the fighter from your list of fighters-available)).
```

The ROSS abbreviations package allows for *personalized* English-like programming, in contrast to languages such as ROSIE (Fain et al., 1981), whose English-like syntax is fixed by the language designers. A personalized English syntax enhances the writability of code, whereas languages whose syntax is fixed often prove difficult to use because users falsely assume that *their* English syntax is the language's. In ROSS, this problem does not exist because users *do* define their own language syntax.

Second, even extensive use of the ROSS abbreviations package carries almost no computational overhead. ROSS expands the abbreviations only once, at load time, somewhat like displacing macros. Other English-like languages may incur high costs in parsing time. In fact, more time can be spent parsing the English-like surface representation into a machine-runnable form than actually executing the runnable code.

3.2.6 ■ Interactive Browsing and Editing Facilities

ROSS encourages the development of highly structured, interactive *browsing* and *editing* facilities. An interactive browser can be thought of as an interface that is an expert in the structure of a simulation and so can quickly guide even a naive user to any piece of a simulation model—any object or behavior. An interactive editor extends the browser by permitting users to modify the code after they have found the part of the simulation model they want to change. Collectively, these features facilitate rapid, coherent modification of models by users who are familiar with the *models*, but not necessarily with the specifics of their *implementation*.

Figure 3.2 shows a user interaction with a simple but effective browser we constructed for the SWIRL simulation. Item (20) is the top-level menu. (Virtually all user interaction with SWIRL involves menu selections.) The user selects option 9, which invokes the browser to guide him or her through the code. If the user has been interacting directly with ROSS, and not with the SWIRL menu, the browser could have been invoked by "(ask browser help)." The browser is a full-fledged ROSS object. At (21), the browser presents a menu of all SWIRL objects it knows about, and the user picks which one to

FIGURE 3.2 Trace of Interactive Browsing in ROSS and SWIRL (user's menu selections in boldface).

(20) Select option:
1 -- Break into ROSS
2 -- Load compiled SWIRL
3 -- Load interpreted SWIRL
4 -- Recompile interpreted SWIRL files
5 -- Load a simulation environment
6 -- Run simulation with graphics
7 -- Run simulation without graphics
8 -- Activate historian and reporter
9 -- Browse or edit behaviors
10 -- Exit SWIRL & ROSS **9**

(21) 1. -- PENETRATOR
2. -- FIGHTER
3. -- GCI
4. -- SAM
5. -- AWACS
6. -- RADAR
7. -- FILTER-CENTER
8. -- COMMAND-CENTER
9. -- FIGHTER-BASE
10. --- TARGET
11. -- MISSILE
12. -- MOVING-OBJECT
13. -- FIXED-OBJECT
14. -- SCHEDULER
15. -- PHYSICIST
16. -- MATHEMATICIAN
Give number of object you want to examine, or NIL to stop: **6**

(22) Documentation is available on the following templates:
1. -- (>THING IS IN YOUR RANGE)
2. -- (TRANSMIT TO YOUR FILTER-CENTER THAT +MESSAGE)
3. -- (>PENETRATOR IS OUT OF YOUR RANGE)
4. -- (TRY TO CHANGE GUIDER OF >FIGHTER TO >PENETRATOR)
5. -- (>PENETRATOR IS DESTROYED)
6. -- (>PENETRATOR HAS CHANGED ROUTE)
7. -- (IS >PENETRATOR STILL IN YOUR RANGE)
8. -- (GUIDE >FIGHTER TO >PENETRATOR)
9. -- (STOP GUIDING >FIGHTER)
10. -- (FIND A NEW GCI TO GUIDE >FIGHTER TO >PENETRATOR)
11. -- (>FIGHTER HAS SIGHTED >PENETRATOR)
12. -- (>FIGHTER UNABLE TO CHASE >PENETRATOR)
13. -- (ARE SATURATED)
14. -- (ARE NOT ECMED OUT BY >PENETRATOR)
15. -- (CHECK FOR NEW PENETRATORS)

(continued)

```
        Give list of messages you want to examine, or T for all, or NIL to stop: 8
(23)     1. -- ENGLISH DESCRIPTION
         2. -- SWIRL CODE
         3. -- BOTH
       Type option, or NIL to stop: 1

       (ask radar documentation for
            (guide >fighter to >penetrator) is
   |Sender: fighter or another radar handing over guidance of a
   fighter. Guides a fighter to a pen. Four cases arise:
   If the radar is destroyed it can do nothing. The fighter just
   follows unguided policy.
   If the fighter seeks guidance towards a penetrator that is not
   currently tracked by the radar, it tries to find another radar
   to guide the fighter. If this fails, it tells the fighter to
   follow unguided policy.
   If the radar is blinded, it tries to find another radar to guide
   the fighter. If this fails, it tells the fighter to follow
   unguided policy.
   Otherwise the radar calculates an intercept point of the fighter
   with the penetrator and tells fighter to vector to this point.|)
```

FIGURE 3.2 Continued

examine. At (22), the message templates of the selected object are displayed, and again the user selects one. Note how both the object-oriented structure of the simulation and the English-like nature of the message templates facilitate finding the exact part of the simulation the user wants to examine. The object-oriented structure imposes a highly modular decomposition of the model, whereas the English-like templates make apparent exactly which behaviors are being modeled. At (23), the user chooses simply to see if the selected behavior embeds the right model. When option 2 is selected, ROSS puts the user into an editor with the code for the behavior.

3.2.7 ■ Using ROSS in the Emacs Editor

ROSS is an interactive programming environment, since it is implemented in Lisp. We have discussed several examples of how this interactivity assists the user in understanding simulations. However, standard interactive programming environments have limitations, most of which stem from the "typewriter" mode of interaction almost all current software enforces. Even though most users run Lisp and ROSS on a terminal with a screen, the screen is useless. Like a typewriter-based terminal, only the current line can be submitted for evaluation. Previous lines cannot be referenced.

We sought to make ROSS a fully screen-oriented interactive environment in several ways. First, we wanted to make each command on the screen referenceable. Second, we wanted to give the user the ability to create multiple windows on the screen, each associated with a different process, such as an editor, a compiler, or a ROSS program. Finally, we wanted to allow users to "program by pointing." The user should be able to move a cursor to any expression on the screen and tell ROSS what to do with the expression.

To achieve these goals, we modified ROSS to run as a process under Emacs (Gosling, 1981), a customizable, screen-oriented editor. In this environment, ROSS is inside an Emacs window, and all forms typed go into the window's buffer. When the user types a carriage return, Emacs takes the form just typed and submits it to the ROSS process for evaluation, printing the value returned just below the form submitted. Thus, in simple interactions, the environment looks just like a standard Lisp session. However, because the user is in a screen-oriented editor, several new capabilities are available. Emacs commands can be used to move the cursor and to mark any previous form in the ROSS buffer. Emacs commands can then be used to apply several operations to the marked item, including the following:

- *Evaluate the item.* If the marked item is a legal Lisp or ROSS form, it can be resubmitted to the ROSS interpreter, and its value will be returned. The expression can be edited with any standard editor commands before reevaluation.
- *Compile the item.* If the marked item is the name or definition of a Lisp function or ROSS behavior, a few keystrokes will tell Emacs to create a Lisp compiler process, associate it with a new window, submit the marked definition to the process, and return the result. In this way, compilation can be much more incremental and interactive than many Lisp dialects permit.
- *Edit the item.* If the marked item is the name or definition of a Lisp function or ROSS behavior, the user can request Emacs to visit the file that contains the function or behavior. The user does not need to know where the function or behavior is defined. Emacs will create a window for the appropriate file and put the user in the file at the location of the specified definition. When the user is in this window, all these capabilities are still at his or her disposal, in addition to the basic editor commands for deleting, adding, moving, and searching text. In particular, he or she

can point to parts of definitions and ask for them to be evaluated. In this fashion, definitions can be rapidly and incrementally modified.

- *Reformat the item.* If the marked item is a Lisp expression, a single command can be used to reformat the expression in a more readable way. This facility is especially useful for cleaning up function or behavior definitions in their files.

The ROSS-Emacs facility reduces the model-builder's memory load by remembering the location of definitions. At the same time, it makes the examination and modification of models a rapid process by automatically handling many low-level programming details.

3.2.8 ■ Textual Output Facilities

We have discussed several features of ROSS that enable even naive users to locate, understand, and change complex simulation models. We now discuss some ways in which ROSS simplifies the analysis of simulation results, which also can be complex.

First, the interactive browsing in ROSS is easily extended to recording simulation events. For example, the recorder and historian we constructed for SWIRL work almost exactly like the browser. The recorder and historian are invoked by selecting option 8 in the SWIRL menu (item (24) in Fig. 3.3). Like the browser, the recorder and historian know all the objects and behaviors that comprise the SWIRL simulation and can guide the user through the code by displaying menus. The menus at (25) and (26) are similar to those at (21) and (22) in Fig. 3.2. However, when the user selects a behavior, the recorder and historian do not display the behavior, as the browser does; rather, they keep a record of each time that behavior is executed during a simulation. An example of a partial record is shown at (28) in Fig. 3.3. It indicates both the simulation time at which the behavior was invoked and the message transmission that caused the invocation.

The recorder and historian allow simulation output to be tailored in several ways. First, because the specification of the objects and behaviors to record is done interactively, recording can be interwoven with running of the simulation (see (27) in Fig. 3.3). Thus, users can rapidly change the parts of the simulation model they are examining. Second, users have a great deal of control over which message transmissions are traced. In standard procedural languages, the only option available is to trace a function or not to trace it. Object-oriented languages such as ROSS allow the user to trace all the message transmissions for all instances of a given class of object, or a specific message transmission for all instances of a class, or even particular types of message transmissions for specific instances of a class of objects. For

FIGURE 3.3 Trace of Interactive Recording in ROSS and SWIRL (user's menu selections in boldface).

---

(24) Select option:
1 -- Break into ROSS
2 -- Load compiled SWIRL
3 -- Load interpreted SWIRL
4 -- Recompile interpreted SWIRL files
5 -- Load a simulation environment
6 -- Run simulation with graphics
7 -- Run simulation without graphics
8 -- Activate historian and reporter
9 -- Browse or edit behaviors
10 -- Exit SWIRL & ROSS **8**

Specify file to record history: **RECORD**

Output to terminal (T or NIL): **T**

(25) 1. -- PENETRATOR
2. -- FIGHTER
3. -- GCI
4. -- SAM
5. -- AWACS
6. -- RADAR
7. -- FILTER-CENTER
8. -- COMMAND-CENTER
9. -- FIGHTER-BASE
10. -- TARGET
11. -- MISSILE
12. -- MOVING-OBJECT
13. -- FIXED-OBJECT
14. -- SCHEDULER
15. -- PHYSICIST
16. -- MATHEMATICIAN
Give list of objects in parentheses, e.g., (1 4 8), or NIL: **(1 2 4 5 6 7 9)**

(26) PENETRATOR has the following message templates:
1. -- (FLY TO >PLACE)
2. -- (DROP >M MEGATON BOMBS EXPLODING AT ALTITUDE >H)
3. -- (>RADAR IS NOW TRACKING YOU)
4. -- (>RADAR IS NO LONGER TRACKING YOU)
5. -- (EVADE)
6. -- (RESCHEDULE YOUR NEXT SECTOR)
7. -- (MAKE A RANDOM TURN)
8. -- (MAKE A TURN >N DEGREES >DIRECTION)
Give list of message numbers to record (T for all): **T**

[*User and recorder interact to specify trace for other objects*]

Select option:
1 -- Break into ROSS
2 -- Load compiled SWIRL

(continued)

```
         3 -- Load interpreted SWIRL
         4 -- Recompile interpreted SWIRL files
         5 -- Load a simulation environment
         6 -- Run simulation with graphics
         7 -- Run simulation without graphics
         8 -- Activate historian and reporter
         9 -- Browse or edit behaviors
        10 -- Exit SWIRL & ROSS 7
(27) Type number of ticks to run: 100
(28) 0.0      (AWACS3 LOOK FOR PEN3)
     0.0      (AWACS3 LOOK FOR PEN2)
     0.0      (AWACS3 LOOK FOR PEN1)
     0.0      (AWACS2 LOOK FOR PEN3)
     0.0      (AWACS2 LOOK FOR PEN2)
     0.0      (AWACS2 LOOK FOR PEN1)
     0.0      (PEN3 FLY TO (880.0 210.0))
     0.0      (PEN2 FLY TO (352.0 700.0))
       0.0      (GCI3 IS PEN2 STILL IN YOUR RANGE)
       0.0      (GCI2 IS PEN2 STILL IN YOUR RANGE)
     0.0      (PEN1 FLY TO (220.0 1085.0))
     492.891342     (AWACS1 PEN2 IS IN YOUR RANGE)
       492.891342     (AWACS1 ARE NOT ECMED OUT BY PEN2).
```

[*Simulation continues for 100 ticks*].

```
Select option:
  1 -- Break into ROSS
  2 -- Load compiled SWIRL
  3 -- Load interpreted SWIRL
  4 -- Recompile interpreted SWIRL files
  5 -- Load a simulation environment
  6 -- Run simulation with graphics
  7 -- Run simulation without graphics
  8 -- Activate historian and reporter
  9 -- Browse or edit behaviors
 10 -- Exit SWIRL & ROSS 10
```

FIGURE 3.3 Continued

example, in SWIRL one can focus on the activities of just *fighter1* rather than all fighters.

3.2.9 ■ Graphical Output Facilities

A primary component of both the SWIRL and TWIRL simulations is their color graphics output facility. Although the graphics package is not an integral part of the ROSS language, we have developed a clean and direct interface between it and ROSS.[4] For each ROSS object, we define a symbol and color. Similarly, we define symbols for events that we want to see graphically represented (e.g., communications between objects, military combat, radar detections). Each time the clock ticks, the graphics screen is updated to show the new locations of the objects and any new events that have occurred since the last clock tick. In a sense, the graphics package creates an animated movie of the simulation as it proceeds over time.

Graphics have provided us with a powerful tool for building and understanding simulations. Being able to watch the simulation as it is running lets the user readily test and verify behaviors, notice global interactions among the objects and events, zoom in on particular areas of interest, and determine the effects of alternative models and behaviors.

3.3 Conclusions

The ROSS language represents our first attempt to develop a relatively complete modeling environment. Ideally, such an environment can help users understand, reason about, and even design a wide variety of complex entities. In this report, we have discussed how ROSS facilitates the construction and viewing of models through object-oriented programming techniques, English-like language syntax, interactive debugging and editing tools, and textual and graphical output facilities. Much work remains. We are presently investigating the Time Warp mechanism (Jefferson and Sowizral, 1982), a methodology for speeding up simulations by distributing them. In addition, we want to develop modeling capabilities that go beyond simulation. We view a simulation as one of several kinds of models. Although other approaches to modeling are less well developed (de Kleer and Brown, 1983), they deserve attention because simulation alone enables users to answer surprisingly few questions about the behavioral characteristics of their models (Davis et al., 1982). To improve modeling as a reasoning and design tool, we must not only make it easier for users to ask questions of their models, we must greatly extend the range of questions they can ask.

[4] SWIRL and TWIRL graphics were written in C by William Giarla. They were built upon graphics work previously developed at Rand for other projects.

References

1. Dahl, O-J., and K. Nygaard, "Simula—An Algol-Based Simulation Language," *Communications ACM*, Vol. 9, 1966, 671–678.
2. Davis, M., S. Rosenschein, and N. Shapiro, *Prospects and Problems for a General Modeling Methodology*, The Rand Corporation, N-1801-RC, June 1982.
3. de Kleer, J., and J. S. Brown, "Assumptions and Ambiguities in Mechanistic Models," in *Mental Models* (D. Gentner and A. Stevens, eds.), Lawrence Erlbaum, Hillsdale, N.J., 1983.
4. Fain, J., D. Gorlin, F. Hayes-Roth, S. Rosenschein, H. Sowizral, and D. Waterman, *The ROSIE Language Reference Manual*, The Rand Corporation, N-1647-ARPA, December 1981.
5. Goldberg, A., and D. Robson, *Smalltalk-80: The Language and Its Implementation*, Addison-Wesley, Reading, Massachusetts, 1983.
6. Gosling, J., *Unix Emacs*, Carnegie-Mellon University, Pittsburgh, 1981.
7. Hayes-Roth, F., D. A. Waterman, and D. B. Lenat, *Building Expert Systems*, Addison-Wesley, Reading, Massachusetts, 1983.
8. Hewitt, C., "Viewing Control Structures as Patterns of Message Passing," *Artificial Intelligence*, Vol. 8, 1977, 323–364.
9. Jefferson, D., and H. Sowizral, *Fast Concurrent Simulation Using the Time Warp Mechanism, Part I: Local Control*, The Rand Corporation, N-1906-AF, December 1982.
10. Kahn, K. M., *Director Guide*, Memo 482B, Massachusetts Institute of Technology Artificial Intelligence Laboratory, Cambridge, Massachusetts, 1979.
11. Kiviat, P. J., R. Villanueva, and H. M. Markowitz, *The Simscript II Programming Language*, Prentice-Hall, Englewood Cliffs, N.J., 1968.
12. Klahr, P., J. Ellis, W. Giarla, S. Narain, E. Cesar, and S. Turner, *TWIRL: Tactical Warfare in the ROSS Language*, The Rand Corporation, R-3158-AF, October 1984.
13. Klahr, P., and W. S. Faught, "Knowledge-Based Simulation," *Proceedings of the First Annual National Conference on Artificial Intelligence*, Palo Alto, California, 1980, 181–183.
14. Klahr, P., D. McArthur, and S. Narain, "SWIRL: An Object-Oriented Air Battle Simulator," *Proceedings of the Second Annual*

National Conference on Artificial Intelligence, Pittsburgh, 1982(a), 331–334.

15. Klahr, P., D. McArthur, S. Narain, and E. Best, *SWIRL: Simulating Warfare in the ROSS Language*, The Rand Corporation, N-1885-AF, September 1982(b).
16. McArthur, D., and P. Klahr, *The ROSS Language Manual*, The Rand Corporation, N-1854-AF, September 1982 (updated September 1985).
17. Narain, S., D. McArthur, and P. Klahr, "Large-Scale System Development in Several Lisp Environments," *Proceedings of the Eighth International Joint Conference on Artificial Intelligence*, Karlsruhe, West Germany, 1983, 859–861.
18. Weinreb, D., and D. Moon, "Objects, Message Passing, and Flavors," *Lisp Machine Manual*, July 1981, 279–313.

SECTION THREE

Applications

In this section we present papers that describe Rand's past and present work in the area of applied artificial intelligence. This work involves a number of expert system applications that use knowledge-engineering tools developed at Rand.

Chapter 4, on expert systems applied to terrorism, describes the use of RITA to develop a model of international terrorism. This application involves defining the basic concepts needed to model terrorist activities and implementing systems to facilitate acquiring and organizing domain knowledge from experts on terrorism. The work is interesting from two perspectives: first, it is one of the early attempts to apply knowledge engineering to a very poorly understood and ill-defined domain, and second, it provides some insight into the effect of the knowledge-engineering methodology on the domain expert. As the authors point out, forcing experts to articulate their basic rules of reasoning sharpens their analytical skills. It makes them more aware, and hence more critical, of their own reasoning; it causes them to examine closely how they arrive at conclusions; and it teaches them to look carefully at any gaps that may exist between their reasoning steps.

Chapter 5, on legal decision making, describes a ROSIE application in the area of product liability law. The expert system, called LDS, assists attorneys and claims adjusters in settling product liability cases by setting a dollar value on the case. To do this, LDS takes into account the extent of the plaintiff's loss, the liability of the defendant, and other factors relevant to the case.

This prototype expert system was developed to explore the feasibility of using rule-based methods to organize and represent knowledge in the legal domain. The authors' experience with LDS indicates that many aspects of the settlement process can be described naturally by such rule-based models. This work is significant because it represents one of the first expert system applications in the legal arena and because it faces problems not encountered in most other application areas. For example, expert systems applied to the legal profession must capture both informal, poorly specified expertise, such as strategies and operating procedures of attorneys, as well as large quantities of information that is formally described, such as statutes, regulations, and other legal text. Whereas the informal strategies may sometimes be expressed quite simply, the formal law is seldom simple and usually requires a means for expressing very complex statements and ideas. The problem then is to provide an adequate means for representing and accessing these complex concepts and rules. The use of ROSIE as a development tool was one approach to alleviating this problem.

Chapter 6, on TATR, describes another ROSIE expert system application, this time in a military domain. Under the interactive direction of the user, TATR assists Air Force tactical targeteers in mission planning. The system helps the user find a preferential ordering of enemy airfields, determines the best targets to attack on those airfields, and identifies weapon systems that are effective against those targets.

TATR is interesting because it is one of a small collection of expert systems developed to handle tasks involving planning. It applies predetermined planning heuristics to generate an initial plan, which can be modified by user guidance or specific instructions. TATR then replans to incorporate the user's changes. By projecting the results of a hypothetical series of activities over a number of days, TATR can assist the user in deciding on the best plan or sequence of plans to implement.

Chapter 7, on TWIRL, describes an extensive ROSS program that simulates ground combat between two opposing forces, including movements and interactions over time. The authors describe the objects that comprise TWIRL and provide examples of object behaviors to explain and illustrate the process of building a simulation in ROSS. TWIRL, like SWIRL (an air battle simulation program written in ROSS), is significant as one of the first object-oriented simulations to use the knowledge-engineering paradigm. Although most simulations separate the design and implementation processes, ROSS-based simulations interweave these processes similar to the way expert systems are typically built. TWIRL and SWIRL were developed incrementally through continual interactions with domain experts. In addition, the domain knowledge embedded in these simulations is highly readable, easily modifiable, and modular.

Chapter 4

Developing Expert Systems to Combat International Terrorism

Donald A. Waterman and Brian M. Jenkins

4.1 Introduction

This chapter describes research on the task of applying knowledge engineering techniques to ill-defined problems in the social sciences, in particular, the problem of international terrorism. Our goal is to explore ways in which expert system technology, in the form of rule-based systems, can be used to help experts understand the domain in which they work and assist them in decision making, particularly in crisis situations. Our approach is to provide experts with an expert system; that is, a set of computer programs that constitute a model of their domain of expertise and that enable them to store information explicitly as rules and data. Experts can then use the system as a tool that guides and stimulates decision making by its ability to explain the lines of reasoning it uses to arrive at each decision it makes.

This chapter is a revised version of P-5811, The Rand Corporation, March 1977. P-5811 also appeared in *Terrorism: Threat, Reality, Response* (R. H. Kupperman and D. M. Trent, eds.), Hoover Institution Press, Stanford, Calif. 1979, 285–324.

An expert system organized as rules representing heuristics (rules of thumb) can be used to describe the dynamics of the situation. It is particularly useful for problem domains that are not well formalized and for which no generally agreed upon axioms or theorems exist. The domain we have chosen for investigation—international terrorism—is just this type of domain. By studying the techniques needed to develop an expert system in this domain we hope to gain insight into how these methods can be applied to other ill-defined domains in the social sciences.

In this study we outline the objectives of our work, describe how information can be represented in rule-based form, describe some preliminary attempts to create programs that help the expert input information into the computer and, finally, discuss the usefulness of providing an expert with this type of tool.

4.1.1 ■ Background

This work is defined by the intersection of two separate research efforts —one involving the application of artificial intelligence techniques to the problem of helping people who are not computer experts interact with computers, and the other involving the study and analysis of international terrorism. The immediate goal is to provide terrorism analysts with computer programs specifically designed to aid them in their analysis of terrorist activities. These programs must be designed so that they can be carefully tailored to the individual needs of each analyst.

The artificial intelligence research effort is based on the premise that a good way to aid computer users is to provide them a personal computer that is sensitive to their needs and desires. This can be accomplished in many ways (via timesharing, intelligent terminals, etc.), but the underlying theme is to have the software designed to accommodate the skills of the user, with more sophisticated software for the less advanced users. The tool we are using for this is called RITA, Rand Intelligent Terminal Agent (Anderson et al., 1976a, 1976b). An intelligent terminal agent is simply a program that can perform some task for the user. Examples of typical tasks are: filing, retrieving, and editing data on local storage files; handling interactive dialogues with external information systems; providing a local tutorial facility; and representing subjective or judgmental information (Waterman, 1978). The most distinctive feature of the RITA architecture is the use of rules to describe judgments. A rule is defined to have the form "IF condition THEN action," meaning "if the given condition is true in the current situation then perform the recommended action." Thus RITA is a *rule-based* expert system building tool.

Since 1973, The Rand Corporation, sponsored jointly by the Defense Advanced Research Projects Agency and the Department of State, has been engaged in research on the phenomena of international terrorism. The theory of terrorism, terrorist tactics, and terrorist groups has been examined, and data on over a thousand incidents of political violence have been amassed. Several hundred of these have been the subject of more detailed examinations. During the course of the research, the participants in the project came naturally to make "expert judgments" or to develop "hunches" regarding various aspects of terrorist activity, such as the responsibility for incidents when credit was not claimed, the objectives of a particular action, and the probable outcome of certain types of episodes. Though often unarticulated, and sometimes unrealized by the participant, these hunches were often based on a series of individual "rules" derived from an understanding of the logic behind the use of terrorist tactics, the observed modi operandi of various terrorist groups, and the outcome of similar episodes in the past. Thus the domain of terrorism is a reasonable area in which to use rule-based expert systems.

Our work is beneficial to both the computer scientists involved in expert system development and the social scientists working on terrorism analysis. The computer scientists benefit by gaining access to a problem domain that can be used to evoke and test ideas about the design and implementation of expert systems. The social scientists benefit by being provided with a requirement and a means for articulating the series of steps that lie behind the intuitive judgments they make in reaching a particular conclusion. In the process of explaining each step, they ask questions they did not ask before simply because the rapid process of thought does not demand such detailed explanations. Previously, in describing why they felt something to be so, it was explained simply as an intuitive judgment, or a hunch. The requirements of machine analysis impose a new degree of rigor on the analysts, lead to new questions, extract articulations about the theory and logic of terrorism, and point to new areas of exploration. In short, it not only provides a useful tool for the analysts to use, but also aids them in formalizing their domain of study.

When fully operational, the expert system will continue to demand that analysts examine each incident in a comprehensive manner and explain each judgment. On the basis of rules provided by the analysts, the system will reach conclusions with which the analysts may disagree. In this case, the analysts will be compelled to reexamine the basis for their deductions, and this may lead to the formulation of new rules for the system. In this way the system will enable analysts to preserve their own judgments and those of others in a form that is easily retrievable and can be made available to decision makers faced with real crisis situations.

4.1.2 ■ Basic Assumptions

This work is based on three major assumptions. The first is that terrorist activities can be analyzed in a formal, rigorous fashion. For the most part, the violence of political extremists is not viewed as a collection of irrational and thus totally unpredictable events. It follows certain rules of logic that can be discerned by the experienced analyst. Patterns emerge that can be translated into operational rules. For example, a study of political kidnappings and hostage incidents shows that political extremist groups that operate in their home territory and have the support of an underground organization generally prefer standard kidnappings as a means of taking hostages. (In a standard kidnapping, the victim is held at an unknown location while the kidnappers bargain by means of telephone or mail with the targets of their demands. This enables them to hold their hostage for months if necessary to increase pressure for concessions.) Groups operating abroad or lacking an underground tend to become involved in barricade-and-hostage incidents (captors seize their hostages in a public place, allowing themselves to become hostages; they bargain for escape along with other demands). This is not always true, but it is generally true. Some of the patterns are based on group characteristics or modi operandi. For example, the Irish Republican Army has shown no inclination to seize hostages for bargaining purposes. Many of the Palestinian and Latin American groups frequently do so.

The second assumption is that although the domain of terrorism is obviously complex and each incident is highly unique, it is still true that even a limited number of rules that prod thinking and formalize the domain will enhance analysis of the topic.

The third assumption is that terrorist activities can be formulated as rule-based systems. One limiting constraint here is the number of rules needed to adequately model the domain. This can be avoided to a certain extent by attempting to model only a small portion of the domain of international terrorism. In this initial effort we have restricted our attention to the problem of terrorist bombings.

4.1.3 ■ Objectives

Our primary objective is to determine the feasibility and utility of developing expert systems within a rule-based framework and to help the user make complex decisions in ill-specified domains that contain large amounts of information that must be coordinated and used in a short amount of time. The secondary objective is to develop a demonstration system that performs interesting and useful deductions within the domain of international terrorism. Such a system would stimulate new ideas about the domain, provide a framework for structuring thinking and guiding problem solving during a crisis situation, and assist in the analysis, understanding and prediction of terrorist activities.

4.1.4 ■ Characteristics of the Expert System

The system under development is a collection of RITA agents that the terrorism analysts will have at their disposal. These agents will constitute a tool that the analysts can use to aid in decision-making or problem-solving tasks. The system will have the following primary characteristics.

1. A *deductive inference capability.* This means that the agents will be capable of not only retrieving information stored in the database but also using that information to make deductions that can cause new information to be added to the database. This capability is a direct result of using a rule-based system, since the rules are, in effect, procedures defining how new information can be deduced from existing data.
2. *Dynamic growth.* In the domain of international terrorism, both data and judgments (or policy) are subject to constant revision. The modularity imposed by the rule-based organization of the agents facilitates such dynamic growth (i.e., it is easy to add, delete, or modify both the data and the rules that constitute the judgments).
3. *Integrated collection of knowledge.* The agents that constitute the system can represent judgments of many experts from various parts of the world. This expertise is stored at one location for later use by experts and nonexperts alike. However, the real utility of such a system is that it will permit a constant exchange of data and judgments by leading experts, and this will lead to the formation of new rules and ideas about the domain.

4.2 Representation of Information in the Form of Rules

A rule-based system is a collection of rules of the form "condition → action" where the conditions are statements about the contents of a database and the actions are procedures that alter the contents of that database. RITA is a rule-based programming language within which one can write specific programs that are sets of rules constituting RITA agents. Rule-based systems evolved from production systems (Newell and Simon, 1972). Production system architectures have been developed to facilitate adaptive behavior (Waterman, 1970, 1975; Waterman and Newell, 1976), to model human cognition and memory (Newell, 1972, 1973), and to create large systems that embody the judgments of a collection of experts (Feigenbaum, et al., 1970; Shortliffe and Buchanan, 1975; Davis, et al., 1977; Lenat, 1976). RITA was designed with the latter task in mind and accordingly has two main constructs: those called rules and those called goals. The rules are antecedent driven. This means that when all the conditions of a rule are true relative to the database, the rule "fires," causing the associated actions to be taken. The goals, however, are consequent driven. This means that the system is given a condition to make true, or, in effect, a question to answer through deductive inference. Here, the right sides or consequents of rules are examined to find one that could make the desired condition true. When such a rule is found, its left side or antecedent is examined to see if all its conditions are true. If they are, the rule is fired; if not, the process continues in the same manner in an attempt to make each condition in the left side of the rule true.

4.2.1 ■ Data Representation in RITA

In RITA the data are represented as objects that can have any number of attribute-value pairs. For example, to represent a person whose name is John Smith, whose age is 32, and whose salary is in the $33,789 to $43,923 range, the object PERSON would have associated with it three attribute-value pairs: NAME = JOHN SMITH, AGE = 32, and SALARY RANGE = $33,789 TO $43,923. This would be written in RITA as:

```
OBJECT person
    name is "John Smith",
    age is "32",
    salary-range is "$33,789 to $43,923";
```

The fact that John Smith, Mary Jones, and Tom Brown are all government service employees and are all part of a group of such employees called GS level 15 can be represented as:

```
OBJECT group
    name is "GS Level 15",
    type is "government service employees",
    members is ("John Smith", "Mary Jones","Tom Brown");
```

Note that the value of an attribute can be either an item such as "John Smith" or a list such as ("John Smith", "Mary Jones", "Tom Brown"). Also, more than one object of the same type can exist simultaneously in the database. The database can contain many distinct persons and groups, each with different attribute-value pairs. Thus Mary Jones might also be in the database as:

```
OBJECT person
    name is "Mary Jones",
    age is "22";
```

4.2.2 ■ Goal and Rule Representation in RITA

Problem domain expertise in RITA is represented as goals and rules. The format for a goal is:

```
GOAL goalname
    IF premise AND premise ... AND premise
    THEN action AND action ... AND action.
```

A few examples will make this format clear. Figure 4.1 shows statements in English and below them the corresponding RITA goals. The format for rules is very similar to that for goals.

```
RULE rulename
    IF premise AND premise ... AND premise
    THEN action AND action ... AND action.
```

Some examples of RITA rules are given in Fig. 4.2. The "deduce" action in Rule 2 is a signal to RITA to process the goals in an attempt to infer the desired information.

The data, goals, and rules just described can be combined to form a RITA agent that will tell the user the name and salary range of each person in the the database if that range is known or can be deduced. This agent is shown in Fig. 4.3.

4.2.3 ■ Example of a Deduction by a RITA Agent

When the agent in Fig. 4.3 is executed, Rule 1 is tested against the database and found to be true since John Smith's salary range is known, but nothing is known about John Smith's status. Since all the premises of Rule 1 are true, Rule 1 "fires," (i.e., the associated action is taken) and the agent writes "John Smith $33,789 to $43,923" at the user's terminal and sets John Smith's status to "accounted for." Again Rule 1 is tested against the database but now fails to fire for John Smith, since the second premise, concerning John Smith's status, is no

1. "The salary range of a government service group can be determined by the salary range of any of its members."

or

"If you don't know the salary range of a government service group but you do know the salary range of a member of that group then the salary range of the group is just the salary range of that member."

GOAL 1:

IF: there is a group whose type is
"government service employees"
and whose salary-range is not known
and there is a person whose salary-range
is known
and the name of the person is in the members
of the group

THEN: set salary-range of the group to the
salary-range of the person;

2. "The salary range of a member of a government service group can be determined by the salary range of the group."

or

"If you don't know the salary range of a member of a government service group but the salary range of the group is known then the salary range of the person is just the salary range of the group."

GOAL 2:

IF: there is a person whose salary-range is not known
and there is a group whose salary-range is known
and the name of the person is in the members
of the group

THEN: set the salary-range of the person to the
salary-range of the group;

FIGURE 4.1 Examples of RITA Goals.

longer true. It also fails to fire for Mary Jones, since the first premise concerning her salary range is not true.

Since the premises in Rule 1 are not true, it cannot fire and Rule 2 is tested. The premise in Rule 2 is true for Mary Jones, so the rule fires and the salary range of Mary Jones is deduced. This deduction involves

1. "Send the name and salary range of each person to the user."

   or

   "If the salary range of a person is known and it has not been sent to the user then send both the name and salary range of the person to the user".

RULE 1:
IF: there is a person whose salary-range is known
and whose status is not known
THEN: send the name of the person to the user
and send the salary-range of the person to the user
and set the status of the person to "accounted for";

2. "Infer the salary range of every person whose salary range is not known."

   or

   "If there is a person whose salary range is not known then infer that salary range."

RULE 2:
IF: there is a person whose salary-range is not known
THEN: deduce the salary-range of the person;

FIGURE 4.2 Examples of RITA Rules.

just the goals. The right sides (action parts) of the goals are checked to see if they could determine the salary range of a person. Only Goal 2 can do this, so its premises are checked to see if they are true so the goal can be fired.

The first premise of Goal 2 is true for Mary Jones, but the second premise is not since the salary range of the group is not known. Now the system does a clever thing. Instead of giving up and deciding that Goal 2 is not true, it tries to deduce the second premise of Goal 2 (i.e., the salary range of the group). The only applicable goal is Goal 1, so its premises are checked. The first premise of Goal 1 is true, since the group is government service employees and its affiliation is not known. The second and third premises of Goal 1 are true for John Smith and the group, so all the premises are true and the goal fires, setting the salary range of the group to "\$33,789 to \$43,923." This makes the second premise of Goal 2 true, and, since the third premise of Goal 2 is true for Mary Jones, all the premises are true and Goal 2 fires, setting the salary range of Mary Jones to "\$33,789 to \$43,923."

```
OBJECT person<1>:
    name        IS  "John Smith",
    age         IS  "32",
    salary-range    IS    "$33,789 to $43,923";
OBJECT person<2>:
    name        IS  "Mary Jones",
    age         IS  "22";
OBJECT group<1>:
    name        IS  "GS Level 15",
    type        IS  "government service employees",
    members     IS  ("John Smith","Mary Jones","Tom Brown");

RULE 1:
      IF:  THERE IS a person WHOSE salary-range IS KNOWN
                AND WHOSE status IS NOT KNOWN
    THEN:  SEND the name OF the person TO user
           & SEND the salary-range OF the person TO user
           & SET the status OF the person TO "accounted for";
RULE 2:
      IF:  THERE IS a person WHOSE salary-range IS NOT KNOWN
    THEN:  DEDUCE the salary-range OF the person;
GOAL 1:
      IF:  THERE IS a group
                WHOSE type IS "government service employees"
                AND WHOSE salary-range IS NOT KNOWN
           & THERE IS a person WHOSE salary-range IS KNOWN
           & the name OF the person IS IN the members OF the group
    THEN:  SET the salary-range OF the group TO the
           salary-range OF the person;
GOAL 2:
      IF:  THERE IS a person WHOSE salary-range IS NOT KNOWN
           & THERE IS a group WHOSE salary-range IS KNOWN & the
           name OF the person IS IN the members OF the group
    THEN:  SET the salary-range OF the person TO the salary-range
           OF the group;
```

FIGURE 4.3 A RITA Agent That Attempts to Deduce the Salary Range of all Persons in the Database.

The deduction is now complete, and control returns to the rules. Rule 1 is checked and this time is true for Mary Jones. It fires, printing "Mary Jones $33,789 to $43,923" at the user's terminal and setting the status of Mary Jones to "accounted for." Now Rule 1 is checked again but is not true, nor is Rule 2, so the agent halts. The database after the deductions are made shows:

```
OBJECT person<1>:
    name          IS  "John Smith",
    age           IS  "32"
    salary-range  IS        "$33,789 to $43,923",
    status        IS  "accounted for";
OBJECT person<2>:
    name          IS  "Mary Jones",
    age           IS  "22"
    salary-range  IS        "$33,789 to $43,923",
    status        IS  "accounted for";
OBJECT group<1>:
    name          IS  "GS Level 15",
    type          IS  "government service employees",
    members IS        ("John Smith","Mary Jones","Tom Brown");
    salary-range  IS "$33,789 to $43,923";
```

Note that not only was the desired information about the salary range of Mary Jones deduced and added to the database, but as a side effect information concerning the salary range of the group was also deduced and stored in the database.

4.3 Expert System Development in RITA

Building an expert system for a domain like terrorism is a complex task regardless of the method chosen for constructing the system. The method used here centers on extracting data and rules from an expert on terrorism in a form that focuses on the essential and relevant information in the domain.

4.3.1 ■ Data and Rule Extraction

The first step in building an expert system in an ill-defined domain is the job of formalizing the domain. This critical step consists of deciding what elements in the domain are relevant to the problem at hand, how they should be categorized, and how they should be defined. It imposes the degree of organization on the data that is needed for later development of relationships between the data elements. The key to formalizing the domain is data extraction — the process of extracting data or knowledge about the domain from an expert. This was accomplished, in our case, by a series of dialogues between the expert and the system-builders, in which the system-builders played the role of protocol analysts (Waterman and Newell, 1973, 1976). Typically the analysts or knowledge engineers will ask pertinent questions of the expert to reveal assumptions and attitudes the expert may not have been conscious of having. These ideas are then expanded by the expert and the analysts into a characterization of the domain.

Rule extraction proceeds in exactly the same manner as data extraction: through an extended dialogue between the expert and the analysts. We have found that trying to extract rules out of context (e.g., issuing the request, "Give me all the rules you know about bombings by the Palestinian Groups.") leads to vague generalizations that are seldom useful. The most successful approach has been to focus on particular events, analyze them in great depth, and then classify the rules generated during the analysis as either specific to a particular context or as a special case that is generally true — one that almost occupies the status of an axiom or tautology in the system. We thus end up with two types of rules: axiomatic ones that are true with near 100 percent probability, and heuristic ones that are true with a lesser probability. Although both types of rules can be used to infer new information, the axiomatic rules can also be used to check the validity of the information being extracted.

Data extraction or domain formalization is not something done in a single step that is followed by the step of rule extraction. In actuality these steps proceed in parallel, progress in each affecting the status of the other. Thus many iterations must be made through the cycle of defining and organizing relevant data, generating rules that relate data elements to each other, and then revising the definitions and organization to accommodate new components of new rules. Eventually we would like to have the job of rule extraction automated, performed perhaps by a RITA agent capable of asking the right questions and using the answers to build RITA rules.

4.3.2 ■ Focal Points for Terrorism

It appears to us that there are three important focal points around which we can build a system for modeling terrorist activities. These are focal points around which information can be gathered and rules can be formulated. They are *event, group,* and *context.* The term *event* stands for a terrorist incident, such as a bombing, hijacking, or kidnapping. The term *group* means a terrorist group, that is, a group that has used terrorist tactics. *Context* is a somewhat less precise label that encompasses local political and economic developments, effectiveness of internal security, and so on. In a specific situation, it may include the circumstances external to the actual incident or event (e.g., the response of a government to the specific terrorist activity).

A useful analogy is to consider these focal points as hubs of wheels: one wheel for group, one for event, and another for context. Radiating from the hub like spokes are the *attributes* that are associated with each wheel. Radiating from the hub labeled *event* are relevant attributes such as its date, time, type, location, target, and victim. Protruding from the hub labeled *group* are attributes such as size, ideology, and composition of membership. Around *context* would be attributes such as the effectiveness of police, and so on. The answer or item of information associated with each attribute, the *value,* is located at the rim of the wheel (see Fig. 4.4).

Rules can relate one attribute or spoke to another on the same focal point or wheel. For example, the answer (or value) to a specific question (that derives from an attribute) will determine the answer to another question. To illustrate, let us use a bombing (an event). One of its attributes is the "target." By stating the target (specific individual, political property, corporate headquarters or offices, etc.) the machine may be led to a deduction about the tactical objective of the event. For example, if the target is "vital systems," the tactical objective may be "disruption."

The rules may also nullify certain questions on the basis of answers to previous questions. For example, if the bomb is identified as a Mol-

FIGURE 4.4 Example of Object-attribute-value Relationship for the Object "Event."

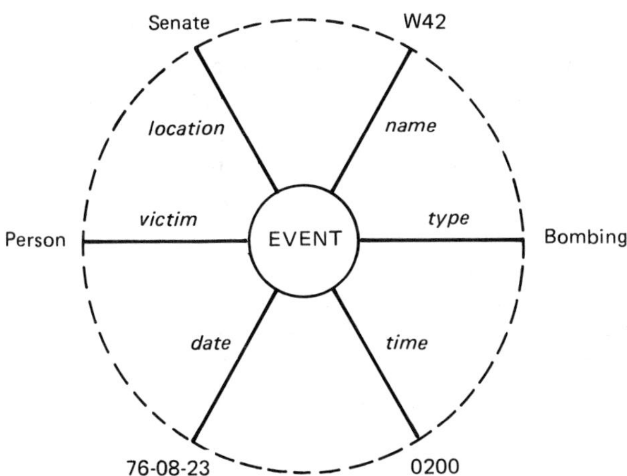

otov cocktail, the machine does not need to ask how the bomb was delivered. (Molotov cocktails are thrown.) It does not need to ask about the size of the bomb since it knows it must have been small. These rules do not represent sophisticated judgments for which experts are required. They are virtually axiomatic. They are included only to expedite the interrogation process by dropping irrelevant or repetitious questions.

Rules may also relate attributes from one focal point to another. For example, if we are talking about bombings, the type of bomb and type of target regularly chosen by a particular group may tell us something about the educational background or the ideology of its members. Such rules are not likely to be axiomatic. The judgments here are likely to be quite complex and based upon several or even many answers to specific questions.

The possible combinations are endless. Rules may be built upon several attributes in each focal point. To arrive at a judgment of what members of the Japanese Red Army who are holding hostages in the French Embassy are most likely to do if its demands are not met requires a very complex chain of reasoning. However, it is important to point out that the deduction does not always have to be correct so long as the users can follow the chain of logic used by the system to arrive at its conclusion. Users then can agree with certain parts or disagree to reach their own conclusion. In the process, they will have been compelled to review their reasoning and examine their assumptions. The system will have assisted, not replaced, the expert or decision maker.

4.4 Current State of Development

At this point we have made one iteration through the cycle of formalizing the domain of terrorist bombings and refining the associated rules. Appendix A illustrates the current formalization.

To help terrorism experts construct the domain, a RITA agent called MODIFY has been implemented. This agent queries the experts, permitting them to add, modify, or delete information from the database that represents the formalization of the domain. The experts use MODIFY first to create the database and then to update and modify it as their conception of the domain becomes clearer. A trace of experts interacting with the MODIFY agent to add a new attribute called *stage* to the object *group* is shown here. The experts' answers are given in italics.

What is to be modified...*group*

What attribute of group is to be modified...*stage*

Now defining the stage of the group:

What is the type number? *?*
Let me rephrase the question...

Do you want to enumerate some of the stages of the group? *yes*
Can any single group have more than one stage? *no*

Give a prompt for the stage of the group
the current stage of the development of the group (1 through 5)

Now enter new values and prompts
[Type only a carriage return to terminate]

A new value for the stage of the group is...*1*
The prompt for "1" is...
violent propaganda stage: sporadic bombings of symbolic targets

A new value for the stage of the group is...*2*
The prompt for "2" is...
organizational growth stage: attacks with specific tactical objectives

A new value for the stage of the group is...*3*
The prompt for "3" is...
guerilla offensive stage: attacks on real rather than symbolic targets

A new value for the stage of the group is...*4*
The prompt for "4" is...
mobilization of masses stage: attack on judiciary to provoke repression

A new value for the stage of the group is...*5*
The prompt for "5" is...
urban uprising stage: mass uprising, full scale urban warfare

A new value for the stage of the group is...

What attribute of group is to be modified...

What is to be modified...
Objects saved on file bomb.objects

After experts create the database that represents the domain they have at their disposal, another RITA agent, called BUILD, that uses the domain just defined to help the experts enter new data about terrorist events or groups into the computer. BUILD uses the domain database to formulate questions about the object to be described. For example, the questions BUILD would ask as a result of the definition given to the MODIFY agent are shown here in an actual trace of experts interacting with BUILD. Again the experts' responses are shown in italics.

Is the stage of the group:
  1? *?*
[violent propaganda stage: sporadic bombings of symbolic targets]
  1? *no*
  2? *?*
[organizational growth stage: attacks with specific tactical objectives]
  2? *no*
  3? *?*
[guerrilla offensive stage: attacks on real rather than symbolic targets]
  3? *no*
  4? *?*
[mobilization of masses stage: attack on judiciary to provoke repression]
  4? *no*
  5? *?*
[urban uprising stage: mass uprising, full scale urban warfare]
  5? *yes*

In this trace, the experts responded to each question of the agent by first typing a question mark to obtain a definition of the term being used and then answering with either yes or no. This feature of being able to ask the agent to explain itself is of critical importance, since the definitions of terms are somewhat arbitrary and not easily inferred. After the expert answered yes to the last question, BUILD created the object shown here:

```
OBJECT group<1>:
    stage IS "5";
```

The BUILD agent helps users enter information about terrorist activities into the system in a form that can be accessed by other RITA agents. However, BUILD does more than just query users and map their replies into RITA data. Before it asks each question, it attempts to deduce the answer itself based on the information it has gathered up to that point. If it can deduce the answer it notifies the user of that fact and does not ask the question. Only when it is unable to deduce the answer does it query the user. Some typical RITA goals that BUILD uses to make deductions about bombing incidents are shown in Fig. 4.5. These goals have the status of axioms in the system (i.e., the probability of their being true is very close to 1). A complete trace of an expert entering data about a hypothetical bombing incident is shown in Appendix B. An informal description of the hypothetical incident plus the resulting RITA description of it are shown in Fig. 4.6.

```
GOAL 1:
      IF:  the time-of-day OF the event IS less THAN 0600
           & the bomb-size OF the event IS "small"
    THEN:  PUT "property damage-no casualties" INTO the
             tactical-objective OF the event AS the LAST MEMBER;

GOAL 2:
      IF:  "no warning" IS IN the recipient-of-warning OF the event
    THEN:  SET the warning-time OF the event TO 0;

GOAL 3:
      IF:  the bomb-type OF the event IS "Molotov-cocktail"
    THEN:  SET the bomb-delivery OF the event TO "thrown"
           & SET the bomb-detonation OF the event TO "impact"
           & SET the secondary-detonation OF the event TO "no detona-
           tion"
           & SET the bomb-sophistication OF the event TO "low"
           & SET the detonation-source OF the event TO "self-detonating"
           & PUT "home-made" INTO the explosive-source OF the event
               AS the LAST MEMBER
           & SET the bomb-size OF the event TO "small";

GOAL 4:
      IF:  the bomb-type OF the event IS "letter or parcel"
    THEN:  SET the bomb-delivery OF the event TO "delivered"
           & SET the bomb-size OF the event TO "small"
           & SET the risk-to-perpetrator OF the event TO "low";

GOAL 5:
      IF:  the bomb-type OF the event IS "land mine"
    THEN:  SET the bomb-delivery OF the event TO "planted"
           & PUT "no warning" INTO the recipient-of-warning
           OF the event AS the LAST MEMBER;
```

FIGURE 4.5 Some of the Goals Used by the BUILD Agent to Deduce Information about Terrorist Bombings.

BUILD is an agent for acquiring data from the user. What is also needed is an agent for acquiring judgments or rules from the user. Such an agent would query the user in much the same manner as BUILD and use the information gathered to construct rules or goals about terrorist activities. To present a clearer idea of how such an agent might work, a hypothetical user-agent dialogue is shown here.

AGENT: What do you want to know about the event that you do not already know?

USER: I want to know the tactical-objective of the event and the political-ideology of the group.

FIGURE 4.6 A Hypothetical Bombing Incident and the Corresponding RITA Description.

The event took place in Washington D.C. at about 1:26 p.m. in the Senate Office Building on August 23, 1976. As Secretary of State Henry Kissinger was exiting the front door a lone individual hurled a Molotov-cocktail at him and then fled on foot. The bomb failed to explode and no one was hurt. Two minutes before the attempted bombing a woman who identified herself as a member of the New World Liberation Front called the Washington Post and claimed credit for the act. She said the reason for the incident was the failure of the government to free SLA political prisoners. The bomb itself was estimated to have weighed about 4 pounds.

```
OBJECT event<2>:
    name      IS    "Washington Incident",
    type      IS    "bombing",
    date      IS    "760823"
    time-of-day          IS    "1326",
    location             IS    "Senate",
    locale               IS    "Washington",
    region               IS    "urban",
    host-country         IS    "United States",
    announced-claimant   IS  ("New World Liberation Front"),
    when-claimed         IS    ("before-bombing"),
    announced-purpose   IS  ("retaliation against government"),
    target      IS    ( "specific individual" ),
    target-symbolic-value    IS    "inherently obvious",
    target-accessibility     IS    "medium",
    victim      IS  ( "person" ),
    bomb-weight       IS    "4",
    bomb-type         IS    "Molotov-cocktail",
    bomb-size         IS    "small",
    bomb-delivery     IS    "thrown",
    bomb-detonation IS      "impact",
    secondary-detonation     IS    "no detonation",
    detonation-source        IS    "self-detonating",
    explosive-source         IS    ( "home-made" ),
    bomb-sophistication      IS    "low",
    audacity            IS    "high",
    risk-to-perpetrator      IS    "high",
    recipient-of-warning     IS    ( "no warning" ),
    warning-time        IS    "0",
    outcome   IS    "malfunction/no detonation",
    tactical-objective       IS    ("publicity/group", "murder"),
    strategic-objective      IS    ( "publicity" ),
    number-killed       IS    "0",
    number-woundedIS          "0",
```

```
      primary-damage  IS      "no damage",
      secondary-damage        IS      "no damage",
      instigator          IS      ("New World Liberation Front"),
      perpetrator         IS      ("New World Liberation Front"),
      unused     IS    ("disclaimant", "bomb-composition");
  OBJECT target<1>:
      name       IS     "Kissinger";
```

FIGURE 4.6 Continued

AGENT: What do you think the tactical-objective might be? ("I don't know" is not acceptable.)

USER: Extortion.

AGENT: What do you think the political-ideology might be? ("I don't know" is not acceptable.)

USER: New left.

AGENT: What pieces of information would you need to validate or negate your answers?

USER: I would want to know the locale of the event, the target of the event, and the announced-purpose of the event.

AGENT: What is a possible locale for extortion and new left?

USER: California.

AGENT: What is a possible target for extortion and new left?

USER: Vital systems.

AGENT: What is a possible announced-purpose for extortion and new left?

USER: Reduce utility rates for the poor.

AGENT: On the basis of your answers, I have constructed the following rule:

```
RULE 1:
      IF:  the locale of the event is "California"
           & the target of the event is "vital systems"
           & the announced-purpose of the event is "reduce
              utility rates for the poor"
    THEN:  set the tactical-objective of the event to
              "extortion-specified philanthropic"
           & set the political-ideology of the group to
              "new left";
```

AGENT: Does this rule strike you as being irrelevant or inaccurate? If so, rewrite it as one or more rules that you believe are more accurate.

This type of rule acquisition capability would be similar to the one developed for MYCIN (Davis, 1976). The agent and the user would work together to develop and refine the rules, with the user always having the final say in the matter. Figure 4.7 shows how some goals acquired this way might look. Note that these goals are more complex than the axiomatic-type goals used by BUILD (see Fig. 4.4). They would be used, in conjunction with many other similar goals, to deduce information about bombing campaigns.

FIGURE 4.7 Goals for Deducing Information about Bombing Campaigns.

GOAL 1:

IF: the public-opinion OF the current-event
IS "anti-terrorist"

THEN: SET the government-response OF the current-event
TO "harsh crackdown on terrorists";

[If the public is strongly against the terrorists, then the government will take harsh measures to suppress the terrorists.]

GOAL 2:

IF: the casualty-level OF the current-event IS "high"
OR THERE IS a campaign WHOSE event-list IS KNOWN
& the name OF the current-event
IS IN the event-list OF the campaign
& the frequency OF the campaign IS "escalating"
OR the time-between-attacks OF the campaign IS "short"

THEN: SET the public-opinion OF the current-event
TO "anti-terrorist";

[If the current event caused many casualties or is part of a campaign whose frequency is escalating or which has a short time between attacks, then the current event will affect public opinion, i.e., the public will become anti-terrorist.]

GOAL 3:

IF: the number-killed OF the current-event IS greater THAN 0

THEN: SET the casualty-level OF the current-event TO "high";

[If 1 or more people are killed, the casualty level is considered high]

GOAL 4:

IF: the attacks-per-month OF the campaign IS NOT less THAN 1

THEN: SET the time-between-attacks OF the campaign TO "short";

[If the attacks average 1 or more per month, they are considered frequent.]

4.5 What We Have Learned So Far

The process of formalizing the domain by identifying the important concepts or objects, their attributes, and the associated values is of major importance in the construction of an expert system. This is because these basic components are all that are available for describing the complex heuristics or rules that define activity in the domain. If these basic building blocks are too narrow in scope, there will be relevant relationships that cannot be expressed. If they are too wide, the system will tend to be inefficient, spending much time processing irrelevant information.

The task of eliciting from experts judgments that the system can use as rules is far more difficult and complex than originally anticipated. Experts, it appears, have a tendency to state their conclusions and the reasoning behind them in general terms that are too broad for effective machine analysis. It is advantageous to have the machine work at a more basic level, dealing with clearly defined pieces of basic information that it can build into more complex judgments. In contrast, the experts seldom operate at a basic level. They make complex judgments rapidly, without laboriously reexamining and restating each step in the reasoning process. The pieces of basic knowledge are assumed and are combined so quickly that it is difficult for them to describe the process. When they examine a problem, they cannot easily articulate each step and may even be unaware of the individual steps taken to reach a solution. They may ascribe to intuition or label a hunch that which is the result of a very complex reasoning process based upon a large amount of remembered data and experience. In subsequently explaining a conclusion or hunch, they will repeat only the major steps, often leaving out most of the smaller ones, which may have seemed obvious at the time.

Knowing what to consider basic and relevant and not requiring further reevaluation is what makes a person a true expert. An economic forecast does not begin with an explanation of why 2 plus 2 equals 4. A political forecast in the United States does not begin with a statement that there are three branches of government and presidential elections every four years. Nor does intelligent discussion about terrorism start with the fact that Palestinians are Arabs or that aerial hijacking means taking over an airplane. And when arguing what a particular group might do in a specific situation, experts seldom state that they base their conclusions perhaps in part on the personality of a particular leader, in part on the modus operandi of a particular group, and in part on recollections of outcomes in similar episodes in the past.

This type of information is considered basic by experts. Nor do they discuss why they chose certain past episodes as relevant and discarded others that nonexperts might have chosen, or what specific aspect of the modus operandi is pertinent to the current circumstances.

Experts are not deliberately mysterious about the process of reasoning, nor are their analyses sloppy or incorrect. They simply do not state every single piece of information and every small component part of every judgment they make. Thus we discovered that the judgments the experts considered simple and basic were actually complex, often composed of many individual steps that could be elicited only by the annoying process of repeatedly asking them to justify each statement, including the statements used to clarify previous statements. Obtaining the basic rules the system needs to mimic the reasoning process of the experts is a difficult and sometimes painful task.

Attempts to extract rules from terrorist experts in the abstract simply by asking them to write all the rules they could think of pertaining to a particular domain did not prove successful for two reasons. First, experts don't usually think of their judgments as being based on a set of rules, and they have trouble putting their ideas into rule form. Second, the rules elicited by this method varied in level of abstraction but generally were all too abstract or complex for the system to use. They had to be broken down into their component parts, which is something the experts had not been required to do and normally were not accustomed to doing.

We discovered that it was far more useful to elicit rules during or immediately after an actual event in which the experts were interested and wanted to discuss anyway. The event provided the stimulus for a lively discussion. During the discussion the experts were asked to offer their opinions or judgments or hunches about some particular aspect of the event. Then they were asked why they felt this to be true. This generally produced a train of rather complex judgments. They were asked to explain how they had made each individual judgment. Each of these produced a train of somewhat less complex judgments that were "pulled apart" by the interrogators, and the process was continued until the critical attributes were identified and basic rules about them articulated.

This by itself was a major achievement. In effect, the extraction process compelled the experts to examine their own train of thought with an unprecedented degree of rigor. The first and most obvious result was the identification of the attributes of an event or group that were generally agreed to be the relevant things to examine. These were the bases for most judgments. The second result was the emergence of some rules about how these attributes interact. But the final and most important result was more than this: *the process itself, the extraction of basic rules, sharpened the experts' analytical skills.* Regardless of whether these rules could ever be assembled into a system that could in any way approach human reasoning in dealing with complex and ill-defined subjects, being forced to articulate every step along the way to a problematic conclusion was a useful exercise for the experts. It made them more aware, and hence more critical, of their own reasoning; it caused them to examine closely how they arrived at conclusions; and it taught them to look carefully at the spaces between the steps they described. Also, it conditioned them not to overlook things that otherwise might have been ignored, especially in crisis situations when they would be compelled to make snap judgments without time for reflection.

This would seem to indicate a potential utility of this effort that transcends the feasibility of being able to represent the entire domain of terrorism by rules in a computer. It is not necessary for the machine alone to duplicate human thought. Nor is it necessary for the experts alone to derive from their subject area a set of judgments that can be stored in a computer. It is the interaction of the two that causes an improvement in the experts' analytical capabilities, in both ordinary and crisis situations, and results in a tool for experts to use.

We anticipate that it will require a large number (perhaps thousands) of rules to deal with a small portion of the domain of international terrorism. This problem could be alleviated to some extent by creating many relatively small agents (300 rules or less), each a specialist in some restricted area of the domain. They could all have access to a large agent containing general information about terrorism and would make use of this agent when necessary. Because of the complexity of the task we will need as much computing power as the state of the art can provide. Thus as the power of computers increases, so will the feasibility of developing expert systems for complex domains like international terrorism.

4.6 Applicability and Future Developments

In addition to the usefulness of expert systems in improving the skills of experts working with the problem of international terrorism, it appears that expert systems may also be extremely useful in the management of crisis situations. Terrorist actions, such as the hijacking of an airliner or the takeover of an embassy, frequently create a crisis situation to which the government must respond. The usual response is to assemble a task force or several task forces at different locations to deal with the crisis. The members of the task force represent different skills (intelligence, public affairs, negotiations, area specialists) and different agencies and departments that are somehow involved in the episode. The task force makes decisions or offers options to the official who must decide the course of action to take. In dealing with these episodes, particularly hostage situations in which lives are at stake, a crisis atmosphere often prevails. Time is critical. (An average barricade-and-hostage incident lasts about 36 hours, and some drag on for days.) Assembling information about the individuals and groups involved is difficult, but this problem can be alleviated with conventional data retrieval systems. Assembling the data that are particularly relevant to a given situation is more difficult. A data retrieval system would not know which special circumstances call for certain actions and which do not. No one has time to read lengthy reports on the group, and skilled specialists themselves might not know which reports to look at first. Moreover there is the problem of decision making by committee. It is difficult to sit around a table for any period of time in silence. People tend to fill the gaps with conversation or discussion about things that may or may not be particularly relevant to the problem at hand. These distractions slow or divert the decision making process.

The system envisioned here provides a straightforward way of proceeding toward a solution. It does this by asking questions already determined to be relevant by experts. In other words, it produces demands for the most relevant information. It summons from its own memory the relevant judgments that have been made about similar groups or events in the past. Furthermore, it enables the committee to explore various options by creating in the system similar artificial events and changing various responses. The system can then display likely outcomes to these events. Interaction between the members of the committee and the system will cause them to carefully examine their own conclusions and decisions.

In other words, the expert system imposes a degree of discipline on the course of the discussion, asks the most relevant questions, provides the best judgments of expert analysis, and allows the committee to explore viable options. It also sharpens the committee's skills during the process. It is not essential that the system be entirely accurate or that its performance be flawless. Again, it is the interaction that leads to good, sharpened answers; it is not the system that reveals them from stored memory or clever deductions.

Expert systems capable of examining terrorist incidents would be especially useful in a crisis if they linked several task forces in a manner similar to the ARPAnet. This would enable the individuals or groups at different locations to see and participate in each aspect of the decision making. Everyone would see the same video display at the same time and could intervene with questions or opinions, and their interventions could be seen by all of the others.

Such a system also has utility as a storehouse of judgmental information compiled by many expert analysts over a period of time. Indeed, it may be seen as a *judgment retrieval system* as opposed to a *data retrieval system*. This would add to the overall amount of expert opinion that is available, would allow interaction between experts at different times and in different locations, and would tend to ameliorate the effect of lost capabilities that results from rotation or unavailability of personnel.

There are many directions in which this research can progress in the future. First, we can introduce the notion of certainty factors, or probability measures on all the rules and goals that give a subjective estimate of their accuracy. This would provide us with a more accurate way to evaluate the results of our deductions. Second, we can expand the scope of the analysis to other terrorist activities, such as kidnappings or barricade-and-hostage events. The scope can also be widened by including data on more groups and incidents. Third, we can develop agents to help the user recognize and define new rules, as described in Section 4.4. Fourth, we can develop agents that are capable of making predictions about future terrorist activities and use them to test the accuracy of our current formalism. Finally, we can attack the problem of inductive inference, recognizing regularities in the data and automatically forming rules to describe these regularities.

References

1. Anderson, R. H., and J. J. Gillogly, *Rand Intelligent Terminal Agent (RITA): Design Philosophy*, The Rand Corporation, R-1809-ARPA, February 1976(a).
2. Anderson, R. H., M. Gallegos, J. J. Gillogly, R. Greenberg, and R. Villanueva, *Rand Intelligent Terminal Agent (RITA): Reference Manual*, The Rand Corporation, R-1808-ARPA, September 1976(b).
3. Davis, R., *Applications of Meta Level Knowledge to the Construction, Maintenance, and Use of Large Knowledge Bases*, Stanford University. Artificial Intelligence Laboratory, Memo AIM-283, 1976.
4. Davis, R., B. G. Buchanan, and E. Shortliffe, "Production

Rules as a Representation for a Knowledge-Based Consultation Program," *Artificial Intelligence,* 8, 1977, 15–45.

5. Feigenbaum, E. A., B. G. Buchanan, and J. Lederberg, "On Generality and Problem Solving: A Case Study Using the DENDRAL Program," in *Machine Intelligence 6* (B. Meltzer and D. Michie, eds.), Edinburgh University Press, 1971, 165–190.
6. Lenat, D. B., *AM: An Artificial Intelligence Approach to Discovery in Mathematics as Heuristic Search,* Stanford University, Artificial Intelligence Laboratory, Memo AIM-286, Ph.D. dissertation, July, 1976.
7. Newell, A., and H. A. Simon, *Human Problem Solving,* Prentice-Hall, Englewood Cliffs, New Jersey, 1972.
8. Newell, A., "A Theoretical Exploration of Mechanisms for Coding the Stimulus," in *Coding Processes in Human Memory* (A. W. Melton and E. Martin, eds.), Winston and Sons, Washington, D.C., 1972.
9. Newell, A., "Production Systems: Models of Control Structures," in *Visual Information Processing* (W. C. Chase, ed.), Academic Press, New York, 1973, 463–526.
10. Shortliffe, E. H., *MYCIN: A Rule Based Computer Program for Advising Physicians Regarding Antimicrobial Therapy Selection,* Stanford University, Ph.D. dissertation, 1974.
11. Shortliffe, E. H., and B. G. Buchanan, "A Model of Inexact Reasoning in Medicine," *Mathematical Biosciences,* 23, 1975, 351–379.
12. Waterman, D. A., "Generalization Learning Techniques for Automating the Learning of Heuristics," *Artificial Intelligence,* 1, 1970, 121–170.
13. Waterman, D. A., "Adaptive Production Systems," *Proceedings of the Fourth International Joint Conference on Artificial Intelligence,* 1975, 296–303.
14. Waterman, D. A., "Serial Pattern Acquisition: A Production System Approach," in *Pattern Recognition and Artificial Intelligence* (C. H. Chen, ed.), Academic Press, New York, 1976, 529–553.
15. Waterman, D. A., *Rule-Directed Interactive Transaction Agents: An Approach to Knowledge Acquisition,* The Rand Corporation, R-2171-ARPA, February 1978.
16. Waterman, D. A., and A. Newell, *Preliminary Results with a System for Automatic Protocol Analysis,* Carnegie-Mellon University, Computer Science Department, 1973.

17. Waterman, D. A., and A. Newell, "PAS-II: An Interactive Task-Free Version of an Automatic Protocol Analysis System," *IEEE Transactions*, C25, 1976, 402–413.

Appendix A

Formalization of a Domain for Terrorist Bombings

event ....

name [give the event to be defined an identifying name]

type
[type of the terrorist event; (e.g., bombing, kidnapping)]
bombing
barricade-and-hostage
kidnapping

date
[use the format yymmdd; (e.g., 760330)]

time-of-day
[a four-digit number; (e.g., 0830, 1635)]

location
[an object, (e.g., embassy, airplane)]

locale
[a place; (e.g., Paris, Madrid)]

region
[environs in which the event occurred]
urban
rural
water
air

host-country
[name of country in which event occurred]

announced-claimant
[name of person(s) or group claiming credit for the event]

when-claimed
[when were claims announced taking credit for the event?]
  before-bombing
  before-publicity
  before-casualty-report
  after-casualty-report

announced-purpose
[announced reason for carrying out event]

disclaimant

[name of person(s) or group disclaiming credit for the event]

target
[who or what was the immediate object of the attack?]
  specific individual
  representative individual
  random individual
  political property
  corporate headquarters or offices
  other commercial property
  private property
  vital systems
  head of state

target-symbolic-value
[what symbolic value did the object of the attack have?]
  inherently obvious
  specified by perpetrator
  none apparent

target-accessibility
[how accessible was the object of the attack to the perpetrators?]
  low
  medium
  high

victim
[who or what was the event intended to affect?]
  person
  organization
  government
  ideal

bomb-weight
[estimated weight in pounds; (e.g., 10)]

bomb-type
[which type of bomb was used in the event?]
  Molotov-cocktail
  other incendiary
  letter or parcel
  pipe
  small explosive charge
  shopping bag
  grenade
  car
  land mine

bomb-size
[estimate the size of the bomb: small, medium, or large]
  small
  medium
  large

bomb-delivery
[how did the bomb arrive at its destination?]
  planted
  delivered
  thrown

bomb-detonation
[what method was used to detonate the bomb?]
  command-line
  command-radio
  impact
  time
  mechanical
  electrical
  chemical
  fuse

x-ray
photoelectric
altitude

secondary-detonation
[what type of backup detonation device did the bomb have?]
no detonation
command-line
command-radio
impact
time
mechanical
electrical
chemical
x-ray
photoelectric
altitude

detonation-source
[who detonated the bomb?]
victim
perpetrator
self-detonating

bomb-composition
[what type of explosive material was used in the bomb?]

explosive-source
[source of the explosive material: commercial, military, etc.]
commercial
military
home-made

bomb-sophistication
[give a subjective estimate of the sophistication of the bomb]
low
medium
high

audacity
[give an appraisal of how brazen and audacious the incident was]
low

medium
high

risk-to-perpetrator
[assess the risk to the perpetrators of capture or death]
low
medium
high

recipient-of-warning
[who received prior warning of the bomb?]
media
target
police
no warning

warning-time
[minutes before the expected detonation the warning was received]

outcome
[what happened to the bomb?]
detonated
discovered/defused
malfunction/no detonation

tactical-objective
[what was the immediate goal of the bombing?]
murder
punishment/retaliation
property damage-no casualties
property damage-casualties
extortion-payoff to perpetrator
extortion-unspecified philanthropic
extortion-specified philanthropic
disruption
publicity/group
publicity/commemorative

strategic-objective
[what was the more global objective of the instigator?]
increase-pain-level
halt-operation

publicity
discredit-government
political-victory
military-victory
defense of the group/movement
intergroup rivalry

number-killed
[number of people killed during incident]

number-wounded
[number of people wounded during the incident]

primary-damage
[what was the damage resulting directly from the bomb itself?]
no damage
low
medium
high

secondary-damage
[what was the damage caused in the aftermath of the bomb?]
no damage
low
medium
high

instigator
[name of person(s) or group who planned the event]

perpetrator
[name of person(s) or group carrying out the event]

group ....
name
[type the full proper name of the group and the acronym, if any]

political-ideology
[political persuasion or connections of group]
fascist
right-wing
Moscow-line communist

independent communist
Trotskyite
Maoist
anarchist
new left

nationality
[country or origin or primary base]

age
[how many years has the group been in existence?]

objective
[what are the strategic objectives of the group?]
enlarge the group
expansion
overthrow of government
discredit the system
territorial independence
limited reforms or concessions
vigilante-like defense

action-frequency
[the approximate number of incidents perpetrated per year]

past-incidents
[type the names of the past incidents instigated by the group]

affiliations
[names of allied groups]

stage-of-development
[stages 1 to 5 allowed]

ethnic-composition
[major nationality or ethnic composition represented in the group]

educational-composition
[what kind of education do the group members have?]
uneducated
high school
university

supporters
[groups, sectors, and organizations that aid and abet the group]
 other terrorist groups
 university-educated population sectors
 working-class sectors
 minority groups
 foreign governments
 nobody

level-of-sophistication
[sophistication of the group in terms of planning and execution]
 low
 medium
 high

tactics
[the typical types of events perpetrated by the group]
 bombing
 barricade-hostage
 kidnapping
 assassinations
 highjackings
 armed assaults
 robbery
 dissemination of propaganda
 sabotage

type
[characterize the goal of the group in terms of the given categories]
 separatist/irredentist
 national revolutionary
 international revolutionary

activity-span
[how many years has the group been active at terrorism?]

targets
[the types of objects or persons typically attacked]
 specific individual
 representative individual
 random individual

government property
political property
corporate headquarters or offices
other commercial property
private property
vital systems

members
[type names of members: first name (alias) last name]

headquarters-location
[where the decision makers are located, (e.g., Berkeley, Beirut)]

territory-of-operations
[the territorial area over which the group spreads its operations]
international
national
regional
state
local

level-of-support
[extent of support for the group: (e.g., local, regional)]
insignificant
local
regional
national
international

type-of-support
[expressions of support for the group]
passive sympathy
limited help
total commitment

person ....

name
[name of person]

nationality
[name of country of national origin]

sex
[male or female]

age
[approximate age in years]

occupation
[what does the person do for a living?]
  police/military
  government
  corporate official
  political-figure
  private-citizen

group-membership
[organizational affiliation]

terrorism-role
[how is this person connected with terrorist activities?]
  target
  perpetrator
  instigator
  hostage

Appendix B

Trace of an Expert using the Build Agent

%rita use.build.goal
use.build.goal:

Fill-in-the-blanks questions can be answered with either a single reply such as "Fred Jones", or with a list of replies, each separated by a comma followed by a space (i.e., "Fred Jones, Mary Smith, John Doe"). To indicate that you don't know, just type <carriage return>.

For questions of the form: "The <a> of the <b> is...", typing "unknown" is equivalent to typing <carriage return>. For questions of the form: "Other <a>s of the <b>...", typing "none" is equivalent to typing <carriage return>.

Yes-or-no questions can be answered with either "y" or "yes" for yes; "n", "no", or carriage return for no; or a single answer, such as "school building" for a qualified yes.

You may type "?" in response to any question to elicit information about the type of answer required.

To terminate the session, type "nothing" in response to the "What is to be defined..." question. Then to see the database that was just created, type "display all objects;".

> The most current event took place in Washington D.C. at about 1:26 p.m. in the Senate Office Building on August 23, 1976. As Secretary of State Henry Kissinger was exiting the front door a lone individual hurled a Molotov-cocktail at him and then fled on foot. The bomb failed to explode and no one was hurt. Two minutes before the attempted bombing a woman who identified herself as a member of the New World Liberation Front called the Washington Post and claimed credit for the act. She said the reason for the incident was the failure of the government to free SLA political prisoners. The bomb itself was estimated to have weighed about 4 pounds.

What is to be defined...*event*

The name of the event is: *Washington Incident*

Is the type of the event:
    bombing? *yes*

The date of the event is: *?*
[use the format yymmdd; (e.g., 760330)]

The date of the event is: *760823*

The time-of-day of the event is: *?*
[a four-digit number; (e.g., 0830, 1635)]

The time-of-day of the event is: *1326*

The location of the event is: *Senate*

The locale of the event is: *Washington*

Is the region of the event:
    urban? *yes*

The host-country of the event is: *United States*

The announced-claimant of the event is: *?*
[name of person(s) or group claiming credit for the event]

The announced-claimant of the event is: *New World Liberation Front*

Is the when-claimed of the event:
    before-bombing? *?*
[when were claims announced taking credit for the incident?
Give one answer for each announced claim]
    before-bombing? *yes*

before-publicity? *no*
before-casualty-report? *no*
after-casualty-report? *no*

Other when-claimed(s) of the event...

The announced-purpose of the event is: *retaliation against government*

The disclaimant of the event is:

Is the target of the event:
specific individual? *Kissinger*
representative individual? *no*
random individual? *no*
political property? *no*
corporate headquarters or offices? *no*
other commercial property? *no*
private property? *no*
vital systems? *no*
head of state? *no*

Other target(s) of the event...

Is the target-symbolic-value of the event:
inherently obvious? *yes*

Is the target-accessibility of the event:
low? *no*
medium? *yes*

[I deduce that the victim(s) of the event includes:
("person")]

The bomb-weight of the event is: *?*

[estimated weight in pounds; (e.g., 10)]

The bomb-weight of the event is: *4*

Is the bomb-type of the event:
Molotov-cocktail? *yes*
[I deduce that the bomb-size of the event is "small"]
[I deduce that the bomb-delivery of the event is "thrown"]
[I deduce that the bomb-detonation of the event is "impact"]
[I deduce that the secondary-detonation of the event is "no detonation"]
[I deduce that the detonation-source of the event is "self-detonating"]

The bomb-composition of the event is:
[I deduce that the explosive-source(s) of the event includes:
("home-made")]
[I deduce that the bomb-sophistication of the event is "low"]

Is the audacity of the event:
  low? *no*
  medium? *no*
  high? *yes*

Is the risk-to-perpetrator of the event:
  low? *no*
  medium? *no*
  high? *yes*

Is the recipient-of-warning of the event:
  media? *no*
  target? *no*
  police? *no*
  no warning? *yes*

Other recipient-of-warning(s) of the event...
[I deduce that the warning-time of the event is "0"]

Is the outcome of the event:
  detonated? *no*
  discovered/defused? *no*
  malfunction/no detonation? *yes*

[I deduce that the tactical-objective(s) of the event includes:
  ("publicity/group", "murder")]
[I deduce that the strategic-objective(s) of the event includes:
  ("publicity")]
[I deduce that the number-killed of the event is "0"]
[I deduce that the number-wounded of the event is "0"]
[I deduce that the primary-damage of the event is "no damage"]
[I deduce that the secondary-damage of the event is "no damage"]
[I deduce that the instigator(s) of the event includes:
  ("New World Liberation Front")]
[I deduce that the perpetrator(s) of the event includes:
  ("New World Liberation Front")]

Finished with the event

What is to be defined...*nothing*

```
The following data were added to
file bomb.data in your file area:

[OBJECTS:]

OBJECT event<2>:
    name        IS      "Washington Incident",
    type        IS      "bombing",
    date        IS      "760823"
    time-of-day         IS      "1326",
```

```
        location            IS      "Senate",
        locale              IS      "Washington",
        region              IS      "urban",
        host-country        IS      "United States",
        announced-claimant  IS  ("New World Liberation Front"),
        when-claimed        IS      ("before-bombing"),
        announced-purpose   IS  ("retaliation against government"),
        target      IS      ( "specific individual" ),
        target-symbolic-value   IS      "inherently obvious",
        target-accessibility    IS      "medium",
        victim      IS  ( "person" ),
        bomb-weight         IS      "4",
        bomb-type           IS      "Molotov-cocktail",
        bomb-size           IS      "small",
        bomb-delivery       IS      "thrown",
        bomb-detonation IS      "impact",
        secondary-detonation    IS      "no detonation",
        detonation-source       IS      "self-detonating",
        explosive-source        IS      ( "home-made" ),
        bomb-sophistication     IS      "low",
        audacity            IS      "high",
        risk-to-perpetrator     IS      "high",
        recipient-of-warning    IS      ( "no warning" ),
        warning-time        IS      "0",
        outcome     IS      "malfunction/no detonation",
        tactical-objective      IS      ("publicity/group", "murder"),
        strategic-objective     IS      ( "publicity" ),
        number-killed       IS      "0",
        number-woundedIS        "0",
        primary-damage      IS      "no damage",
        secondary-damage        IS      "no damage",
        instigator          IS      ("New World Liberation Front"),
        perpetrator         IS      ("New World Liberation Front"),
        unused      IS      ("disclaimant", "bomb-composition");
OBJECT target<1>:
        name        IS      "Kissinger";

        exiting.
        %
```

Chapter 5

Models of Legal Decisionmaking

Donald A. Waterman and Mark A. Peterson

5.1 Introduction

The American civil justice system operates principally through the extrajudicial behavior of litigators.[1] The vast majority of civil claims are settled out of court, and the outcomes for most of these are entirely determined by negotiations among plaintiffs' and defendants' lawyers or insurance company claims adjusters.[2] Even when a settlement is not reached, the arguments, decisions, and negotiations made during the settlement process influence the nature of the formal trial.

Despite the importance of this process, we know very little about how lawyers and adjusters go about settling cases. Research provides a general description of settlement practices but almost no information about how litigators pursue or respond to civil claims, or about how

[1] Throughout this report, we use the term *litigation* broadly, to include all acts in evaluating, negotiating, advancing, or defending against a claim, whether or not the claim results in the filing of a lawsuit. The term *litigators* includes all professionals who conduct litigation—insurance company claims adjusters as well as lawyers.

[2]See page 136.

This chapter originally appeared as R-2717-ICJ. The Rand Corporation, 1981.

their actions affect the outcomes of settlements. Nor do we have good information on the effects of changes in legal rules or procedures on litigators' behavior and settlement outcomes. Traditional methods of research have provided neither the complex data that are needed to understand litigators' behavior nor the means to analyze even the limited existing data about settlements.

In this chapter we describe how an innovative research method, the development of rule-based computer models, might be used to obtain and organize comprehensive information about the actions of lawyers and claims adjusters in settling cases. Interviews used to develop rule-based models would provide data about experts' decisions, and the models would provide a method for systematically analyzing these data.

We begin, in Section 5.2, with a theoretical overview of the settlement process and the role that litigators' decisions play within that process. This overview serves as both a summary of our existing knowledge and a background for the discussion of how rule-based models might contribute to research on settlements.

Section 5.3 describes the method of rule-based computer modeling, its past use in analyzing decision making in different areas of expertise, and the application of the model to the study of settlement decisions. We then discuss a prototype rule-based model that we have developed to examine initial technical questions about models of legal decisions. This preliminary work indicates that it is technically feasible to develop simple rule-based models of litigants' settlement decisions, and that exploration of more comprehensive models is warranted.

Section 5.4 describes empirical research that will permit development of a more comprehensive model and presents some of the technical issues that must be addressed in developing such a model.

Section 5.5 describes proposed research using the comprehensive models, including (1) tests of the validity and generality of the models;

[2] This chapter focuses on settlements in personal injury claims. In California, 97 percent of the claims arising from automobile accidents are settled without a lawsuit being filed; only 0.4 percent of such claims go to trial (California Citizens Committee on Tort Reform, 1977, p. 53). Over 80 percent of the closed product-liability insurance claims surveyed by the Insurance Services Office (ISO) in a national study were settled before a lawsuit was filed; and over 95 percent of the claims (representing 81 percent of the payments for bodily injury and 89 percent of the claims for property damage) were settled before trial (Insurance Services Office, 1977, pp. 95–96). Settlements are also the primary means for disposing of other types of legal disputes, including divorce (Friedman and Percival, 1976) and medical malpractice (Danzon, 1979).

(2) research on multiparty strategies and negotiations; and (3) research on the effects of changes in legal rules and procedures on litigators' decisions. Finally, Section 5.6 summarizes the conclusions derived from our current work.

5.2 An Overview of the Settlement Process

A thorough understanding of settlement practices requires consideration of the effects of procedures, legal rules, and parties' characteristics, stakes, and interests on those practices (Mnookin and Kornhauser, 1979; Eisenberg, 1976). This section provides a framework within which these aspects of the settlement process can be discussed. We begin by examining prior empirical and theoretical considerations of settlement behaviors. We then present a number of hypotheses about settlement behaviors and describe the limitations of existing research methods for exploring these hypotheses.

Because settlement practices are complex and heterogeneous, it would be unrealistic to attempt to develop a detailed description of all civil settlements. Therefore, we shall focus on the settlement of tort claims,[3] which constitute a major proportion of civil disputes.[4] Tort law raises interesting and pressing issues about how settlement behaviors are affected by changes in legal procedures and rules (e.g., bases of liability, impacts of contributory negligence, constriction of the privity rule).[5]

5.2.1. ■ The Role of Case Worth in Settlement

Decisions to settle liability claims are the result of both private behaviors (decisions by each party) and multiparty behaviors (communications and

[3] Since there is great variation in legal rules, strategies, and party interests even among tort cases, our description of rule-based models in later sections of this chapter focuses even more narrowly on product-liability cases.

[4] Friedman and Percival (1976) found that in two California counties, tort cases constituted 27 percent and 19 percent of all 1970 civil court filings, and 56 percent and 50 percent of all nonfamily cases. Of course, most tort claims are settled without a filing of a civil claim.

[5] California Citizens' Commission on Tort Reform, 1977.

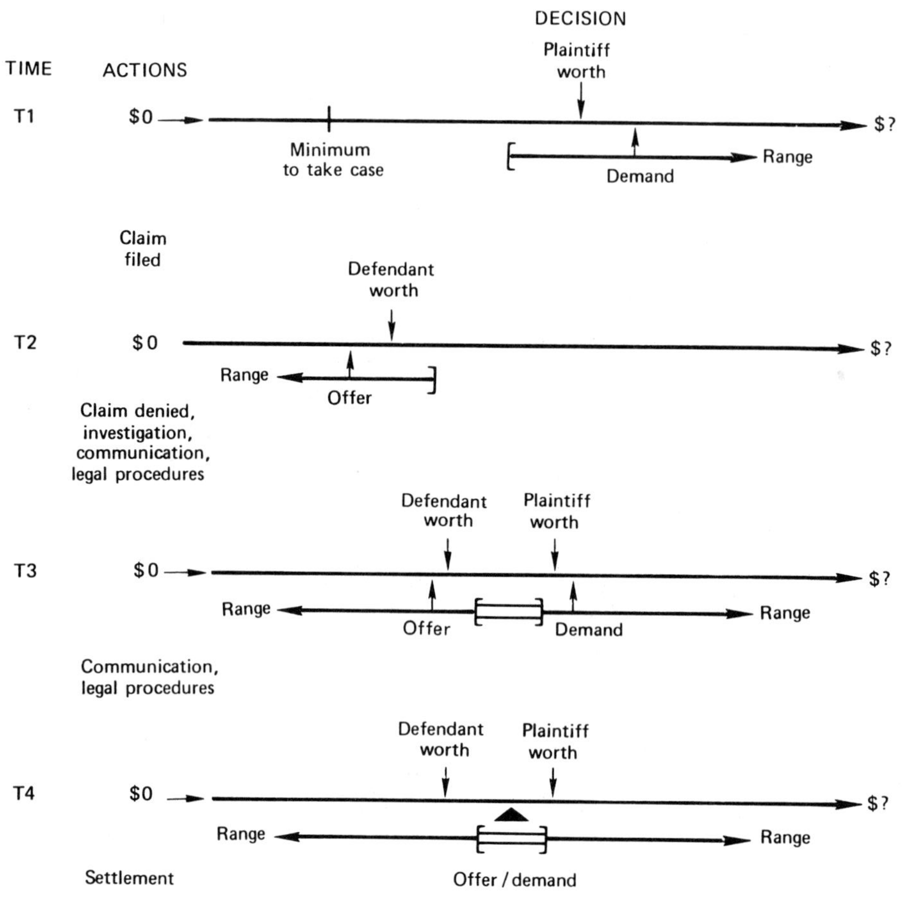

FIGURE 5.1 Schema of Settlement Process.

negotiations that influence those private decisions).[6] Figure 5.1 shows a schema of the private decision-making process of litigators. It summarizes the theoretical assumptions about decisions that each litigator must make, the relationships among these private decisions, and the relationships between these decisions and the settlement of a claim.[7]

Trial lawyers and claims adjusters report that they routinely make

[6] To simplify the modeling task, we assume that the interests and decisions made by litigators correspond to those of their clients. This assumption is clearly a simplification, particularly for plaintiffs (cf. Rosenthal, 1974). In future work, we expect to include consideration of the various interests and decisions made by both the litigators and their clients.

[7] The schema is based in part on Posner (1977) and Danzon (1980).

private evaluations of the "worth" of civil claims with which they are involved. These evaluations are apparently related to the litigators' expectations of the verdict for the case if it were tried. Presumably, they reflect the litigators' assessments of the facts of the case in light of (1) formal legal rules; (2) informal rules that guide interpretations of indefinite legal terms (e.g., general principles that suggest whether or not an act was reasonable or undertaken with "ordinary care"); (3) informal rules for calculating the value of damages (e.g., valuing pain and suffering at some multiple of medical expenses; and (4) expectations about jurors' or a judge's affective response to the facts or parties (e.g., their reactions to sensational injuries or how they may be influenced by the age, race, sex, demeanor, and sympathetic quality of the parties).

Legal practitioners seem able to make these evaluations of worth without considering adversarial factors, since they must make them at the beginning of cases when little or no knowledge of the opposing party or of the likely trier of fact is available.

We assume that evaluations of worth are central to litigators' other decisions and behavior. As the first step in pursuing a liability claim, at time T1 in Fig. 5.1, a plaintiff's lawyer decides whether or not to accept a case by estimating the worth of the claim and comparing the estimated worth with some minimum value for taking a case. The lawyer will also consider the costs of pursuing the claim. If after these costs are subtracted the estimated worth still exceeds the minimum for accepting the case (as show in Fig. 5.1), the plaintiff's lawyer will file a claim, forcing the defendant's lawyer or an insurance company claims adjuster also to estimate the worth of the case (at time T2).

In addition to deciding the worth of cases, both litigators must decide upon the range of settlements they would accept. This decision is based upon the estimated worth of the case and the litigator's anticipation of the costs that will arise from further litigation. Because a settlement avoids additional litigation costs, the parties are usually willing to accept a settlement that is less favorable to them than their estimated worth of the case (Danzon, 1980).[8] The plaintiff will accept settlements

[8] The costs of further litigation include uncertainties about sustaining an unfavorable verdict. The risks of further litigation differ for parties and insurance companies. Insurance companies defend most claims, and their risks of losing a verdict can be offset against the verdicts that they win. In contrast, a plaintiff has one claim and can hedge against the possibility of an unfavorable verdict only by settling (Ross, 1970; Galanter, 1974). On the other hand, insurance companies face the risk that some adverse verdicts might serve as a stronger precedent than a settlement would. An insurance company may face numerous actual and potential claims similar to the one being litigated. An adverse verdict could both increase the costs of resolving similar claims and induce potential claimants to pursue claims they would not otherwise have brought.

below his or her estimate, and the defendant will accept settlements above his or her estimate. In Fig. 5.1, the defendant rejected the plaintiff's claim because it exceeded the defendant's acceptable range.

Finally, each party must decide what case value it will communicate to its adversary. As a part of its bargaining strategy, each side will make a demand or offer that is more favorable to it than its estimate of case worth[9] (cf. the description of plea bargaining in Nagel and Neff, 1976).[10]

At various points in the case, a lawyer or adjuster will become involved with legal procedures, collect further information (sometimes investing substantially), and communicate with the other party. As a result of any of these activities, a litigant may change his or her decisions about worth, acceptable range, and offer/demand. One of the principal purposes of the rule-based modeling effort described in this study is to examine the effects of these activities and information on such decisions. However, for this overview, the effects of such developments are represented simply in Fig. 5.1, with developments between times T2 and T3 producing changes in litigators' decisions.[11]

At time T3, the acceptable ranges of settlements for the two parties overlap. The plaintiff will accept an offer that is, in fact, below the maximum demand to which the defendant will agree.[12] If either party

[9] Initial offers and demands must leave litigators with sufficient room for bargaining up to the time of a trial verdict. Unless new developments occur in a case, it is difficult for parties to take a more extreme position later in negotiations (Ross, 1972).

[10] The demands/offers may be particularly extreme when a litigator is uncertain about case worth—to avoid "giving the case away." Extreme demands/offers might also indicate an inexperienced litigator who can not easily value the case. (W.L.F. Felstiner, personal communication).

[11] We have shown both estimates moderating, because uncertainty has been reduced. Additional information could move both estimates up (e.g., injuries are greater than previously believed) or down (e.g., injuries are less severe).

[12] As the result of developments between T2 and T3, the plaintiff might increase his or her acceptable range and demand, even if new information causes him or her to reduce the estimate of case worth. Ross (1970) argues that a party who has undertaken a substantial investment between T2 and T3 will increase the demand and the minimum settlement he or she will accept. At time T2, a settlement would have avoided this substantial expense; however, at T3, the plaintiff will expect compensation for this expense. If the expense is greater than the reduction in the estimate of the case worth, the plaintiff will demand and accept a higher settlement at T3 than at T2 even though the plaintiff valued the case more highly at T2. Ross reports that claims adjusters recognize the need to provide greater settlements to claimants who have undertaken investments in pursuing the case.

makes an offer or demand within this overlap, the parties will agree and settle the case. However, at time T3, neither party has indicated a willingness to settle at a value within this acceptable range; therefore, no settlement occurs.[13] At time T4, the parties still hold to the same judgments about worth and acceptable ranges, but one of the parties has made an offer/demand that falls within the overlap of acceptable ranges. The other party finds the offer/demand acceptable and the case is settled.[14]

5.2.2 ■ Settlement Strategies, Communications, and Procedures

Figure 5.1 is intended merely to show the relationships among litigators' decisions and the settlement of a case; therefore, it does not indicate the potentially intricate strategies, communications, and procedures that occur within negotiations (Engel and Steele, 1979). It also does not indicate that litigators' actions and the resulting changes in their decisions will most likely occur in a few important periods. Because litigators' multiple caseloads prevent their constant attention to any one case, they will consider cases only periodically, depending upon procedural demands, actions by their adversary, developments in information, client demands, and so forth.

For most cases, strategies, communications, and procedures are probably not very intricate. Drawing on interviews with claims adjusters and plaintiffs' lawyers and also on observations of adjusters' settlements of automobile accident cases, Ross (1970) found that even when a claimant was represented by a lawyer, few cases involved anything beyond the simplest negotiations. Our preliminary examination of correspondence in closed insurance claims files supports this. We found that most communications between parties simply conveyed information necessary for evaluating the case (e.g., copies of doctors' or laboratory reports) or emphasized a particular chain of reasoning that was either rejected by the other party as irrelevant or accepted by both parties. Communications frequently appealed to norms that served as

[13] One of the objectives of third-party mediators is to discover undisclosed overlaps in acceptable settlements.

[14] The parties do not have to agree on the value of the case. Since each side will accept a settlement less favorable to it than its estimate of case worth, it is sufficient that the parties' acceptable ranges overlap and that one party proposes a settlement within this overlap.

standard bases for evaluating cases (e.g., a tacit agreement that pain and suffering is worth *n* times medical expenses; Ross, 1970).[15]

Ross's study suggests that these generally accepted norms or rules for deciding cases are the bases both for litigators' private decisions about cases and for negotiations among the parties. Ross found that litigators' decisions ignored fine points of law: Adjusters and plaintiffs' lawyers both evaluate the facts of a claim in terms of a simplified set of operating rules to determine whether the claim should be settled with payment and, if so, approximately how much the payment should be. Our preliminary interviews corroborated this finding. The lawyers and adjusters we interviewed also reported using simplified rules for analyzing case worth. Moreover, rules used by different litigators addressed similar factors (e.g., extent of medical expenses, characteristics of the parties, past and future lost wages). As a result, the adversaries usually agree about the worth of a case. In short, the simplified rules have resulted in a routinized claims settlement process. In many cases, the application of legal rules is so clear that there is no question about whether or not liability exists. And even when liability is not clear, negotiations are usually based on simple rules that ignore the complexities of the formal law.

Ross concluded that this simplification results from litigators' attempts to satisfy conflicting objectives. Faced with the large volume of claims and the bureaucratic structure of insurance companies, adjusters must try to expeditiously settle cases and achieve equitable results while minimizing payments. Plaintiffs' lawyers also face a conflict between expeditious settlement and maximizing payments. The simple rules provide expeditious and roughly just bases for settling the bulk of cases.

Matheny (1980) argues that the considerable uncertainty of litigation might also contribute to this simplification. Because it is difficult for parties to evaluate cases in the face of this uncertainty, parties can exploit the ambiguity. To protect themselves from exploitation, litigants may have developed norms for providing each other with information. These simple rules also permit parties to dispose of cases without requiring precise, unambiguous information.

[15] The simplified interactions among litigators found in Ross's research and our preliminary work closely resemble Matheny's (1980) theoretical description of plea-bargaining practices. Matheny describes plea negotiation as "uncertainty reduction rather than convergence through simple haggling and bluffing in a sentence market-place" (1980, p. 277). Since the tasks and problems faced by civil and criminal litigators are very similar, the behavior of both kinds of litigators should be similar (Engel and Steele, 1979).

5.2.3 ■ Research Questions and Hypotheses

This overview raises many general questions about litigators' behavior in resolving liability claims: How do litigators evaluate case worth? Are their decisions based on the settlement amounts of other, similar cases (cf. Matheny, 1980)? Are litigators' decisions about case worth based on the verdicts they would expect if the cases went to trial (Danzon, 1980)? Are those decisions based on some intrinsic consideration of just or appropriate compensation (Ross, 1970)? To what degree do litigators in the same jurisdiction use common rules or norms to evaluate cases? Do plaintiffs' lawyers differ systematically from defense lawyers and claims adjusters in the way they evaluate case worth? How are judgments about clients' characteristics and appeal considered in litigators' evaluations of case worth? How do legal rules affect decisions about case worth? Do litigators base their decisions on a general assessment of whether liability is certain or uncertain and not on refined considerations of legal doctrine? Do fine points of law become more important as the facts or legal issues become clearer?

How are decisions about the acceptable range related to decisions about case worth? Do litigators adjust case worth by their estimates of further litigation costs, so that when costs are greater they will accept settlements that are further away from their estimates of the case's worth (cf. Danzon, 1980)? What other matters influence decisions about an acceptable settlement?

How are decisions about demands/offers related to decisions about case worth or the acceptable range of settlements? Do litigators use patterns of demands/offers to communicate relative willingness to settle (cf. Ross, 1970)? If so, how are these patterns interpreted? Do demands/offers usually tend to converge as a case proceeds? In what circumstances will a plaintiff's lawyer increase a demand or a defendant decrease an offer? Does such intransigence occur only when a party receives new facts, or does it also occur in the absence of new facts?

Previous research and our own preliminary review suggest a number of hypotheses about the effects of particular facts, legal doctrines, litigator characteristics, and strategies upon litigators' behavior. For illustration, we shall briefly discuss the hypotheses that neither the adoption of strict liability nor the adoption of comparative negligence will change settlement practices in product-liability cases.

Schwartz (1979) and others argue that the adoption of strict liability would have little effect on the resolution of product-liability claims because juries do not decide cases tried under negligence differently from cases decided under strict liability. In theory, negligence and strict liability differ. Negligence requires a finding of an unreasonable act attributable to a defendant—the theory focuses on the defendant's acts and requires a finding that the risks from those actions outweigh their benefits. Strict liability focuses on the product, requiring a finding that a product was defective, which appears to involve only a consideration of risk.

However, in practice there may be little difference between the two bases of liability. If a product is claimed to be defective because of an unsafe design or inadequate warning, the determination of a defect requires a balancing of the risks and benefits of at least some attributes of products. Also, in most states, the defect must make a product unreasonably dangerous; again, the determination of unreasonableness seems to retain a balancing of risks and benefits.[16] Moreover, negligence has been extended to permit liability without finding that a defendant acted unreasonably. The doctrine of *res ipsa loquitor* permits a jury to infer negligence on the basis of the product defect, without any direct evidence concerning the defendant's behavior. Doctrines of vicarious liability hold manufacturers accountable for negligence by employees, suppliers, and subsequent fabricators.[17]

If litigators base their decisions about the worth of cases on expected jury verdicts, and if they (as well as commentators) believe that juries would decide cases similarly under either theory, the availability of a theory of strict liability should have no impact on settlements. However, if litigators' decisions about case worth are based on considerations other than case worth, or if they believe that juries would decide product-liability cases differently under the two theories, then the adoption of strict liability might change settlements.[18] Litigators may expect verdicts under strict liability to be more favorable to defendants, since jurors sometimes fail to understand or agree with the assumption of negligence under *res ipsa loquitor*. Also, if strict liability reduces the plaintiff's costs in pursuing a product-liability claim, plaintiffs may demand higher settlements when that doctrine becomes available.

Untested hypotheses also exist about the effects of the adoption of the legal theory of comparative negligence. Under the traditional, contributory negligence doctrine, a plaintiff was not entitled to recover a verdict from a negligent defendant if the plaintiff's own carelessness

[16] Restatement (second) of Torts 402a. But California requires only that a product be dangerous, not unreasonably dangerous (Schwartz, 1979).

[17] See Schwartz, 1979.

[18] Sole reliance on strict liability might, ironically, reduce the worth of cases. Some lawyers expect larger verdicts for cases tried under a theory of negligence, since a central issue presented to the jury under that theory is the defendant's alleged insensitivity to the risks he or she was imposing. See Cotchett and Cartwright (1977).

contributed to an injury. Under the newer doctrine of comparative negligence, a careless plaintiff can recover a verdict, but the verdict amount will be reduced in an amount proportional to his or her own responsibility for the injury. Ross (1970) argues that comparative negligence will have little impact on settlements, a view that seems to be broadly held. He found that litigators were providing settlement payments to negligent plaintiffs who should have been barred from recovery under the doctrine of contributory negligence. Ross attributed these settlements to adjusters' judgments that it is unfair to bar recovery when a defendant's greater negligence was principally responsible for the plaintiff's injury; in these cases, adjusters applied a *de facto* comparative negligence rule.

As an alternative hypothesis, settlements under comparative negligence might increase if previous payments to negligent plaintiffs were based on litigants' expectations about potential jury verdicts for the case. This hypothesis would imply that adjusters (or defense lawyers) settle under contributory negligence because they are not certain that a jury would find the plaintiff to have been negligent. Many juries in contributory negligence jurisdictions avoid the unpopular harshness of that doctrine by applying their own lay form of comparative negligence. Rather than barring recovery by careless plaintiffs by finding them to be negligent, these juries reduce the plaintiffs' awards to reflect their carelessness. Thus, adjusters may agree to settle claims by careless plaintiffs because they expect that a jury would award them some damages anyway.

If juries award larger verdicts to careless plaintiffs under contributory negligence or, more precisely, if litigators expect that juries would do so, then settlements should increase under that rule. However, verdicts and settlements might decrease. Juries might be more likely to find a plaintiff negligent under comparative negligence because they would not need to avoid the harshness of the contributory negligence rule. Thus, a change to comparative negligence could have an uncertain effect upon verdicts by increasing the probability of finding a plaintiff negligent, but also by increasing the amount of damages awarded if such negligence is found. In turn, the effect of comparative negligence on settlements would depend upon litigators' perceptions of how these two theories will affect jury verdicts.

5.2.4 ■ Research on Litigant Behavior

No past research has examined litigator behavior in sufficient detail to address either the general questions or the specific hypotheses previously considered. Ross's work attempts to provide a description of the general settlement process, rather than a detailed analysis of settlements of individual cases.[19] Similarly, analyses of closed-claims files (Danzon, 1980; Insurance Services Office, 1977) and studies using retrospective interviews with attorneys or parties (Civil Litigation Research Project, 1979) have not attempted to describe systematically the operating rules that determine settlements of civil liability claims.

It seems unlikely that existing methods used by Ross or other researchers can provide data sufficiently detailed or objective to permit a systematic description of litigators' behaviors. Even the most complete closed-claim file or retrospective interview can provide only limited information about the legal, factual, and strategic issues that arise in different cases. The data would not include details needed to describe how claims adjusters and attorneys decide those cases or to examine how various legal doctrines combine to determine settlements. Also, the integrity of these types of data must be seriously questioned. Material in closed-claim files that is relevant to legal or other rules may be biased by the litigators' tendency to "build a file" to support the outcome that they feel is appropriate (Ross, 1970). Retrospective interviews also suffer from the bias of interviewees toward presenting material in the best light, as well as from memory losses and other biases. Further, neither closed-claim studies nor retrospective analyses of claims pursued can deal with the issue of access to representation. Both sources provide information only for actual claims.[20] Finally, the great factual variation among claims and the complexity of legal issues that might pertain to any case limit the utility of standard statistical procedures for analyzing data about settlements.

5.3 Rule-based Computer Modeling of Litigants' Decisions

Rule-based computer modeling combines a method that can be used to extract thorough and detailed information about litigators' settlement decisions with a means for systematically exploring and organizing that

[19] Ross provided descriptions of some of the simplified operating rules, but even these rules may have changed with important recent changes in the tort law. Thus, Ross's work may be too dated to be useful for examining current issues about legal policy.

[20] Retrospective interviews can examine plaintiffs' lawyers' reasons for not taking cases, but they can probably provide only limited information about characteristics of unrepresented cases.

information. The rule-based model provides a sophisticated means for exploring these decisions and behaviors, formulating hypotheses about them, and testing those hypotheses quickly. In turn, the modeling results can be elaborated and tested through other research, some of which is described in Section 5.5.

In this section we will first briefly consider uses of rule-based and other computer models to study legal processes. We will then describe in more detail features of rule-based models of settlement decisions, illustrating these features with a simple prototype rule-based model that we have developed.

5.3.1 ■ Computer Modeling of Legal Decisions

The use of computer modeling techniques to study legal decision-making processes is not new. Some progress has been made in creating a language for expressing legal concepts (Stamper, 1976; Jones, et al., 1979), analyzing cases on the basis of legal doctrine (Meldman, 1977; Popp and Schlink, 1975), investigating the tax consequences of corporate transactions (McCarty, 1980; McCarty and Sridharan, 1980), automating the assembly of formal legal documents (Sprowl, 1979), and performing knowledge-based legal information retrieval (Hafner, 1980). However, rule-based modeling differs from this more conventional approach by developing a structure for both analyzing and explaining the reasoning processes of litigators.

Rule-based models have not been used to study legal decisions, but they have been used successfully to describe other complicated expert decision processes, such as those involved in the analyses of molecular structures (Buchanan, et al., 1976; Nii and Feigenbaum, 1978; Carhart, 1979), medical diagnoses (Weiss and Kulikowski, 1979; Pople, 1977; Shortliffe, 1976), mineral exploration (Duda, et al., 1979; Duda, et al., 1978), electrical circuit design (Sussman, 1977), and international terrorism (Waterman and Jenkins, 1979). These models have been used to construct "expert systems," computer programs that embody expertise and knowledge supplied by human experts and that use artificial intelligence techniques to provide inferences for the people who will work with the information these expert systems produce (Feigenbaum, 1977).

In developing an expert system, researchers (typically computer scientists with some knowledge of the area of expertise) "pick the brains" of a small number of experts. To do this, they present an expert with a hypothetical case that requires a decision. The expert then indicates which decisions should be made and why. The researchers can systematically explore the decision process by varying facts presented to the expert and noting how changes in facts change both the decision and the chain of reasoning supporting that decision.

The researchers will usually describe the decision process revealed through this experimental approach in terms of a set of heuristics or "rules of thumb," each of which describes a portion of the decision process. If the heuristics are stated in the form of "if-then" rules, the result is a rule-based model of expertise.

The model is a collection of rules, each of which has the form: if *conditions* then *conclusions*. That is, if a given set of conditions exists, then the experts reach the following intermediate conclusions. The data, or facts, that match the "if" part (the premises) of a rule are often provided by the conclusion of one or more other rules. In this way, individual rules are chained together to describe the decision process. Complicated decisions such as those found in legal analyses can be represented by long or complex chains of rules.

Rule-based models of litigators' decisions would be generally similar to those developed for other applications, although new technical issues are raised by the adversarial quality of litigators' decisions and the nature of legal rules (i.e., their dependence upon normative judgments, real or hypothetical statements of the parties, past knowledge, and so on.

5.3.2 ■ A Prototype Rule-based Model

To explore the feasibility of modeling litigators' settlement decisions, we developed a simple prototype rule-based model that describes how litigators decide about the value of product-liability cases. In constructing the prototype, we were concerned principally with determining whether legal and other rules involved in settlements could be transformed into the precise and unambiguous syntax needed for a computer program of the model, or whether features of legal rules (e.g., concepts of time, intent, or foreseeability) created particular transformational or programming problems.[21] We also used the prototype to see how a full rule-based model might look and to develop initial means by which lawyers and claims adjusters could interact with the model.

[21] Our prototype legal decision-making system, LDS, is implemented in ROSIE (Waterman, et al., 1979), a rule-oriented language designed to facilitate the development of large expert systems using English-like syntax. For an example of a typical ROSIE rule, see Fig. 5.1. ROSIE is a direct descendant of RITA (Anderson and Gillogly, 1976; Waterman, 1976), and more distantly of MYCIN (Shortliffe, 1976).

Because we were concerned principally with the technical feasibility of the model, we did not conduct the substantial research that would be necessary to develop a full model of litigators' decisions about the value of cases. The rules included within the prototype model were primarily formalized statements of the California legal doctrine for product liability as stated in statutes, court opinions, and legal treatises. These doctrines present an appropriate test of our ability to formalize legal concepts as statements in a computer program. The prototype also included rules for calculating damages; these rules were suggested by interviews with claims adjusters and plaintiffs' lawyers, by Commerce Clearing House and other professional guides to product-liability practice, and by closed product-liability insurance claims that we examined. Our development of the prototype permitted us to examine the feasibility of transforming some bases of settlements into a rule-based model, but did not provide us with a complete or necessarily accurate representation of product-liability law and practice. The prototype also provides a simple example of the basic features of rule-based models of settlement decisions.

Each rule of the prototype model explicitly describes a relationship between some facts of a case, inferences (i.e., conclusions) from other rules, and the conclusion that litigators would reach, based on these premises. Legal principles, such as the theory of strict liability, practitioners' strategies, and bases for calculating damages, can be thought of as ways of organizing facts and intermediate conclusions into rules. Within the prototype model, we have formalized only rules that describe legal principles and bases for calculating damages. We assume that other bases of litigators' decisions can also be organized into rules, but that effort was beyond the limited purposes of the prototype.

The rule defining the theory of strict liability is given in Fig. 5.2 to illustrate how the rules are formalized. Like all the rules in the model, it is in the form of "if-then" statements, with the premises joined by conjunctions or disjunctions of terms. The premises are a mixture of facts (e.g., the loss is a personal injury) and intermediate conclusions from other rules within the model (e.g., the incidental-sale defense is not applicable).

The model reproduces practitioners' inference processes by chaining together individual rules. The conclusion of one rule or a number of rules produces intermediate conclusions that match the premises for other rules, thus producing the model's inference chains. For example, the model examines rules that determine whether the defendant was responsible for the use of the product (see Rule 1, Appendix A) and whether the incidental-sale defense is applicable (see Rule 2, Appendix A) to determine whether or not the premises of the rule defining strict liability are satisfied.

```
IF (the plaintiff is injured by the product
     or (the plaintiff does represent the decedent
        and (the decedent is killed by the product
           or the decedent is injured by the product
           or the decedent's property is damaged by the product))
     or the plaintiff's property is damaged by the product)
   and the incidental-sale defense is not applicable
   and (the product is manufactured by the defendant
     or the product is sold by the defendant
     or the product is leased by the defendant)
   and the defendant is responsible for the use of the product
   and (California is the law of the case*
     or the user of the product is the victim
     or the purchaser of the product is the victim)
   and the product is defective at the time of the sale
   and the defendant did not reasonably expect
        'the defect will be eliminated before the sale'
THEN assert the theory of strict-liability does apply
        to the plaintiff's loss.
```

* The reference to California is included to show how the model can incorporate the different substantive law of different jurisdictions. The prototype can be run for four "jurisdictions" that have identical laws, except for two doctrines: whether or not bystanders can sue (shown in this rule), and whether contributory negligence or comparative negligence is used in the jurisdiction.

FIGURE 5.2 Definition of Strict Liability.

Just as other rules or chains of rules provide conclusions that match the premises for the rule defining strict liability, the conclusion of this rule (i.e., that the defendant is liable under the theory) will match the premises of other rules within the model, such as a rule that states the impact of the plaintiff's possible negligence upon the amount of the settlement (Rule 7, Appendix A).

In short, rules link facts and conclusions, and the rules themselves are linked through chains that represent the inference process. The facts of each case determine the sequence of rules involved in the chain; as a result, the inference chain will differ among cases presenting different facts. For each case, the inference chain continues until it reaches a final conclusion about the likely worth of the case.

5.3.3 ■ Case Analysis with the Prototype Rule-based Model

The operation and use of the prototype rule-based model can be illustrated by the analysis of a hypothetical case. The case described here is similar to one in our sample of closed-case insurance claims. The description includes only a small part of the information that was considered by the model:

> On the afternoon of August 2, 1978, the plaintiff, Mr. Samuel Willis, was cleaning a bathtub drain with a liquid cleaner in an apartment complex located in Flagstaff, Arizona,[22] and managed by Harvey Craton. During this process, the cleaner exploded out of the drain and onto the left arm and hand of the plaintiff, causing extensive injury in the form of burns and permanent scarring. The plaintiff was employed by Mr. Craton to effect minor repairs in the apartment and was doing so at the time of the accident. Medical expenses for the plaintiff were $6000. He was unable to work for 200 working days during which time his rate of pay was $47 per day. The cleaner was manufactured and sold by the defendant, Stanway Chemical Company. The contents of the product were judged to be defective by experts retained by the defendant. The product's label warned of potentially explosive chemical reactions from improper use of the product, but the label did not give a satisfactory description of means to avoid chemical reactions. The plaintiff was not familiar with the product. The plaintiff did not know what had been placed in the drain before he used the cleaner, and he did not flush out the drain before using the cleaner. The amount of the claim was $60,000.

The inference process performed by our model on the drain-cleaner case suggests that litigators would probably evaluate the worth of the case at between $35,000 and $41,000. Figure 5.3 shows a portion of the inference chain involved in considering this case. The rules were not invoked in one sequential chain; rather, they form a decision tree in which several chains of rules come together as premises that lead to the use of a single rule.

Seven conditions were needed to reach a conclusion that the defendant was liable under strict liability (Rule 4).[23] Although Fig. 5.3 shows only four of the conditions, all were satisfied. Some were satisfied by simple facts (e.g., the plaintiff was injured by the product), but most conditions required processing of other rules or would require such processing in a fully developed model. For example, the strict liability rule (Rule 4) requires a premise that the defendant was responsible for

[22] The model will process cases other than those for which California law applies (i.e., the three other hypothetical jurisdictions). California is mentioned in Rule 4 to illustrate that the law of particular jurisdictions can be represented in a model that applies to multiple jurisdictions. For this case, Rule 4 is met because the victim used the product.

[23] The figure does not trace the inference process all the way to the facts of the case; it omits some rules that lead to conclusions listed at the left margin, as well as other rules that provided premises for those shown in the figure.

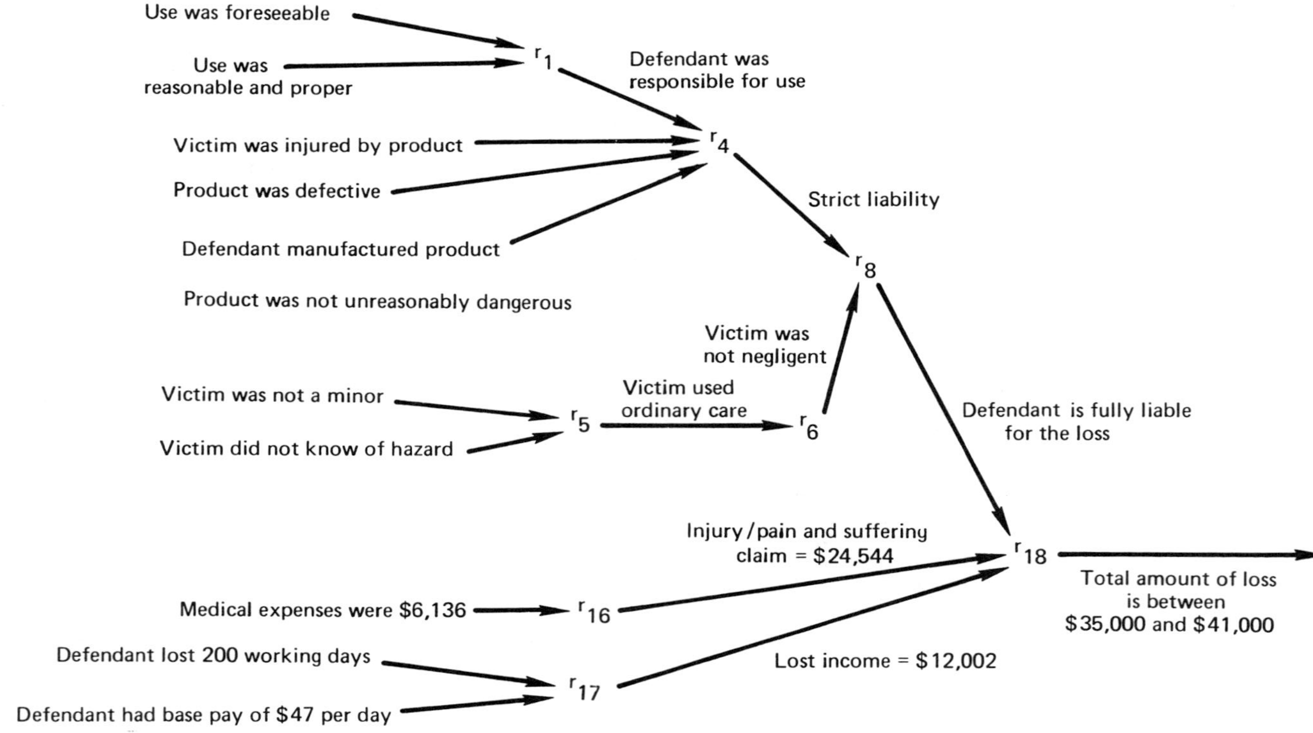
Use was foreseeable
Use was reasonable and proper
r1
Defendant was responsible for use
Victim was injured by product
Product was defective
Defendant manufactured product
r4
Strict liability
Product was not unreasonably dangerous
r8
Victim was not negligent
Victim was not a minor
Victim did not know of hazard
r5
Victim used ordinary care
r6
Defendant is fully liable for the loss
Injury/pain and suffering claim = $24,544
Medical expenses were $6,136
r16
r18
Total amount of loss is between $35,000 and $41,000
Defendant lost 200 working days
Defendant had base pay of $47 per day
r17
Lost income = $12,002

FIGURE 5.3 Representation of Computer Output for Drain-cleaner Case.

the product's use. This premise is satisfied by the conclusion of Rule 1. In turn, the conclusion of Rule 1 was reached because that rule's two premises were satisfied (i.e., the product was used in a reasonable and proper manner and its use was foreseeable). A fully developed model would include rules that define *reasonable and proper* and *foreseeable* as used in this context. The derivation of rules to describe such imprecise terms would be among the more technically difficult tasks in developing a comprehensive rule-based model.

Other rules determine that the plaintiff was not negligent in his use of the product and calculate the special damages for the case. Together, these three separate chains of rules lead to the conclusion that the defendant is liable for the total amount of the plaintiff's injuries.

As we indicated, the facts presented to the model determine the inference chain that will be applied to the case. If the facts in this example are changed to indicate that the plaintiff had a means for protecting himself from the danger but did not do so, the model then uses a different chain of rules (see Fig. 5.4). The model uses Rule 5 to conclude that a user of the product who is an adult, who knows its hazards, and who fails to use available precautions against those hazards failed to use due care in the use of the product. This conclusion then matches a premise in Rule 6, so that that rule now leads to the conclusion that the plaintiff was negligent in his use of the product.

Both conclusions—that the defendant is liable under a theory of strict liability (a conclusion resulting from the same chain of reasoning as in the first example) and that the plaintiff was negligent in his use of the product—become premises in a comparative negligence rule. Since the other five premises of this rule are satisfied, the rule determines that the defendant is responsible for only a portion of the plaintiff's loss. Because of the limited objectives of the prototype model, we have not attempted to develop a rule that calculates the degrees of comparative liability of the plaintiff and of the defendant. Under an assumption that the plaintiff is responsible for 30 to 40 percent of his injury, the model determines that the case should settle for between $21,000 and $29,000.

5.4 Development of Comprehensive Rule-based Models

Our development of a prototype model indicates that it is technically feasible to develop simple rule-based computer models that describe some bases of decisions made by litigators in civil liability claim settle-

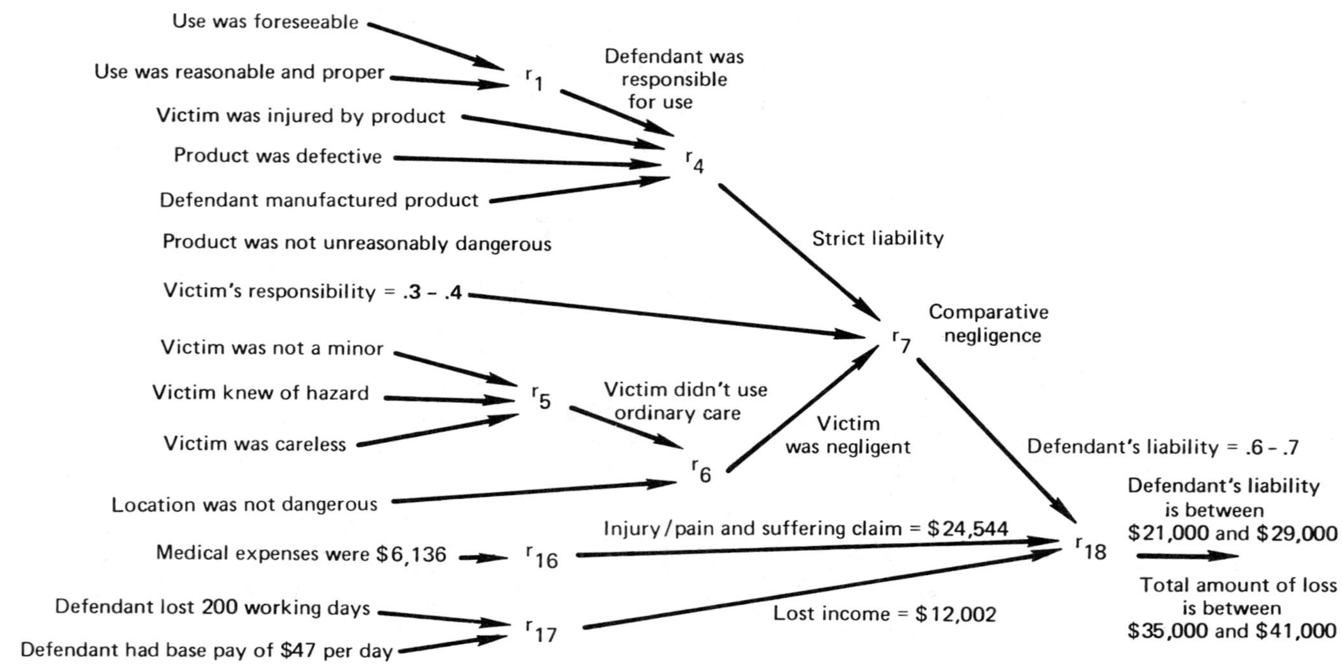
Use was foreseeable
Use was reasonable and proper
Victim was injured by product
Product was defective
Defendant manufactured product
Product was not unreasonably dangerous
Victim's responsibility = .3 - .4
Victim was not a minor
Victim knew of hazard
Victim was careless
Location was not dangerous
Medical expenses were $6,136
Defendant lost 200 working days
Defendant had base pay of $47 per day
r1
Defendant was responsible for use
r4
Strict liability
r5
Victim didn't use ordinary care
r6
Victim was negligent
r7
Comparative negligence
r16
Injury/pain and suffering claim = $24,544
r17
Lost income = $12,002
Defendant's liability = .6 - .7
r18
Defendant's liability is between $21,000 and $29,000
Total amount of loss is between $35,000 and $41,000

FIGURE 5.4 Representation of Computer Output for Drain-cleaner Case with Changed Facts.

ments. Some elements of the decisions can be described in terms of "if-then" rules, using a limited number of terms that can be precisely described. These rules can be chained together by the model to provide a reasonable, simple description of settlement decisions. Our initial success with the prototype warrants further work to see whether a broader range of determinants of settlement decisions can be successfully described by more elaborate rule-based models.

In this section we describe how rule-based models of case worth could serve as a central focus of research on settlement practices. We describe the empirical research that would be needed to develop comprehensive models of litigators' evaluations and then consider a number of technical issues that would have to be addressed during the development of such comprehensive models.

5.4.1 ■ Rule-based Models of the Worth of Liability Claims

As described in Section 5.2, litigators must make a number of decisions in pressing or responding to a civil liability claim. These include decisions about the worth of a claim, whether to represent a claimant, the acceptable range for settlement, offers or demands, communications with other parties, and the use of legal procedures. Litigators' decisions about case worth seem central to their other decisions and actions; therefore, research to develop models of case worth should provide a convenient and appropriate initial step toward evaluation of this complex series of decisions and actions.

Focusing on this one type of decision would simplify the initial research and would, at the same time, provide information that is critical for understanding other aspects of the settlement process. Lawyers' and adjusters' decisions about case worth are closely related to other decisions, such as whether to accept a plaintiff's case, what offers or demands the parties will make, and what settlements they will find acceptable. Although these related decisions are interesting and important, research on them would best be deferred until models of case worth have been developed and studied.

By themselves, models of case worth would address many of the research questions raised in Section 5.2. Work on developing the models would reveal how litigators consider legal doctrine in evaluating cases. It would examine the hypothesis that in evaluating cases, litigators avoid detailed consideration of legal issues and consider only whether liability is certain or uncertain. It would examine the alternative hypotheses that decisions about worth: are based on litigators' perceptions of expected jury verdicts; are based on general patterns of settlements; and are guided, in part, by litigators' abstract considerations of just or appropriate compensation. This research could also provide information on whether litigators' decisions about case worth differ markedly among individuals; whether they differ among plaintiffs' lawyers, defense lawyers, and claims adjusters; and whether they differ among jurisdictions.

In addition to being of central importance, decisions about case worth are most readily modeled. Rule-based models would be developed primarily through repeated interviews and experiments with a small number of lawyers and claims adjusters, who would decide the value of hypothetical cases and describe the bases for their decisions. We expect that litigators should be able to perform this research task readily, since they routinely evaluate the worth of civil claims, often on the basis of limited and even hypothetical information.[24]

In contrast, interviews based on hypothetical cases may not provide a sufficient method to examine negotiating and bargaining strategies in which a lawyer or adjuster must respond to and anticipate actions by an adversary. Strategic issues involving negotiations, decisions about offers and demands, or the use of alternative legal procedures might be examined more effectively through simulated gaming situations, in which lawyers and adjusters play against each other or a programmed opponent. Such gaming research could build upon our proposed models of case worth. By knowing a litigator's estimate of a case's worth and the basis for that estimate, we could more effectively structure research questions about negotiations.

Initial models of case worth could be supplemented by later research that is based, in part, on the initial models. Rule-based models can be developed in an incremental fashion because the results of subsequent research can be incorporated as additional rules in the inference chains that drive the models. In Section 5.5, we describe further research for elaborating initial models of case worth.

5.4.2 ■ Research Methods for Developing the Models

As previously stated, data needed to develop the initial models would be obtained through intensive interviews with plaintiffs' lawyers, defense lawyers, and claims adjusters.[25] Each interview would center on

[24] Also, because the Socratic method of legal education relies heavily on varying hypothetical cases, this experimental approach seems particularly appropriate for analyzing the decisions of legal experts.

[25] The modeling research will not attempt to produce statistical analyses providing probability statements about litigators' decisions or behavior in handling liability claims. Rather, it is a procedure that should permit us to explore those decisions and develop models that can be tested in other research.

a number of hypothetical cases. The litigator would consider one hypothetical case at a time and indicate his or her decision about its worth. The interviewer would then ask the expert to explain why he or she decided on that value, probing to discover as much as possible about the decision. The interviewer would attempt to reformulate the expert's explanations into "if-then" rules of the type used in the model. The expert would then review the reformulations to verify that they accurately describe the basis for a decision and to obtain modifications of the rules.

As computer programs incorporating the models are developed, they would be used in the interviews. The interviewer would present the computer analysis of particular cases and determine whether the expert agrees with the model's conclusions and reasoning chains. In light of the experience of others who have developed rule-based models, we expect that this procedure will produce considerable refinement of the model.

The nature of the models will be determined by the litigators upon whose expertise they are based. Models derived from interviews with highly experienced and expert litigators will describe sophisticated settlement practices. Thus, in addition to providing research information, such models would be useful as teaching devices, or as expert systems, that less-skilled litigators could draw upon for advice. Issues of variations in the quality of legal services could be studied by comparison of sophisticated models derived from expert litigators, with models derived from litigators who are not specialists in the studied legal area.

Rule-based models can also be used to explore the similarity of decisions among litigators. We would expect to find systematic differences between plaintiff's lawyers and defense lawyers or claims adjusters, and between professionals practicing in different jurisdictions. However, we also expect to find common bases among litigators in evaluating the worth of cases. The great frequency of communications among lawyers and adjusters, their use of common professional guides, and the high rate of settlement suggest that there are common approaches among litigators in how they evaluate cases. Common models could be developed if many of the same rules could be used to describe decisions, at least for litigators representing the same side in the same jurisdiction.

On the other hand, if the research should show marked differences in decisions made by particular types of litigants, the method could be used to develop individual models of their decisions. Further work with the individual models could then attempt to account for these differences and could examine negotiations by using gaming techniques.

5.4.3 ■ Technical Issues in Developing the Models

Although rule-based modeling has been used to describe expert decisions in other areas, several technical problems must be addressed in developing a large rule-based system dealing with legal settlements.

A model of settlement decisions should be complete enough to make useful predictions, and small enough to be a manageable computer program. Our experience with representing product-liability law and associated legal practices in rule form suggests that a model for a narrow domain of inquiry (e.g., automobile accidents that raise issues of product liability) might require up to several thousand rules. A model of this size presents special problems, mostly about efficient access to rules and data, that are not encountered in the development of a smaller prototype. It would be premature to propose a solution to this difficult problem at this time, but a possible approach for fast access might be to use data structures with explicit links to the rules, and to partition the data and rules to minimize the need for large, time-consuming searches.

The model should also incorporate a facility for explaining why a conclusion was reached, preferably by graphically displaying the inference chain. Our prototype model provided such explanations (see Appendix B), but did not provide an accompanying graphic display. A sophisticated explanation facility would be useful during both model development and interviews, when it could show experts why the model reached a given conclusion.

The model should also include a facility for explaining why an expected conclusion was not reached. To determine why an expected answer was not obtained, the system must search for a way to obtain that answer, hypothesizing facts or intermediate conclusions that could be used to arrive at it. The search should produce a list of facts or conditions that need to be true for the model to obtain the desired answer. This explanation facility would provide additional insights into the operation of the model.

The model should work toward reducing imprecise terms that occur in legal doctrines and other rules describing litigants' decisions. Interpretations of imprecise terms could be derived inferentially from instances of the terms used in past situations. The hypothetical cases used in the expert interviews will provide many instances in which the expert must decide, for example, if a jury is likely to find a particular act to be reasonable, undertaken with ordinary care, and so forth.

The model can use several methods to interpret imprecise terms. First, it can provide rules that describe how an imprecise term was used previously in particular contexts. Second, it can display brief descriptions of instances of prior use of the imprecise term and let the user decide whether or not the term applies in the current instance. Third, the model can ask a series of questions to elicit information about the specific case in which the imprecise term is at issue, compare the answers with prior cases in which the term applied, and provide a numeric rating that indicates the degree of certainty that the rule defining the term applies presently. Fourth, the model might use a system of gradual refinement by query to determine whether or not a term applies. To do this it would ask a series of increasingly specific questions. Each of these might have imprecise terms that would be further refined by even more specific query lists.

Finally, since settlements are affected by litigators' uncertainties about proving factual issues and applicable legal doctrine, the models must incorporate methods for dealing with these uncertainties. Our prototype model has no provision for such uncertainty; rather, it uses a binary approach in which facts are classified as present or absent.

Discussions about the preferred approach to this issue will necessarily await further work, since the model's treatment of uncertainty should represent how practitioners actually deal with uncertainties. Lawyers and adjusters may treat uncertainties as additional premises within operating rules used to reach decisions. Presumably, this could be incorporated within the overall approach of the model. Alternatively, practitioners might consider a case independently of matters of uncertainty, reach a tentative conclusion, and then adjust that conclusion by some probabilistic factor that represents their overall uncertainty about the case. This would suggest that uncertainties should not be incorporated as premises within each rule but should be treated as a separate rule that is applied after other rules have been considered. A third approach to this issue might be the use of certainty factors (Shortliffe, 1976). Here, numbers representing the expert's confidence in the accuracy of the data and rules might be incorporated into the model to provide a more accurate reflection of his or her decision processes.

5.5 Tests and Uses of the Models

Once the models of case worth are developed, they must be validated by tests of their performance on well-understood problems. Then they can be used to study interesting and complex issues such as the use of multiparty strategies in negotiations and the effect of changes in legal rules on litigators' decisions.

5.5.1 ■ Validation of the Models

Like all models, rule-based models tend to oversimplify. The research method of presenting hypothetical cases to litigators may be ineffective for studying some matters that influence litigators' decisions, such as how actively a client participates (Rosenthal, 1974), and how lawyers' and adjusters' decisions are affected by their own characteristics (i.e., their experience, ability, and economic motivation).

Experiments or survey questionnaires based on the models could examine the models' generality and more thoroughly examine differences in decision making among litigators. For example, hypothetical cases could be presented to groups of practitioners not involved in the models' development. The practitioners would be asked to decide the value of these cases and describe the bases for their decisions. The models' outcomes and inference processes could then be compared with those of the test group to examine whether the models are representative of decisions made by the relevant group of practitioners (e.g., plaintiffs' lawyers in the jurisdiction covered by the model), how the model might be unrepresentative, and what types of practitioners might reach conclusions significantly different from those of the model.

The models might also be tested by a comparison of the processes described in them with patterns of actual settlements as revealed in analyses of other data. For example, models of the worth of product-liability cases could be tested through analysis of data from the Insurance Services Office (ISO) survey of closed product-liability cases. The ISO survey is based on detailed information from 23 property insurance companies about all product-liability claims closed between July 1, 1976, and March 15, 1977 (Insurance Services Office, 1977). The file contains detailed information on the type and extent of bodily injuries, medical expenses, lost wages, and other direct economic costs for 24,452 claims.

The ISO data do not provide simple criteria for determining whether models of case worth are valid. Nor do they include information about some matters that are likely to be relevant to litigators' decisions (e.g., characteristics of the parties, information about defenses). Also, as a closed-claim study, the ISO data present problems of biased reporting, and the ISO sampling plan oversamples recent cases that were settled quickly. Moreover, the ISO data provide information about actual settlements, whereas models would describe decisions made by each side.

Nevertheless, analyses of the ISO data can provide independent tests of some hypotheses derived from the rule-based models. In particular, if both plaintiffs' lawyers and claims adjusters regard a certain issue as having the same impact on case value, then analyses of the

ISO data should reveal that the issue has a predicted impact on settlements. Some issues influencing litigators' decisions might be present in every case (e.g., larger settlements for claimants who suffer greater losses in future income); for these we would predict statistical main effects across all cases. Other issues would operate differently for particular cases (e.g., negligence by the injured party might be less important when that party was killed); for these we would predict statistical interactions or effects only for selected cases.

5.5.2 ■ A Laboratory for Studying Civil Litigation

Models of case worth can be used in further research to examine the complicated set of behaviors that occur in resolving claims and to explore how those behaviors are affected by changes in legal rules, procedures, and litigators' strategies. The models could be used as a first step in a "laboratory" that examines other decisions made by litigators, negotiations, the effects of negotiations on litigators' decisions, and the effects of changes in legal doctrines on decisions and behavior.

Other decisions made by litigators can be studied, in part, through further interviews with experts who participated in developing the models of case worth. These interviews would ask only limited questions about the worth of the cases, primarily to confirm existing models. Most questions would examine decisions about acceptable settlements, offers, and demands, the relationship among these decisions and decisions about case worth. The interviews might then be used to develop models of these other decisions.

5.5.3 ■ Research on Negotiations Through Gaming

The use of rule-based models in gaming research provides a powerful means for conducting controlled research on negotiations, organizing the complex information involved, and testing hypotheses.[26] In the gaming situation, plaintiffs' lawyers and claims adjusters not only make decisions about a hypothetical case, they also negotiate with an adversary. The adversary can be either a computer program or another litigator participating in the research.

Models of litigators' decisions about case worth, possibly supplemented by models of acceptable range and of initial offer/demand, would provide an excellent basis for gaming research. Rule-based mod-

[26] Because of these advantages, Rand is currently using rule-based models in research on international negotiations and defense strategies.

els could be used to describe each litigator's position at the beginning of negotiations, informing researchers of the important decisions made by each litigator and the bases for those decisions. Negotiations would then alternate between the two parties. Each party would provide current decisions about case worth, the acceptable range, and their next step, based on their own prior actions and those of the adversary. The parties would have opportunities for making offers or demands and otherwise communicating with each other. A party's involvement in legal procedures or its research on legal or factual issues could be simulated as events involving costs but possibly producing useful information. The litigators would be asked to discuss their actions and strategies and the actions of their adversaries, indicating why the actions were taken, what was expected as a result, how they interpreted the adversary's actions, and so on.

Gaming research can extend the rule-based model in two ways. First, it can provide a basis for developing rules to describe the broader range of decisions and behaviors that occur during negotiations. Second, actions by the adversary could be added as premises in the rules describing litigators' decisions. By comparing the rule-based models at successive points, we could see how litigators' actions and those of their adversaries affect the litigators' decisions. The gaming method also provides an opportunity for testing models as they are being developed. Models could be used to predict a party's next action, and the resulting prediction could then be compared with the action actually taken by the party.

5.5.4 ■ The Effects of Changes in the Law

Rule-based models can be used to examine how litigators' decisions and behaviors might be affected by changes in legal doctrine or procedures. The effects of legal changes are difficult to predict, particularly since the effects of any single change often depend upon other legal rules and strategies operating within the settlement process. For example, the expansion of liability in product cases that would result from adoption of a comparative negligence rule depends upon whether the jurisdiction applies the doctrine to strict liability cases. To appreciate the significance of a change in doctrine, it is necessary to consider the influence of legal rules, strategies, and characteristics of the legal system on the magnitude and direction of the change. Because these determinants of settlements are complex and numerous, a computer model provides a unique and powerful basis for analyzing potential changes.

To examine the effects of legal changes, we would begin by modifying one or more rules within the model. Changing one rule may change the entire inference process for many cases. As an example drawn from our prototype model, we could change the legal rule defining strict liability (Fig. 5.2), adding a requirement that the defendant will be strictly liable only if, in addition to the other conditions, the product was unreasonably dangerous when sold. Figure 5.5 shows how the inference process changes for the case used previously as an illustration.

Throughout our earlier discussion, the drain-cleaner case included the fact that the product was not unreasonably dangerous, a fact not previously used in any rule. Because we have now added to the rule defining strict liability (Rule 4) the premise requiring that a product be unreasonably dangerous, the presence of this fact now prevents the application of that rule. Further, since the defendant is no longer strictly liable, the inference chain no longer includes Rule 7 (the comparative negligence rule) or Rule 18, which determines a likely settlement amount for the case. Instead, Rules 10 and 20 are applied to obtain the result that the defendant was not liable.[27] The calculation regarding the value of the loss was unchanged, although no settlement is made under the revised definition of strict liability. Of course this example, based on the formal law, is obvious. But it illustrates how changes in one rule can affect the chain of reasoning that a litigator uses to value a case.

Modifications to the model, by themselves, can represent only simple changes in the inference process, that is, how settlements should change if part of the inference process changed and lawyers or claims adjusters did not adapt by modifying other parts of that process. However, we know that decisions about settlements are the result of complex behaviors. By changing one part of the decision process, we are likely to produce secondary changes in other parts of that process. For example, when a legal doctrine is changed, lawyers and claims adjusters may adapt their strategies, their interpretations of the law, or other practices to produce consequent changes in settlements that were not intended by the court or legislature that imposed the change.

The model can contribute to comprehensive research exploring these secondary changes. First, formal changes in the model can suggest hypotheses about where secondary changes in the inference process are likely to occur. Secondary change occurs because lawyers and claims adjusters do not accept the simple change that would occur from modifying a legal doctrine or a strategy. They make further changes in their decisions to ameliorate or take advantage of what was

[27] Rule 20 is not included in Appendix A.

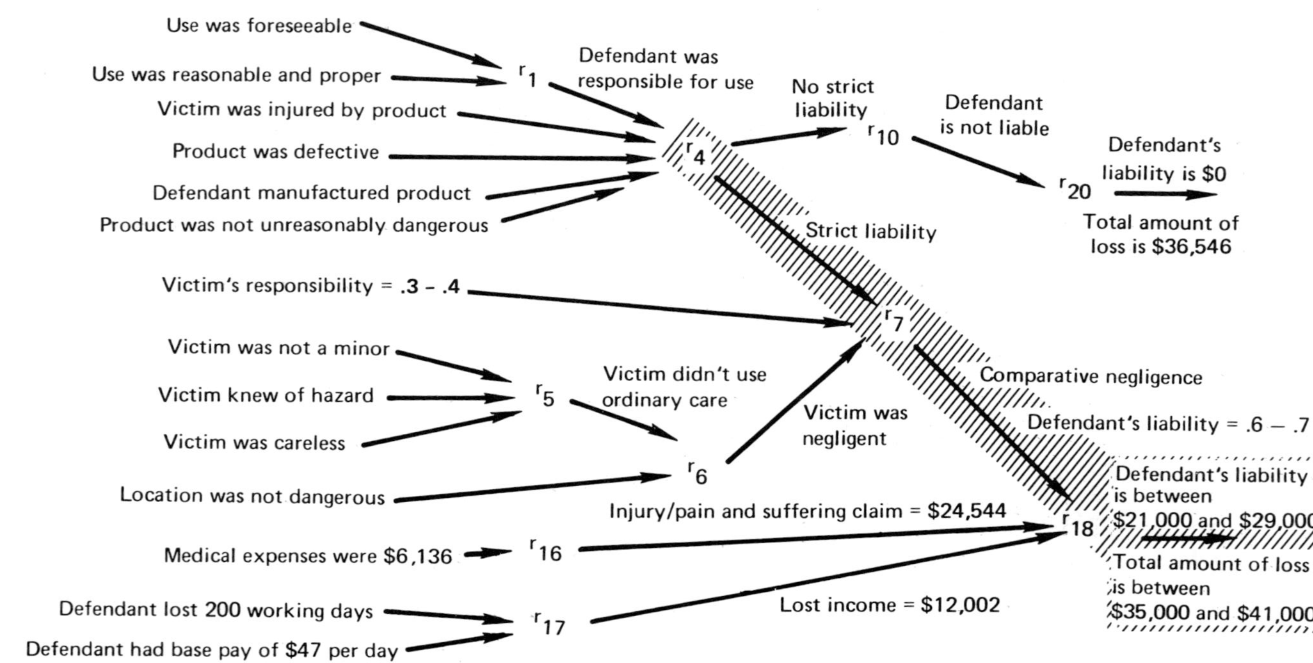
Use was foreseeable
Use was reasonable and proper
Victim was injured by product
Product was defective
Defendant manufactured product
Product was not unreasonably dangerous
Victim's responsibility = .3 - .4
Victim was not a minor
Victim knew of hazard
Victim was careless
Location was not dangerous
Medical expenses were $6,136
Defendant lost 200 working days
Defendant had base pay of $47 per day
r1
Defendant was responsible for use
r4
No strict liability
r10
Defendant is not liable
r20
Defendant's liability is $0
Total amount of loss is $36,546
Strict liability
r7
r5
Victim didn't use ordinary care
r6
Victim was negligent
Comparative negligence
Defendant's liability = .6 — .7
Injury/pain and suffering claim = $24,544
r16
r17
Lost income = $12,002
r18
Defendant's liability is between $21,000 and $29,000
Total amount of loss is between $35,000 and $41,000

FIGURE 5.5 Representation of Computer Output for Drain-cleaner Case with a Change in the Definition of Strict Liability.

intended to be a simple change. By showing what the simple changes in the inference process would be, the model can suggest areas of tension where secondary changes are likely to occur.

Second, the model provides a tool for empirically examining secondary changes in the inference process. We can present hypothetical cases that include relevant changes in the law. Hypotheses about primary and secondary changes in the decision process can then be compared with lawyers' and adjusters' decisions for these cases. We can consider how a given change affected the experts' decisions about acceptable settlements, offers, demands, and other negotiation strategies. We can also use these tests to explore the decisions resulting from unexpected secondary changes. By comparing the simple changes in the inference process suggested by the model with actual changes in lawyers' and claims adjusters' decisions, we may gain some understanding of the more subtle ramifications of changing legal rules.

Third, we can use the rule-based model to represent a theory of secondary change in decision processes. Rules can be developed within the model to make secondary changes that reflect our understanding of how lawyers and claims adjusters adapt to new strategies or changes in legal rules. The rules we develop will then permit us to test and refine our theories of secondary change.

Research on the effects of changes in the law would be facilitated if models were developed in two jurisdictions. Changes could be studied by comparing decisions made by experts in each jurisdiction under different legal doctrines. Within each jurisdiction, experts would consider cases using laws that apply in their jurisdiction and the same set of cases using the law of the other jurisdiction. Using this strategy, we could study differences in decisions among jurisdictions and compare these differences with changes in decisions that experts indicate they would make if they were working with a different legal doctrine. The comparison of models across jurisdictions draws upon the experts' actual knowledge derived from working with their own legal doctrine. By looking at the changes in practices for each expert, we can avoid having to analyze the competing explanations for differences in practices between jurisdictions.

5.6 Conclusions

The U.S. system of civil justice operates primarily through the private decisions and actions of litigators—lawyers and, to an important extent, insurance company claims adjusters. Rule-based computer models offer a promising method for developing both a theoretical understanding of these settlement decisions and the empirical data needed to test those theories.

Rule-based modeling has several advantages for studying litigators' decisions. First, the model's use of rules captures the actual basis of those decisions. Legal decisions, including those involved in litigating claims, are based primarily on sets of rules. Most legal doctrine is stated as a set of rules that can be translated into the "if-then" statements of a rule-based model. Lawyers and claims adjusters typically use rules to describe their decisions (e.g., "if medical expenses are 'padded,' then pain and suffering should not be three times the medical expenses"; or "if the plaintiff is unattractive, then settle for a lower value"). Because practitioners actually use rules in deciding about settlements, a model based on rules can describe those decisions. The common use of rules would also ensure that lawyers and claims adjusters could understand and contribute to the model development.

Second, the modeling method can provide data about the litigators' decision processes through experimental variation of the hypothetical facts presented to them. Researchers who have developed rule-based models in other areas of expertise have found this experimental approach appealing to the experts whose decisions are modeled. In our preliminary interviews, we found that lawyers and adjusters will readily provide estimates of worth for hypothetical cases and that they regard making estimates for hypothetical cases a routine part of their work. Of course, the model derived through this experimental approach will be hypothetical, but its validity can be tested by comparing its results with decisions made by lawyers and claims adjusters in actual cases (see Section 5.5).

Third, a rule-based model provides a particularly appropriate means for organizing the great number of factors that might influence litigators' decisions. Again, the analytic structure of rule-based modeling captures the structure of litigators' actual decisions. Those decisions are not made by applying the same fixed set of rules to all cases; rather, lawyers and claims adjusters draw from a large set of rules and apply only some of those rules in resolving any particular claim. Rule-based models are dynamic. Thus, the rules that are used to describe the decision for a particular case are determined by the facts presented by the case. These rules will vary from case to case as the facts of the cases vary.

Fourth, the models provide a methodology for studying negotiating strategies and the effects of negotiations and legal procedures on the decisions of individual litigators (see Section 5.5). By explicitly describing the decisions and strategies of a party going into a multiparty negotiation, we can refine rules that describe that party's strategies and add rules that describe reactions to the opponents' strategies.

Fifth, rule-based models provide a convenient means to organize and study the effects of different legal rules and procedures on the settlement decisions made by litigators. The models can be used not only to identify changes in settlement practices that are likely to occur, but also to indicate why these changes are likely.

Acknowledgments

Many colleagues have taken an interest in, encouraged, and helpfully criticized our attempt to apply rule-based modeling as a research tool for studying legal settlements. Their support and criticism have been invaluable in helping us refine our approach. In particular, we would like to thank Stephen Carroll, David Seidman, Frederick Hayes-Roth, and Gary Martins for their continuing support and frequent suggestions. David Seidman and Philip Klahr reviewed several drafts of this report, providing suggestions about both the report and our basic approach. Edward Feigenbaum provided useful suggestions about developing and utilizing rule-based models of litigators' decisions. Finally, we wish to thank the Institute for Civil Justice, the Institute's director Gustave Shubert, and deputy director Charles Nelson for their confidence in and support for our work in developing a new technology for studying the process of civil litigation.

References

1. Buchanan, B. G., D. H. Smith, W. C. White, R. J. Gritter, E. A. Feigenbaum, J. Lederberg, and C. Djerassi, "Automatic Rule Formation in Mass Spectrometry by Means of the Meta-DENDRAL Program," *Journal of American Chemical Society,* Vol 98, 1976.
2. California Citizens' Commission on Tort Reform, "Writing the Liability Balance," Los Angeles, September 1977.
3. Carhart, R. E., "CONGEN: An Expert System Aiding the Structural Chemist," in *Expert Systems in the Micro Electronic Age* (D. Michie, ed.), Edinburgh University Press, 1979.
4. Civil Litigation Research Project, Law School, University of Wisconsin, Madison, 1979.
5. Cohen, L. J., *The Probable and the Provable,* Oxford University, Oxford, 1977.

6. Cotchett, J. O., and R. E. Cartwright, *California Products Liability Actions*, Matthew Bender, San Francico, 1977.

7. Danzon, P., *The Disposition of Medical Malpractice Cases*, The Rand Corporation, R-2622-HCFA, June 1980.

8. Duda, R., J. Gaschnig, and P. Hart, "Model design in the Prospector Consultant System for Mineral Exploration," in *Expert Systems in the Micro Electronic Age* (D. Michie, ed.), Edinburgh University Press, 1979.

9. Duda, R. O., P. E. Hart, N. J. Nilsson, and G. Sutherland, "Semantic Network Representations in Rule-based Inference systems," in *Pattern-Directed Inference Systems* (D. A. Waterman and F. Hayes-Roth, eds.), Academic Press, New York, 1978.

10. Eisenberg, M. A., "Private Ordering Through Negotiations: Dispute-settlement and Rulemaking," *Harvard Law Review*, Vol. 89, 1976, 637–681.

11. Engel, D. M., and E. H. Steele, "Civil Cases and Society: Process and Order in the Civil Justice System," *American Bar Foundation Research Journal*, Spring, 1979, 295–346.

12. Feigenbaum, E. A., "The Art of Artificial Intelligence: I. Themes and Case Studies of Knowledge Engineering," *Proceedings of the Fifth International Joint Conference on Artificial Intelligence*, Cambridge, Massachusetts, 1977, 1014–1029.

13. Friedman, L. M., and R. V. Percival, "A Tale of Two Courts: Litigation in Alameda and San Benito Counties," *Law and Society Review*, Vol. 10, 1976, 267–302.

14. Galanter, M., "Why the 'Haves' Come out Ahead," *Law and Society Review*, Vol. 5, 1974, 95–160.

15. Gould, J. P., "The Economics of Legal Conflicts," *Journal of Legal Studies*, Vol. 2, 1973, 279–290.

16. Hafner, C. D., "Representation of Knowledge in a Legal Information Retrieval System," in *Research and Development in Information Retrieval, Proceedings of the Third Annual SIGIR Conference*, Cambridge, England, 1980.

17. Insurance Services Office, "Insurance Services Office Product Liability Closed Claim Survey: A Technical Analysis of Survey Results," New York, 1977.

18. Interagency Task Force on Product Liability, "Product Liability Legal Study," The Research Group, 1977.

19. Jones, S., P. J. Mason, and R. K. Stamper, "LEGOL-2.0: A Relational Specification Language for Complex Rules," *Information Systems*, Vol. 4, No. 4, December, 1979.

20. Jones, W., *Simulating International Crises: The Applications and Limitations of Free-form Games*, The Rand Corporation, WN-9510-PR, June 1976.

21. Landes, W. L., "An Economics Analysis of the Courts," *Journal of Law and Economics*, Vol. 14, 1971, 61.

22. Matheny, A. R., "Negotiation and Plea Bargaining Models," *Law and Policy Quarterly*, Vol. 2, No. 3, 1980, 267–284.

23. McCarty, L. T., "The TAXMAN project: Towards a Cognitive Theory of Legal Argument," in *Computer Logic and Legal Language* (B. Niblett, ed.), Cambridge University Press, 1980.

24. McCarty, L. T., and N. S. Sridharan, "The Representation of an Evolving System of Legal Concepts, Part One: Logical Templates," *Proceedings of the Third National Conference of the Canadian Society for Computational Studies of Intelligence*, Victoria, British Columbia, 1980.

25. Meldman, J. A., "A Structural Model for Computer-aided Legal Analysis," *Journal of Computers and Law*, Vol. 6, 1977, 27-71.

26. Mnookin, R. H., and L. Kornhauser, "Bargaining in the Shadow of the Law: The Case of Divorce," *Yale Law Journal*, Vol. 88, 1979, 950–997.

27. Nagel, S. S., and M. Neff, "Plea Bargaining, Decision Theory, and Equilibrium: Part I," *Indiana Law Journal*, Vol. 51, 1976, 987–1024.

28. Nagel, S. S., and M. Neff, "Plea Bargaining, Decision Theory, and Equilibrium: Part II," *Indiana Law Journal*, Vol. 52, Fall, 1976, 1–61.

29. Nii, H. P., and E. A. Feigenbaum, "Rule-based Understanding of Signals," in *Pattern-Directed Inference Systems* (D. A. Waterman and F. Hayes-Roth, eds.), Academic Press, New York, 1978.

30. Pople, H., "The Formation of Composite Hypotheses in Diagnostic Problem Solving," *Proceedings of the Fifth International Joint Conference on Artificial Intelligence*, Cambridge, Massachusetts, 1977, 1030–1037.

31. Popp, W. G., and B. Schlink, "JUDITH: A Computer Program to Advise Lawyers in Reasoning a Case," *Jurimetrics Journal*, Vol. 15, No. 4, 1975, 303–314.

32. Posner, R. A., *An Economic Analysis of Law* (2nd ed.), Little Brown, Boston, 1977.

33. Rosenthal, D. E., *Lawyers and Their Clients: Who's in Charge?*, Russell Sage, New York, 1974.

34. Ross, H. L., *Settled Out of Court: The Social Process of Insurance Claims Adjustments*, Aldine Publishing Co., Chicago, 1970.

35. Schum, D. A., and A. W. Martin, "Empirical Studies of Cascaded Inference in Jurisprudence: Methodological Considerations," Rice University, Houston, Texas, 1980.

36. Schwartz, G. T., "Foreword: Understanding Product Liability," *California Law Review*, Vol. 67, No. 3, 1979, 453–496.

37. Shortliffe, E. H., *Computer-Based Medical Consultations: MYCIN*, American Elsevier, New York, 1976.

38. Sprowl, J. A., "Automating the Legal Reasoning Process: A Computer that Uses Regulations and Statutes to Draft Legal Documents," *American Bar Foundation Research Journal*, No. 1, 1979, 3–81.

39. Stamper, R. K., "The Legol Project: A Survey," UK Scientific Centre Report, IBM United Kingdom Limited, 1976

40. Sussman, G. J., "Electrical Circuit Design: A Problem for Artificial Intelligence Research," *Proceedings of the Fifth International Joint Conference on Artificial Intelligence*, Cambridge, Massachusetts, 1977, 894–900.

41. Waterman, D. A., *An Introduction to Production Systems*, The Rand Corporation, P-5751, 1976.

42. Waterman, D. A., R. H. Anderson, F. Hayes-Roth, P. Klahr, G. Martins, and S. J. Rosenschein, *Design of a Rule-Oriented System for Implementing Expertise*, The Rand Corporation, N-1158-ARPA, 1979.

43. Waterman, D. A., and B. Jenkins, "Heuristic Modeling Using Rule-based Computer Systems," in *Terrorism, Threat, Reality, Response* (R. Kupperman and D. Trent, eds.), Hoover Institution Press, Stanford University, 1979.

44. Weiss, S. M., and C. A. Kulikowski, "EXPERT: A System for Developing Consultation Models," *Proceedings of the Sixth International Joint Conference on Artificial Intelligence*, Tokyo, Japan, 1979, 942–950.

Appendix A

A Representative Set of Rules from the Prototype System

The following rules are representative of the rules in the protoype legal decision-making system. These rules are more English-like than those illustrated in an earlier version of the system (see Appendix B).

```
[RULE1:  RESPONSIBILITY FOR USE OF PRODUCT]
IF  the use of (the product) at the time of the plaintiff's loss
       is foreseeable
    and (that use is reasonable-and-proper
       or that use is an emergency
       or (there is a description by the defendant of that use
          and that description is improper)
       or there is not a description by the defendant of that use)
THEN assert the defendant is responsible for the use of the product.

[RULE2:  INCIDENTAL SALE DEFENSE][1]
IF  (manufacturing is the defendant's business
       and the defense1 of the defendant is applicable)
    or (sales is the defendant's business
       and the defense2 of the defendant is applicable)
    or (leasing is the defendant's business
       and the defense3 of the defendant is applicable)
THEN assert the incidental-sale defense is applicable.

[RULE3.2:  DEFINITION OF LOSS]
IF  the type of the plaintiff's loss is 'decedent'
THEN assert the plaintiff does represent the decedent
    and the decedent is killed by the product.
```

[1] Defense1 is applicable if the defendant manufactured only a component part of the defective product and if the part manufactured by the defendant had nothing to do with the product being defective. Defense2 is applicable if the defendant did not manufacture the defective product but was an occasional seller of that product and was not engaged in selling that product as part of his or her business. Defense3 is applicable if the defendant did not manufacture or sell the defective product but was a casual lessor or renter of that product and was not engaged in leasing or renting as part of his or her business.

```
        and the defense2 of the defendant is not applicable)
      or (leasing is the defendant's business
        and the defense3 of the defendant is not applicable)
THEN assert the incidental-sale defense is not applicable.

[RULE3.1:   DEFINITION OF LOSS]
IF   the type of the plaintiff's loss is 'injury'
THEN assert the plaintiff is injured by the product.

[RULE3.2:   DEFINITION OF LOSS]
IF   the type of the plaintiff's loss is 'decedent'
THEN assert the plaintiff does represent the decedent
      and the decedent is killed by the product.

[RULE3.3:   DEFINITION OF LOSS]
IF   the type of the plaintiff's loss is 'property-damage'
THEN assert the plaintiff's property is damaged by the product.

[RULE4:   STRICT LIABILITY DEFINITION]
IF   (the plaintiff is injured by the product
        or (the plaintiff does represent the decedent
          and the decedent is killed by the product)
        or the plaintiff's property is damaged by the product)
      and the incidental-sale defense is not applicable
      and (the product is manufactured by the defendant
        or the product is sold by the defendant
        or the product is leased by the defendant)
      and the defendant is responsible for the use of the product
      and (California is the jurisdiction of the case
        or the user of the product is the victim
        or the purchaser of the product is the victim)
      and the product is defective at the time of the sale
      and (the product is unchanged from the manufacture to the sale
        or (the defendant's expectation is 'the product is unchanged
              from the manufacture to the sale'
          and the defendant's expectation is reasonable-and-proper))
THEN assert the theory of strict-liability does apply
        to the plaintiff's loss.

[RULE5:   ORDINARY CARE DEFINITION]
IF   the victim is an adult who does know the proper use of the product
      and (the victim does know 'the product is defective'
        and the victim does continue the use of the product)
      or ((the victim does know 'the product is dangerous'
        or the victim does know 'the product is defective')
        and (the victim is careless in the use of the product
          or the victim is inattentive in the use of the product))
      or (the victim is improper in the use of the product
        and ((there is a warning by the manufacturer
```

```
            and that warning does describe the improper use of the product)
            or (there is a warning by the seller
          and that warning does describe the improper use of the product)))
    or (the victim does know 'the victim is sensitive to the product'
      and the victim does continue the use of the product)
    or the victim does use poor-practices in the use of the product
    or (there is a means for protection from the hazard of the product
      and the victim does not use that means)
THEN assert the use of (the product) by the victim does not involve
        ordinary-care.

[RULE5.1:  LACK OF ORDINARY CARE]
IF  the use of (the product) by the user does not involve ordinary-care
THEN create a lack of ordinary-care by the user.

[RULE5.2:  LACK OF ORDINARY CARE]
IF  there is a lack of ordinary-care by the user
THEN assert the danger does [not] cause that lack.

[RULE6:  NEGLIGENCE DEFINITION]
IF  (the product's user is not working in some area of some possible danger
    and the use of (the product) by the user
        does not involve ordinary-care)
     or (the product's user is working in some area
        of some possible danger (d)
      and the use of (the product) by the user
         does not involve ordinary-care
      and the danger (d) does cause the lack of ordinary-care
        by the user)
    or the victim does accept 'the product is dangerous'
THEN assert the use of (the product) by the user is negligent.

[RULE7:  COMPARATIVE NEGLIGENCE - PARTIAL LIABILITY]
IF  the theory of strict-liability does apply to the plaintiff's loss
    and the product's user is the victim
    and (California[2] is the jurisdiction of the case
      or Arizona is the jurisdiction of the case)
    and the victim does know 'the product is dangerous'
    and the victim does appreciate 'the product is dangerous'
    and the use of (the product) by the user is negligent
    and the user of the product does contribute to the plaintiff's loss
THEN assert the defendant is liable for the plaintiff's loss
    and the liability of the defendant is partial
    and 1 - the maximum proportion of the responsibility
        for the plaintiff's loss
```

[2] The identification of states is arbitrary.

```
        is the minimum proportion of the defendant's liability
      and 1 – the minimum proportion of the responsibility
          for the plaintiff's loss
        is the maximum proportion of the defendant's liability.

[RULE8:  COMPARATIVE NEGLIGENCE - TOTAL LIABILITY]
IF  the theory of strict-liability does apply to the plaintiff's loss
    and (the use of (the product) by the user is not negligent
      or the product's user is not the victim)
THEN assert the defendant is liable for the plaintiff's loss
    and the liability of the defendant is total.

[RULE9:  CONTRIBUTORY NEGLIGENCE]
IF  the theory of strict-liability does apply to the plaintiff's loss
    and the product's user is the victim
    and (Colorado is the jurisdiction of the case
      or Delaware is the jurisdiction of the case)
    and the use of (the product) by the user is negligent
    and the user of the product does contribute to the plaintiff's loss
    and the maximum proportion of the responsibility
      for the plaintiff's loss is greater than 0
THEN assert the defendant is not liable for the plaintiff's loss
    and the theory of contributory-negligence
      does apply to the plaintiff's loss.

[RULE10:  NO LIABILITY]
IF  the theory of strict-liability does not apply to the plaintiff's loss
THEN assert the defendant is not liable for the plaintiff's loss.
    and display 10.

[RULE11:  EXIT]
quit.
end law.
```

Appendix B

Trace of a User Interaction with the Prototype System

The following is a trace of a user interacting with an earlier version of our prototype legal decision-making system (LDS). The user input is italicized to distinguish it from the models' response. The rules in this version are not as English-like as those in our most recent version (see Appendix A). The most recent version does not yet have an explanation facility, so the earlier version of ROSIE is shown here.

@rosie

This program demonstrates the use of a rule-based model for studying legal decision-making processes. It consists of a set of rules for processing product liability cases. We have already entered some information about an actual case. Important aspects of the case are summarized here.

The program will process the case and present its conclusions. Then, by answering a series of program questions, you will be able to change certain key aspects of the case and rerun the model to see the effect of the changes.

On the afternoon of August 2, 1978, the plaintiff, Mr. Samuel Willis was cleaning a bathtub drain with a liquid cleaner in an apartment complex located in Flagstaff Arizona and owned and managed by Harvey Craton. During this process the cleaner exploded out of the drain and onto the left arm and hand of the plaintiff, causing extensive injury in the form of burns and permanent scarring. The plaintiff was employed by Mr. Craton to effect minor repairs in the apartment and was doing so at the time of the accident. Medical expenses for the plaintiff were $6000. He was unable to work for 200 working days during which time his rate of pay was $47 per day. The cleaner was manufactured and sold by the defendant, Stanway Chemical Company. The contents of the product were judged to be defective by experts retained by the defendant. The product's label warned of potentially explosive chemical reactions from improper user of the product, but the label did not give a satisfactory description of means to avoid chemical reactions. The plaintiff was not familiar with the product. The plaintiff did not know what had been placed in the drain before he used the cleaner, and he did not flush out the drain before using the cleaner. The amount of the claim was $40,000.

The case is now being analyzed.

The defendant is liable under the theory of strict liability. The plaintiff is not responsible for his loss. The amount of defendant liability is between $35000 and $41000, which represents the value of the case.

You may now process the case again, changing a few of the key pieces of data describing the case. Or instead, you may examine the rules that led to the decisions just reached.

Would you like to process the case again? ***n***

Would you like an explanation of the model's current decision-making process? ***yes***

What would you like explained?
a) defendant's liability
b) product user's negligence
c) victim's liability
d) what rule led to a given deduction?
e) why the rule was applicable
f) nothing

? ***a***

THE LIABILITY OF THE DEFENDANT WAS CALCULATED BECAUSE:

A: At cycle #394 RULE4 fired.
The rule is:
[STRICT LIABILITY DEFINITION]
IF LIABILITY OF DEFENDANT IS NOT KNOWN
AND (TYPE OF LOSS OF PLAINTIFF IS INJURY
OR TYPE OF LOSS OF PLAINTIFF IS PROPERTY-DAMAGE
OR TYPE OF LOSS OF PLAINTIFF IS DECEDENT)
AND PRODUCT OF DEFENDANT IS CAUSE OF LOSS OF PLAINTIFF
AND INCIDENTAL-SALE-DEFENSE OF DEFENDANT IS NOT-APPLICABLE
AND RESPONSIBILITY OF ACTUAL-USE OF PRODUCT OF DEFENDANT IS DEFENDANT'S
AND (JURISDICTION OF CASE IS CALIFORNIA
OR JURISDICTION OF CASE IS COLORADO
OR USER OF PRODUCT OF DEFENDANT IS NAME OF VICTIM
OR PURCHASER OF PRODUCT OF DEFENDANT IS NAME OF VICTIM)
AND STATUS-WHEN-SOLD OF PRODUCT OF DEFENDANT IS DEFECTIVE
AND (SECONDARY-PROCESSING OF PRODUCT OF DEFENDANT IS NONEXISTENT
OR (SECONDARY-PROCESSING-EXPECTATION OF DEFENDANT IS NO-REMOVAL-OF-DEFECTS
AND VALIDITY OF SECONDARY-PROCESSING-EXPECTATION OF DEFENDANT IS
REASONABLE-AND-PROPER))
THEN SET LIABILITY OF DEFENDANT TO STRICT-LIABILITY ;

THIS RULE FIRED BECAUSE:

B.1: The LIABILITY of DEFENDANT was not known
B.2: The LOSS of PLAINTIFF was BURNS-AND-PERMANENT-SCARRING
B.3: The TYPE of BURNS-AND-PERMANENT-SCARRING was INJURY
B.4: The PRODUCT of DEFENDANT was DRAIN-CLEANER
B.5: The CAUSE of BURNS-AND-PERMANENT-SCARRING was DRAIN-CLEANER
B.6: The INCIDENTAL-SALE-DEFENSE of DEFENDANT was NOT-APPLICABLE
B.7: The ACTUAL-USE of DRAIN-CLEANER was CLEANING-DRAIN

B.8: The RESPONSIBILITY of CLEANING-DRAIN was DEFENDANT'S
B.9: The JURISDICTION of CASE was ARIZONA
B.10: The USER of DRAIN-CLEANER was SAMUEL-WILLIS
B.11: The NAME of VICTIM was SAMUEL-WILLIS
B.12: The STATUS-WHEN-SOLD of DRAIN-CLEANER was DEFECTIVE
B.13: The SECONDARY-PROCESSING of DRAIN-CLEANER was NON-EXISTENT

What would you like explained?
a) defendant's liability
b) product user's negligence
c) victim's liability
d) what rule led to a given deduction?
e) why the rule was applicable
f) nothing

? ***e***

Why ***B.8***?

C: At cycle #291 RULE1 fired.
The rule is:
[RESPONSIBILITY FOR USE OF PRODUCT]
IF RESPONSIBILITY OF ACTUAL-USE OF PRODUCT OF DEFENDANT IS NOT KNOWN
AND (NATURE OF ACTUAL-USE OF PRODUCT OF DEFENDANT IS FORESEEABLE
AND (ACT OF ACTUAL-USE OF PRODUCT OF DEFENDANT IS REASONABLE-AND-PROPER
OR CIRCUMSTANCE OF ACTUAL-USE OF PRODUCT OF DEFENDANT IS FORESEEABLE-EMERGENCY
OR NATURE OF DESCRIPTION OF INTENDED-USE OF PRODUCT OF DEFENDANT IS IMPROPER
OR AUTHOR OF DESCRIPTION OF INTENDED-USE OF PRODUCT OF DEFENDANT IS NOT NAME OF DEFENDANT))
THEN SET RESPONSIBILITY OF ACTUAL-USE OF PRODUCT OF DEFENDANT TO DEFENDANT'S ;

THE RULE FIRED BECAUSE:

D.1: The PRODUCT of DEFENDANT was DRAIN-CLEANER
D.2: The ACTUAL-USE of DRAIN-CLEANER was CLEANING-DRAIN
D.3: The RESPONSIBILITY of CLEANING-DRAIN was not known
D.4: The NATURE of CLEANING-DRAIN was FORESEEABLE
D.5: The ACT of CLEANING-DRAIN was REASONABLE-AND-PROPER

What would you like explained?
a) defendant's liability
b) product user's negligence
c) victim's liability
d) what rule led to a given deduction?

e) why the rule was applicable
f) nothing

? ***d***

What set the degree of liability of defendant?

THE DEGREE OF LIABILITY OF DEFENDANT WAS SET BECAUSE:

I: At cycle #450 RULE8 fired.
The rule is:
[COMPARATIVE NEGLIGENCE - TOTAL LIABILITY]
IF LIABILITY OF DEFENDANT IS STRICT-LIABILITY
AND DEGREE OF LIABILITY OF DEFENDANT IS NOT KNOWN
AND (METHOD OF ACTUAL-USE OF PRODUCT OF DEFENDANT IS NOT NEGLIGENT
OR USER OF PRODUCT OF DEFENDANT IS NOT NAME OF VICTIM)
THEN SET DEGREE OF LIABILITY OF DEFENDANT TO TOTAL-LIABILITY ;

THE RULE FIRED BECAUSE:

J.1: The LIABILITY of DEFENDANT was STRICT-LIABILITY
J.2: The DEGREE of STRICT-LIABILITY was not known
J.3: The PRODUCT of DEFENDANT was DRAIN-CLEANER
J.4: The ACTUAL-USE of DRAIN-CLEANER was CLEANING-DRAIN
J.5: The METHOD of CLEANING-DRAIN was not known

What would you like explained?
a) defendant's liability
b) product user's negligence
c) victim's liability
d) what rule led to a given deduction?
e) why the rule was applicable
f) nothing

? ***f***

Would you like to process the case again? *yes*

Please answer the following questions concerning the case. Respond with the letter that matches your answer. If you need help type a question-mark, if you don't know the answer just type a carriage-return.

What is the jurisdiction of the case?
a) Arizona
b) California
c) Colorado
d) Delaware

? ***a***

Was the victim either the user or purchaser of the product?
a) Yes

b) No

? ***a***

What was the status of the product when it was sold by the defendant?

a) Defective
b) Non-defective

? ***a***

Was the product modified after manufacture by parties other than the defendant?

a) Yes
b) No

? ***b***

Was the nature of the use of the product foreseeable?

a) Yes
b) No

? ***a***

What is the legal status of the victim?

a) Adult
b) Minor

? ***a***

Did the victim know the product was defective before he used it?

a) Yes
b) No

? ***b***

Did the victim continue using the product, even after he found it defective?

a) Yes
b) No

? ***b***

Did the victim have a means for protecting himself from the dangers of using the product?

a) Yes
b) No

? ***a***

Did the victim use this means to protect himself?

a) Yes
b) No

? ***b***

Did the victim know and appreciate the danger involved in the use of the product?

a) Yes
b) No

? ***a***

What were the medical expenses of the plaintiff?
    $6000

The case is now being analyzed.
The defendant is liable under the theory of strict liability. The plaintiff is partially responsible for his loss under the theory of comparative negligence. The total amount of the loss is between $35000 and $41000. The amount of defendant liability is between $21000 and $29000.

Would you like to process the case again? ***no***

Would you like an explanation of the model's current decision-making process? ***yes***

What would you like explained?
- a) defendant's liability
- b) product user's negligence
- c) victim's liability
- d) what rule led to a given deduction?
- e) why the rule was applicable
- f) nothing

? ***a***

THE LIABILITY OF THE DEFENDANT WAS CALCULATED BECAUSE:

K: At cycle #3482 RULE4 fired.
The rule is:
[STRICT LIABILITY DEFINITION]
IF LIABILITY OF DEFENDANT IS NOT KNOWN
AND (TYPE OF LOSS OF PLAINTIFF IS INJURY
OR TYPE OF LOSS OF PLAINTIFF IS PROPERTY-DAMAGE
OR TYPE OF LOSS OF PLAINTIFF IS DECEDENT)
AND PRODUCT OF DEFENDANT IS CAUSE OF LOSS OF PLAINTIFF
AND INCIDENTAL-SALE-DEFENSE OF DEFENDANT IS NOT-APPLICABLE
AND RESPONSIBILITY OF ACTUAL-USE OF PRODUCT OF DEFENDANT IS DEFENDANT'S
AND (JURISDICTION OF CASE IS CALIFORNIA
OR JURISDICTION OF CASE IS COLORADO
OR USER OF PRODUCT OF DEFENDANT IS NAME OF VICTIM
OR PURCHASER OF PRODUCT OF DEFENDANT IS NAME OF VICTIM)
AND STATUS-WHEN-SOLD OF PRODUCT OF DEFENDANT IS DEFECTIVE
AND (SECONDARY-PROCESSING OF PRODUCT OF DEFENDANT IS NONEXISTENT
OR (SECONDARY-PROCESSING-EXPECTATION OF DEFENDANT IS NO-REMOVAL-OF-DEFECTS
AND VALIDITY OF SECONDARY-PROCESSING-EXPECTATION OF DEFENDANT IS
REASONABLE-AND-PROPER))

THEN SET LIABILITY OF DEFENDANT TO STRICT-LIABILITY ;
THIS RULE FIRED BECAUSE:

L.1: The LIABILITY of DEFENDANT was not known
L.2: The LOSS of PLAINTIFF was BURNS-AND-PERMANENT-SCARRING
L.3: The TYPE of BURNS-AND-PERMANENT-SCARRING was INJURY
L.4: The PRODUCT of DEFENDANT was DRAIN-CLEANER
L.5: The CAUSE of BURNS-AND-PERMANENT-SCARRING was DRAIN-CLEANER
L.6: The INCIDENTAL-SALE-DEFENSE of DEFENDANT was NOT-APPLICABLE
L.7: The ACTUAL-USE of DRAIN-CLEANER was CLEANING-DRAIN
L.8: The RESPONSIBILITY of CLEANING-DRAIN was DEFENDANT'S
L.9: The JURISDICTION of CASE was ARIZONA
L.10: The USER of DRAIN-CLEANER was SAMUEL-WILLIS
L.11: The NAME of VICTIM was SAMUEL-WILLIS
L.12: The STATUS-WHEN-SOLD of DRAIN-CLEANER was DEFECTIVE
L.13: The SECONDARY-PROCESSING of DRAIN-CLEANER was NONEXISTENT

What would you like explained?
a) defendant's liability
b) product user's negligence
c) victim's liability
d) what rule led to a given deduction?
e) why the rule was applicable
f) nothing

? ***e***

Why ***L.6***?
M: At cycle #3430 RULE3 fired.
The rule is:

[INCIDENTAL SALE DEFENSE]
IF INCIDENTAL-SALE-DEFENSE OF DEFENDANT IS NOT KNOWN
AND ((TYPE OF BUSINESS OF DEFENDANT IS MANUFACTURING
AND PRODUCT OF DEFENDANT IS OUTPUT OF BUSINESS OF DEFENDANT
AND DEFENSE1 OF DEFENDANT IS NOT-APPLICABLE)
OR (TYPE OF BUSINESS OF DEFENDANT IS SALES
AND PRODUCT OF DEFENDANT IS MERCHANDISE OF BUSINESS OF DEFENDANT
AND DEFENSE2 OF DEFENDANT IS NOT-APPLICABLE)
OR (TYPE OF BUSINESS OF DEFENDANT IS LEASING
AND PRODUCT OF DEFENDANT IS MERCHANDISE OF BUSINESS OF DEFENDANT
AND DEFENSE3 OF DEFENDANT IS NOT-APPLICABLE))
THEN SET INCIDENTAL-SALE-DEFENSE OF DEFENDANT TO NOT-APPLICABLE ;

THE RULE FIRED BECAUSE:

N.1: The INCIDENTAL-SALE-DEFENSE of DEFENDANT was not known
N.2: The BUSINESS of DEFENDANT was DRAIN-CLEANER-MANUFACTURING
N.3: The TYPE of DRAIN-CLEANER-MANUFACTURING was MANUFACTURING
N.4: The PRODUCT of DEFENDANT was DRAIN-CLEANER
N.5: The OUTPUT of DRAIN-CLEANER-MANUFACTURING was DRAIN-CLEANER
N.6: The DEFENSE1 of DEFENDANT was NOT-APPLICABLE

What would you like explained?

a) defendant's liability
b) product user's negligence
c) victim's liability
d) what rule led to a given deduction?
e) why the rule was applicable
f) nothing

? ***b***

THE METHOD OF ACTUAL USE OF THE PRODUCT
WAS CALCULATED BECAUSE:

O: At cycle #3589 RULE6 fired.
The rule is:
[NEGLIGENCE DEFINITION]
IF METHOD OF ACTUAL-USE OF PRODUCT OF DEFENDANT IS NOT KNOWN
AND ((STATE OF LOCALE OF USER OF PRODUCT OF DEFENDANT IS NOT DANGEROUS
AND CAREFULNESS OF ACTUAL-USE OF PRODUCT OF DEFENDANT IS NOT-ORDINARY-CARE)
OR (STATE OF LOCALE OF USER OF PRODUCT OF DEFENDANT IS POSSIBLY-DANGEROUS
AND STYLE OF ACTUAL-USE OF PRODUCT OF DEFENDANT IS CARELESS
AND CAUSE OF STYLE OF ACTUAL-USE OF PRODUCT OF DEFENDANT IS STATE OF LOCALE OF
USER OF PRODUCT OF DEFENDANT)
OR (PRODUCT-IS-DANGEROUS IS IN ACCEPTANCE OF VICTIM))
THEN SET METHOD OF ACTUAL-USE OF PRODUCT OF DEFENDANT TO NEGLIGENT ;

THIS RULE FIRED BECAUSE:

P.1: The PRODUCT of DEFENDANT was DRAIN-CLEANER
P.2: The ACTUAL-USE of DRAIN-CLEANER was CLEANING-DRAIN
P.3: The METHOD of CLEANING-DRAIN was not known
P.4: The USER of DRAIN-CLEANER was SAMUEL-WILLIS
P.5: The LOCALE of SAMUEL-WILLIS was BATHTUB

P.6: The STATE of BATHTUB was SAFE
P.7: The CAREFULNESS of CLEANING-DRAIN was NOT-ORDINARY-CARE

What would you like explained?
a) defendant's liability
b) product user's negligence
c) victim's liability
d) what rule led to a given deduction?
e) why the rule was applicable
f) nothing

? ***e***
Why ***P.7***?
Q: At cycle #3535 RULE5 fired.
The rule is:

```
[ ORDINARY CARE DEFINITION ]
IF CAREFULNESS OF ACTUAL-USE OF PRODUCT OF DEFENDANT IS
    NOT KNOWN
AND ( LEGAL-STATUS OF VICTIM IS INFORMED-MINOR
OR LEGAL-STATUS OF VICTIM IS ADULT )
AND ( ( PRODUCT-IS-DEFECTIVE IS IN KNOWLEDGE OF VICTIM
AND STATUS OF ACTUAL-USE OF PRODUCT OF DEFENDANT IS CON-
    TINUED-USE )
OR ( PRODUCT-IS-HAZARDOUS-OR-DEFECTIVE IS IN KNOWLEDGE OF
    VICTIM
AND ( ATTENTIVENESS OF ACTUAL-USE OF PRODUCT OF DEFEN-
    DANT IS INATTENTIVE
OR STYLE OF ACTUAL-USE OF PRODUCT OF DEFENDANT IS CARE-
    LESS ) )
OR ( ACT OF ACTUAL-USE OF PRODUCT OF DEFENDANT IS IM-
    PROPER
AND ( ( AUTHOR OF WARNING OF DANGERS OF IMPROPER-USE OF
    PRODUCT OF DEFENDANT IS
MANUFACTURER OF PRODUCT OF DEFENDANT )
OR ( AUTHOR OF WARNING OF DANGERS OF IMPROPER-USE OF
    PRODUCT OF DEFENDANT IS
SELLER OF PRODUCT OF DEFENDANT ) ) )
OR ( SENSITIVE-TO-PRODUCT IS IN KNOWLEDGE OF VICTIM
AND STATUS OF ACTUAL-USE OF PRODUCT OF DEFENDANT IS CON-
    TINUED-USE )
OR ( MEANS OF ACTUAL-USE OF PRODUCT OF DEFENDANT IS POOR-
    PRACTICES )
OR ( THERE IS PROTECTION OF DANGERS OF ACTUAL-USE OF
    PRODUCT OF DEFENDANT
AND STATUS OF PROTECTION OF DANGERS OF ACTUAL-USE OF
    PRODUCT OF DEFENDANT IS
UNUSED-BY-VICTIM ) )
```

```
THEN SET CAREFULNESS OF ACTUAL-USE OF PRODUCT OF DEFEN-
    DANT TO NOT-ORDINARY-CARE;

THE RULE FIRED BECAUSE:

R.1: The PRODUCT of DEFENDANT was DRAIN-CLEANER
R.2: The ACTUAL-USE of DRAIN-CLEANER was CLEANING-DRAIN
R.3: The CAREFULNESS of CLEANING-DRAIN was not known
R.4: The LEGAL-STATUS of VICTIM was ADULT
R.5: The KNOWLEDGE of VICTIM was (PRODUCT-IS-DANGEROUS
    PRODUCT-IS-DANGEROUS)
R.6: The MEANS of CLEANING-DRAIN was GOOD-PRACTICES
R.7: The DANGERS of CLEANING-DRAIN was EXPLODES-IN-WATER
R.8: The PROTECTION of EXPLODES-IN-WATER was COVER-DRAIN
R.9: The STATUS of COVER-DRAIN was UNUSED-BY-VICTIM

What would you like explained?
    a) defendant's liability
    b) product user's negligence
    c) victim's liability
    d) what rule led to a given deduction?
    e) why the rule was applicable
    f) nothing
? c

THE THEORY OF NEGLIGENCE WAS CALCULATED BECAUSE:

S: At cycle #3644 RULE7 fired.
The rule is:
[ COMPARATIVE NEGLIGENCE - PARTIAL LIABILITY ]
IF LIABILITY OF DEFENDANT IS STRICT-LIABILITY
AND DEGREE OF LIABILITY OF DEFENDANT IS NOT KNOWN
AND USER OF PRODUCT OF DEFENDANT IS NAME OF VICTIM
AND ( JURISDICTION OF CASE IS CALIFORNIA
OR JURISDICTION OF CASE IS ARIZONA )
AND PRODUCT-IS-DANGEROUS IS IN KNOWLEDGE OF VICTIM
AND PRODUCT-IS-DANGEROUS IS IN APPRECIATION OF VICTIM
AND METHOD OF ACTUAL-USE OF PRODUCT OF DEFENDANT IS NEG-
    LIGENT
AND CAUSE OF CONTRIBUTING-FACTORS OF LOSS OF PLAINTIFF IS
    NAME OF VICTIM
THEN SET DEGREE OF LIABILITY OF DEFENDANT TO PARTIAL-LIABIL-
    ITY
AND SET MINIMUM-PROPORTION OF DEGREE OF LIABILITY OF DE-
    FENDANT TO 1 -
MAXIMUM-PROPORTIONATE-VICTIM-RESPONSIBILITY OF LOSS OF
    PLAINTIFF
```

AND SET MAXIMUM-PROPORTION OF DEGREE OF LIABILITY OF DEFENDANT TO 1 –
MINIMUM-PROPORTIONATE-VICTIM-RESPONSIBILITY OF LOSS OF PLAINTIFF
AND SET THEORY OF NEGLIGENCE TO COMPARATIVE-NEGLIGENCE ;

THIS RULE FIRED BECAUSE:

T.1: The LIABILITY of DEFENDANT was STRICT-LIABILITY
T.2: The DEGREE of STRICT-LIABILITY was not known
T.3: The PRODUCT of DEFENDANT was DRAIN-CLEANER
T.4: The USER of DRAIN-CLEANER was SAMUEL-WILLIS
T.5: The NAME of VICTIM was SAMUEL-WILLIS
T.6: The JURISDICTION of CASE was ARIZONA
T.7: The KNOWLEDGE of VICTIM was (PRODUCT-IS-DANGEROUS PRODUCT-IS-DANGEROUS)
T.8: The APPRECIATION of VICTIM was (PRODUCT-IS-DANGEROUS-PRODUCT-IS-DANGEROUS)
T.9: The ACTUAL-USE of DRAIN-CLEANER was CLEANING-DRAIN
T.10: The METHOD of CLEANING-DRAIN was NEGLIGENT
T.11: The LOSS of PLAINTIFF was BURNS-AND-PERMANENT-SCARRING
T.12: The CONTRIBUTING-FACTORS of BURNS-AND-PERMANENT-SCARRING was NO-USE-OF-DRAIN-LID
T.13: The CAUSE of NO-USE-OF-DRAIN-LID was SAMUEL-WILLIS

What would you like explained?

a) defendant's liability
b) product user's negligence
c) victim's liability
d) what rule led to a given deduction?
e) why the rule was applicable
f) nothing

? ***f***

Would you like to process the case again? ***no***

Would you like an explanation of the model's current decision-making process? ***no***

Finished

Chapter 6

TATR: A Prototype Expert System for Tactical Air Targeting

Monti D. Callero, Donald A. Waterman, and James R. Kipps

6.1 Introduction

During wartime, tactical air planners determine the intended operation of tactical air resources in a future operation (usually the next day) and prepare the necessary orders and instructions for operational units, such as fighter wings, to execute the planned missions. The selection of enemy target elements to be attacked is a core task in the planning process. Target selection depends primarily on human judgment to integrate information about friendly and enemy force posture, capability, operations, and objectives and thereby determine effective, efficient courses of action. Human decision making is inherently unstructured, and its predominance in target selection has inhibited the development of automated tools to perform this task.

Because we believe that automated aids specifically designed to reflect the human decision process can contribute to better judgments, we have developed a prototype expert system to help tactical air tar-

This chapter is an edited version of R-3096-ARPA, The Rand Corporation, August 1984.

geteers select and prioritize target elements. This program, the tactical air target recommender (TATR),[1] applies a *knowledge-engineering* problem-solving approach in which human domain knowledge is essential, and judgment, experience, and intuition play a larger role than mathematical algorithms and stochastic formalisms.

Based on decision-making techniques provided by experienced Air Force tactical air targeteers, TATR performs the following tasks under the interactive direction of a user:

- Preferential ordering of enemy airfields;
- Determination of the target elements to attack on those airfields; and
- Identification of the weapon systems that can be most effective against those target elements.

It also updates the status of database elements both through user input and projections of the effects of friendly air operations.

6.1.1 ■ Tactical Air Planning

Figure 6.1 shows the tactical air planning-process cycle. The cycle contains four major steps: target file generation, targeting, force application, and Air Tasking Order (ATO) preparation. (The current version of TATR addresses only the targeting step.)

Target File Generation

Intelligence data (information about the enemy) are collected continuously, in peacetime as well as wartime. The process increases in pace and focus, however, after hostilities commence. Raw data are gathered from many sources, through a wide variety of techniques, ranging from strictly human efforts to applications of highly advanced technology. Intelligence analysts reduce the raw data to identify and classify enemy resources and force elements; they then construct a target base composed of large data files on potential target elements. During the course of conflict, the status of the potential target elements can change rapidly as a result of actions against them or of the enemy's own operations; hence, the target base must be modified frequently as new intelligence is reported and analyzed.

This target base provides the main source of information about the

[1] The version of TATR reported here is a step in an iterative process. Previous prototype development efforts that contributed to the development of TATR are reported in Callero et al. (1981, 1982).

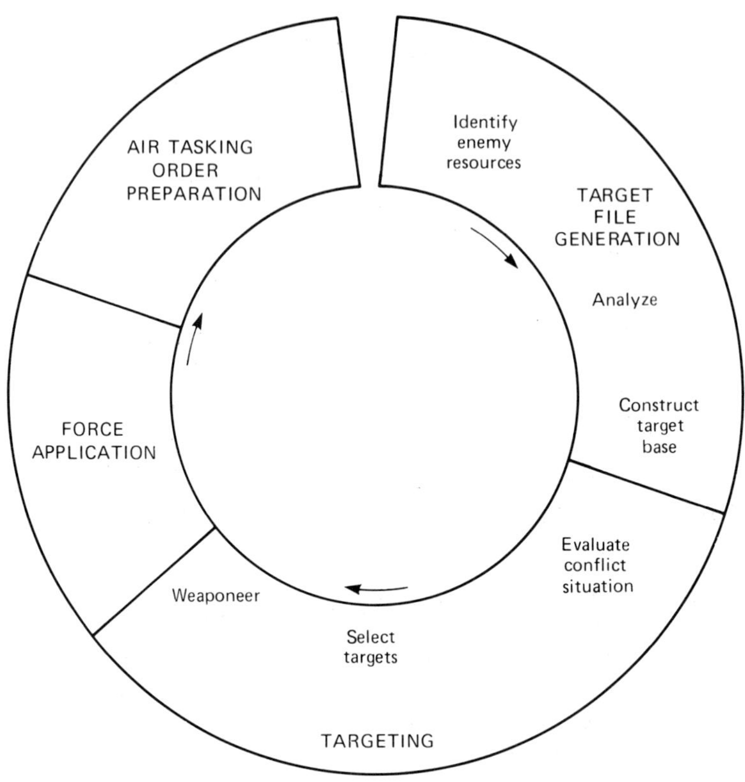

FIGURE 6.1 Tactical Air Planning Cycle.

enemy for the tactical planning process. For each potential target (e.g., airfields), the information may include target type, location, organizational linkages, supporting elements, recent movements, and estimates of capabilities. For airfield targets, similar data are provided for *target elements* located at the airfield, (e.g., aircraft, maintenance, and petroleum storage).

In the USAF Tactical Air Control Center (TACC), where the tactical air planning process takes place, the target base is partially automated by the Data Communication, Storage and Retrieval System (DC/SR). The remainder of the target base resides in hard-copy text, maps, and photographs.

Targeting

The targeting function consists of selecting from the target base specific target elements for attack and identifying weapon systems that can achieve the desired damage expectancies (a task called weaponeering). Targeting involves three overlapping and iterative activities: evaluation of target elements in the target base to assess their military value and relevance; selection of a candidate subset of target elements and determination of the effects desired against them; and weaponeering to determine both ability to achieve the desired effects and expected resource costs.

Selection of a subset of target elements from the many candidates in the target base is determined by the significance, accessibility, and vulnerability of target elements; objectives and strategies set forth in apportionment instructions and other guidance documents; rules of engagement; principles of air warfare; and tactics. Effects expected to be achieved against selected target elements are determined from target analysis information such as vulnerability, perishability, utility value, relationship to other target elements, location and mobility, and the validation of the target information. Weaponeering calculations array both damage criteria and weapons effects against forces, weapons, fuzing, and delivery tactics. They provide numbers of aircraft required to attain the expected damage levels on each target, and they specify the munitions the aircraft should carry. Information on enemy defenses is also analyzed, and a defense-suppression target list is prepared for each target.

The targeting process results in a prioritized list of target elements for attack during the following day, based on all of the considerations and information accumulated from the activities just described. The list, weaponeering data, and defense-suppression target elements are passed to the next step in the planning process.

Force Application

Force application produces a plan to match friendly air resources and enemy target elements. Input to the process includes the prioritized target list, the defense-suppression target list, and weaponeering data prepared in the targeting process; threat estimates; availability and capability of friendly forces; weather; and combat objectives, strategies, and tactics. The goal is to assign available force to the target set to achieve the best possible trade-off between results and cost (attrition, resource consumption, etc.). For example, forces are generally assigned in strike packages that may include defense-suppression aircraft, fighter escorts, electronic-countermeasure aircraft, and reconnaissance aircraft, in addition to the aircraft actually attacking the target. Overflight coordination with friendly ground fire-support elements may also be required.

The plan specifies the units that are to fly the missions, the types of aircraft, the munitions to be carried, the controlling agencies (e.g., ground radar sites) to be used to and from the target, and the timing of the critical points in the mission, such as rendezvous with tanker and escort aircraft and time over the target.

Air Tasking Order Preparation

The final step in the planning process is to format the agreed-upon plan as an ATO that is communicated to all appropriate organizations. It directs them to perform the attacks as specified.

6.1.2 ■ Rationale for An Expert Aid

In every step of the tactical planning process, people must make judgments about complex problems under time constraints. Decisions are made by Air Force officers with a variety of backgrounds. At the outbreak of hostilities, the officers cannot be expected to have broad experience in tactical planning. Because of this, and because of the inherent complexity of tactical planning, there is clearly a need for sophisticated, automated aids to help regularize the process and assist the targeteer in making the best possible selections. Such aids would be particularly important in large-scale modern conflicts, in which the most targeting help would be needed and the greatest returns would be expected.

The scattered distribution of expert targeteers in peacetime and the general lack of expertise in dealing with modern forces in large-scale war have important implications for the utility and structure of the targeting aid. From the utility standpoint, the targeting aid would provide a focal point and could serve as the repository for the development and accumulation of (prewar) targeting concepts by Air Force targeteers. If the distributed knowledge can be used in a tool that permits experimentation, evaluation, and modification, the Air Force might have a dependable targeting capability at an outbreak of war. In fact, alternative plans could be developed and made available as a basis for fighting the first day of war. On the other hand, the targeting aid must be adaptable to changing ideas about war fighting that evolve in peacetime as well as during an actual war, since to a large degree it will be necessary to learn to fight the war as it unfolds. Hence, the structure of the targeting aid must permit rapid adaptation within the operational environment.

An aid that can accumulate knowledge, consider heuristics, adapt to the user as well as the situation, and communicate easily with the user would significantly improve the force employment process. Continuing advances in the tools and techniques of artificial intelligence (AI) have brought knowledge engineering to a point where it can serve as the basis for such an aid. A prototype expert system can serve as a vehicle for investigating the current utility of knowledge engineering and may also have the potential to evolve into a useful operational capability.

We have chosen to focus on the targeting step of the tactical planning cycle because it is separable in both concept and practice. It contains sufficient elements to fully challenge current knowledge-engineering capabilities, and a successful automated aid would fulfill a real need for the targeteer. The focus of targeting interest in this study is on selecting and attacking enemy airfields.

6.1.3 ■ Knowledge Engineering

Knowledge engineering requires many iterations of system implementation. The knowledge that human experts possess is often difficult to articulate because it may not be complete, definitive, or consistent. Translating such knowledge into computer programs produces precise and rigorous interpretations that lead to deeper understanding and new perceptions about the problem domain. These, in turn, stimulate changes in the knowledge base that translate into new, precise, and rigorous interpretations in the program. Hence, system development requires an evolutionary approach.

For the tactical targeting aid, two categories of knowledge must be acquired:

1. Knowledge people use to process information about the conflict situation so they can make decisions about the use of tactical air resources; and
2. Information about the conflict environment that is known (or at least reported) and is available to the decision makers (such information is generally stored in data files or databases).

The unclassified conflict environment developed for our prototype system is based on airfield information developed by the Air Force and used extensively by the Air/Ground Operations School and others. To support the weaponeering function (relating expected target damage and specific attacks by various aircraft/munitions combinations) without using classified information and procedures, we developed a representative weaponeering procedure and generated an unclassified weaponeering database that is sufficiently realistic for research purposes.[2]

[2] In an actual operational environment, automated weaponeering calculations and database updates could be accomplished by interfacing with existing programs on the DC/SR.

The human knowledge to be used in a knowledge-engineering system must be acquired directly from people who are expert (or at least very knowledgeable) in performing the targeting tasks. Targeting-knowledge acquisition must be an ongoing process, even in an actual war. The knowledge must evolve over time through iterations of trial and evaluation, and the targeting aid must contribute to that process.

We acquired our initial set of targeting knowledge through extensive discussions of targeting techniques with highly qualified Air Force tactical targeteers. After eliciting an initial set of targeting heuristics, we formalized and structured those heuristics and iteratively, with the targeteers, improved our interpretation and the conciseness and precision of their rules. After sufficient agreement, we implemented the heuristics in the TATR program, which became the primary vehicle for evolving further heuristics. From that point, TATR evolved through hands-on use by selected targeteers.

6.1.4 ■ ROSIE

A key feature of TATR is that it is programmed in the ROSIE (Rule-Oriented System for Implementing Expertise) programming language (Fain et al., 1981). ROSIE was developed at Rand to support knowledge-based programming tasks. It readily accommodates heuristic logic and has an English-like syntax that helps nonprogrammers understand and verify the program. Its readability also enables the user to determine appropriate program modifications as the knowledge base evolves. Hence, TATR can provide a vehicle for the development and evolution of targeting concepts and approaches.

6.2 TATR Functions and Interface

6.2.1 ■ Overview

TATR is an interactive program that performs its functions and produces output only at the direction of a user. *Its primary functions are to provide a plan for attacking enemy airfields and to project the effects of implementing the plan.* The plan results from a user/program interchange. TATR applies predetermined planning heuristics to generate an initial plan that can then be modified by user guidance or specific instructions. The program then replans to incorporate the user's directions.

By projecting the results of a series of plans over a number of days, TATR can help the user select the best plan or sequence of plans to implement.

In addition to the basic planning function, TATR also interactively maintains its databases by processing updates from the user, and, in response to user requests, it provides detailed information about plans, friendly force capabilities, and enemy force posture and status.

To facilitate understanding of TATR functions, output, and interfaces, and to introduce key definitions and terminology, we will sketch the automatic plan-generation function, briefly discuss database information, and describe how the user can interface with TATR to modify the TATR-generated plan. A more extensive discussion of the program logic, heuristics, and calculations follows in Section 6.3. An example of a planning session is given in Appendix A.

Plan-generation Function

TATR uses a database of information describing the airfields, the target elements on the airfields (e.g., aircraft, runways, maintenance facilities), and the types of friendly forces available for the attack. When a user calls upon TATR to execute the plan-generation function, the program applies a qualitative rating process to each target on each airfield. The first step in the process is to examine each target's vulnerability to attack. Next, target elements with capacity characteristics (e.g., petroleum storage) are assessed according to their ability to withstand attack. Based on these assessments, the target's operational status, factors pertaining to the airfield (e.g., sortie activity), and the tactical objectives of friendly counter-air activities, TATR rates each target as excellent, very good, good, or unrecommended.

Once the target elements are rated, the program "weaponeers"[3] each target rated as excellent, very good, or good, and determines the effects that attacks on those targets would have on the sortie-generation capability of each airfield. TATR displays target ratings and the results of each step in the sortie-generation calculation as they are determined.

The program then orders the airfields by the reduction the attacks are expected to produce in the number of sorties each airfield can generate in a day and forms a target development list (TDL). The TDL

[3] The weaponeering process can either identify weapon systems that are effective against a target and determine the number of those systems necessary to achieve a specified damage expectancy, or calculate damage expectancy against a target, given a specified type and number of weapon systems. Both approaches are used in TATR, but the present discussion assumes use of the former.

contains the ordered list of airfields with the target elements on each airfield that have been determined best to attack, and the types and number of aircraft that could be assigned to the attacks. The TDL is the product of the plan-generation function and forms the basis for interactive plan development with the user.

The Database

The TATR program requires a database of general information about enemy airfields and specific information regarding the composition of each airfield. The general information includes the types of target elements that might be found on each airfield, the types of enemy aircraft that might be present, the types of friendly aircraft and weapons available to attack the enemy airfields, and parameters of weapon system capability and friendly-aircraft effectiveness. The specific information includes a detailed description of each enemy airfield, usually containing 80 or more assertions. An abbreviated example of the airfield information is shown in Fig. 6.2.

The initial TATR database is generated in advance and updated dynamically as the program is being executed. This dynamic updating capability is an absolute necessity, since the status of the enemy airfields changes during the battle. Changes result from enemy operations that either diminish or increase resources and from actions against them by friendly forces.

Changes in the enemy's status are recognized and processed in two different ways: First, friendly aircrews and intelligence systems observe and report changes; the information is extracted from the intelligence reports and entered by the user prior to or during interactive plan development. Second, TATR recognizes that friendly actions were previously planned to have been carried out against an enemy airfield, hence changes are expected to have occurred that have not yet been reported. In this case, the user can enter the actual (if known) number and type of weapon systems and target elements attacked, and the program will calculate the effects and reflect them as status estimates in the database. If no actual information about a previously planned attack is available, the effects of the planned attack are projected and reflected as estimates in the database. Reported information takes precedence over projected effects.

6.2.2 ■ Interface

A user interfaces with TATR primarily through menu-driven communications. TATR presents a menu of things the user can choose to do at any given time, and the user selects the thing he or she wants to do

```
Let the name of Afld #1 be ...
Assert Afld #1 does have a nuclear capability.
Let the ceiling at Afld #1 be 4500 feet.
Let the visibility at Afld #1 be 5 miles.
Let the primary mission of Afld #1 be OCA.
Let the number of double bay shelters at Afld #1 be 75.
Assert Afld #1 does not have underground facilities for aircraft.
Assert each of floggers and farmers is a type of aircraft
    at Afld #1.
Assert maintenance hard is accessible at Afld #1.
Let the number of maintenance hard areas at Afld #1 be 2.
Let the average-size of maintenance hard areas at Afld #1
    be 5000 ft**2.
Let the percentage-expectation for finding aircraft in
    maintenance hard at Afld #1 be 0.75.
Assert munitions assembly area is accessible at Afld #1.
Let the number of munitions assembly areas at Afld #1 be 1.
Let the munitions-assembly-area at Afld #1 be 9000 ft**2.
Let the operating-efficiency of munitions assembly at Afld #1
    be 0.85.
Assert pol hard is accessible at Afld #1.
Let the number of pol hard areas at Afld #1 be 2.
Let the average-number of pol hard tanks per area at Afld #1 be 50.
Let the average-capacity of pol hard tanks at Afld #1 be 8000 gals.
Assert pol soft is accessible at Afld #1.
Let the number of pol soft storage areas at Afld #1 be 2.
Let the average-number of pol soft tanks per area at Afld #1 be 5.
Let the average-capacity of pol soft tanks at Afld #1 be 5000 gals.
    etc.
    etc.
```

FIGURE 6.2 Illustrative Data Entries for an Enemy Airfield.

next by identifying it on the menu. Following selection of a menu item, the user is presented with either (1) the final result of the action, (2) another menu, (3) a question requiring a direct answer, or (4) access to modify the TATR rulesets or database. The top-level menu is shown in Fig. 6.3.

The *Display* portion of the menu allows the user to look at information he or she might need to develop a final target list. For instance, item [A] gives the user a display of the TDL, an example of which is shown in Fig. 6.4. The sortie reduction (SR) at each airfield is shown in the first column, and the sortie capability (SC) before and after the attack is also indicated. The third column shows the target ratings (EX for excellent and G for good). The fourth column indicates the change

Display:
- [A] Target Development List (TDL)
- [B] Designated Weapon Packages
- [C] Target Recovery Tables
- [D] Target Status Tables
- [E] (not implemented)
- [F] Additional Target Information

Modify:
- [G] Target Development List
- [H] Weapon Packages
- [I] Attack Projections
- [J] Data & Rulesets

Tasking Commands:
- [K] Attack Targets Specified by TDL
- [L] Advance To The Next Time Period
- [M] Initiate Target Rating & Weaponeering Program
- [N] Move To A Previously Seen Day
- [O] Exit From This TATR Session

FIGURE 6.3 Top-level Menu.

in status of each target element—in this case, all change from 1.0 (perfect) to 1 minus their damage expectancy (DE) from an attack carried out by the number, type, and munitions load of the weapon packages shown in the fifth column. The last column indicates the expected aircraft attrition.

Item [B], designated weapon packages, displays additional information about the damage expectancy and the weapon packages that could be used against each of the target elements on each base. Items [C] and [D] display the expected rate of reconstitution and the current

FIGURE 6.4 Illustrative Target Development List (TDL).

Current TDL (Target Development List): Day 1 v3 — Time Frame = MEDIUM

SR	*Elements*	*Rating*	*Status*	*Weapack*	*DE*	*Attrit'n*
	AFLD #1			SC: 640 -> 238		
402	Main Hard	EX	1.0 -> 0.26	8 F-16X/1	0.74	0.48
	Mun Assem Area	EX	1.0 -> 0.25	4 F-16X/2	0.75	0.24
	Munitions Hard	EX	1.0 -> 0.23	5 F-111X/1	0.77	0.3
	Mun Load Area	EX	1.0 -> 0.25	4 F-16X/2	0.75	0.24
	POL Hard	EX	1.0 -> 0.26	3 F-111X/2	0.74	0.18
	AFLD #3			SC: 288 -> 270		
18	Munitions Soft	G	1.0 -> 0.26	8 F-111X/1	0.74	0.48
	Mun Load Area	G	1.0 -> 0.28	11 F-16X/2	0.72	0.66
	POL Hard	G	1.0 -> 0.23	5 F-111X/1	0.77	0.3

status of each target attacked, respectively. Item [F], additional target information, gives the user access to the entire target data file.

The modify and tasking items are described here.

[G] *Modify target development list.* Allows the user to add airfields to or delete airfields from the TDL.

[H] *Modify weapon packages.* Allows the user to investigate the effect of using different weapon packages against target elements on the TDL. Any combination of aircraft and munitions load may be investigated. The number of weapon systems may be either specified or program-determined to meet TATR's desired damage expectancy. Once a preferred weapon package has been identified, this item also allows the user to designate it for use on the TDL.

[I] *Modify attack projections.* Allows the user to investigate the effect of changing the target elements to be attacked on an airfield. Once a preferred set of target elements has been identified, this item allows the user to designate it for use on the TDL.

[J] *Modify data and rulesets.* Allows the user to reflect changes to the database resulting from intelligence reports, changes in general planning guidance, and/or changes in weaponeering approaches. This item also allows the user to change TATR's targeting rules or any other ruleset in the program.

[K] *Attack targets specified by TDL.* Causes TATR to calculate the results of implementing a TDL. A copy of the modified database containing resultant target status is saved and tagged for future reference and/or return during a planning session. In this manner, item [K] allows the user to *look ahead* into future time periods to investigate the longer-term effects of an attack or series of attacks.

[L] *Advance to the next time period.* Simulates moving ahead in time to the next day. This item is used in conjunction with [K] for investigating the longer-term effects of attacks.

[M] *Initiate Target Rating and Weaponeering Program.* Initiates the plan-generation function described earlier.

[N] *Move to a previously seen day.* Recalls the database and TDL previously generated using [K]. This item is used in conjunction with [K] and [L] to look ahead.

[O] *Exit from this TATR session.* Terminates the TATR session.

The information that would appear on the user's terminal during an illustrative plan-generation interface is shown in Appendix A.

6.3 The TATR Program

6.3.1 ■ Overview

The main components of the TATR program are listed in Table 6.1 and described in the following subsections.

Target Database

The target database currently stored in TATR contains a selected set of enemy airfields extracted from an unclassified exercise database used by the Air Force in the Air/Ground Operations School. In addition to general airfield data, each entry contains detailed information about the important targets located at the airfield, including the current number and types of enemy aircraft and their characteristics (e.g., range, munitions, POL[4] requirements). The following target elements are considered by TATR:[5]

- Aircraft;
- Access taxiways;
- Maintenance soft;
- Maintenance hard;
- Munitions loading area;
- Munitions assembly area;
- Munitions storage hard;
- Munitions storage soft;
- Refueling soft;
- Rapid turn area;
- POL storage hard; and
- POL storage soft.

Weather forecasts are also included because TATR can limit the weapon systems it considers to those whose delivery parameters are below the ceiling and visibility forecast for a target. Some illustrative

[4] Petroleum, oil, and lubricants.

[5] A target element is considered *hard* if it has been hardened against attack (e.g., a concrete bunker). The designation as *hard* or *soft* appears as part of the name of the element.

TABLE 6.1 TATR Program Components.

Component	*Contents*
Target database	Airfield target elements; enemy aircraft capability; weather
Operational status	Target element status; battle damage; target element reconstitution
Rules	Tactical file; policy file; users file
Weaponeering	Probability-of-arrival tables; probability-of-damage tables; computation functions
Displays	Target development list; weapon systems packages; strike results; target operational status

airfield database entries are shown in Fig. 6.2. Based on user input, the program dynamically updates the target database to reflect rapidly changing conditions that would be expected in a combat environment.

Operational Status

The operational status (opstat) component of the program includes the current status of the airfield targets and the target reconstitution at each airfield. *The opstat is displayed as the percentage of the target element that is still operational*. For example, if the target element is undamaged, its status is 1; if it is completely destroyed, its status is 0. Battle damage resulting from each strike may be entered by the user as an input from an intelligence battle damage report. If such an input is not made, the program assumes that all planned strikes occur and achieve the damage estimated. Opstat incorporates provisions for the reconstitution of targets, based on estimates of the expected improvement in a target's capability in each time period after a strike. This increment of improvement is applied to a target's opstat for each time period unless it is overridden by an input of confirmed target status.

Rules

As stated earlier, TATR is programmed in the ROSIE language. The program consists of English-like rules organized in logical, procedural rulesets. The organization and form of the rules facilitate the user's comprehension of the program flow and logic. The main body of rules, the tactical file, performs the primary tasks of developing the attack plan, interacting with the user, dynamically updating data files, and controlling the sequence of program events. These rules fall into three major categories: target-element capability, target-element rating, and airfield selection.

Target-element Capability Rules. These rules define various capabilities, such as the rate at which targets are reconstituted (repaired or resupplied), the current activity level at the airfield, and the capacity of various critical resources at the airfield, such as munitions storage, munitions assembly, and maintenance. A portion of the ROSIE ruleset defining the munitions soft capability in TATR is shown in Fig. 6.5.

Since these rules define the terms used by the program (e.g., munitions soft capacity, daily consumption of POL by an aircraft type), they are fixed and would not normally be modified by the user.

Target-element Rating Rules. These rules evaluate each target element at an airfield and rate it as either excellent, very good, good, or unrecommended. The rating considers the criticality of the target relative to maintaining the airfield's primary mission, the vulnerability of the target element to attack, and the current status and effectiveness of the target element. A portion of the ROSIE ruleset for rating aircraft as targets is shown in Fig. 6.6.

Once all the targets are rated, the program uses those rated excellent, very good, or good to project the effect of an attack against them.

Airfield-selection Rules. These rules provide a basis for choosing a particular airfield to attack from among a set of possible candidates. The rules assess the sortie capability of each airfield and the reduction in sortie capability that could be achieved by attacking the recom-

FIGURE 6.5 Portion of ROSIE Ruleset Defining Munitions Soft Capability.

```
To generate a capacity of an area at an airfield:

  [1] Select the area:

  <MUNITIONS SOFT>

Produce (the number of munitions soft areas at the airfield)
× (the average-size of munitions soft bunkers at that airfield)
× (the average-number of munitions soft bunkers per area
       at that airfield)
× (the status of munitions soft at that airfield)
/ (the average-space-requirement for munitions storage).
```

```
To rate-aircraft at an airfield:
[1]  If the airfield does have exposed aircraft,
         choose situation:
     If the number of aircraft in "the open" at the airfield
         is greater than .25 × the total-number (TOTAL)
         of aircraft at that airfield,
       let EXCELLENT be the rating for aircraft at that airfield;
     If that number [of exposed aircraft] is greater than .20 × TOTAL,
       let VERY GOOD be the rating for aircraft at that airfield;
     If that number [of exposed aircraft] is greater than .15 × TOTAL,
       let GOOD be the rating for aircraft at that airfield;
     Default: let UNRECOMMENDED be the rating for aircraft
         at that airfield.
End.
```

FIGURE 6.6 Portion of ROSIE Ruleset for Rating Aircraft.

mended targets. The program applies the rules and uses the results to compile a TDL, which contains each airfield under consideration, ordered by the sortie reduction achievable from attacking the preferred targets. Also included are the weapon packages needed to effect the desired damage on each target element.

The airfield selection rules calculate the sortie reduction that would result from attacking each recommended target element separately and then combine these reductions to determine the effect of attacking groups of elements. A portion of a ROSIE airfield selection ruleset is shown in Fig. 6.7. This ruleset determines the percentage reduction in aircraft after an attack by F-16X/1 or F-4X/4 aircraft on aircraft, maintenance hard, or the munitions loading area at an airfield.[6]

Although the tactical file can be modified, like any TATR rule or database item, we consider its rules to be firm in the sense that a user would not normally change them for any particular operational run. Needed operational flexibility is provided by two sets of rules and parameters called the policy file and the user file.

Policy and User Files. The policy and user file sets are those rules and parameters that would normally be changed by a user to account for situational variation, command guidance and direction, and indi-

[6] The use of these rules to determine aircraft reduction is illustrated in Appendix A.

```
To generate percentage-reduction to aircraft
     after an attack on a target at an airfield:

[1]  If the current-DE (for the target) at the airfield~= 0,
     select the target:
<AIRCRAFT>
  Produce ((that current-DE)
           × (the number of exposed aircraft)
           /  (the total-number of aircraft at that airfield));
<MAINTENANCE HARD>
  Choose situation:
     If the weapon-system for use against maintenance hard
          at that airfield = F-16X/1,
        produce (that current-DE)
                  × ((the number of aircraft sent against maintenance hard
                       at that airfield)
                  /  1 [aircraft required to destroy each shelter])
                  × .75 [probability of finding aircraft in a shelter]
                  × 2 [aircraft per shelter]
                  /  (the total-number of aircraft at that airfield));
     If that weapon-system = F-4X/4,
        produce (that current-DE)
                  × ((the number of aircraft sent against maintenance hard
                       at that airfield)
                  /  2 [aircraft required to destroy each shelter])
                  × .75 [probability of finding aircraft in a shelter]
                  × 2 [aircraft per shelter]
                  /  (the total-number of aircraft at that airfield));
<MUNITIONS LOADING AREA>
     If the total-number (TOTAL) of aircraft at the airfield > 20
               and that current-DE > .25,
        produce ((that current-DE)
     × ((the capacity of central MLA [munitions loading area]
               at that airfield)
               / (1 × that current-DE))
          / (TOTAL));
     End.
```

NOTE: The times sign(×) and slash(/) are standard programming symbols for multiplication and division. The term *current-DE* refers to the damage expectancy for the target element, based on previous attacks.

FIGURE 6.7 Portion of ROSIE Ruleset for Determining Percentage Reduction in Aircraft after an Attack.

vidual targeteer approaches. The policy file contains things that targeteers have no independent authority to establish or change and would be procedurally bound not to change. Policies and directions from higher authorities (e.g., command, theater, national) fall in this category. They might include rules of engagement, political and geographical limitations, and weapon system employment constraints. The user file contains items that targeteers have complete control over in interacting with TATR to develop an attack plan. These items include attack objectives, desired damage expectancy, and rules, data, and parameters for TDL generation that allow for exploring variations in TDLs under different conditions.

A portion of the policy rules is shown in Fig. 6.8. These ROSIE rules determine whether or not a given weapon system satisfies current policy for use against a particular target element. For example, they prohibit the use of F-16/X aircraft against airfields more than 400 nautical miles from the battle area and the use of F-4X/4 aircraft to attack specified target elements during poor weather.

Weaponeering

The weaponeering component determines which combinations of aircraft type, munitions load, and delivery tactics are effective against a given target element and calculates how many aircraft are required to achieve a desired damage expectancy against that element. Effective combinations are determined by applying rules such as those shown in Fig. 6.8 and using a table of preferred weapon systems for each target element type. Note that the choice of attack aircraft and target is influenced by the weather.

During the weaponeering process, the weaponeering component considers the probability of the aircraft arriving at the target and the probability of those that arrive damaging the target with the munitions being carried and the delivery tactic used. These probabilities are provided to the program in tabular form. The computational procedure is far simpler than the damage computation routines normally used by the Air Force. However, the procedure provides sufficient weaponeering capability for our immediate needs. In an operational implementation of TATR, the TATR system would be interfaced with an official Air Force weaponeering program.

The weaponeering subroutine that calculates weapon effects is programmed in the C programming language (Kernighan and Ritchie, 1978). Aircraft types, munitions loads, and delivery tactics are determined by ROSIE rules in the main body of the TATR program. All data reflecting aircraft capability are constructive and unclassified.

```
To decide a weapon-system does satisfy policy-rule
     for use against a target at an airfield:

[1]  Select the type of attack aircraft used by the weapon-system:
     <F-111X>
        If the distance from home base to the airfield > 1000 miles,
           conclude false [weapon system does not satisfy policy];
     <F-4X, F-16X>
        If the distance from home base to the airfield > 400 miles,
           conclude false [weapon system does not satisfy policy].
[2]  If the ceiling at the airfield is less than 3500 feet or
        the visibility at that airfield is less than 3 miles,
        let the weather be poor,
     otherwise, let the weather be good.
[3]  Select the target:
     <AIRCRAFT>
        If the weapon-system = either F-16X/2 or F-4X/3,
           conclude true [weapon system does satisfy policy];
     <MAINTENANCE HARD>
       If (the weather = good and
           the weapon-system = either F-4X/4 or F-16X/1) or
          (the weather = poor and
           the weapon-system = either F-111X/1 or F-4X/1),
          conclude true [weapon system does satisfy policy];
     <MUNITIONS HARD>
       If the weapon-system = F-111X/1 or
             (the weather = good and that weapon-system = F-4X/4),
          conclude true [weapon system does satisfy policy];
     <POL HARD>
       If (the weather = good and
           the weapon-system = either F-4X/4 or F-111X/2) or
          (the weather = poor and the weapon-system = F-111X/1),
          conclude true [weapon system does satisfy policy];
Default: Conclude false [weapon system does not satisfy policy].
End.
```

NOTE: The term *weapon system* refers to the attack aircraft plus its delivery aids and the munitions it carries.

FIGURE 6.8 The Portion of the ROSIE Ruleset that Defines TATR Policy.

Displays

Since TATR is an interactive program, all output is provided to the user online at a terminal. Online displays from video terminals can be saved and printed in hard-copy form. Illustrative displays are shown in Appendix A.

6.3.2 ■ TATR Logic Flow

The TATR program follows six major steps to create an airfield attack plan.

1. Rate target elements at each airfield to determine acceptable targets;
2. Weaponeer target elements at airfields containing acceptable targets;
3. Form strike packages of airfield attack aircraft;
4. Determine the sortie reduction achievable by each attack;
5. Display an initial TDL containing recommended airfields, target elements to attack, and weapon packages needed for the attack; order the airfields according to the sortie reduction achievable by the attacks; and
6. Interact with the user to develop a final TDL.

These steps are discussed in the following subsections.

Rate Target Elements

The first step in the plan-generation process is to determine the acceptability of the target elements at each airfield. The TATR program automatically evaluates every target element at every airfield and assigns each a rating of excellent (EX), very good (VG), good (G), or unrecommended (U). Generally, to be rated EX, VG, or G, target elements must be considered both critical to the operation of the airfield and vulnerable to attack. The rating rules also take into account other factors, including:

- The objective of the attack (sortie reduction, sortie suppression, or capability neutralization);
- The capability of the target element to support the maximum sortie rate (e.g., munitions, POL, and maintenance would be rated as having either an extensive, adequate, or limited capability);

- Recovery time (the time required for the target element to recover from an attack);
- The current status of the target element (the percentage of the element that is still operational);
- The number and quantity of the target elements; and
- The activity level at the airfield (high or low).

These ratings provide an indication of how acceptable each target element is as a target and a preliminary estimate of the relative payoff from a successful attack.

Weaponeer Target Elements

The second step in the plan-generation process is to determine the best combination of aircraft, munitions load, and delivery tactic for attacking the recommended target elements on each of the TDL airfields. A target element is recommended if it is evaluated as EX, VG, or G by the rating rules.

The user has three strike objectives from which to choose: sortie reduction, sortie suppression, and capability neutralization. The objectives are defined in Table 6.2. The emphasis in the current TATR implementation has been on refining and extending the rules for sortie reduction; thus the rating rules addressing this objective are the most sophisticated.

For each recommended target element, the program identifies feasible combinations of aircraft, munitions load, and delivery tactic by using data that represent weapons-effects calculations from operational tests. The feasible combinations are then screened by rules (such as those shown in Fig. 6.8) that reflect policy, user, or operational (e.g., range) constraints. Combinations that survive the screening are submitted to a weaponeering component. At present, the best combination is considered to be the one that requires the least attrition to achieve the desired damage expectancy.

TABLE 6.2 Definition of TATR Objectives.

Objective	*Definition*
Sortie reduction	Reduce overall airfield sortie rate for a period of days
Sortie suppression	Reduce overall airfield sortie rate for a period of hours
Capability Neutralization	Destroy the airfield's capability to perform a special function

TABLE 6.3 Weaponeering Component of TATR.

Source of Information	*Input to Weaponeering Subroutine*	*Output from Weaponeering Subroutine*
TDL	Airfield	Airfield
TATR rules	Target element	Target element
TATR rules	Aircraft/munitions/ tactic	Aircraft/munitions/ tactic
User	Strike objective	Quantity of aircraft
User	Desired damage expectancy	Expected attrition
Opstat	Previous strike results	Desired damage expectancy; actual damage expectancy

Table 6.3 shows the input and the output of the weaponeering component. This component determines how many of each type of aircraft are needed to attack each target element at each airfield on the TDL. The aircraft type and number, called the attack force, forms the strike package. At present, the best strike package is considered to be the one that requires the least attrition to achieve the desired damage expectancy. Of course, the targeteer has the option of changing the recommended strike package or selecting another one to take into account the difference in cost and availability of the different types of aircraft in the strike packages.

In the current implementation of TATR, defense suppression and air-defense escort aircraft are not included in the strike package. These factors would have to be incorporated before the program could be used in an operational tactical air-planning environment.

The user may set the desired damage expectancy (the default is 0.70). The actual damage expectancy usually will exceed the desired damage expectancy because the weaponeering component always satisfies the desired DE and applies only integer numbers of aircraft.

Calculate Sortie Reduction

TATR assists the targeteer in deciding which airfield to attack by rating each airfield in terms of the sortie reduction an attack would cause. After TATR forms the strike package, it determines the sortie reduction achievable by attacking each recommended target element at each airfield. Sortie reduction is obtained by subtracting an airfield's postattack sortie capability from its preattack capability. The sortie capability of each airfield is determined for the time period of interest (some number of days). For example, the sortie capability over a two-day period would be the sum of the capabilities for each of the two days, taking into account target reconstitution and resupply. The program assumes that each target element is reconstituted and resupplied on a daily basis, the rate depending on the target element type.

TATR determines an airfield's sortie capability by examining the current description (quantity, area, operational status, etc.) of certain key target elements at the airfield and calculating the maximum number of sorties each element can support. *The smallest of these maximum numbers is the limiting factor and thus the maximum sortie capability of the airfield.*[7] For example, suppose there are only enough aircraft to support a sortie rate of 110, enough munitions to support a sortie rate of 120, enough POL to support a sortie rate of 100, and enough maintenance capability to support a sortie rate of 150. Also suppose that all other target elements can support a sortie rate of 140 or more. TATR would decide that the airfield's sortie capability is 100, since this is the best the airfield can do with its limited POL supply.

The key target elements used to estimate airfield sortie capability are shown in Table 6.4, which also lists some (but not all) of the factors used in calculating the sortie capability each target element can support.

TATR assumes that maintenance takes place in shelters and hangars; thus an attack on maintenance will destroy a certain percentage of the aircraft at the airfield. It will therefore reduce sorties by reducing both aircraft and the airfield's maintenance capability. Similarly, TATR assumes that an attack on the munitions loading area will destroy some aircraft. The program estimates the loss of aircraft when maintenance or munitions loading is attacked and incorporates it into the sortie reduction caused by the attack (see Fig. 6.7).

Order and Display TDL

The fifth step in the plan-generation process adjusts the TDL order to reflect the sortie reduction achievable by attacking each airfield and displays the TDL to the user. Airfields for which a high sortie reduction can be attained are listed ahead of those with a lower achievable sortie reduction. A sample TDL is shown in Fig. 6.9. The TDL is ordered by number of sorties reduced, regardless of the type of aircraft

[7] Note that the targeteer can choose not to attack any of the less effective target elements on the airfield, and the sortie reduction (as estimated by the program) will remain the same, unless aircraft would be destroyed by an attack on any of these other elements (see Appendix A).

TABLE 6.4 Target Elements Used to Estimate Airfield Sortie Capability and Factors Considered.

Target Element	*Factors Considered*
Aircraft	Number; type; maximum sortie rate; munitions/mission; POL/mission
Munitions storage (soft, hard)	Status; number of areas; bunkers per area; bunker size; munitions/aircraft type
POL storage (soft, hard)	Status; number of areas; tanks per area; tank capacity; POL/aircraft type
Maintenance (soft, hard)	Status; number of areas; size of areas; space requirements/aircraft
Munitions loading	Status; number of areas; central area loading time for each aircraft type; dispersed area loading time for each aircraft type
Munitions assembly	Status; number of areas; size of areas; space requirement/aircraft; permanent area assembly capacity; dispersed area assembly capacity; operating efficiency of munitions assembly at the airfield

making up those sorties. Thus the targeteer may choose to reorder the TDL, because, for example, 98 sorties from airfield #4 may be more of a threat than 138 sorties from airfield #2.

The TDL includes the airfields, recommended target elements, estimated change in target-element status, weapon package needed to effect that change, damage expectancy, attrition, and overall change in the sortie capability of the airfield. Thus, in Fig. 6.9, attacking maintenance hard, munitions soft, and POL soft at airfield #4 would change the sortie capability of that airfield from 190 to 92, a reduction of 98; and the preferred weapon package for attacking maintenance hard at airfield #4 is 3 F-16X/1s, which would produce a damage expectancy of 0.77 and attrition of 0.24.

User Interaction

The final step in the plan-generation process permits direct interaction with and involvement by the user. The user can directly modify the plan or investigate the effect of changes to operational conditions and/or parameters assigned to the user file. This interaction will cause TATR to reaccomplish one or more of the previous steps in the plan-generation process. As explained in Section 6.2, the user may modify

Target Development List: Day 1 Version 1 — Time Frame = MEDIUM

SR	Targets	Rating	Status	Weapack	DE	Attrit'n
AFLD #1				SC: 640 -> 211		
429	Main Hard	VG	1.0 -> 0.27	8 F-16X/1	0.73	0.64
	Mun Assem Area	VG	1.0 -> 0.26	4 F-16X/2	0.74	0.32
	Munitions Hard	VG	1.0 -> 0.25	5 F-111X/1	0.75	0.5
	Mun Load Area	VG	1.0 -> 0.26	4 F-16X/2	0.74	0.32
	POL Hard	VG	1.0 -> 0.28	3 F-111X/2	0.72	0.3
AFLD #2				SC: 292 -> 154		
138	Main Hard	VG	1.0 -> 0.28	18 F-111X/1	0.72	1.8
	Munitions Hard	VG	1.0 -> 0.25	5 F-111X/1	0.75	0.5
	POL Hard	G	1.0 -> 0.25	5 F-111X/1	0.75	0.5
AFLD #4				SC: 190 -> 92		
98	Main Hard	VG	1.0 -> 0.23	3 F-16X/1	0.77	0.24
	Munitions Soft	VG	1.0 -> 0.27	8 F-16X/2	0.73	0.64
	POL Soft	G	1.0 -> 0.17	2 F-16X/1	0.83	0.16
AFLD #3				SC: 288 -> 272		
16	POL Hard	VG	1.0 -> 0.25	5 F-111X/1	0.75	0.5
	Munitions Hard	G	1.0 -> 0.25	5 F-111X/1	0.75	0.5
	Munitions Soft	G	1.0 -> 0.27	8 F-111X/1	0.73	0.8

FIGURE 6.9 Illustrative TDL Produced by TATR.

the TDL, the weapon packages, the attack projections, and even the data and rulesets. The user decides when to calculate the results of attacking targets on the TDL, when to move ahead (or back) in time to a different day, and when to generate a new TDL. Appendix A contains a detailed trace of a user-TATR interactive planning session, illustrating the many ways the user can interact with the system.

6.4

Potential Benefits From A Fully Operational TATR

This report has described TATR in its current stage of development. To be made operational, TATR would have to be linked to the operational weaponeering programs and database systems in the combat planning center. It would also need to be further iterated to improve its targeting performance and to reflect more accurately the targeting concepts and procedures in use. The potential benefits of making TATR operational (in addition to providing a direct aid to the targeteer in making real-time decisions) would include the following:

- *A repository of targeting knowledge.* The English-like linguistic structures of the ROSIE programming language allow the heuristic model used in TATR to be readily understandable by targeting professionals. As a result, TATR could evolve into the main document for recording targeting concepts, doctrine, procedures, and skills. It would incorporate the knowledge of all who worked with it and contributed to its evolution.
- *A learning tool.* Newly assigned targeteers could use TATR to orient themselves quickly on all the airfield targeting factors in a given theater. Both experienced and new targeteers could use TATR to regularly exercise and enhance their planning acuity.
- *A research tool.* An advanced version of TATR could remain dedicated to targeting research to develop greater insight into the targeting problem.
- *A preplanning tool in an operational context.* In any theater where U.S. air forces may have to be employed, there will be a high premium attached to having attack plans on the shelf and ready to be implemented. TATR will allow air planners to keep such a plan updated and optimized daily.
- *A force structuring tool.* In an era of limited resources, the Air Force may be able to deploy only a limited number of forces to a theater or theaters. Determining the optimum minimum force mix to achieve desired conflict objectives will remain a continuing problem. TATR could help decision makers identify this optimum force mix and quantify the capability of many possible force combinations.
- *A tool for identifying intelligence requirements.* TATR can identify required information for the intelligence community. The intelligence information gathered today is so voluminous that air planners must continually work toward determining exactly what is required, as opposed to desired, information. By exercising and evolving TATR, the intelligence requirements can be readily recognized because they must be specified in detail. Also, the effect of having or not having an item of information is immediately apparent from the quality of the TATR output.

References

1. Callero, M., D. Gorlin, F. Hayes-Roth, and L. Jamison, *Toward an Expert Aid for Tactical Air Targeting*, The Rand Corporation, N-1645-ARPA, January 1981.
2. Callero, M., L. Jamison, and D. Waterman, *TATR: An Expert Aid for Tactical Air Targeting*, The Rand Corporation, N-1796-ARPA, January 1982.
3. Fain, J., D. Gorlin, F. Hayes-Roth, S. Rosenschein, H. Sowizral, and D. Waterman, *The ROSIE Language Reference Manual*, The Rand Corporation, N-1647-ARPA, December 1981.
4. Fain, J., F. Hayes-Roth, H. Sowizral, and D. Waterman, *Programming in ROSIE: An Introduction by Means of Examples*, The Rand Corporation, N-1646-ARPA, February 1982.
5. Hayes-Roth, F., D. Gorlin, S. Rosenschein, H. Sowizral, and D. Waterman, *Rationale and Motivation for ROSIE*, The Rand Corporation, N-1648-ARPA, November 1981.
6. Hayes-Roth, F., D. Waterman, and D. Lenat (eds.), *Building Expert Systems*, Addison-Wesley Publishing Company, Inc., Reading, Massachusetts, 1983.
7. Kernighan, B., and D. Ritchie, *The C Programming Language*, Prentice-Hall, Inc., Englewood Cliffs, New Jersey, 1978.
8. Waterman, D., and F. Hayes-Roth, *An Investigation of Tools for Building Expert Systems*, The Rand Corporation, R-2818-NSF, June 1982.

Appendix A

Illustrative User-TATR Interactive Planning Session

This appendix provides a listing of the information appearing on the user's terminal during an illustrative user-TATR plan-generation interaction. Some editing has been done for brevity—once a lengthy TATR output has been shown, repetition provides no new insight into the interaction process.

This illustrative interaction begins after the database has been updated in preparation for a plan-generation session. The updates reflect data from operational reports on the previous days' missions against the airfields, including the actual number of weapons systems that arrived over the targets, as well as adjustments for intelligence reports of observed target status.

TATR's output is shown in roman type; the user's input is shown in boldface; and the authors' annotations are shown in brackets.

TATR — Tactical Air Target Recommender

The attack objective is SORTIE REDUCTION.
The time period is 2 DAYS and the time frame is MEDIUM.
The desired effect on aircraft is KKILL.

— TOP LEVEL MONITOR —

Display:
- [A] Target Development List
- [B] Designated Weapon Packages
- [C] Target Recovery Tables
- [D] Target Status Tables
- [E] (not implemented)
- [F] Additional Target Information

Modify:
- [G] Target Development List
- [H] Weapon Packages
- [I] Attack Projections
- [J] Data & Rulesets

Tasking Commands —
- [K] Attack Targets Specified By TDL
- [L] Advance To The Next Day
- [M] Generate a TDL
- [N] Move To A Previously Seen Day
- [O] Exit From This TATR Session

What would you like to do? **m**

Recomputing TDL (Target Development List). . .

Rating target elements at AFLD #1 . . .(please wait)

[There follows a stream of comments designed to show the user what steps are being computed and to keep him or her informed of interim data. We omit it here for brevity.]

What would you like to do? **a** [Display the TDL]

Current TDL (Target Development List): Day 1 — Time Frame = MEDIUM

SR	*Elements*	*Rating*	*Status*	*Weapack*	*DE*	*Attrit'n*
AFLD #1				*SC: 640 -> 238*		
402	Main Hard	EX	1.0 -> 0.26	8 F-16X/1	0.74	0.48
	Mun Assem Area	EX	1.0 -> 0.25	4 F-16X/2	0.75	0.24
	Munitions Hard	EX	1.0 -> 0.23	5 F-111X/1	0.77	0.3
	Mun Load Area	EX	1.0 -> 0.25	4 F-16X/2	0.75	0.24
	POL Hard	EX	1.0 -> 0.26	3 F-111X/2	0.74	0.18
AFLD #3				*SC: 288 -> 270*		
18	Munitions Soft	G	1.0 -> 0.26	8 F-111X/1	0.74	0.48
	Mun Load Area	G	1.0 -> 0.28	11 F-16X/2	0.72	0.66
	POL Hard	G	1.0 -> 0.23	5 F-111X/1	0.77	0.3

What would you like to do? **g** [Modify the TDL]

[In this sequence we show how to add an airfield that the user wants to attack but that TATR did not include on the TDL.]

TDL Modification Commands —

- [A] Display TDL
- [B] Delete Airfields from TDL
- [C] Add Airfields to TDL
- [D] Exit to Top Level

What would you like to do? **c**

Not included in the target development list

SR	*Elements*	*Rating*	*Status*	*Weapack*	*DE*	*Attrit'n*
[A] AFLD #2				*SC: 292 -> 278*		
14	Munitions Hard	EX	1.0 -> 0.23	5 F-111X/1	0.77	0.3
	POL Hard	EX	1.0 -> 0.23	5 F-111X/1	0.77	0.3
	Mun Load Area	G	1.0 -> 0.25	4 F-16X/2	0.75	0.24
[B] AFLD #4				*SC: 190 -> 176*		
14	Main Hard	EX	1.0 -> 0.23	3 F-16X/1	0.77	0.18
	Munitions Soft	EX	1.0 -> 0.26	8 F-16X/2	0.74	0.48
	POL Soft	G	1.0 -> 0.15	2 F-16X/1	0.85	0.12

Specified entries will be added to the target development list. . .

Select entries (hit * for all): **a**

Current TDL (Target Development List): Day 1 — Time Frame = MEDIUM

SR	*Elements*	*Rating*	*Status*	*Weapack*	*DE*	*Attrit'n*
AFLD #1				*SC: 640 -> 238*		
402	Main Hard	EX	1.0 -> 0.26	8 F-16X/1	0.74	0.48
	Mun Assem Area	EX	1.0 -> 0.25	4 F-16X/2	0.75	0.24
	Munitions Hard	EX	1.0 -> 0.23	5 F-111X/1	0.77	0.3
	Mun Load Area	EX	1.0 -> 0.25	4 F-16X/2	0.75	0.24
	POL Hard	EX	1.0 -> 0.26	3 F-111X/2	0.74	0.18
AFLD #3				*SC: 288 -> 270*		
18	Munitions Soft	G	1.0 -> 0.26	8 F-111X/1	0.74	0.48
	Mun Load Area	G	1.0 -> 0.28	11 F-16X/2	0.72	0.66
	POL Hard	G	1.0 -> 0.23	5 F-111X/1	0.77	0.3
AFLD #2				*SC: 292 -> 278*		
14	Munitions Hard	EX	1.0 -> 0.23	5 F-111X/1	0.77	0.3
	POL Hard	EX	1.0 -> 0.23	5 F-111X/1	0.77	0.3
	Mun Load Area	G	1.0 -> 0.25	4 F-16X/2	0.75	0.24

What would you like to do? **d** [Exit to Top Level]

Returning to the Top Level Monitor. . .

What would you like to do? **i** [Modify Attack Projections]

[In this sequence we show how a user can investigate the effects of attacking a target element combination on an airfield other than the one TATR included in the TDL.]

Commands for Projecting Attack Results —

[A] Display Projected Attack Results At An Airfield
[B] Add Attacks To An Airfield's Projections
[C] Delete Attacks From An Airfield's Projections
[D] Redesignate Preferred Target Elements To Attack
[E] Exit To Top Level

What would you like to do? **b**

Which airfield would you like to use? **b** [Afld #2]

Attack projections for AFLD #2: Day 1 — Time Frame = MEDIUM

SR	*Elements*	*Rating*	*Status*	*Weapack*	*DE*	*Attrit'n*
14	Munitions Hard	EX	1.0 -> 0.23	5 F-111X/1	0.77	0.3
	POL Hard	EX	1.0 -> 0.23	5 F-111X/1	0.77	0.3
	Mun Load Area	G	1.0 -> 0.25	4 F-16X/2	0.75	0.24

[A] Access Taxiways
[B] Aircraft
[C] Landing Surfaces
[D] Maintenance Hard
[E] Maintenance Soft
[F] Muns Assembly Area
[G] Munitions Hard
[H] Munitions Soft
[I] Muns Loading Area
[J] POL Hard
[K] POL Soft
[L] Rapid Turn Area
[M] Refueling Soft

Which target elements would you like to use? **i**

Simulating an attack on target elements at AFLD #2 . . .

The sortie capability of AFLD #2 before the attack = 292

Results of attack:

Target Elements	Status
Munitions Loading Area	1.0 -> 0.25

Calculating reductions in aircraft at AFLD #2:

	FLOGGERS	FARMERS
Munitions Loading Area	40 -> 38	30 -> 28

Calculating AFLD #2:

Sortie throughput for DAY 1:

Aircraft Type	*Number*	*Sortie Rate*	*Sorties*	*Excess Capability*
FLOGGERS	38	2.0	76	
FARMERS	28	2.2	61	
Total aircraft sorties:			137	
Munitions Storage (Hard & Soft)			137	1402 TONS
Munitions Assembly Area			137	687 TONS
Munitions Loading Area			144	21 MINUTES
POL Storage (Hard & Soft)			137	439680 GALS

Cumulative sorties through DAY 1 = 137

Reconstituting target elements at AFLD #2. . .(please wait)

[Note that the excess capacity refers to the capacity of the target element to support more than the required sorties. Thus, we see that besides the munitions needed to support 137 sorties, there were an additional 1402 tons of munitions at airfield #2.]

Sortie throughput for DAY 2:

Aircraft Type	*Number*	*Sortie Rate*	*Sorties*	*Excess Capability*
FLOGGERS	39	2.0	78	
FARMERS	29	2.2	63	
Total aircraft sorties:			141	
Munitions Storage (Hard & Soft)			141	1967 TONS
Munitions Assembly Area			141	680 TONS
Munitions Loading Area			141	1157 MINUTES
POL Storage (Hard & Soft)			141	563920 GALS

Cumulative sorties through DAY 2 = 278

The projected sortie capability after the attack =278

The projected sortie capability reduction =14

Attack projections for AFLD #2: Day 1 — Time Frame =Medium

SR	*Elements*	*Rating*	*Status*	*Weapack*	*DE*	*Attrit'n*
14	Mun Load Area	G	1.0 -> 0.25	4 F-16X/2	0.75	0.24
14	Munitions Hard	EX	1.0 -> 0.23	5 F-111X/1	0.77	0.3
	POL Hard	EX	1.0 -> 0.23	5 F-111X/1	0.77	0.3
	Mun Load Area	G	1.0 -> 0.25	4 F-16X/2	0.75	0.24

[We note here that even though munitions and POL storage were determined to be excellent targets by the TATR planning rules, they did not impact directly on sortie generation capability within the medium time frame. The planning rules consider more than just sortie generation, but the user need not, as exemplified here.]

Would you like to add another entry? **no**

Would you like to try another target? **no**

What would you like to do? * [The user calls for the menu again.]

Commands for Projecting Attack Results —
- [A] Display Projected Attack Results At An Airfield
- [B] Add Attacks To An Airfield's Projections
- [C] Delete Attacks From An Airfield's Projections
- [D] Redesignate Preferred Target Elements To Attack
- [E] Exit To Top Level

What would you like to do? **b**

Which airfield would you like to use? **a** [Afld #1]

Attack projections for AFLD #1: Day 1 — Time Frame = MEDIUM

SR	*Elements*	*Rating*	*Status*	*Weapack*	*DE*	*Attrit'n*
402	Main Hard	EX	1.0 -> 0.26	8 F-16X/1	0.74	0.48
	Mun Assem Area	EX	1.0 -> 0.25	4 F-16X/2	0.75	0.24
	Munitions Hard	EX	1.0 -> 0.23	5 F-111X/1	0.77	0.3
	Mun Load Area	EX	1.0 -> 0.25	4 F-16X/2	0.75	0.24
	POL Hard	EX	1.0 -> 0.26	3 F-111X/2	0.74	0.18

Which target elements would you like to use? **d i f**
[Maintenance hard, munitions assembly area, and munitions loading area.]

Simulating an attack on target elements at AFLD #1 . . .

The sortie capability of AFLD #1 before the attack = 640

The projected sortie capability after the attack = 253

[The same series of information items shown in the preceding similar run are omitted here for brevity.]

The projected sortie capability reduction = 387

Attack projections for AFLD #1: Day 1 — Time Frame = MEDIUM

SR	*Elements*	*Rating*	*Status*	*Weapack*	*DE*	*Attrit'n*
402	Main Hard	EX	1.0 -> 0.26	8 F-16X/1	0.74	0.48
	Mun Assem Area	EX	1.0 -> 0.25	4 F-16X/2	0.75	0.24
	Munitions Hard	EX	1.0 -> 0.23	5 F-111X/1	0.77	0.3
	Mun Load Area	EX	1.0 -> 0.25	4 F-16X/2	0.75	0.24
	POL Hard	EX	1.0 -> 0.26	3 F-111X/2	0.74	0.18
387	Main Hard	EX	1.0 -> 0.26	8 F-16X/1	0.74	0.48
	Mun Load Area	EX	1.0 -> 0.25	4 F-16X/2	0.75	0.24
	Mun Assem Area	EX	1.0 -> 0.25	4 F-16X/2	0.75	0.24

Would you like to add another entry? **no**

Would you like to try another target? **no**

What would you like to do? **e** [Return to Top Level]

Returning To The Top Level Monitor. . .

What would you like to do? **h** [Modify Weapon Packages]

[In this sequence we show how a user can select a different preferred weapon system for attacking a target element from the one selected by TATR.]

Weapon Package Modification Commands —

- [A] Display Weapon Packages For Use Against Target Elements
- [B] Modify Weapon Packages For Use Against Target Elements
- [C] Redesignate A Preferred Weapon Package
- [D] Exit To Top Level

What would you like to do? **b**

Which airfield would you like to use? **a** [Afld #1]

Your choice of target element? **i** [Munitions Loading Area]

Weapon packages for use against Munitions Loading Area at AFLD #1:

Weapon Packages	*Nos.*	*DE*	*Delivery Tactic*	*Attrit'n*	*Ceiling: 4500 FEET Visibility: 5 MILES*
F-16X/2	4	0.75	LOW	0.24	
F-4X/3	4	0.74	LOW	0.32	

- [A] F-16X/2 (MK82, CBU)
- [B] F-4X/3 (CBU)

Which weapon systems would you like to use? **b**

Do you wish to specify the number of F-4X/3 to use? **no**

Do you wish to specify a desired DE? **no**

Recomputing weapon package for Munitions Loading Area. . .

Weapon packages for use against Munitions Loading Area at AFLD #1:

Weapon Packages	*Nos.*	*DE*	*Delivery Tactic*	*Attrit'n*	*Ceiling: 4500 FEET Visibility: 5 MILES*
F-4X/3	4	0.74	LOW	0.32	
F-16X/2	4	0.75	LOW	0.24	

Would you like to add other weapon packages? **no**

What would you like to do? **d** [Return to Top Level]

Returning To The Top Level Monitor. . .

What would you like to do? **i** [Modify Attacks]

[In this sequence we show how a user can change the target elements to attack on an airfield from the set on the TDL to another set that has been investigated earlier and is preferred by the user.]

What would you like to do? **d** [Redesignate Preferred Attack]
Which target would you like to use? **a** [Afld #1]

Attack projections for AFLD #1: Day 1 — Time Frame = MEDIUM

SR	*Elements*	*Rating*	*Status*	*Weapack*	*DE*	*Attrit'n*
402	Main Hard	EX	1.0 -> 0.26	8 F-16X/1	0.74	0.48
	Mun Assem Area	EX	1.0 -> 0.25	4 F-16X/2	0.75	0.24
	Munitions Hard	EX	1.0 -> 0.23	5 F-111X/1	0.77	0.3
	Mun Load Area	EX	1.0 -> 0.25	4 F-16X/2	0.75	0.24
	POL Hard	EX	1.0 -> 0.26	3 F-111X/2	0.74	0.18
[A] 387	Main Hard	EX	1.0 -> 0.26	8 F-16X/1	0.74	0.48
	Mun Assem Area	EX	1.0 -> 0.25	4 F-16X/2	0.75	0.24
	Mun Load Area	EX	1.0 -> 0.26	4 F-4X/3	0.74	0.32
[B] 387	Main Hard	EX	1.0 -> 0.26	8 F-16X/1	0.74	0.48
	Mun Load Area	EX	1.0 -> 0.25	4 F-16X/2	0.75	0.24
	Mun Assem Area	EX	1.0 -> 0.25	4 F-16X/2	0.75	0.24

Select 1 entry: **a**

What would you like to do? **e**

Returning To The OCA Top Level Monitor. . .

What would you like to do? **a**

Current TDL (Target Development List): Day 1 — Time Frame = MEDIUM

SR	Elements	Rating	Status	Weapack	DE	Attrit'n
AFLD #1				*SC: 640 -> 253*		
387	Main Hard	EX	1.0 -> 0.26	8 F-16X/1	0.74	0.48
	Mun Assem Area	EX	1.0 -> 0.25	4 F-16X/2	0.75	0.24
	Mun Load Area	EX	1.0 -> 0.26	4 F-4X/3	0.74	0.32
AFLD #3				*SC: 288 -> 270*		
18	Munitions Soft	G	1.0 -> 0.26	8 F-111X/1	0.74	0.48
	Mun Load Area	G	1.0 -> 0.28	11 F-16X/2	0.72	0.66
	POL Hard	G	1.0 -> 0.23	5 F-111X/1	0.77	0.3
AFLD #2				*SC: 292 -> 278*		
14	Mun Load Area	G	1.0 -> 0.25	4 F-16X/2	0.75	0.24

[At this point the user has investigated other ways to attack Afld #1 and has opted for a lesser sortie reduction level in favor of a smaller weapons package. Also, the user has opted to show both F-4Xs and F-16Xs as viable candidates for this attack.]

[The following sequence is another example of investigating an alternate attack to conserve friendly weapon systems.]

What would you like to do? **i**

Commands For Projecting Attack Results —

[A] Display Projected Attack Results At An Airfield
[B] Add Attacks To An Airfield's Projections
[C] Delete Attacks From An Airfield's Projections
[D] Redesignate Preferred Target Elements To Attack
[E] Exit To Top Level

What would you like to do? **b**

Which target would you like to use? **c**

Attack projections for AFLD #3: Day 1 — Time Frame = MEDIUM

SR	*Elements*	*Rating*	*Status*	*Weapack*	*DE*	*Attrit'n*
18	Munitions Soft	G	1.0 -> 0.26	8 F-111X/1	0.74	0.48
	Mun Load Area	G	1.0 -> 0.28	11 F-16X/2	0.72	0.66
	POL Hard	G	1.0 -> 0.23	5 F-111X/1	0.77	0.3

Which target elements would you like to use? **i**

[Munitions Loading Area]

Simulating an attack on target elements at AFLD #3 . . .

Attack projections for AFLD #3: Day 1 — Time Frame = MEDIUM

SR	*Elements*	*Rating*	*Status*	*Weapack*	*DE*	*Attrit'n*
18	Mun Load Area	G	1.0 -> 0.28	11 F-16X/2	0.72	0.66
18	Munitions Soft	G	1.0 -> 0.26	8 F-111X/1	0.74	0.48
	Mun Load Area	G	1.0 -> 0.28	11 F-16X/2	0.72	0.66
	POL Hard	G	1.0 -> 0.23	5 F-111X/1	0.77	0.3

What would you like to do? **e**

Returning To The OCA Top Level Monitor. . .

What would you like to do? **a**

Current TDL (Target Development List): Day 1 — Time Frame = MEDIUM

SR	*Elements*	*Rating*	*Status*	*Weapack*	*DE*	*Attrit'n*
AFLD #1				*SC: 640 -> 253*		
387	Main Hard	EX	1.0 -> 0.26	8 F-16X/1	0.74	0.48
	Mun Assem Area	EX	1.0 -> 0.25	4 F-16X/2	0.75	0.24
	Mun Load Area	EX	1.0 -> 0.26	4 F-4X/3	0.74	0.32
AFLD #3				*SC: 288 -> 270*		
18	Mun Load Area	G	1.0 -> 0.28	11 F-16X/2	0.72	0.66
AFLD #2				*SC: 292 -> 278*		
14	Mun Load Area	G	1.0 -> 0.25	4 F-16X/2	0.75	0.24

What would you like to do? **k** [Attack targets specified by TDL]
Saving this planning session as version 1 of day 1.
Attacking target elements at AFLD #1
What would you like to do? **d** [Display Target Status Tables]
Which targets would you like to use? **a b c** [Airfields 1, 2 and 3]
Which target elements would you like to use? **all**

Status Table: (percentage of target undamaged)

	AFLD #1	*AFLD #2*	*AFLD #3*
Access Taxiways	100	100	100
Aircraft	98	95	92
Landing Surfaces	100	100	100
Maintenance Hard	26	100	100
Maintenance Soft	100	100	100
Muns Assembly Area	25	100	100
Munitions Hard	100	100	100
Munitions Soft	100	100	100
Muns Loading Area	26	25	27
POL Hard	100	100	100
POL Soft	100	100	100
Rapid Turn Area	100	100	100
Refueling Soft	100	100	100

What would you like to do? **o** [Exit from this TATR session]

Chapter 7

TWIRL: Tactical Warfare in the ROSS Language

Philip Klahr, John W. Ellis, William D. Giarla, Sanjai Narain, Edison M. Cesar, and Scott R. Turner

7.1 Overview and Goals

During the past few years, we have been exploring methods for improving simulation technology. These studies have applied and extended recent advances in artificial intelligence, expert systems, computer networking, parallel processing, and graphics to the area of simulation. We have sought to create an environment, or simulation laboratory, in which credible simulations can be easily built, easily understood and modified, and run at speeds acceptable for human use.

This research has produced ROSS (McArthur and Klahr, 1982; McArthur et al., 1984), an object-oriented message-passing language ideally suited for developing simulations; the SWIRL simulation (Klahr et al., 1982a, 1982b), a strategic air battle simulation written in ROSS; and the Time-Warp mechanism (Jefferson and Sowizral, 1982), an approach to using parallel processing to significantly speed up simulation runs. This report describes our most recent development, TWIRL (Tactical Warfare in the ROSS Language), a ground combat simulation.

This chapter is an edited version of R-3158-AF, The Rand Corporation, October 1984.

The TWIRL development was undertaken primarily to

- Further explore and experiment with the ROSS environment to better determine its strengths and weaknesses for simulating military battles;
- Determine how to represent and visually depict electronic systems operating on the battlefield;
- Design and implement a prototype simulation that could serve as a tool for exploring various strategies and tactics in electronic combat; and
- Develop a (prototype) capability that allows a person to take the role of one of the objects involved in a battle. For use in analysis or training, this facility would enable a person to play an active, decision-making role during a simulation run.

Our experience with the development of the SWIRL air battle simulation convinced us that the ROSS language is fully capable of representing and simulating military battles, primarily because of its object-oriented framework for expressing the simulation domain. Briefly, one formulates a set of *objects* representing classes (radars, aircraft, missiles, etc.) or individual members of those classes (e.g., radar14), and specifies their attributes and behaviors. Objects are organized in a hierarchy of class-subclass links (e.g., GCI radars might be a subclass of ground-based radars, which in turn might be a subclass of radars). This hierarchy allows an object to inherit automatically the attributes and behaviors of the classes to which it belongs. Thus, for example, ground-based radars, being a subclass of radars, would inherit knowledge associated with the radar class (the general class of all radars). The organization of knowledge around objects facilitates modularity, modifiability, and maintenance of the simulation (Klahr and Faught, 1980).

Within ROSS, objects communicate with one another by sending *messages*. These messages are patterns or templates that typify the real-world messages that objects would normally send to one another in a battle (e.g., airborne surveillance radar to operations center: "Enemy aircraft detected 120 km west of Berlin"). When receiving a particular message, an object searches through its behaviors to match the message and then takes the corresponding specified action (e.g., operations center launches defensive fighters). The concepts of *objects, messages,* and *messages triggering actions* form the basis of the ROSS language.

Following the success of using ROSS for the SWIRL simulation, we wanted to expand its application to other environments, in particular, a tactical, land-based combat environment. Because of the growing interest in electronic combat (EC), both at Rand and in the military, we decided to focus on representing communications and exploring various strategies for interfering with communications during combat. For our prototype simulation, we chose to model destruction (by artillery fire), disruption (by jamming), and some limited air operations.

Section 7.2 describes the TWIRL domain. Sections 7.3 through 7.5 describe the TWIRL implementation, the various design decisions that were made, and how they evolved into ROSS code. Section 7.5 also provides examples of how the TWIRL simulation could be used as a training facility. In particular, we have developed an initial capability to allow a person to play one of the simulation objects. The human player receives and sends the messages the corresponding automated object would typically receive and send in a simulation. This *human-in-the-loop* facility adds another dimension to the interactivity of ROSS. A person could also use this facility to force certain decisions to be made and thereby direct the simulation to whatever experimental situation is desired. Thus, this capability can contribute to analysis, training, and the development of tactics.

The reader should keep in mind that the particular operation we have simulated is a fictitious one. Our primary concern is with methodology—we are building tools and exploring methods to help people better depict and understand complex phenomena. Therefore, some of the particular objects and behaviors we have chosen to represent are simplistic and some may even be incorrect.[1] The main point we are attempting to make is that the ROSS environment is rich enough to allow one to easily understand and modify the objects and behaviors to create whatever simulation model is desired.

A primary objective of this report is to indicate what it is like to build a battle simulation in ROSS. We often specify various objects and behaviors in ROSS code; a knowledge of ROSS is not necessary, however, for understanding the material.

7.2 General Description of TWIRL

TWIRL simulates ground combat between two opposing forces (hereafter referred to as Red and Blue). We view TWIRL as a prototype of a

[1] Some of the behaviors presented here have been even further simplified for exposition purposes. Also, many objects and behaviors that normally figure in ground combat have been omitted to reduce the scope and complexity of our prototype effort.

design tool for military strategists working in command, control, and communications countermeasures (C^3CM), electronic warfare (EW), and electronic combat (EC). TWIRL consists of a set of ROSS-defined objects that represent the players in the simulation, along with their specified attributes and possible behaviors. Given an initial configuration of Red and Blue forces, TWIRL simulates their movements and interactions over time.

A highly useful component of TWIRL is its color graphics facility. The use of color greatly aids in differentiating between different types of objects (e.g., Red and Blue); in contrasting movable objects with the physical setting (e.g., mountains, rivers, streams, roads); and in locating the various activities performed by the objects (i.e., bombing, artillery firing, communicating, jamming, and direction finding).

In a TWIRL simulation, the user receives both textual information about the simulated events and visual information that depicts the battle as it proceeds over time. In addition to the usual map display of unit identities and locations, TWIRL incorporates visual indications of communications traffic, identifying originator and recipient(s), and selected EW activities (direction finding and jamming). In a sense, the simulation presents an animated movie of the participating units, augmented by displays of the activities in the electromagnetic spectrum.

Since the graphics interface directly with the simulation, the user sees the simulation as it is produced. Also, because ROSS is highly interactive, the user may stop the simulation and graphics at any time, zoom or pan, examine or change various attributes or behaviors, and so on. Although the graphics must be viewed in a live demonstration to appreciate their scope and utility, we have included several color plates of TWIRL's graphical output to give at least some indication of this capability.

7.2.1 ■ Problem Domain: Hasty River-crossing Operation

The domain we chose for TWIRL is a hasty river-crossing operation by Red forces (i.e., one executed directly from the approach march without delay for assembling massive assault forces and fire support). Such a military maneuver employs a combined arms team (infantry, artillery, armor, electronic combat, etc.), with complex interactions and critical timing requirements among the various arms and activities. These characteristics make it a suitable vehicle for examining and illustrating the potentially disruptive effects of EC. In addition, descriptions of typical Red river-crossing operations that include doctrine, timing, force composition, tactics, procedures, and norms can be found in readily available sources (Department of the Army, 1977, 1978; Reznichenko, 1966; Sidorenko, 1970).

In our scenario, Red forces are on the offensive as they near a sizable river obstacle. As the scenario opens, both the Red division chosen to force the crossing and the likely defending Blue mechanized regiment are in assembly areas some distance from the river. Red's plan calls for two regiments, moving forward abreast, to mount the assault directly from the approach march in an attempt to secure the crossing before defending Blue forces can establish a deliberate defense of the river line. Once in its hasty defense posture, Blue has two main methods of interfering with Red's planned operation: through artillery fire, or by communications jamming (it could also use some combination of the two).[2]

Each Red unit is assigned a movement schedule designed to fit its contribution to the division's overall advance and assault crossing of the river. These schedules (called *track plans*) would be carried out as long as no Blue-induced obstacle or disruptive actions interfere. The assault units' track plans call for the crossing to begin at "H-hour." Thus, the simulation begins at H − 7:00 (H minus 7 hours), when the vanguards of the lead regiments move out of the divisional assembly area about 70 km from the river. The Red regiments and supporting division artillery units proceed according to their track plans. Along the way, at preplanned halts, maneuver and artillery units deploy into smaller elements (each with its own track plan). This process continues until all Red units reach their assigned assault positions. There they halt, deploy into combat formations, and await the assault order from their parent regiments.[3] Blue, of course, will seek to disrupt Red's planned advance. Klahr et al. (1984) describes the planned deployment and movement of all Red units included in the TWIRL simulation.

As the Red attack units continue moving forward along the road network, Blue aerial reconnaissance discovers them and communicates this to the Blue ground force commander. The commander, in turn, orders the defending Blue mechanized regiment to move out of its assembly area and take up defensive positions along the river opposing

[2] Blue offensive air support operations are simulated in only very rudimentary form, primarily to illustrate feasibility and the scope and volume of the additional actors and behaviors needed to couple air activity to the ground combat. To date, only the results of interdiction attacks on bridge and road junction targets have been included in our computations (see Section 7.4). Although allowed for in the code, Red air operations are not part of the present TWIRL simulation.

[3] To simplify the simulation and still incorporate the description and effects of vital command and control communications, we include only objects at regiment level and below. In practice, the assault order would more likely be the responsibility of the division. In TWIRL, division-level objects play no active role in the simulation.

the expected Red attack axes. In our simulation, each Blue unit also has a predefined track plan of movements. However, for the purpose of this simulation, and unlike Red, no obstacles are permitted to interfere with Blue unit movements to their assigned defensive positions. This ensures that a hasty defense is established before Red units begin their assault crossing, thereby providing the necessary context within which to simulate the disruptive effects of jamming and/or artillery fire on the Red time table. Klahr et al. (1984) also describe the movement and deployment of all Blue units.

As each Red unit proceeds on its track plan, it communicates to its parent regiment when it begins or completes a phase of its deployment to its assault positions. No attempt has been made to replicate faithfully the volume and entire range of communications traffic that might accompany such operations. These two types of messages (announcements of the start of road movement and of planned stopovers) were deemed sufficient to allow simulation of Blue ELINT (electronics intelligence), COMINT (communications intelligence), SIGINT (signals intelligence), and target location and generation activities.

Once in their defensive positions and alerted, Blue's direction finders attempt to locate the positions of enemy combat units. When a direction finder learns that a unit has stopped, it notifies the Blue regimental commander of a potential target at a particular position. The Blue commander must then decide, given its jamming and artillery assets, what to do about the target. Jamming blocks a unit from receiving messages on one or more channels, causing a delay in that unit's reception of messages (we assume that when the recipient of a message is jammed, the sender knows it and retransmits the message on another channel or dispatches it by other, nonelectronic means). Artillery fire causes attrition and movement delay when units are fired upon and hit. Red can similarly jam and fire against Blue's units.

Blue can initiate air reconnaissance to detect Red's position and movement, and can initiate air attacks on various road junctions and bridges along Red's route to slow the advance. (Section 7.4 discusses how TWIRL could be extended to allow Blue air forces to engage Red ground or air forces.)

Currently, the major measure of effectiveness of Blue's various jamming, artillery, and air support strategies in TWIRL is the time delay involved in Red's planned assault.[4] If Red were to proceed unimpeded, the Red assault units would begin to cross the river at H-

[4] In addition, provision has been made in the TWIRL code to calculate damage to units under artillery fire and to record their current strength. Thus, the force ratio at the point of contact could be calculated as another measure of merit or for use to control movement once combat was joined.

hour. Blue's attempts to stop Red are expected to result in delays to Red's advance, providing a measure of how well Blue has done.[5] A graphic display of the disruption to individual Red unit plans (contributing to the overall delay in the scheduled assault time) would assist greatly in judging the results of different Blue strategies. We have provided simultaneous presentation of an unimpeded and a delayed assault by using two regiments assaulting abreast. One is programmed to be immune to Blue actions directed at its subordinate units so that all proceed according to their scheduled track plans. The two regiments have identical orders of battle, and both are scheduled to begin the river crossing at H-hour. Consequently, the graphic display, at any given time in the simulation, will illustrate the cumulative deviation from the schedule of any unit that has been affected by Blue's defensive efforts.

Even with this brief description, one can begin to see how such a simulation can be used to examine various situations and problems. Some hypothetical questions a military analyst might address include:

- What units and actions are affected if specific Red communications are disrupted?
- Are any of Red's communication networks critical?
- What happens when Blue jams a crucial node in a network?
- How effective are redundant communications?
- What effects result from Red jamming Blue's communications?
- How can Blue best disrupt a Red river-crossing operation?

7.2.2 ■ The Players

TWIRL contains approximately 50 objects that represent classes (or subclasses) and approximately 90 objects that represent actual instances of those classes (i.e., particular Red and Blue units). The number of classes represented may appear high relative to the number of instances. However, many of the class objects serve as intermediate objects in the object hierarchy and do not have instances as direct descendants. For example, MOVING-OBJECT contains the subclasses RED-UNIT and BLUE-UNIT, which, in turn, eventually spawn partic-

[5] Section 7.6 contains a brief description and analysis of the events resulting from an exemplary Blue disruption effort and compares those results with the Red scheduled attack plan as given in Klahr et al. (1984).

ular artillery units, regiments, and so on. Also, most behaviors are associated with classes rather than instances. For our purposes, we are more concerned with the ability to represent various types of military units than we are with the ability to represent large quantities of any particular type of unit. Once we define a division artillery unit, for example, it is of little concern whether we have 4 or 40 of them. Essentially, they all exhibit similar behaviors (in our simulation), and only their particular attributes (e.g., position, strength) may vary.[6]

The main objects that comprise the TWIRL domain are briefly described in this subsection. More detail on many of these objects is presented in subsequent sections. Most of the objects correspond to real-world entities, but some, such as the MATHEMATICIAN and the PHYSICIST (Klahr et al., 1982b), are auxiliary objects (they do not have real-world correlates, but they function as full objects, in the ROSS sense, to perform certain computations). Objects are organized hierarchically and may belong to many classes simultaneously, thereby giving rise to multiple inheritance hierarchies.

General, high-level objects include the following:

SIMULATOR. The top-level object in TWIRL. All other TWIRL objects are descendants of SIMULATOR (i.e., its subclasses include MOVING-OBJECT, which has subclasses RED-UNIT and BLUE-UNIT, and so on).

MOVING-OBJECT. Contains behaviors used for movement (e.g., stopping, starting, turning, waiting, etc.). All Red and Blue units are moving objects (i.e., the objects RED-UNIT and BLUE-UNIT are subclasses of MOVING-OBJECT).

COMMUNICATING-OBJECT. Represents the class of TWIRL objects that can communicate (in the real-world sense, rather than in the ROSS sense) with other objects in the simulation. It contains all the behaviors objects use to send messages over the various communication channels defined in TWIRL. All Red and Blue units are communicating-objects (i.e., the objects RED-UNIT and BLUE-UNIT are subclasses of COMMUNICATING-OBJECT).

A few objects have behaviors that can apply to both Red and Blue forces (currently they exist for Blue only). Most of these are involved

[6] Certainly when one is working with large numbers (perhaps thousands) of objects, other issues arise, particularly computer memory and speed. Some of these are addressed in Jefferson and Sowizral (1982). Our concern here centers on how best to represent domain knowledge.

in air operations, which have been modeled only at a very general level in TWIRL. They include:

TACC. Tactical air control centers; they initiate air reconnaissance and offensive air support operations, and communicate mission results to the appropriate Red or Blue ground force command element.

AIRBASE. Airbases that launch air missions as requested by TACCs.

MISSION. Aircraft assigned for reconnaissance or attack.

Objects on the Red side include:

RED-UNIT. The broadest generic class, representing all Red units. Only very general, default behaviors and attributes for Red units are stored here. RED-UNIT is a subclass of both COMMUNICATING-OBJECT and MOVING-OBJECT.

DIV. A subclass of RED-UNIT, representing the command elements and other specified units of Red divisions (in general). TWIRL contains three command elements of a single Red division: DIVTAC, DIVMAIN, and DIVREAR.

DIVTAC. The forward tactical division headquarters, which controls the advance to the river and the crossing operations of the two first-echelon (assault) regiments.

DIVMAIN. The fully staffed operational division headquarters; also the two second-echelon maneuver regiments, and organic and attached division, Army, and front fire and combat support units not otherwise identified individually.

DIVREAR. The administrative and logistical support headquarters of the division.

REGT. A subclass of RED-UNIT, representing the headquarters (CP) of the first-echelon (assault) motorized rifle regiment of the division (reinforced), its two second-echelon maneuver battalions, and organic and attached subordinate fire and combat support units not otherwise identified individually.

ASSAULT-UNIT. A subclass of RED-UNIT, assigned to force the river crossing operation; ASSAULT-UNIT includes battalions (ADV) and companies (FWD).

ADV. A subclass of ASSAULT-UNIT, representing first-echelon (assault) motorized rifle battalions of a first-echelon regiment (reinforced); they act as advanced guard for the main body of the regiment.

FWD. A subclass of ASSAULT-UNIT, representing assault companies of a first-echelon battalion that act as a forward detachment.

ARTILLERY. A subclass of RED-UNIT, representing artillery units (in general) that support the advance through artillery fire (both barrage and directed).

DIVARTY. A subclass of ARTILLERY, representing organic division artillery assets, plus those attached from Army and front for the river-crossing operation. We postulate that the division will control the equivalent of two artillery regiments.

REGTARTY. A subclass of ARTILLERY, representing all organic and attached artillery assets under operational control of a first-echelon (assault) regiment. We postulate that each assault regiment will control the equivalent of two artillery battalions.

BNARTY. A subclass of ARTILLERY, representing attached artillery assets under operational control of a first-echelon battalion of an assault regiment. We postulate that each assault battalion will control the equivalent of two artillery batteries.

ENG. A subclass of RED-UNIT, representing engineer units assigned to provide route and river-crossing site reconnaissance and other preparations, augmented to operate as crossing control teams. We postulate the equivalent of one reinforced engineer reconnaissance platoon for each assault regiment crossing sector.

ELECTRONIC-WARFARE-UNIT. A subclass of RED-UNIT, which includes units with active and passive EW functions.

DFERS. A subclass of ELECTRONIC-WARFARE-UNIT, which performs passive functions and represents COMINT and ELINT units with direction-finding capability.

EH. A subclass of DFERS, which represents high-frequency (HF) radio intercept and direction-finding platoons organic to division reconnaissance battalions. We postulate that a division will possess only one such platoon.

EV. A subclass of DFERS, representing very high-frequency (VHF) radio intercept and direction-finding platoons organic to divisional reconnaissance battalions. We postulate that a division will possess two of these platoons, one to support each regimental crossing sector.

JAMMERS. A subclass of ELECTRONIC-WARFARE-UNIT. JAMMERS are active EW units.

JH. A subclass of JAMMERS, representing HF radio-jamming companies attached to the division for the river-crossing operation. We postulate that the division will be allocated one such company.

JV. A subclass of JAMMERS, representing Army VHF radio-jamming companies attached to the division for the river-crossing operation. We postulate that the division will be allocated two of these companies, one to support each regimental crossing sector.

Objects on the Blue side include:

BLUE-UNIT. The broadest generic class, representing all Blue units. Only very general, default behaviors and attributes for Blue units are stored here. BLUE-UNIT is a subclass of both COMMUNICATING-OBJECT and MOVING-OBJECT.

BLUE-DIV. A subclass of BLUE-UNIT, representing the parent division (and all superior Blue ground force elements) of the defending Blue regiment. This object enters the simulation only to provide the source of the message to the defending mechanized infantry regiment ordering it to move into defensive positions along the river and, once there, to issue a subsequent tactical alert order.

BLUE-TACC. The Air Force tasking element that schedules (frags) air missions in response to self-generated or ground force requirements.

BLUE-AIRBASE. The aircraft sortie-generation capability available to respond to BLUE-TACC frags.

BLUE-AIRMISSION. The response (i.e., a specific number of aircraft assigned a specific task at a specific time) of BLUE-AIRBASE to a BLUE-TACC frag.

BLUE-FIRING-UNIT. A subclass of BLUE-UNIT, representing the artillery units that attempt to slow Red's movement through directed artillery fire. (Because Blue's artillery units behave differently from Red's, they were not set up as subclasses of a more general artillery class.)

ARTYBN. A subclass of BLUE-FIRING-UNIT, representing the senior artillery CP/fire direction center (FDC) for all the organic and attached artillery (taken to be the equivalent of three batteries) supporting the defending mechanized infantry regiment; it also represents the heavy artillery battery.

ARTYBTRY. A subclass of BLUE-FIRING-UNIT, representing organic or attached medium artillery batteries that support the defending mechanized infantry regiment. We postulate the regiment controls two such batteries.

MECH-REGT-HQ. A subclass of BLUE-UNIT, representing the command element and CP functions of the defending mechanized infantry regiment. In TWIRL, MECH-REGT-HQ1, an instance of MECH-REGT-HQ, decides the appropriate response (EW or fire support) to targets nominated by direction-finding units.

MECHBN. A subclass of BLUE-UNIT, representing the class of maneuver elements organic to the defending Blue regiment. Four instances of MECHBN exist in TWIRL, but once deployed in their defensive positions, they currently play no further role in the simulation.

DFPLT. A subclass of BLUE-UNIT, representing the class of EW units capable of intercepting and direction-finding all tactical communication nets in use by the attacking Red division. TWIRL contains two instances of DFPLT.

JAMCO. A subclass of BLUE-UNIT, representing the class of active EW units capable of jamming receivers on any of the tactical communication nets in use by the attacking Red division.

Objects used to represent communication channels and networks include:

CHANNEL. The class of communication media over which objects can communicate within the simulation. Its subclasses include BROADCAST-CHANNEL and POINT-TO-POINT-CHANNEL.

BROADCAST-CHANNEL. The class of communication networks over which objects can broadcast messages simultaneously to other objects in the network (which may include the enemy listening in).

POINT-TO-POINT-CHANNEL. The class of direct, point-to-point communication channels.

Objects used to represent *terrain* include:[7]

TERRAIN-OBJECT. The only terrain objects represented in TWIRL are manmade objects, that is bridges and road junctions. (Obviously one could introduce such objects as rivers, streams, lakes, hills, roads, obstacles, minefields, flatlands, etc.) Basically, a terrain object "knows" how to determine whether a unit can cross it and either allows the unit to cross or notifies it of its current status.

BRIDGE. A subclass of TERRAIN-OBJECT, representing the class of bridges that exist on Red's route to the major river crossing. Bridges can be destroyed by Blue air interdiction, delaying Red's advance.

ROAD-CROSSING. A subclass of TERRAIN-OBJECT, representing the class of road junctions in the road network that Red's units will be

[7] Strictly speaking, all the features included in the TERRAIN-OBJECT class need not be (and are not) actual terrain elements. However, as they affect the simulated events in a similar manner, their inclusion is convenient.

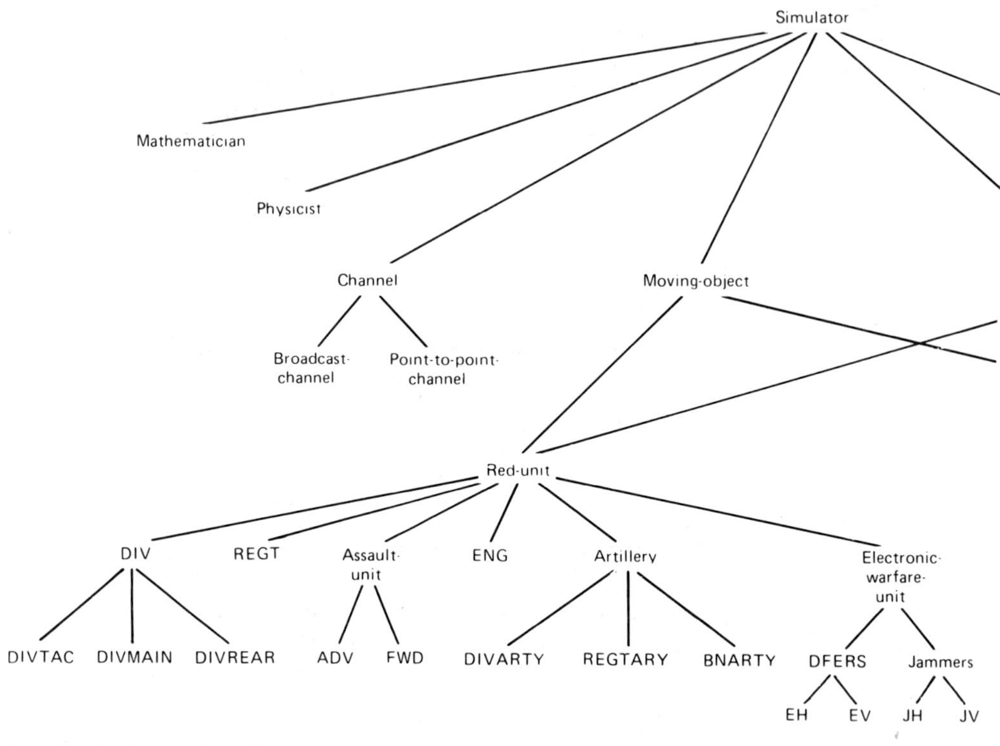

FIGURE 7.1 TWIRL Hierarchy of Objects.

crossing en route to the river. Road junctions can be destroyed by Blue air interdiction, delaying Red's advance.

And finally, two auxiliary objects serve primarily as computational objects:

MATHEMATICIAN. The MATHEMATICIAN does most of TWIRL's computations (e.g., computing distances traversed and updating locations of objects).

PHYSICIST. The PHYSICIST determines the effects of various physical phenomena such as bomb explosions and artillery fire.

Figure 7.1 presents a ROSS hierarchy of the main objects in the simulation. (This is not a military command hierarchy!) Each object represents a subclass of its parent classes (e.g., ASSAULT-UNIT is a subclass of RED-UNIT, which, in turn is a subclass of both MOVING-

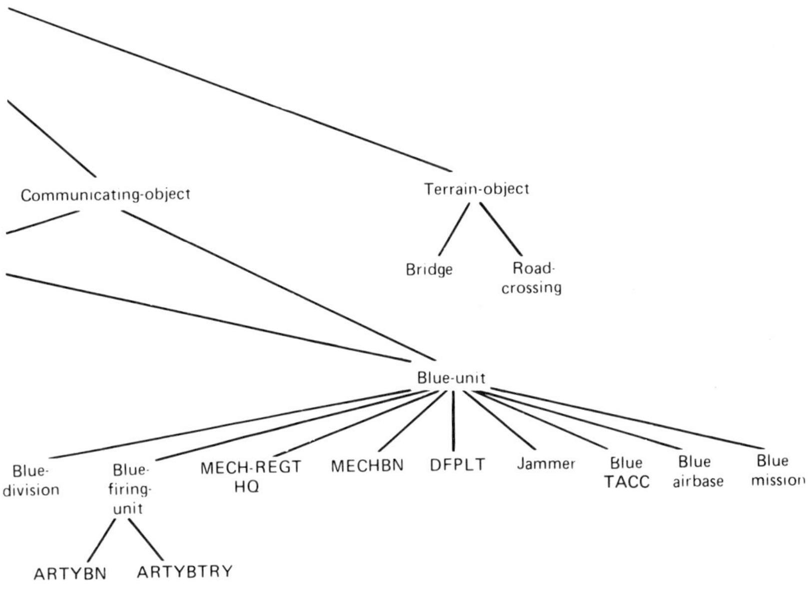

OBJECT and COMMUNICATING-OBJECT). Color Plate 1 provides a list of the objects (and other features) that are displayed graphically.

7.3 Representing Communications

Representing the communications between objects is quite straightforward in ROSS. Objects communicate by sending messages to one another. However, real-world communications can be quite complex, exhibiting a variety of characteristics and behaviors. For example, there are different types of communication techniques (e.g., voice, teletype, Morse code), different types of signals (e.g., telephone, radio: AM, FM, SSB), different frequencies, and so on. Also, when a message is sent, many things can happen to it en route to the intended receiver (e.g., noise on the channel can garble the message, jamming on a particular frequency can prevent receipt of the message, or other objects can be listening in and also receive the message, unbeknownst to either the sender or the intended receiver).

To accommodate such possibilities and complexities, we created a ROSS object called CHANNEL to represent the class of all communication media. Instances of CHANNEL represent particular communicating channels, each with its own set of characteristics (attributes). When an object sends a message to another object, the message always passes through a communication channel. The channel (like any other ROSS object) has a set of behaviors to respond to various situations (messages sent to jammed or dead objects, enemies listening in, etc.).

The CHANNEL object allowed us to model the communications process effectively. It also suggested a particular strategy for modeling processes within an object-oriented framework:

> To model a set of effects that seem external to the other objects being modeled, create an object to represent those effects and define appropriate behaviors for executing them.

We applied this principle in the development of SWIRL, in particular to create objects representing a scheduler (e.g., to determine proximities of objects), a mathematician, and a physicist (e.g., to determine the effects of electromagnetic pulses). Its full impact, however, came in the TWIRL development, primarily in the modeling of communications and combat, as we shall see. With a little imagination, one can readily envision creating objects to represent weather, geographical entities, functional entities (segmenting an object into several objects representing the different functions of the object), plans and procedures, hypotheses and beliefs, and even alternative futures.

7.3.1 ■ The Channel Object

The top-level object in TWIRL is called SIMULATOR. We tell that object to create a new generic (class) object called CHANNEL:

```
(1)  (ask SIMULATOR create generic CHANNEL with
          normal-delay      0
          jammed-delay      30).
```

The two attributes specify any delays involved in sending a message; for example, if the intended receiver is jammed, the message is delayed 30 minutes. (The 30-minute delay, an arbitrarily selected value, represents the time interval necessary for the sender to find another channel, retransmit the message on a new channel, and have the message get through to the intended receiver. We could, of course, model this process explicitly, but for simplicity we represent it here as a delay.)

Next, we define a behavior for CHANNEL that allows an object to send a message through a channel to a receiver:

```
(2) (ask CHANNEL when receiving
                    (send from >sender to >receiver +message)
   (if (member receiver (~your units-jammed))
    then (~requiring (~your jammed-delay) minutes
                           tell ~the receiver ~that message)
    else (~requiring (~your normal-delay) minutes
                          tell ~the receiver ~that message))).
```

When a channel object (any member of the CHANNEL class) receives a message such as "(send from regiment1 to artillery5 begin preparatory fire)," the channel object will first test if artillery5 (the receiver) is a member of the channel's list of units-jammed. If artillery5 is not jammed, the message "begin preparatory fire" will go through without delay; otherwise, there will be a 30-minute delay.

Before creating particular channel instances, we first create a subclass of CHANNEL representing broadcast networks:

```
(3) (ask CHANNEL create generic BROADCAST-CHANNEL)
```

with the behavior:

```
(4) (ask BROADCAST-CHANNEL when receiving
                         (broadcast from >sender +message)
   (loop for friend in (~your friendly-listeners) do
          (~you send from ~the sender to ~the friend ~that message))
   (loop for enemy in (~your enemy-listeners) do
        (~you send from ~the sender to ~the enemy ~that message))).
```

Thus, when a broadcast-channel broadcasts a message, it sends it to all friendly listeners as well as any enemy listeners on the channel. (The "send ..." messages used in (4) trigger the behavior defined in (2).)

And, finally, we create a particular channel:

```
(5) (ask BROADCAST-CHANNEL create instance CHANNEL1 with
      frequency           vhf
      type                voice
      used-for            command
      side                red
      friendly-listeners  (regt1 regtarty11 regtarty21 divarty1)
      units-jammed        nil
      enemy-listeners     nil).
```

Thus, CHANNEL1 is an instance of BROADCAST-CHANNEL, which is a subset of CHANNEL. CHANNEL1 has an initial set of attributes as defined in (5). These attributes (as well as everything else in ROSS) can be dynamically modified by the user or as the result of actions occurring in a simulation run. Also, since BROADCAST-CHANNEL is a subset of CHANNEL, CHANNEL1 inherits the two attributes defined in (1), as well as the behaviors defined in (2) and (4), so it knows how to broadcast a message and send it to particular receivers.

7.3.2 ■ Displaying Communications

In the TWIRL development, we wanted users to understand the communication and EW activities that go on in a battle. We wanted to display both graphical and textual information about communications and EW. The graphics facility we developed for TWIRL significantly extended the capabilities of our SWIRL graphics, providing techniques to portray communications, jamming, and artillery fire. Much of the work was experimental, trying alternative displays with different colors, highlights, menus, and so on, and getting feedback on the various alternatives.

Color graphics represents a critical component of TWIRL. Only a live demonstration, however, can convey its impact. Nevertheless, we include several snapshots of a TWIRL simulation to give the reader at least some idea of the graphics facility. Color Plate 2 shows a TWIRL snapshot of Red communications during Red's march toward the river. The sender of the message is displayed in yellow; the arrows indicate the receivers to whom the message is being sent (in this case, it is being sent over a broadcast channel); those objects that actually receive the message are displayed in orange. The message is printed in the lower left corner. The various times in the top part of the photo specify a *raw* time (in seconds) since the start of the simulation, an *operational* time relative to Red's projected crossing of the river at H-hour, a *day* time indicating time of day, and a *simulation* time relative to the start of the simulation.

The communications are shown schematically on a color graphics monitor, and are simultaneously explained in more detail in a textual display on an adjacent terminal. The following examples of textual display are excerpted from a TWIRL simulation:

```
***** BROADCAST MESSAGE SENT *****
      Time:          H - 6.0
      Channel:       red channel1
      Sender:        red divarty1
      Receivers:     (divarty1 regtarty11 regtarty21 regt1)
      Message:       (divarty1 beginning to move from (71.0 45.0) at time
                         3600)
```

```
*** POINT-TO-POINT MESSAGE SENT ***
    Time:           H - 5.917
    Channel:        red channel5
    Sender:         red regt2
    Receivers:      divtac
    Message:        (regt2 stopping at (67.25 51.0) at time 3898)
*** POINT-TO-POINT MESSAGE SENT ***
    Time:           H - 1.8
    Channel:        blue channel6
    Sender:         blue mech-regt-hq1
    Receivers:      artybn1
    Message:        (open fire on bnarty211 at (12.75 38.0) with 1 unit for
                        15 minutes)
***** BROADCAST MESSAGE SENT *****
    Time:           H - 1.75
    Channel:        blue channel2
    Sender:         blue mech-regt-hq1
    Receivers:      (jamco1)
    Message:        (execute jamming on channel1 against adv21 at
                        (12.25 43.0))
```

Since all messages flow through channel objects, these objects are responsible for printing the information. Note that the Time entry is stated as *operational* time in hours relative to H-hour, but the Message entry (in the first two messages) shows time as *simulation* time in seconds (from the start).

7.4 Representing Combat

Because we were primarily interested in simulating and displaying EW, the present version of TWIRL makes no attempt to represent maneuver unit combat or the effects of air attack on such ground forces. The primary combat interactions modeled included EC (jamming), artillery fire, and some limited air operations. At the conclusion of this section, we discuss briefly how maneuver unit combat and close air support might be treated.

7.4.1 ■ Electronic Warfare (Direction Finding, Jamming)

Jamming refers to the process of electronically blocking objects from receiving messages. Direction finders attempt to locate enemy units by intercepting enemy communication activities on specific channels and frequencies. In the TWIRL simulation, when the Blue direction finders learn that Red units are stopping (and will be stationary for some time), the Blue commander is notified about the enemy unit. The Blue commander then decides what to do (e.g., jam or fire artillery).[8] In this section, we look at the process of jamming as it evolved into TWIRL code.

In behavior (4), described in Section 7.3, a broadcast-channel object will send messages to all friendly listeners on the channel, as well as to any enemies that may be listening in. How are direction finders (the enemy listeners) placed on the channel's list of enemy-listeners?

We define an object called DFPLT, a direction-finder platoon, to represent the aggregate functions involved in direction finding. When the Blue commander, called MECH-REGT-HQ1, sends out a "go on alert" message to its units, the Blue units set their status attribute to "alert." The DFPLT does one other thing:

```
(6)  (ask DFPLT when receiving (go on alert)
          (~requiring 5 minutes set your status to alert)
          (~you plan after 5 minutes listen)).
```

That is, it also schedules itself, after a 5-minute delay (modeling the delay required to activate its equipment), to start listening:

```
(7)  (ask DFPLT when receiving (listen)
          (loop for channel in (~your enemy-channels) do
          (tell ~the channel direction finder ~me listening))).
```

Thus, the DFPLT sends a message to each of the enemy-channels it knows about (e.g., various frequencies it can listen in on), notifying the channel that it is listening.

The receiving channel-object then records the fact that the direction finder is listening:

```
(8)  (ask CHANNEL when receiving (direction finder >df listening)
          (~you add ~the df to your list of enemy-listeners)
          (print-df-listening df myself)).
```

The channel adds the direction finder to its list of enemy-listeners. The call on the function "print-df-listening" results in a textual display, such as

```
### DIRECTION FINDER LISTENING ###
     Time:              H - 2.02
     Listener:          blue dfplt1
     Channel:           red channel1       Type: broadcast-channel
```

[8] Obviously, the commander could decide to do both (jam and strike). At times there are benefits to be gained from this tactic; however, our objective was to demonstrate representative capabilities, not wide latitude in options.

When a direction finder subsequently hears a message, the graphics will also depict this information. An example of this is shown in Color Plate 3.

Let's consider a concrete example. We first create a particular DFPLT:

```
(9)  (ask DFPLT create instance DFPLT1 with
     position          (-1.0 41.0)
     enemy-channels    (channel1)
     track-plan        ((advance to (1.5 39.0) arriving at 4.97 hours))).
```

Suppose DFPLT1 receives a "go on alert" message after it arrives at its final position. Behavior (6) is triggered and, after a five-minute delay, DFPLT1's sets its "status" (a new attribute is created for DFPLT1) to "alert" and starts to "listen." This would trigger behavior (7), which would result in the message "direction finder DFPLT1 listening" being sent to CHANNEL1. This message, in turn, triggers behavior (8), which causes CHANNEL1 to add DFPLT1 to its list of enemy-listeners. Now, when a Red unit sends a broadcast message through CHANNEL1, behavior (4) is triggered, which results in CHANNEL1 forwarding the message to all friendly listeners as well as DFPLT1, an enemy-listener.

As it listens in, a DFPLT looks for those messages that indicate that an object has stopped its movement and will be stationary for a while. When it hears such a message, it notifies the Blue commander MECH-REGT-HQ1:

```
(10)(ask DFPLT when receiving (>unit stopping at >position +anything)
     (if (and (eq (~your status) 'alert) (is-not-friendly unit))
      then (~requiring 15 minutes broadcast to mech-regt-hq1
                          that potential target ~the unit at ~the position))).
```

(Note that this broadcast message is slightly different from the one shown in (4). It is directed to a particular member on the broadcast channel.)

If the MECH-REGT-HQ1 decides to jam the unit (MECH-REGT-HQ behaviors are discussed in Section 7.5), it will send a message to its jamming company to execute jamming against the unit on the appropriate channel. This would trigger the jamming company to execute the following behavior:

```
(11)  (ask JAMCO when receiving
            (execute jamming on >channel against >enemy at >position)
        (~you set your jamming-status to jamming)
        (~you decrement your available-capacity by 1)
        (tell ~the channel ~me jamming ~the enemy)
        (~you add ~the enemy to your list of targets-serviced)).
```

The message sent to the channel would trigger the behavior:

```
(12)  (ask CHANNEL when receiving (>jammer jamming >unit)
          (~you add ~the unit to your list of units-jammed)
          (print-jamming jammer unit myself)
          (tell ~the unit your communications is jammed)).
```

The channel-objects keep track of the units jammed and will delay messages sent to jammed units (see behavior 2). The call to the function "print-jamming" results in a textual display, such as:

```
##### JAMMING #####
    Time:                  H - 1.75
    Jammer:                blue jamco1
    Channel:               red channel1    Type: broadcast-channel
    Jammee:                red fwd111
```

At the same time this information is printed on a terminal, the graphics screen shows the particular jammer JAMCO1 jamming unit FWD111. A barrier is placed around FWD111 to indicate that messages would not get through to it on CHANNEL1. The graphics indicating a barrier to communications consist of a bracket on each side of the unit's military symbol. The bracket's line is sawtoothed and color-coded. Color Plate 4 shows a Blue jammer jamming four Red units. Color Plate 5 shows a subsequent Red message being broadcast. Those Red objects that are jammed do not receive the message; that is, they do not show up as orange.

In summary, the jamming process in TWIRL consists of objects (direction finders) listening in on communications of the opposing side (through channel-objects), commanders being notified, jamming companies being ordered to jam, and the jamming objects having messages delayed.

7.4.2 ■ Artillery Fire

As an alternative, or addition, to jamming, the Blue commander may decide to command artillery to fire on Red targets. In Section 7.5, we will see how the Blue commander decides whether to fire or jam. Here, we describe how artillery fire is represented in TWIRL.

To initiate artillery fire, the Blue commander sends a message to a BLUE-FIRING-UNIT (an artillery battalion or artillery battery) to open fire:

```
(13)  (ask BLUE-FIRING-UNIT when receiving
         (open fire on >target at >position with >n units for >m minutes)
           (~you decrement your available-capacity by ~the n)
```

```
(~you add ~the (list target n) to your list of assignments)
(print-firing myself target)
(tell physicist ~me assigning ~the n units to ~the target
   for ~the m minutes)
(~you plan after ~the m minutes stop firing on ~the target)).
```

The call to the function "print-firing" results in a textual display, such as:

```
XXXXX     BLUE OPENING FIRE     XXXXX
    Time:                          H - 1.75
    Firing Unit:                   artybtry1
    Target:                        bnarty121
```

Also, the color graphics screen will update to show artillery fire directed toward the target from the firing unit. (Color Plate 6 shows an example of two artillery units firing at two targets. Color Plate 7 provides some examples of Red's combat activities, including artillery fire and jamming.) The "stop firing ..." message (the last action in behavior 13) will also subsequently result in a textual display indicating that the artillery fire has stopped; the color graphics screen is updated accordingly.

The PHYSICIST serves primarily as an intermediary between artillery firing objects and targets (similar to the way CHANNEL objects act as intermediaries between communicating objects). The message to the PHYSICIST in (13) results in the PHYSICIST notifying the target that it is under fire. The PHYSICIST also computes any damage that results from artillery fire. There are, of course, many alternative methods for calculating damage. In TWIRL, damage consists of attrition and delay. Each combat unit in TWIRL is assigned an initial strength (e.g., an artillery unit would have a specified number of guns). Attrition would reduce the strength available according to the PHYSICIST's calculations. Delay would simply modify a unit's track plan.

There are also many options for deciding when to compute damage. For simplicity, the PHYSICIST computes damage once, after the artillery ceases fire on the target:

```
(14)  (ask PHYSICIST when receiving
          (>arty ceasing fire on >target with >n units after >m minutes)
            (~you tell ~the target to decrement your current-capacity by
              !(~you determine attrition to ~the target resulting from
                artillery fire of ~the n units for ~the m minutes))
            (~you tell ~the target to plan after
              !(~you determine delay to ~the target resulting from
                artillery fire of ~the n units for ~the m minutes)
              seconds resume plan)
            (tell ~the target artillery from ~the arty has stopped)).
```

(As an alternative to calculating damage all at one time, the PHYSICIST could calculate damage every minute or even every second. Calculations for attrition and delay are based on volume of the artillery fire and duration of firing.[9]

7.4.3 ■ Air Operations

A TACC object initiates air operations by commanding (sending messages to) airbases to scramble aircraft. In TWIRL, a TACC can assign reconnaissance missions (either to cover specific locations or to survey an extended area) and ground attack missions (for interdiction attacks on bridges and road junctions). As an example of the former, suppose we wanted Blue's TACC1 (an instance of TACC) to initiate surveillance missions periodically over a particular area. In TWIRL, this would look like:

```
(15)  (ask TACC1 when receiving
                        (execute periodic surveillance over >destination)
          (~you send point-to-point to !(~your airbase)
              fly surveillance recon over ~the destination)
          (~you plan after 5400 seconds
              execute periodic surveillance over ~the destination)).
```

This behavior causes TACC1 to command its airbase to initiate an area surveillance mission every 90 minutes. The last action in (15) resembles a recursive function call. After a 90-minute delay, the same behavior is executed again. The message to the airbase causes a reconnaissance aircraft to be scrambled and directed toward the desired destination.

Blue interdiction operations begin when TACC1 is notified by one of its reconnaissance aircraft that enemy units are moving toward the river (Color Plate 8 shows an aircraft sending a message to TACC1, which is offscreen to the left), that is,

```
(16)  (ask TACC1 when receiving (red units heading toward the river)
          (~you plan after !(~your command-delay) seconds
              send point-to-point to !(~your airbase)
              attack bridge1 at position (40.9 42.0)
              with 2 aircraft arriving in 30 minutes)
          (~you plan after !(~your command-delay) seconds
              send point-to-point to blue-div1
              commence advance to block red operation)).
```

[9] The volume and duration of fire can be measured in any units suitable for the analyst's purpose.

TACC1 commands its airbase to initiate an attack on BRIDGE1, a bridge that several Red units will need to cross, and at the same time notifies Blue's ground operations commander BLUE-DIV1 to begin ground operations to block Red's advance.[10]

Currently, aircraft can be assigned to attack bridges and road junctions. When an airbase receives an "attack ..." message, it formulates a mission that consists of one or more aircraft and a scheduled plan of operations (e.g., actual time of takeoff, time of arrival over target, etc.). The bombing component triggers the behavior:

```
(17)  (ask MISSION when receiving (bomb >target)
          (tell physicist ~the target being bombed by
              !(~your number-of-aircraft) aircraft)
          (print-bombing myself target)
          (~you plan after !(~your bomb-delay) seconds next event)).
```

Once again, the PHYSICIST serves as an intermediary to calculate the effects of bombings on targets. The call to the function "print-bombing" results in a textual display, such as:

```
**** BOMBING OCCURRED ****
     Time:                       H - 5.5
     Mission:                    blue airmission2
     Planes:                     2
     Target:                     bridge1
     Position:                   (40.9 42.0)
     Capacity:                   0 (totally out)
```

Suppose TACC1 initiates an attack on BRIDGE1. When the attack occurs, the PHYSICIST is notified, and it computes the resulting damage to the bridge. Each bridge has an associated "capacity" that indicates its current operational strength (measured in percentages). If a bridge is at 100 percent capacity, it is fully operational; 0 percent capacity indicates the bridge is totally destroyed; values between 0 and 100 percent indicate fractional damage. No moving object (Red or Blue unit) that approaches the bridge can cross unless the bridge is sufficiently operational to allow the unit to cross. This calculation should be a function of the type of unit crossing and the characteristics of the bridge itself. Currently in TWIRL, however, the bridge must be at full capacity to allow a unit to cross it, that is,

[10] In practice, the TACC would not directly order ground units into action. For simplicity, we have short-circuited the path that air intelligence data would normally follow to ground force command channels, where it could then influence or trigger ground force commanders' actions.

```
(18)  (ask MOVING-OBJECT when receiving (at >bridge)
         (if (lessp (ask ~the bridge recall your capacity) 100)
          then (~you broadcast to all that stopped at obstacle !bridge
                  and repairing)
            (~you set your velocity to (0.0 0.0))
            (setq repair-time (ask mathematician compute repair
                time for ~the bridge))
            (~you plan after ~the repair-time seconds tell physicist
                ~the bridge is repaired)
            (~you plan after ~the repair-time seconds resume plan)
         else (~you resume plan))).
```

In this behavior, the unit approaching the bridge repairs it. The MATHEMATICIAN calculates the repair time. One could make this process more complicated by allowing only certain types of units to repair bridges. Those units that cannot repair bridges would need to summon the repair units, which could cause further delays to planned movements.

Currently, offensive air support operations in TWIRL are initiated against only bridges and road junctions. It is easy to envision how this could be extended to allow attacks on Blue and Red units as well. Basically, one could still use behavior (17), but the PHYSICIST behavior for determining damage would need to consider the type of target hit and would compute damage differently for the different types of objects.

The ability to provide air attacks on enemy units would give the Blue commander yet a third option for dealing with enemy targets (in addition to jamming and artillery fire). The Blue commander could send messages to its TACC to initiate air interdiction, just as it sends messages to its jamming companies to jam and to its artillery units to fire.

7.4.4 ■ Additional Features

Currently, when the track plans of opposing Red and Blue ground forces bring the forces into close proximity with each other, no interaction occurs and each proceeds on its original plan as if the other were not there. This situation could not be tolerated if it was essential to simulate maneuver unit combat activities. A simple example will illustrate how one might approach the simulation of maneuver unit combat in TWIRL.

Each unit might be assigned attributes that specify its initial strength, the range at which it could detect and engage various types of enemy units, the attrition it might inflict and suffer in a given engagement, how long the engagement might last, and how the unit's subsequent behavior might be modified. Once a ground unit approaches to within detection range of an enemy unit, the PHYSICIST could be notified to calculate the mutual attrition rates. The resulting rates and directions of movement for the two combatants could be determined periodically (as a function of force ratio, for example) to provide a record trace of the FLOT (forward line of own troops). Behaviors specifying the circumstances under which a unit would break contact, hold, fight a withdrawal, call for artillery or other fire support, and so on, could also be included to expand the repertoire of simulated activities.

Inclusion of on-call artillery or aerial fire support requires a mechanism to originate the request. As suggested previously, an engaged ground unit could originate the request (i.e., send a message through the proper channels) when, for example, its strength, the force opposing it, or its retrograde move rate reached a specified threshold value. The channel could be simulated to any level of complexity the analytical problem dictates. This includes some or all of the ground force and air echelons that are involved in present Service doctrine. Higher ground force echelons could introduce delays for assessment and consolidation of multiple requests, substitute artillery for a requested air strike, or exercise veto power, for example. But once an approved request reaches the Air Force's TACC, the procedure could be similar to that previously described: The TACC would decide the number and type of aircraft to commit, the air unit to execute the mission, the ordnance, and the desired time on target, and would then send a message to the airbase to execute the mission.

These simple examples of additional combat interactions illustrate how one could begin to build into TWIRL far more complexity than is incorporated in our prototype simulation.

7.5 Decision Making: the Blue Commander

7.5.1 ■ Automating the Decision-making Process

As an example of how to model decision making in TWIRL, we consider the Blue commander called MECH-REGT-HQ1, which is an instance of the general class of commanders MECH-REGT-HQ (mechanized regiment headquarters). The Blue direction finder alerts its MECH-REGT-HQ when it determines that a Red unit has stopped at a particular location (see behavior 10). This triggers the following behavior:[11]

```
(19)  (ask MECH-REGT-HQ when receiving
                (potential target >unit at >position)
            (if (~you determine there is an artillery priority for ~the unit)
             then (~you assign artillery to ~the unit at ~the position
                based on targets to be serviced)
            else (~you assign jammer to ~the unit at ~the position))).
```

The first thing the MECH-REGT-HQ does is determine the artillery priority of the unit. Basically, the MECH-REGT-HQ examines its "target-priority-list" attribute to see if the enemy unit falls into any of the classes of targets listed there. If it does not, the MECH-REGT-HQ decides to assign a jammer to the enemy unit. This evolves into the MECH-REGT-HQ sending an "execute jamming ..." message to a jamming company that is triggering the behavior shown in (11).

Next, MECH-REGT-HQ checks to see if there are any enemy targets waiting to be serviced (which might be the case, for example, if there were more targets than available artillery):

```
(20)  (ask MECH-REGT-HQ when receiving
              (assign artillery to >unit at >position based on
                                          targets to be serviced)
            (if (~your targets-waiting-to-be-serviced)
             then (assign artillery to ~the unit at ~the position based on
                target priorities)
             else (~you assign artillery to ~the unit at ~the position))).
```

If there are no other enemy targets waiting to be serviced, the MECH-REGT-HQ assigns artillery to the new target (see behavior (23), to follow). Otherwise, the artillery priority of the new enemy target is compared with the priorities of the targets waiting to be serviced:

```
(21)  (ask MECH-REGT-HQ when receiving
          (assign artillery to >unit at >position based on target priorities)
            (if (greaterp
                    (~you determine artillery priority of ~the unit)
                    (~you determine highest-priority of waiting targets))
            then (~you assign artillery to ~the unit at ~the position)
            else (~you add-by-priority ~the unit to your list of
                        targets-waiting-to-be-serviced)
                (~you assign jammer to ~the unit at ~the position))).
```

[11] We must reemphasize that the particular behaviors we have developed for TWIRL are exemplary only and not meant to portray realistically the behaviors of any corresponding real-world entity. The goal is to show how it is possible to do so.

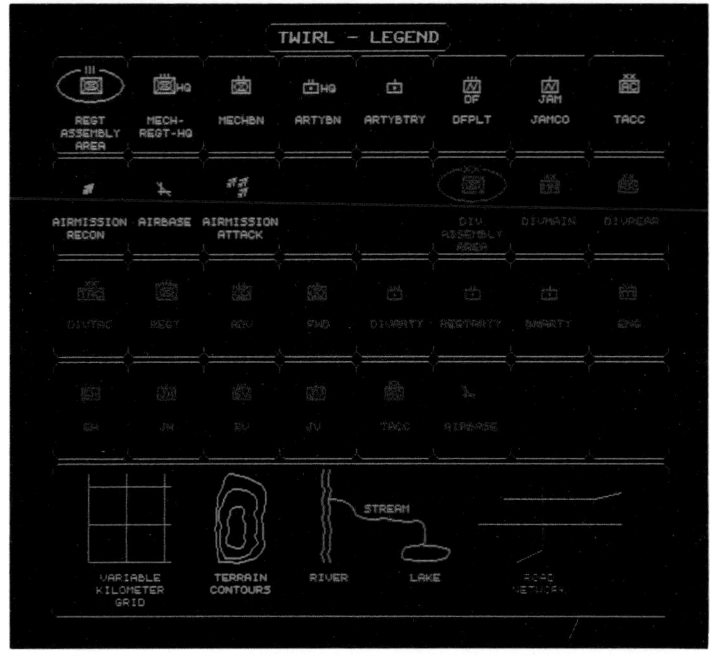

PLATE 1 TWIRL Graphics Legend.

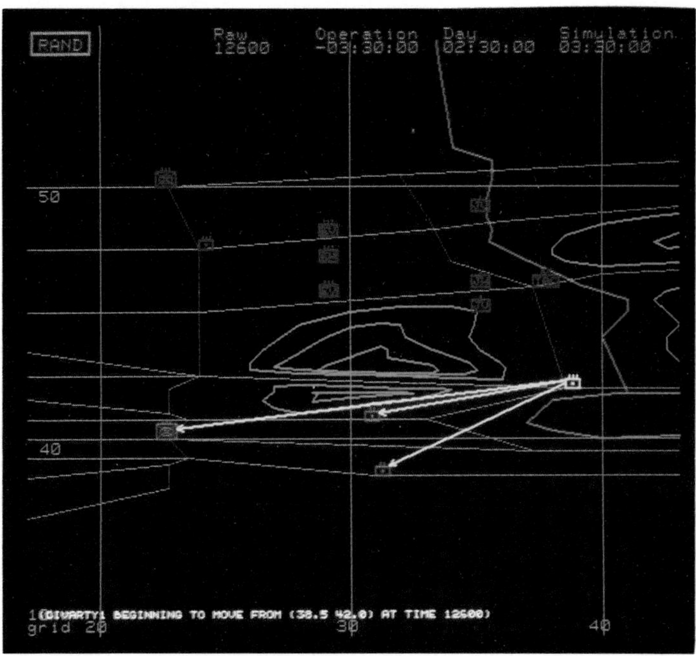

PLATE 2 Communications Display in TWIRL.

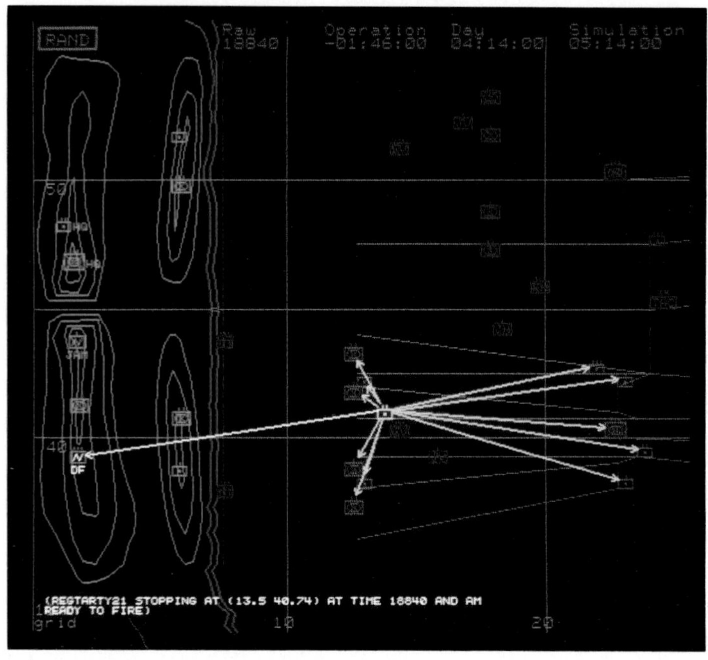

PLATE 3 Direction Finding.

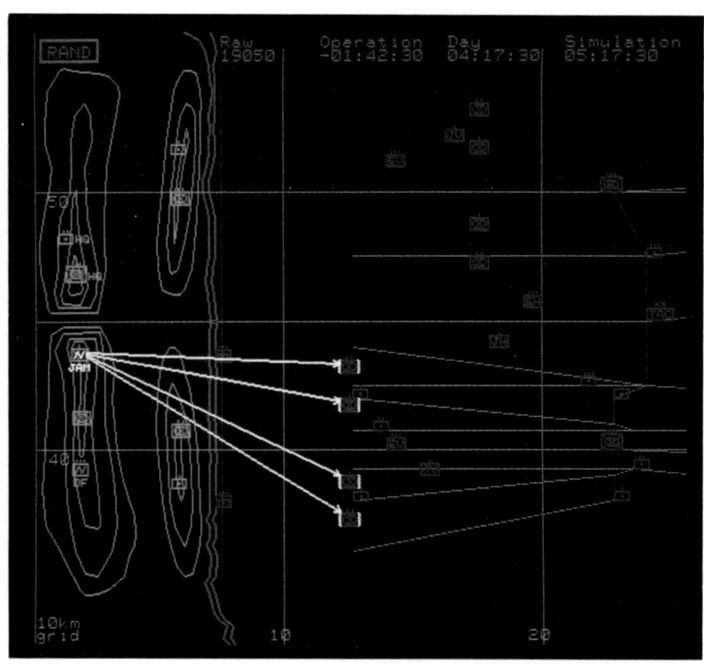

PLATE 4 Jamming Communications.

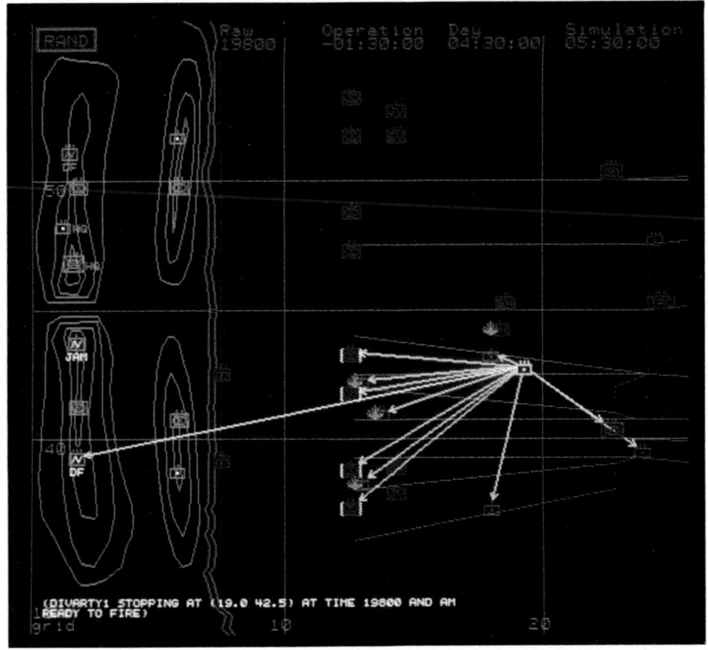

PLATE 5 Jammed Communications.

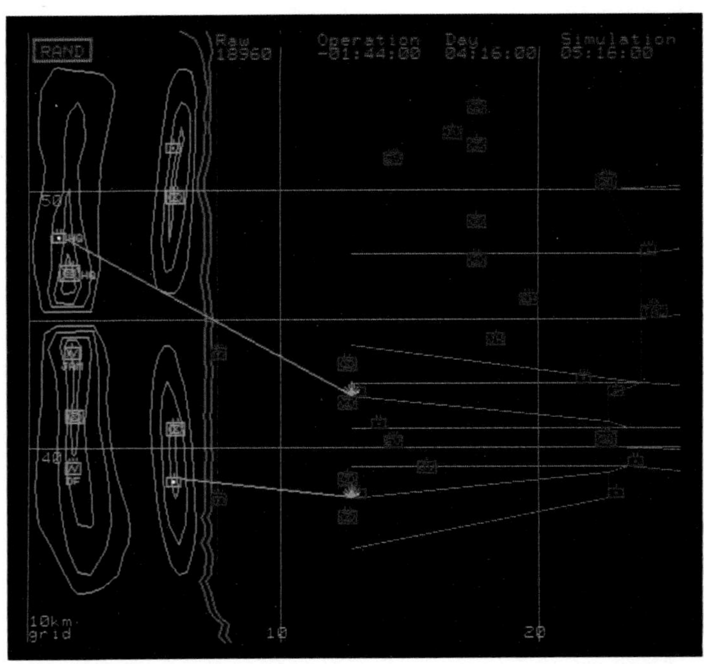

PLATE 6 Blue Artillery Fire.

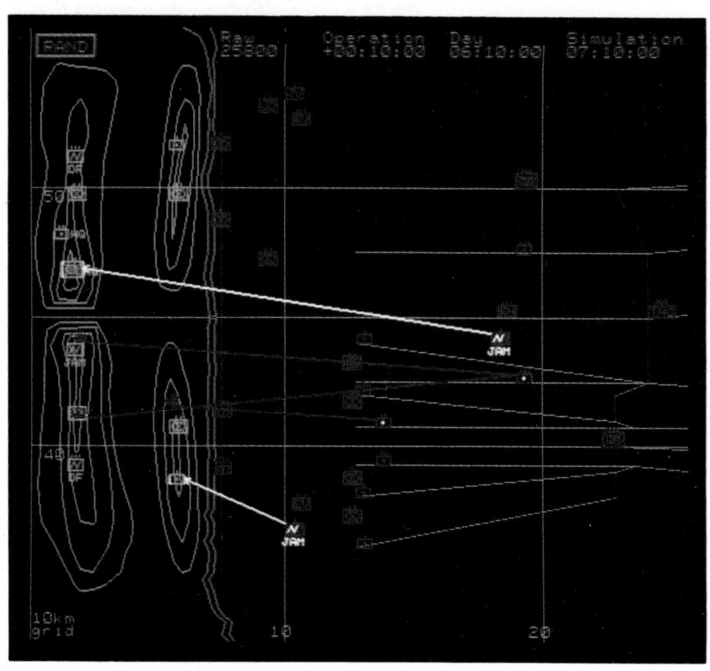

PLATE 7 Red Artillery Fire and Jamming.

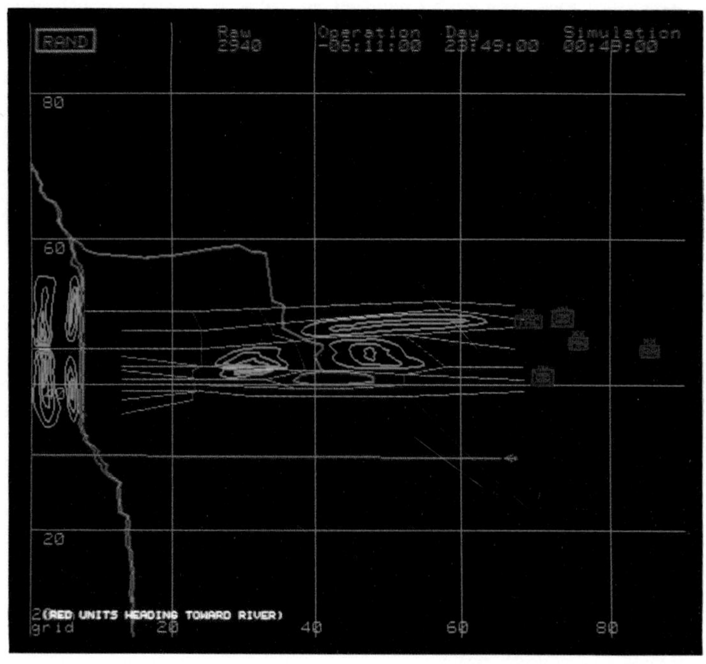

PLATE 8 Air Surveillance.

If the priority of the new enemy target is greater, the MECH-REGT-HQ assigns artillery to the new target. If it is not, the MECH-REGT-HQ adds the new target to its "targets-waiting-to-be-serviced" list and in the meantime assigns a jammer to the new target. Note that the MECH-REGT-HQ still wants to bring artillery fire to bear on the new target. (Behaviors (19), (20), and (21) could be combined into one large behavior. We chose to represent them separately to indicate the three decision points.)

Two loose ends remain. First, when, if ever, do the enemy units waiting to be serviced actually get serviced? This occurs when an artillery unit reports that it has ceased firing on its assigned target (artillery fire occurs for particular intervals of time determined by the MECH-REGT-HQ):

```
(22)  (ask MECH-REGT-HQ when receiving
                    (>artillery ceasing fire on >target)
         (if (~your targets-waiting-to-be-serviced)
          then (setq newtarget
                    (~you determine highest-priority of waiting targets))
               (~you remove ~the newtarget from your list of
                    targets-waiting-to-be-serviced)
               (~you assign artillery to ~the newtarget at
                    !(~you determine position of ~the newtarget)))).
```

Second, the MECH-REGT-HQ has to assign artillery to targets:

```
(23)  (ask MECH-REGT-HQ when receiving
                  (assign artillery to >target at >position)
         (if (~you determine that no artillery are available)
          then (~you consider reassigning artillery with lowest
                priority target to ~the target at ~the position)
          else (~you send point-to-point to
                !(~you find best available artillery)
                open fire on ~the target at ~the position with
                !(~you determine number of firing units for ~the target)
                units for
                !(~you determine duration to fire at ~the target)
                minutes))).
```

If no artillery is available, the MECH-REGT-HQ considers reassigning a currently firing artillery unit to the new target (see behavior 24). Otherwise, it decides to fire on the target and looks for the best available artillery unit (based on available capacity of the artillery and distance from the target). It then sends a point-to-point message to the artillery unit to open fire, which triggers behavior (13). The number of firing elements to assign and the duration of firing are determined by the MECH-REGT-HQ, based on the target type (a list relates target types to number of firing elements and firing duration).

Finally, we show how MECH-REGT-HQ can reassign artillery:

```
(24)  (ask MECH-REGT-HQ when receiving
              (consider reassigning artillery with lowest priority
                  target to >new-target at >position)
            (setq low-artillery (~you find artillery with lowest target))
            (setq low-target (~you find target with lowest priority))
            (if (greaterp
                    (~you determine artillery priority of ~the new-target)
                    (~you determine artillery priority of ~the low-target))
             then (~you send point-to-point to ~the low-artillery
                        cease fire on ~the low-target)
               (~you assign jammer to ~the low-target at
                    !(~you determine position of ~the low-target))
               (~you send point-to-point to ~the low-artillery
                 open fire on ~the new-target at ~the position with
                 !(~you determine number of firing units for ~the
                 new-target) units for
                 !(~you determine duration to fire at ~the new-target)
                 minutes)
               (~you add-by-priority ~the low-target to your list of
                 targets-waiting-to-be-serviced)
             else (~you assign jammer to ~the new-target at ~the position)
               (~you add-by-priority ~the new-target to your list of
                 targets-waiting-to-be-serviced))).
```

We can summarize the decision-making process of the Blue commander as follows: It can assign jammers and artillery to enemy units. It prefers to assign artillery for those enemy units that are on its artillery priority list. It jams those enemy units not on the artillery list. If it prefers to assign artillery to an enemy unit but cannot, it jams the unit but still intends to assign artillery in the future, if at all possible. It will assign artillery to enemy units, based on its priority list, until all of its artillery is in use. Artillery units can be reassigned at any time if targets with higher priorities are detected. When artillery units are freed up, they are reassigned to any enemy units waiting to be serviced.

This behavior is obviously only one of many possible sets of behaviors. For example, additional complexity could be added to the list of possible behaviors by expanding or limiting the number of available artillery tubes per battery, the number and types of artillery rounds, the accuracy of target acquisition and of placing rounds on targets, and so on.

Alternatively, instead of automating the Blue commander, a human player may be allowed to make those decisions as they arise within an actual simulation run. This capability is discussed in the following section.

7.5.2 ■ Incorporating Human Decisions (Human in the Loop)

The object-oriented organization of ROSS provides an excellent environment in which to allow a person to play one of the simulation objects (or, more generally, to allow any number of people to play any number of simulation objects). The person becomes a ROSS object just as the automated simulation players are ROSS objects, that is, the person receives and sends messages just like any other ROSS object.

To illustrate this capability, we have developed a prototype facility in TWIRL in which a person can play the role of a Blue commander, the MECH-REGT-HQ1. Recall that a direction finder, when it locates an enemy unit (behavior 10), notifies the MECH-REGT-HQ1, who in turn decides what to do about the enemy (behavior 19). We can redefine behavior (19) for our Blue commander MECH-REGT-HQ1 to be the following:

```
(25)  (ask MECH-REGT-HQ1 when receiving
               (potential target >unit at >position)
             (print-target-menu unit position)).
```

Note that behavior (19) applies to the class of all MECH-REGT-HQ, whereas (25) applies to only one particular instance of that class, MECH-REGT-HQ1. All other Blue commanders still have behavior (19).

When MECH-REGT-HQ1, which a person is now playing, is notified of a potential enemy target, the function "print-target-menu" is called to list the available options. Since the person playing MECH-REGT-HQ1 would probably not know what the options are or what messages he or she can send, we decided to facilitate the interaction by means of a menu. Figure 7.2 shows a typical interaction.

The options available to the person in Fig. 7.2 correspond to particular messages to be sent or actions to be taken. For example, Option 1, the one actually selected by the person, causes an "open fire ..." message to be sent to ARTYBTRY1, which triggers a behavior similar to (13). Option 2, if selected, would trigger the chosen jamming company to execute behavior (11). Option 3 would result in a "cease fire ..." message being sent, and so on. Option 7 would eliminate behavior (25) and result in the MECH-REGT-HQ1 again exhibiting behavior (19).

We should clarify that what we have done in behavior (25) and Fig. 7.2 is allow a person to decide what to do about potential enemy targets as they occur in a simulation. In a sense, the person is acting as a part of MECH-REGT-HQ1, but not necessarily all of MECH-REGT-HQ1. We have redefined only one behavior, behavior (19), which can be complex and might trigger behaviors (20), (21), (23) and (24). Other behaviors for MECH-REGT-HQ1 have not been changed. Thus, the

TIME = H − 1.5

UNIT	POSITION	TARGET	ASSIGNED	TOTAL CAPACITY	AVAILABLE	T_BEG	T_END
artybn1	(1.0 48.0)	bnarty121	1	2	1	18910	19810
artybtry2	(5.5 51.5)	bnarty211	1	1	0	18960	19860
artybtry1	(5.5 38.5)	-	0	1	1	-	-
jamco1	(1.5 43.5)	adv12	yes	8	6	18300	20100
		adv11	yes			19400	21200

Target sited by dfplt1
Target: fwd111 Position: (12.25 38.5)

You may:

1. assign artillery
2. assign jammer
3. cease fire on a target
4. cease jamming a target
5. seek information
6. evaluate Lisp form
7. have automated blue regiment take over decision making
8. ignore the object

Please type the appropriate number: **1**

Specify artillery you wish to assign: **artybtry1**

XXXXX BLUE OPENING FIRE XXXXXXX
Time: H - 1.5
Firing Unit: artybtry1
Target: fwd111

FIGURE 7.2 Human Decision Making in TWIRL (human responses in boldface).

person need not replace an object completely, but may replace only part of the object, for example those behaviors of importance or focus. The person can be allowed to replace as much of an object as desired by redefining the appropriate behaviors.

Allowing a person to play an object, or certain functions of an object, has great utility for training and analysis. For training, this facility allows the trainee to make decisions in a combat simulation and see their impact as the simulation progresses. For analysis, it is possible to make decisions to direct the simulation toward various situations and alternatives and to explore various strategies and tactics, again seeing their impact in the simulation.

7.6 Results of an Exemplary Simulation

In Section 7.2, we briefly described the problem domain simulated by TWIRL. Here we assess the sequence of events produced by the current TWIRL code and indicate where (in that sequence) and how Red and Blue combat actions cause deviations in each others' planned activities. Recall that in TWIRL each object's intended movements and planned combat actions are specified in a *track plan*. In essence, track plans embody each side's operational plans or goals. This analysis of an exemplary TWIRL simulation focuses mainly on how Blue actions cause Red to alter its track plans, which, in turn, cause delays in Red's commencing the assault phase of the operation.

To describe and explain the actions and reactions of the simulated Red and Blue combat units, we refer to specific instances of the classes (generic objects) defined in Section 7.2. Figure 7.1 illustrated the hierarchical relationships of those classes in the ROSS code. Specific instances of a class (e.g., a certain motorized rifle regiment is an instance of the class of all Red motorized rifle regiments) are given unique identification numbers. These, together with the class name, indicate position in the military command hierarchy. Figure 7.3 shows the unit numbering system adopted for the Red command structure in the cur-

FIGURE 7.3 Simulated Red Military Command Hierarchy.

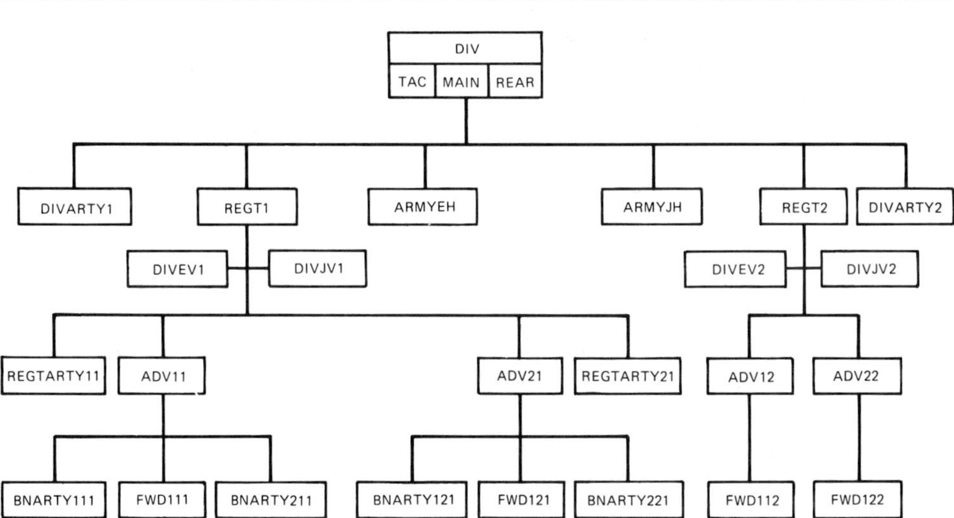

rent TWIRL simulation. Note that REGT2 is not simulated in as much detail as REGT1, that is, no fire support units below the motorized rifle division level (REGTARTY or BNARTY units) are included for REGT2. Their absence introduces no difficulties, as REGT2 plays only the role of a baseline control case. We purposely designed the ROSS code not to allow Blue's disruptive efforts to affect REGT2's scheduled track plans.[12]

Basically, the Red operational plan, collectively defined by the individual Red unit track plans, calls for the major units (maneuver and fire support) to depart from a rear assembly area and move over designated lines of communication (LOCs) toward assault positions near the river. The actual assault crossing is scheduled for a specified H-hour, when all essential units are to be in place and ready. During the approach march, each major assault unit (i.e., REGT1 and REGT2) moves independently, periodically detaching subordinate or attached subunits (e.g., ENG1, DIVEV2), each of which then continues separately toward its own assault location. Also, during the approach march, the track plans of the fire support units instruct them to halt from time to time to set up a firing position from which to provide on-call fire support to cover the march routes of the maneuver units. The timing of the halts produces a leapfrogging pattern to ensure continuous fire support coverage during the march (see Klahr et al., 1984).

Once the major maneuver and fire support units reach their forward assembly areas, the subordinate assault and fire support units (e.g., FWD111, BNARTY121) detach and deploy to their assault positions to await the assault order.

In the current TWIRL code, delay in executing a unit's scheduled track plan provides a measure of the collective effectiveness of three means of disruption: air attacks on the LOCs, artillery fire on the units themselves, and jamming of their communications. The consequences to Red if Blue were to employ all three are described in this section. The Red responsive behaviors are those described in Section 7.4.

Blue reconnaissance flights discover Red units moving out of the division assembly area (see Color Plate 8). Upon receipt of this information, the Blue air component commander (through his or her TACC) plans to interdict the likely Red LOCs, choosing two bridges and five road junctions as targets. Attacks on four road junctions and both bridges create obstacles that are sufficient to stop movement at those points until repairs are made. These obstacles are on routes to be used

[12] As mentioned earlier, the use of REGT2 as a control facilitates identification of the impact of disruptive measures on the behavior of REGT1. This is particularly useful when viewing the graphic display.

by DIVTAC, REGT1, DIVARTY1, and REGTARTY21, with the latter two sharing a portion of a single route.

When an obstacle is encountered, Red unit behavior calls for the unit to stop and clear the obstacle or repair damaged facilities, using its organic engineer assets. This action is assumed to occur at the rate of restoring 4 percent of capacity per minute (i.e., for damage preventing any movement across the obstacle, full movement is restored in 25 minutes). If several units share the same route, and following units arrive at the obstacle before an earlier unit has cleared it, the new unit's repair capability is added, thereby increasing the repair rate proportionately.

In our example, DIVARTY1 and REGTARTY21 start out on separate routes that merge at one of the damaged road junctions, continue together over a damaged bridge, then diverge on separate routes. DIVARTY1 arrives at the damaged road junction first, finds it damaged, repairs it, and moves on, having suffered a 25-minute delay in its track plan. REGTARTY21, arriving somewhat later, finds the road junction at full capacity and suffers no delay, but the interval between it and DIVARTY1 has now been decreased by 25 minutes.

Upon arriving at the damaged bridge, DIVARTY1 begins repairs and, some 20 minutes later, is joined by REGTARTY21. Their combined repair capacity completes the job in a total of 22 minutes, rather than the 25 minutes it would have taken DIVARTY1 working alone. As movement begins again, a following unit's behavior requires it to remain 5 minutes behind any leading unit. Hence, the bridge repairs cost DIVARTY1 a delay of 22 minutes and REGTARTY21 a delay of 7 minutes. These two units then continue with their track plans.

As a result of these delays, DIVARTY1 is 47 minutes behind time (H − 3:43 vs. H − 4:30) in arriving at a temporary halting site from which it was intended to provide on-call fire support for all REGT1 units during their approach march. However, unimpeded units would probably have outdistanced the effective reach of DIVARTY1's guns, as the supported units have widened the interval by some 20 to 25 km. Hence, this mission would probably be unfulfilled unless suitable adaptive behavior were added to Red units to maintain the intended timing among all the advancing Red units.[13] These behaviors were not essential for our purposes, so DIVARTY1 remains in its temporary firing site the scheduled 60 minutes, departing at H − 2:43 instead of H − 3:30. DIVARTY1 encounters no further obstacles on its approach

[13] For this simple example, no attempt has been made to incorporate behaviors that could sense the developing maltiming among units and attempt to adjust movement schedules to compensate.

march, closing its assault firing position at H − 0:43, 47 minutes late. The consequences of this late arrival are now discussed.

REGTARTY21 has no enroute supporting fire responsibilities and was scheduled to continue directly to its forward assembly area. However, it encounters a bombed road junction further along the way, repairs it in 25 minutes, and closes its assembly area 32 minutes behind schedule, at H − 2:43 instead of H − 3:15. The original schedule called for REGTARTY21, having arrived at its forward assembly area, to organize two artillery task groups (BNARTY121 and BNARTY221) and to prepare them to move forward in support of the motorized rifle assault units. The first of these (BNARTY121) was scheduled to depart from the forward assembly area at H − 2:30, 45 minutes after REGTARTY21 arrived. The current TWIRL code allows this schedule to be met. (However, if that 45-minute period were the minimum time required for REGTARTY21 to organize an artillery task group, then BNARTY121's schedule would have slipped here also.) REGTARTY21's offspring (BNARTY121 and BNARTY221) arrive at their respective assault positions on their original schedules. However, the behavior code for REGTARTY21 requires it to spend its scheduled 60-minute residence time in its forward assembly area. Hence, REGTARTY21 does not arrive at its assault position until H − 1:13, 32 minutes late.

En route to its forward assembly area, REGT1 encounters two damaged road junctions, repairs each one, and arrives at its assembly area at H − 3:10, 50 minutes late. Upon arrival, REGT1 planned to designate and dispatch two engineer units (ENG1 and ENG2) to survey battalion crossing sites and establish crossing control points—ENG1 was to continue forward immediately, while ENG2 was to depart from the assembly area 15 minutes after arrival. Since REGT1 arrives 50 minutes late, ENG1 and ENG2 each depart 50 minutes later than intended. Hence, ENG1 would not complete its mission until H − 0:40 instead of H − 1:30, and ENG2 would complete its mission at H − 0:25 instead of H − 1:15.[14] Since REGT1 was to remain at this position monitoring and controlling its units' approach until H-hour, the 50-minute delay in arrival would not prevent it from moving then, as required.

In addition, during REGT1's halt in its forward assembly area, it organizes and deploys its assault companies (FWD111 and FWD121) and battalions (ADV11 and ADV21). With the current TWIRL behaviors, these actions proceed according to the original track plans, with

[14] As the original schedule called for REGT1 to issue the assault order at H − 0:45, these delays could have been critical. Behaviors to make the assault order dependent upon timely completion of the missions of ENG1 and ENG2 were not (but could easily have been) included in the TWIRL code.

no attempt to shorten the stay in the assembly area to make up lost time. As a result, FWD111, FWD121, ADV11, and ADV21 close their final assault positions at H − 1:10 instead of H − 2:00 (since REGT1 arrived in the assembly area 50 minutes late).

As DIVTAC moves forward toward the location planned for its interim command post (CP), it encounters a damaged bridge, repairs it, and arrives at its CP site at H − 4:05, 25 minutes late. Its direction-finder units (ARMYEH, DIVEV1, and DIVEV2) were scheduled to depart for their assault positions 27 minutes after DIVTAC's arrival, and the jammer units (ARMYJH, DIVJV1, and DIVJV2) an additional 15 minutes later. All EW units adhere to their original schedules, with no adjustments to make up lost time. Thus, the jammer units supporting REGT1 (ARMYJH and DIVJV1) reach their assault positions 25 minutes later than planned (because of DIVTAC's 25-minute delay)—ARMYJH at H − 1:28 instead of H − 1:53, and DIVJV1 at H − 0:38 instead of H − 1:03.

As Red units continue to move into their assault positions, Blue DFPLT1 intercepts their messages, causing MECH-REGT-HQ1 to allocate artillery and jamming against selected targets. An artillery mission against a unit results in the unit being out of action during the mission plus a subsequent recovery period, which depends on the strength and duration of the fire mission. Jamming delays the receipt of, and response to, orders during the duration of jamming.[15] These two mechanisms can disrupt Red's preparations for assault enough to cause REGT1 to delay the assault order. REGT1 plans to issue the assault order at H − 0:45, but its behavior requires all designated assault units (motorized rifle, artillery, and jammer) to have reported being in position and ready to assault. The delays described previously cause two assault units, DIVARTY1 and DIVJV1, not to be in their assault positions at H − 0:45. Therefore, REGT1 does not issue the assault order. REGT1's behavior provides for reassessment of readiness every 15 minutes thereafter. DIVARTY1 reports ready to assault at H − 0:43 and DIVJV1 at H − 0:38. Hence, REGT1 issues the assault order at H − 0:30, 15 minutes late.

However, one other behavior affects the content of the assault order. If all assault units have unjammed communications, the series of actions commanded by the assault order commences immediately. If

[15] However, movements scheduled in the unit's track plan will be executed on time, even though incoming communications are jammed. We judged this behavior to be more reasonable than to have such movements held in abeyance in case the presence of jamming *might* be blocking an incoming message that *might* contain revised movement orders.

jamming currently affects communications to at least one assault unit, the execution time in the assault order is delayed 40 minutes. As explained in Section 7.4, this delay provides an allowance to account for working around the jamming or adapting to other nonelectronic means of communication. In this scenario, at H − 0:30, REGT1 finds that communications with four of its assault units (FWD111, FWD121, ADV11, and ADV21) are jammed, and thus incorporates a 40-minute delay in the execution times contained in the assault order.

In the original schedule, the assault order (issued at H − 0:45) would result in ARMYJH and DIVJV1 commencing jamming immediately; DIVARTY1, REGTARTY11, and REGTARTY21 opening barrage fire on Blue positions at H − 0:30; and FWD111, FWD121, ADV11, and ADV21 advancing toward the river with BNARTY111, BNARTY211, BNARTY121, and BNARTY221 in support at H − 0:15. However, with the previously described delays (and given no further Blue disruptive actions), each of these activities would occur 55 minutes later than originally scheduled (15 minutes delay in assault order plus 40 minutes allowance for the presence of jamming). Thus, with the 55-minute delay, ARMYJH and DIVJV1 should begin jamming at H + 0:10. ARMYJH responds, but DIVJV1 does not, as it was taken under fire by Blue ARTYBTRY1 from H − 0:23 to H − 0:08 and is still out of action at H + 0:10.

Both DIVARTY1 and REGTARTY11 open barrage fire on the new assault schedule at H + 0:25. But, from H − 0:58 to H − 0:43 REGTARTY21 was taken under artillery fire of strength sufficient to reduce its firing capacity to zero, and thus it cannot respond to the assault order.

All four motorized rifle assault units move out on the assault as ordered at H + 0:40, accompanied by their supporting artillery. The latter set up positions (on the new assault schedule) at H + 0:45 and open direct fire on the crossing sites. Two of the supporting artillery units, BNARTY121 and BNARTY211, were under Blue artillery fire from H − 1:45 to H − 1:30, and the other two, BNARTY111 and BNARTY221, from H − 1:00 to H − 0:45, resulting in reduced capacity to provide direct fire support for the initial crossings.

In short, the exemplary TWIRL behaviors for Blue air interdiction attacks produced delays and mistimings among some Red units. Delays to two units proved meaningful in that their arrivals at their assault positions were late enough to require postponing the final assault order. Blue jamming of some assault units' communications caused Red to allow additional time for orders to get to intended recipients, adding to the cumulative delay in executing the assault. Blue artillery fire reduced Red jamming capability beginning shortly before the final assault, thus mitigating a potential Red threat to its own targeting capabilities. In addition, Blue artillery was able to reduce the strength of Red artillery available for preparatory fires and for direct support of the assault unit crossings.

7.7 Concluding Remarks

7.7.1 ■ Simulation Development

A primary objective of our research was to test the utility of the ROSS environment for building combat simulations. In particular, we wanted to design and implement a prototype battle simulation that could be used for experimenting with alternative strategies and tactics for using EW in a combat environment. Through the presentation of approximately 25 examples of TWIRL code (written in ROSS), we have tried to provide an understanding of how one builds a simulation in ROSS, and to show that, in fact, ROSS provides an excellent environment for structuring and understanding combat simulations. Other research projects using ROSS have reached similar conclusions (Dockery, 1982; Gunsch and Hebert, 1983; Nugent, 1983; Conker et al., 1983; Steeb et al., 1984).

The object-oriented message-passing framework of ROSS is well matched to the requirements of a combat simulation such as TWIRL. The discrete components of the simulation map directly onto objects, and communications among the objects map onto messages. The object-oriented organization also conveniently allows one to create objects to model special effects within a simulation (e.g., the CHANNEL and PHYSICIST objects in TWIRL).

Other features of ROSS that enhanced TWIRL's development were ROSS's fairly easy syntax; its readable, English-like appearance, which can be tailored to a user's taste; its interactive capability; its modularity (which made the human-in-the-loop feature easy to implement); and the ease with which users can extend a simulation. This last feature deserves to be particularly highlighted.

Building TWIRL was an incremental process. A few objects were created, some behaviors were designed and tested, and then the simulation was run. In about three weeks, we had a dozen objects and two dozen behaviors for TWIRL. Feedback from simulation runs was used to debug the existing behaviors and decide where further detail was required. This led to more objects and more behaviors, and again, further simulation testing. Thus, seeing results of a small, initial simulation fed the knowledge-building process. Gaps and hidden assumptions were discovered and filled in, incorrect behaviors were modified or replaced, and so on. This process is in sharp contrast to the way most simulations are developed, where the design process is separate from the implementation. In ROSS, design and implementation occur together and influence each other continually as the system evolves.

The incremental model development process in ROSS has some very useful features. First, an initial, fairly simple, running prototype can usually be developed in a few weeks. From this point onward, a demonstrable system always exists. Second, knowledge is debugged incrementally, in small chunks. Third, having a visual display of simulations, at even general levels, suggests areas where further knowledge should be added to increase complexity and fill in gaps. Finally, having a workable, continually expanding system with visual feedback keeps motivation and interest high.

We must again emphasize what we consider to be a crucial component for work in simulation—color graphics. The ability to see simulations as they are running not only helped us debug behaviors and verify their interactions, but also tremendously enhanced our understanding of the simulation. Global interactions and patterns are not readily discernible from printed output of events and aggregated statistics. The ability to view simulations dynamically significantly enhances the building of them and, we feel, will determine their ultimate utility and impact. All of the underlying schemes for representing knowledge, for executing simulations, and for verification become secondary unless the computer simulation can communicate effectively with the ultimate user.

We must present two potential problems or warnings about using ROSS: First, there is the issue of speed and the ability to scale up to larger simulations. Our work with TWIRL did not directly address this problem. ROSS is not computationally fast when run simultaneously with graphic displays. For our TWIRL simulation, however, speed was not a major issue. The compiled TWIRL system containing approximately 140 objects and 200 behaviors ran at acceptable speeds on a stand-alone, dedicated VAX 11/750. (The Appendix describes the TWIRL computing environment.) When scaling up to larger simulations, however, we will need to address the speed issue. Jefferson and Sowizral (1982), in their work on Time Warps, directly address this problem, proposing a new method for distributing simulations among several computers operating in parallel.

The second issue involves the completeness of ROSS as a programming language. ROSS was developed within the LISP language environment. When operating in ROSS, one is actually within LISP, with ROSS loaded. Therefore, one must be familiar with LISP to use Ross. In fact, various LISP functions must often be used, particularly for arithmetic operations and list processing.

7.7.2 ■ Analytic Considerations

Another goal of our research was to demonstrate that a TWIRL-like simulation could provide insight into the nature and usefulness of electronic combat. Therefore, we purposely limited the scope of the phenomena explicitly modeled in our river-crossing scenario. We chose to focus on the disruptive effects of only a few of the means available to a commander to counter a prospective enemy operation. Three means of attack were included in the simulation: air attacks on lines of communications, artillery fire directed at enemy units, and communications jamming.

All three means of disruption impose a delay on an affected unit's intended mission. Hence, in our prototype simulation, the magnitude of delay provides a first-order indicator of the effectiveness of disruption. Typically, delays imposed on units force adjustments in the schedules of their subsequent actions or of coordinated or supporting actions of other units. The total impact of the individual deviations from scheduled track plans comes together where coordinated action occurs. In the river-crossing scenario, this coordinated action is the division-wide direct assault on the river, ordered only after all critical participants have reached their assigned jump-off areas. TWIRL's graphic depiction of disruptive actions and effects, together with the transparency of the ROSS code, allows the individual and cumulative delays to be traced to their sources more easily than do other simulation techniques.

In dealing with delay, the TWIRL prototype does not explicitly model the processes by which delay is generated. That is, delays due to LOC attacks and communications jamming are assigned arbitrary values. To do otherwise would have meant greatly expanding the scope of our simulation in terms of additional objects and behaviors—an investment deemed unnecessary for a prototype demonstration. However, analysis of substantive questions of fire support or electronic combat would require such expansion. For instance, an investigation of differing strategies and tactics of electronic warfare would require adding the behaviors of actors sufficient to define the functions and instrumentalities of the portion of the enemy command and control apparatus that is of interest. The degree and specificity of detail included in the simulation of the enemy C^3 system would have to match that of the friendly countermeasure strategies, tactics, and systems subject to analysis.

In summary, we believe that the TWIRL prototype has demonstrated the ability to produce and display (textually and graphically) the effects of selected specific combat activities. Moreover, TWIRL provides a convenient mechanism to trace cause and effect as they propagate and multiply through a complex set of interconnected activities. Although the TWIRL prototype was never intended to produce substantive analytical results or insights, we believe that its operation has clearly illustrated that a useful analytical tool can be built upon it by simply adding those behaviors and actors needed to define the operational environment at a level of detail commensurate with the analytic questions of interest.

7.7.3 ■ Applications and Utility

We believe that the development of the ROSS language and its application through SWIRL and TWIRL can lead to significant improvements in the analysis of problems characterized by complex interactions among many components. The examples noted here illustrate the range of applicability of the technique and some idea of its utility.

Vulnerability assessment. All systems, particularly large and complex ones such as field forces, are bound to have inherent vulnerabilities, many of which may not be apparent to their commanders. TWIRL would be useful for identifying the critical functions and components of a combat force and hence their vulnerable features. This technique could be applied to identify enemy vulnerabilities for exploitation or seek deficiencies in Blue for remedial action.

Red activities. By incorporating knowledge of Red field operations, doctrine, and tactics gained from observing exercises and actual combat, a composite, consistent picture of Red behavior could be built up over time. A knowledge-based simulation of the Red combat system (including air- and ground-based fire support, EC, maneuver unit control, firepower distribution and norms, logistics, air defense, sensor platform deployment, etc.) would help to provide insight into doctrine and procedures and to assess the individual and collective component contributions to Red combat capability.

Doctrine library. The TWIRL technique could support development of a computer database for Red and Blue doctrine, providing a single source for up-to-date, integrated Red combined arms operational doctrine, as well as NATO joint and combined doctrine, rules of engagement, procedures, norms, and so on. Such a repository would enable analysts to compare differences between U.S. Service doctrine and U.S. joint doctrine, for example, and to identify and assess the effects of those differences.

Training. A comprehensive combat simulation could help teach U.S. and NATO commanders how to make good decisions rapidly during combat by incorporating enemy doctrine, rules, limitations, and other behavioral patterns, as well as orders of battle and equipment capabilities. This tool could be used by candidate Blue commanders and their staffs to test their knowledge of current Red and Blue doctrines, their decision-making capabilities, and the operational procedures for the theater in scenarios that simulate combat situations.

Critical-node analysis. The TWIRL methodology could be used to help identify the nodes in enemy combat systems and to identify their characteristics when they are critical and when they are not. By analyzing simulated, potentially critical nodes at various times during the scenario (for example, when they are known to be critical), one could isolate the observable, characteristic behavior patterns associated with them, that is, their discernible physical and electronic (COMINT, SIGINT, ELINT, and other) signatures. Field commanders need such data to determine which sensors and other combat information systems to deploy, where, and at which times.

Blue doctrine development. The TWIRL methodology could help develop and test new Blue operational doctrine and modify current doctrine and procedures. It could also provide a means (now nonexistent) of harmonizing individual arms employment doctrine throughout the combined arms systems.

Evaluating contingency plans. Currently, contingency plans go largely untested, at least in their operational content. A TWIRL-like simulation could provide a tool for commanders' staffs to test developed plans, suggest deficiencies, identify potential successes, and help construct or modify plans to respond to new requirements.

This list is certainly not exhaustive, yet the applications described here are representative of the wide range of problem areas that need new tools to help in experimentation and analysis. The TWIRL development attempts to provide a step in that direction.

Acknowledgments

TWIRL embodies considerable knowledge about tactical ground combat and electronic warfare. We want to thank Lt. Gen. (Ret.) John Cushman, U.S. Army, and John Callahan and Kenneth Smith of Defense Systems Corporation for sharing their views and knowledge in these areas. We have also benefited greatly from discussions with Rand colleagues David McArthur, Milton G. Weiner, and Willard Naslund, and with Dennis Bennett of TRW, who provided the much-needed initial impetus and motivation for this work.

References

1. Conker, R. S., J. R. Davidson, P. K. Groveston, and R. O. Nugent, *The Battlefield Environment Model,* The Mitre Corporation, MTR-83W00245, September 1983.
2. Department of the Army, *Opposing Forces—Europe,* Field Manual FM 30-102, Washington, D.C., 18 November 1977.
3. Department of the Army Intelligence and Security Command, *Soviet Army Operations,* U.S. Army Intelligence and Threat Analysis Center, JAG-13-U-78, April 1978.
4. Dockery, J. T., *Structure of Command and Control Analysis,* Shape Technical Center, The Netherlands, 1982. Presented at the Symposium on Modeling and Analysis of Defense Processes, Brussels, July 1982.
5. Gunsch, G. H., and B. S. Hebert, *A Proposed Military Planning Task Simulator Using the ROSS Language,* Masters Thesis, Air Force Institute of Technology, AFIT/GE/EE/83D-24, 1983.
6. Jefferson, D., and H. Sowizral, *Fast Concurrent Simulation Using the Time Warp Mechanism, Part I: Local Control,* The Rand Corporation, N-1906-AF, December 1982.
7. Klahr, P., J. Ellis, W. Giarla, S. Narain, E. Cesar, and S. Turner, *TWIRL: Tactical Warfare in the ROSS Language,* The Rand Corporation, R-3158-AF, 1984.
8. Klahr, P., and W. S. Faught, "Knowledge-Based Simulation," *Proceedings of the First Annual National Conference on Artificial Intelligence*, Palo Alto, 1980, 181-183.
9. Klahr, P., D. McArthur, and S. Narain, "SWIRL: An Object-Oriented Air Battle Simulator," *Proceedings of the Second Annual*

National Conference on Artificial Intelligence, Pittsburgh, 1982(a), 331-334.

10. Klahr, P., D. McArthur, S. Narain, and E. Best, *SWIRL: Simulating Warfare in the ROSS Language*, The Rand Corporation, N-1885-AF, September 1982(b).
11. McArthur, D., and P. Klahr, *The ROSS Language Manual*, The Rand Corporation, N-1854-AF, September 1982.
12. McArthur, D., P. Klahr, and S. Narain, *ROSS: An Object-Oriented Language for Constructing Simulations*, The Rand Corporation, R-3160-AF, December 1984.
13. Nugent, R. O., *A Preliminary Evaluation of Object-Oriented Programming for Ground Combat Modeling*, The Mitre Corporation, Working Paper WP-83W00407, 27 September 1983.
14. Narain, S., D. McArthur, and P. Klahr, "Large-Scale System Development in Several Lisp Environments," *Proceedings of the Eighth International Joint Conference on Artificial Intelligence*, Karlsruhe, West Germany, 1983, 859-861.
15. Reznichenko, V. G., *Tactics (The Officer's Library)*, Moscow, 1966, translated by USAF Foreign Technology Division, FTD-MT-67-35, NTIS, AD659928, 1967.
16. Sidorenko, A. A., *The Offensive (A Soviet View)*, Moscow, 1970, translated and published by U.S. Air Force, Washington, D.C., 1975.
17. Steeb. R., D. McArthur, S. Cammarata, S. Narain, and W. Giarla, *Distributed Problem Solving for Air Fleet Control: Framework and Implementation*, The Rand Corporation, N-2139-ARPA, April 1984.

Appendix

Computing Environment

ROSS has been operational for several years and has been implemented in a wide variety of Lisps (Narain et al., 1983), including Maclisp, Franzlisp, Interlisp-20, Vax-Interlisp, Interlisp-D, and Zetalisp. Our primary research environment, and the one in which TWIRL is implemented, includes the Franzlisp version of ROSS running under UNIX 4.1bsd on either a VAX 11/780 or a VAX 11/750.

A file containing Franzlisp (Opus 38.50, dated February 1983) requires 605,302 bytes of storage. Adding compiled ROSS requires an additional 146,432 bytes. TWIRL contains approximately 140 objects and 200 behaviors. A system including Franzlisp, ROSS, and compiled TWIRL code requires 1,203,318 bytes of storage.

Our graphics software is written in the C language and loaded directly into the Franzlisp environment. Our primary graphics processor is an AED 512 with a color monitor. We have interfaced ROSS directly with an EMACS editor. Rand's E editor can also be used to edit ROSS files, but editing with E must be performed external to ROSS.

SECTION FOUR

Techniques

In this section we present papers that describe Rand's past and present work in the areas of knowledge acquisition, knowledge representation, and distributed problem solving.

Chapter 8 discusses exemplary programming and shows how knowledge can be acquired from experts through the use of examples. The authors describe a prototype EP (exemplary programming) system that allows computer programs to be created by example, and discuss research issues involved in developing such systems.

EP was designed as a programming aid for nonexpert computer users. The EP paradigm is as follows: the user performs some task on a computer, such as retrieving information from a database while the EP system "watches over the user's shoulder," recording the interaction. As the task is performed, EP creates an algorithm or model of the interaction and uses it to construct a program to perform that task or some variant of it. User comments or advice are combined with prestored knowledge about the task domain to create a general-purpose program for performing tasks illustrated by the example.

This work represents a first step toward developing a system that can acquire knowledge from a programming-naive user and organize it into a form executable by a computer. The work is noteworthy because the problem involves applying induction techniques to a "real world," rather than "toy," application, and because solutions to this problem have an extremely high payoff. There are a few other systems that have been developed to create individual rules from examples in complex application areas; they are somewhat static, however, and do not attempt to handle a dynamic sequence of events.

Chapter 9, on knowledge acquisition and refinement, describes the authors' experiences and recommendations in developing machine-aided systems for knowledge acquisition and learning. After exploring alternative approaches, the authors focus on an incremental process in which initial knowledge is formulated by human experts. The machine-aided program iteratively refines this knowledge as indicated by the expert system's performance and experience. This process involves predicting probable consequences of actions, noticing unfulfilled expectations, isolating weaknesses in the existing knowledge base, and remedying them.

In this framework, a learning system must use existing knowledge to plan reasonable courses of action, carry out those plans, and then diagnose weaknesses that explain observed failures or unexpected successes. The processes of planning, acting, and evaluation cooperate to produce new knowledge by refining and extending prior knowledge. This approach blends machine capabilities with human expertise in the generation and iterative improvement of expert systems.

Chapter 10, on plausible inference, addresses the problems expert systems have in drawing inferences from domain knowledge when both the knowledge and its implications are less than certain. These problems include devising effective techniques to represent the uncertainty and propagating the certainty measures during the inference process. This work is particularly significant since domain knowledge is rarely certain and mechanisms for incorporating and effectively using uncertainty are critical for developing usable expert systems.

Methods typically used for plausible inference include subjective Bayesian reasoning, measures of belief and disbelief, and the Dempster-Shafer theory of evidence. Analysis of systems based on these methods reveals important deficiencies in areas such as the reliability of deductions and the ability to detect inconsistencies in the knowledge from which deductions were made. The system developed by Quinlan, called INFERNO, addresses some of these points. Its approach is probabilistic but makes no assumptions whatsoever about the joint probability distributions of pieces of knowledge; thus the correctness of inferences can be guaranteed. INFERNO informs the user of inconsistencies that may exist in the information presented to it, and makes suggestions about changing the information to make it consistent. Quinlan reworks an example from a Bayesian system and compares its conclusion with that reached by INFERNO.

Chapter 11, on distributed problem solving, reports on the results of an ongoing investigation of distributed problem solving for air fleet control. Distributed problem solving, or multiple-agent problem solving, refers to the process by which several agents interact to achieve common or related goals. This research is particularly noteworthy because it is one of the few efforts involved in the fairly new area of *distributed artificial intelligence,* and uses knowledge-based simulation to test various cooperative strategies and behaviors.

In this paper the authors describe the development of organizational structures for cooperative planning in complex, spatially distributed systems. They discuss the implementation of multiple cooperative agents, first in a domain-independent fashion, and then in the context of two task domains. The authors contrast the methodologies, difficulties, and opportunities of distributed and centralized problem solving. From this analysis, they postulate a set of requirements on the information-gathering and organizational policies of group problem-solving agents, and develop a general framework for implementing such policies. The authors then present a set of distributed problem solvers developed for air-traffic control and remotely piloted-vehicle fleet control. Finally, they describe some experimental findings that use the cooperative strategies, with particular emphasis on role assignment within the group and communications between group members.

Chapter 8

Exemplary Programming: Applications and Design Considerations

Donald A. Waterman, William S. Faught, Philip Klahr, Stanley J. Rosenschein, and Robert B. Wesson

8.1 Introduction

It would be useful, indeed, if each of us had a personal assistant to help us at the terminal. Many times we've had to rename a dozen files according to some simple criterion, or had to do some infrequent operation that we didn't quite remember how to do but never had time to construct a macro-program to do it for us. With the tremendous increase in useful program libraries and activities available through the terminal, such an assistant seems almost essential for everyone from the professional who doesn't have the time to learn every detail of a system to the office clerk who needs to do highly repetitive tasks but thinks DO loops are some kind of breakfast cereal.

This chapter is a revised version of N-1484-RC, The Rand Corporation, April 1980, and R-2411-ARPA, The Rand Corporation, February 1980. N-1484-RC also appeared in *Automatic Program Construction* (A. W. Biermann, G. Guiho, and Y. Kodratoff, eds.), Macmillan Publishing Co., N.Y., 1984, 433–460.

We are researching the ways and means of creating machine-based versions of a personal assistant. After analysis and the actual construction of two preliminary versions, we are ready to tackle the design of a program that can itself learn to mimic example tasks and remember how to perform the routine ones it has seen before. We call the method *exemplary programming* (EP), a type of program synthesis based on program specifications from examples of the task to be performed (Biermann & Krishnaswamy, 1976; Siklossy & Sykes, 1975; Green, 1976).

In many respects, EP relates to research in automatic programming (Balzer et al., 1978; Green, 1977; Heidorn, 1976; Manna & Waldinger, 1978). This research has examined various forms of program specification, including natural language, functional description, and predicate assertions of states or values to be obtained. Whereas these systems form a program from a given set of specifications, EP synthesizes a program from a user-system trace or protocol that represents an example of the task the user wants EP to synthesize into a program. In this sense it is related to the QBE (query-by-example) system developed by IBM for database retrieval. This system retrieves information based on examples of the type of information desired (Girdonsky & Neudecker, 1976).

Synthesizing programs by example has been studied from various viewpoints. Biermann emphasized step-by-step acquisition (Biermann & Krishnaswamy, 1976) and algorithms to locate branch points and loops within a program's control flow (Biermann et al., 1975). Work by Bauer (1979) has focussed on the need for a specification language within the paradigm for specifying branch conditions and functions—program constructs that are nearly impossible to infer by example.

8.1.1 ■ The EP Paradigm

The EP system "looks over the shoulder" of the user as he or she performs a task on the computer, and from this example creates a program called an *agent* to perform the same task. User comments or *advice* are combined with stored knowledge about the task domain to create a general-purpose program for performing tasks illustrated by the example.

The basic EP paradigm is illustrated in Fig. 8.1. The user interacts with an application program or operating system to perform a task. The EP program watches and saves the record or *trace* of the interaction as one example of how to perform the task. During the interaction the user may provide the EP program with advice clarifying the example. The trace, advice, and built-in knowledge about the task domain are used by the EP program to construct an *agent* for performing the task.

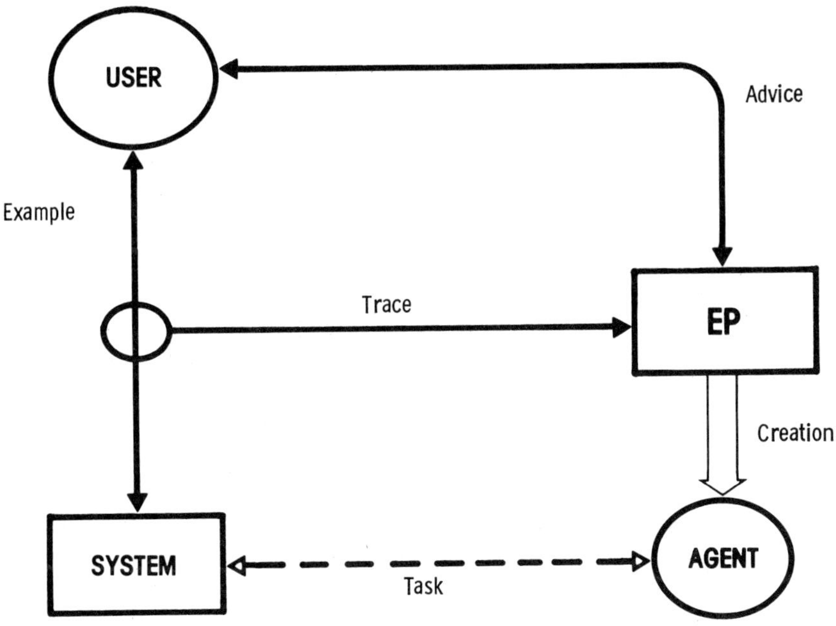

FIGURE 8.1 EP Paradigm.

As the agent attempts to perform the task, it may encounter conditions that did not occur during the example. At this point the user is notified and asked to interact again to provide an example of what to do in this new situation. The EP program monitors the interaction and augments the agent, enabling it to recognize and respond to the new situation when it occurs again. Thus, the agent is developed incrementally based on a number of different examples of task execution.

8.1.2 ■ Important Ideas in EP

The EP approach to program synthesis is based on four important ideas. The most fundamental idea is that of the *user agent* (Anderson, 1976b; Waterman, 1978a, 1978c). This is a program that can act as an interface between users and the computer systems they want to access. A user agent is typically a small program residing in a user's terminal or in a portion of a central timesharing system. It may display many of the characteristics of a human assistant, such as the ability to carry on a dialogue with the user or external computer systems or even other agents. The user agent is the target program we are attempting to create through use of the EP system.

Another important idea that pervades the EP system design is that of *concurrent processing*, an organization that permits the user-system interaction to take place concurrently with its analysis by the EP system and the subsequent creation of a user agent. Instead of having the EP system situated between the user and the external system, it sits off to one side (see Fig. 8.1), analyzing the trace as it is being generated. In our current prototype, EP-2, the EP system actually runs on a remote computer linked to the user-system interaction on the user's local computer. Thus the delay in response time seen by the user during agent creation is minimized. Debugging is facilitated by having the EP system execute the agent as the user watches. After debugging is complete, the agent can be compiled into an efficient form that runs directly on the user's local machine.

An important idea that has dominated the EP design philosophy has been *learning from examples* (Hayes-Roth, 1978). Example-based learning has been studied by researchers in artificial intelligence and cognitive psychology, particularly in the areas of concept formation (Hunt, 1962; Hayes-Roth and Hayes-Roth, 1977; Winston, 1975), serial pattern acquisition (Simon and Kotovsky, 1963; Waterman, 1976), and rule induction from examples (Hayes-Roth, 1976a, 1976b; Vere, 1978; Waterman, 1975). It is our contention that traces of the activity one would like performed in a human-machine environment contain a wealth of information about the task, the user, and the approach suggested by the user for attaining goals. Specification by example is a natural means of conveying information, one that minimizes the need for training the user in the operation of the program-synthesis technique. When supplemented with advice from the user about intentions and built-in knowledge about the task domain, the example becomes a powerful tool for program specification.

The final important idea incorporated into the design of both the EP system and the user agents it creates is that of *rule-based systems* (Waterman and Hayes-Roth, 1978a, 1978b). The rule-directed approach to knowledge acquisition has been the basis for a number of successful research projects, including MYCIN (Shortliffe, 1976), a system that contains condition-action rules that encode heuristics for diagnosis and treatment of infectious diseases, TIERESIAS (Davis, 1976), a rule-based approach for transferring expertise from a human to the knowledge base of a high-performance program, and Meta-DENDRAL, a program designed to formulate rules of mass spectrometry which describe the operation of classes of molecular structures (Buchanan, 1974). Other related systems include AM (Lenat, 1976, 1977; Lenat and Harris, 1978), which uses heuristic rules to develop concepts in mathematics, and SLIM and SPROUTER (Hayes-Roth, 1973, 1976a, 1976b; Hayes-Roth and McDermott, 1976, 1978), which infer general *condition -> action* rules from before-and-after examples of their use. The rule-based system design imposes a high degree of structure on the code, leading to a simple organization that facilitates debugging, verifiability, and incremental modification (Hayes-Roth et al., 1978).

8.1.3 ■ Applying EP: Task Domains and Difficulties

The EP paradigm is applicable to tasks that require repetitive, personalized user-system dialogue and can be described by one or more sequences of actions on some external system. Examples of these user-interactive tasks include computer network tasks (e.g., file transfers), operating systems tasks (e.g., file maintenance), database retrievals, and edit macros. Development of an advanced EP system will permit us to make inroads into the following problem areas involving effective use of computers: (1) the difficulty of correctly interacting with numerous systems and facilities, each of which requires a unique syntax and protocol; (2) the problem of remembering how to do something that an expert previously demonstrated; (3) the frustrating problem of repeating the same sequence of instructions to accomplish a frequently occurring task; and (4) the problem of generalizing specific command sequences to handle a more varied set of problem conditions.

There are, however, certain difficulties associated with the use of example-based programming. First is the basic problem of specifying a complex algorithm from examples of behavior traces. For most interesting classes of algorithms, a single behavior trace will generally be consistent with a large number of alternative algorithms. Since users of an EP system are trying to build a realization for an algorithm that could be arbitrarily complex, they can never be absolutely sure that the approximation constructed by example is close enough to the desired algorithm to meet their needs. This implies the necessity for an open-ended algorithm-construction paradigm, that is, the ability to extend the algorithm by example at any time during its construction or application by the user.

Implicit in all the EP work are the following conjectures: (1) interesting classes of algorithms can be defined by specification of behavior traces; (2) there are specific bases for choosing one algorithm over another; and (3) programs can be implemented to make this choice and synthesize the algorithms. Reasonable computer scientists may not agree that the first two conjectures are plausible. The skeptic might feel that the approach lacks merit because of the idiosyncratic nature of interesting algorithms. However, our previous work with exemplary programming has led us to believe that not only do such classes of algorithms exist, but they provide the basis for interesting and practical applications.

Another fundamental problem is how to integrate diverse sources of knowledge in the synthesis of an algorithm. For any particular application domain there will be several unique knowledge sources that can be used to help interpret the behavior trace. For example, in the operating system domain they might include expected input and output strings for each system command, simplified flowcharts of system commands, typical connected sequences of user actions (e.g., telnetting to a remote site and then logging in), and user advice for branches and loops. The problem of integrating knowledge sources necessitates the use of a special mechanism or representational technique, such as cooperating specialists (see Subsection 8.4.5).

Another problem is that a strict example-based paradigm tends to present information at a very low level only. High-level information, such as a description of the task, algorithm, and so on, can also be quite useful. Such a high-level language would effectively condense the information in many examples into a few concise statements. In our approach we touch on this idea through the application of *user advice* and defined *scripts* (see Subsection 8.5.1) that represent high-level abstractions of potential algorithms the user may want to implement.

Since much knowledge about the task domain is needed to help the system interpret the examples, the task domain must be well defined ahead of time. Thus, unexpected results during the execution of the example will be difficult to handle. Even worse, the examples must be error-free, or the EP system must have a way of recognizing errors when they occur. These errors can come from either the user or the system that is being accessed. We feel that the requirement of providing error-free examples is not so great a restriction as to negate the usefulness of the approach.

EP applies only to domains where there is an abundance of low-level feedback at short intervals, that is, a dialogue that represents or describes the relevant ongoing behavior. Consequently, the exemplary programming approach would not apply to synthesizing a sort function by giving examples of input–output pairs. However, if the algorithm could be demonstrated by actually sorting a list of items, showing all intermediate steps, then this approach might possibly be applicable.

Another problem is that in some interactions involving human-machine dialogue, the human performs crucial activities in his or her head that are relevant to the task. How to present these activities to the EP system is the question here. For example, a user lists files and deletes those with the prefix "bin" if he or she knows what is in the file. The

EP system might be able to infer that files with the prefix "bin" were being deleted but would not be able to deal with the later information.

The ideas we describe for an advanced EP system are clearly speculative, since they have not been implemented and tested. Our inital EP systems are only a beginning and do not prove that an advanced EP system such as the one we describe here can be developed. Many researchers have been stymied by the complexities of developing an automatic programming system. In our approach we hope to simplify the problem by limiting the automatic programming system to one that creates programs from examples rather than general specifications. But the task is still complex and difficult. Our approach is based on the deficiencies uncovered in developing previous EP systems. Although these previous systems produced only simple programs, they were both operational and useful. We hope the discussion that follows will shed light on new issues and ideas in the area of program synthesis.

Section 8.2 of this paper discusses EP-1, our initial version of an exemplary programming system. Section 8.3 describes the design and implementation of EP-2, our current EP System. Section 8.4 discusses design goals for an advanced version of EP, and Section 8.5 describes architectural considerations. The conclusions are presented in Section 8.6.

8.2 The EP-1 System

The first EP system, EP-1 (Waterman, 1978b, 1978c), was written in RITA (Anderson et al., 1977; Anderson & Gillogly, 1976b). In its acquisition mode, EP-1 "watches" the user perform some interactive task, queries the user about the task, and then produces a set of RITA rules to perform that task. Questioning the user is necessary because EP-1 contains no domain-specific knowledge.

The operation of EP-1 consists of two parts: *initialization* and the *basic cycle*, as follows:

1. *Initialization.* The user supplies a name for each type of data object relevant to this task.
2. *Basic Cycle.*
   a) The user sends a message to the external system and receives its reply.
   b) The user is asked for the current values of the data objects declared relevant during initialization.

c) A RITA rule is created. Its premises reflect the values of the data objects before the user sent his or her last message to the external system. Its actions reflect the content of the last message and its effect on the data objects.

d) The user continues by repeating the cycle and quits by typing "*finished*."

During initialization the user supplies a name for each type of data object relevant to the task. The basic cycle involves EP-1 watching the user interacting with the external system, querying the user, and creating appropriate RITA rules.

As an example, we will consider the New York Times Information Bank (NYTIB), which contains abstracts of recent newspaper articles. For a NYTIB retrieval task, the user might specify that the following two types of information are relevent.

- The status of the interaction (a term that describes the current status of the program, such as "define date range," or "search for abstracts"); and
- The value of the response (the response the user receives from the external system, e.g., "> " from the NTYIB program).

The user would also specify that "value of the response" is output information from the external system. EP-1 creates a new rule at the juncture of two cycles, using the information gained in the first cycle to define the premises of the rule and the information gained in the second cycle to define the actions. Figure 8.2 gives an example of the dialogue needed for rule creation in the NYTIB retrieval task.

The NYTIB retrieval task consists of logging into their computer system and answering from 10 to 20 queries designed to elicit the information necessary to retrieve and display abstracts of news articles relevant to the topic of interest. In the example of Fig. 8.2, the user had indicated interest in the "PLO" and "bombs," and immediately prior to cycle-1, the system had asked the user to specify the dates of interest. The user responded with the range April to June 1976. The system then displayed the current set of active topics and asked for a boolean expression to define the search. The user specified a search for topic 1 alone and received information regarding the number of relevant abstracts found.

The rule created from the two cycles of dialogue in Fig. 8.2 is shown here. Note that the premises are extracted from cycle-1 and the actions from cycle-2.

```
RULE M:
  IF:    the status OF the interaction IS "search for abstracts"
         & the value OF the response CONTAINS {"> "}
```

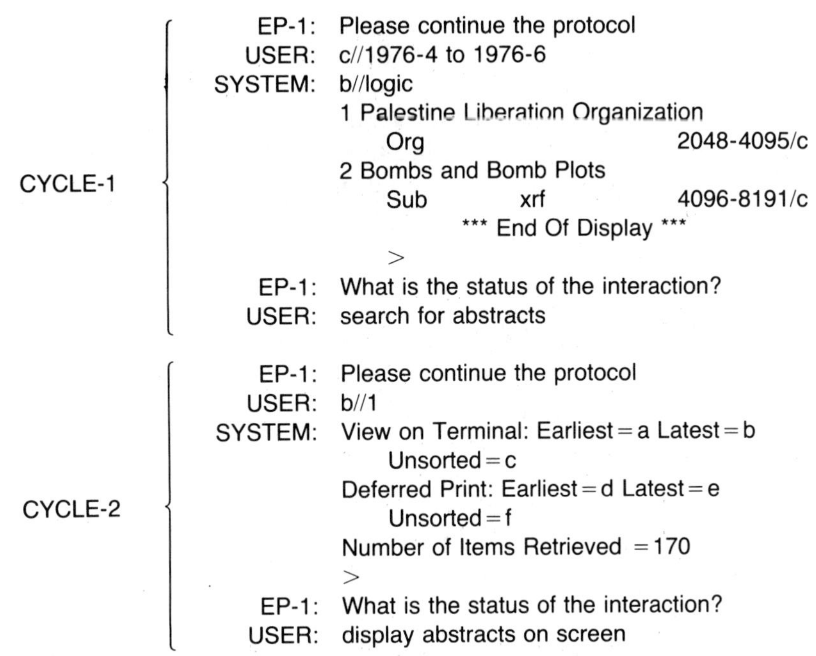

```
CYCLE-1
     EP-1:  Please continue the protocol
     USER:  c//1976-4 to 1976-6
   SYSTEM:  b//logic
            1 Palestine Liberation Organization
                 Org                          2048-4095/c
            2 Bombs and Bomb Plots
                 Sub          xrf             4096-8191/c
                         *** End Of Display ***
                 >
     EP-1:  What is the status of the interaction?
     USER:  search for abstracts

CYCLE-2
     EP-1:  Please continue the protocol
     USER:  b//1
   SYSTEM:  View on Terminal: Earliest=a Latest=b
                 Unsorted=c
            Deferred Print: Earliest=d Latest=e
                 Unsorted=f
            Number of Items Retrieved  =170
            >
     EP-1:  What is the status of the interaction?
     USER:  display abstracts on screen
```

FIGURE 8.2 Two Cycles of Dialogue Needed for Rule Creation in EP-1.

```
THEN:  SET the status OF the interaction TO
            "display abstracts on screen"
       & SET the value OF the response TO " "
       & SET the reply OF the agent TO "b//1";
```

This rule could be paraphrased as, "If it is the time to search for abstracts and the system (NYTIB) has indicated it is ready by giving the appropriate response (in this case, a prompt character), then note that the next step will be to display the abstracts on the screen, set the value of the response to the empty string, and note that the choice 'b//1' should be sent to the system (NYTIB)." The "reply OF the agent" is an EP-1 variable that is sent to the external system by other rules in the set.

EP-1 employs generalization only in limited ways. It generalizes the response of the external system by considering only the first few characters of the last line of output. This was adequate for many tasks, but to expand the range of tasks it could handle, EP-1 would need specific knowledge about the tasks, including rules describing which components of the system response are likely to be invariant. EP-1 also generalizes the task agents by permitting the user to specify which replies to the external system are invariant and which should be acquired by the task agent as it is executing. The result is an interactive task agent that queries the user and passes replies to the system. In the preceding example, the user might indicate that the date range and the boolean expression defining the range of the search were variables. In this case the task agent would query the user for these values instead of always retrieving abstracts concerning the PLO from April to June 1976.

The main drawback to EP-1 is that the user has to supply extensive information after each user-system interaction. In addition, EP-1 has no user aids such as a library of agents or separation of communication channels. As a first test of EP design principles, however, EP-1 was effective.

8.3 The EP-2 System

The latest EP system, EP-2, is patterned after EP-1. EP-2, however, extends and develops the ideas in that initial prototype.

8.3.1 ■ Basic Structure

EP-2 operates in three stages: *trace acquisition, trace interpretation,* and *program creation*. First, EP-2 watches the user perform a series of operations on the computer and saves the trace of the user-system interaction. Next, EP-2 maps the trace into a model of the interaction that is more general than the trace and is in the form of a graph describing the flow of control during the interaction. Finally, EP-2 transforms the model into a program composed of rules whose conditions represent nodes in the graph and whose actions represent transitions from one node to the next. The program or agent is stored in the user's library under a name supplied by the user. To activate the agent, the user supplies the agent name, usually a natural language command (e.g., "print 2 copies of file foo").

The EP-2 system requires three major information channels: *user-system, user-EP,* and *EP-system*. A switch called the *front end* (FE), situated on the user's local system, coordinates and directs the information flow along these channels. The user-system channel is used by EP-2 to obtain trace information during agent creation, and the user-EP channel permits the exchange of advice and instructions between EP-2 and the user. The EP-system channel is used to send input to the system when executing stored agents.

EP-2 has three basic modes: *dormant*, *create*, and *execute*. When the system is in the dormant mode, the user interacts with it through the front end while EP-2 does nothing. When the system is in the agent-creation mode, the user first gives it the name of the agent, that is, the *agent call*. The call may have *variable* items in it. Values for the variables are subsequently assigned when the user executes the agent. The user then interacts with the system through the FE, and the FE marks and sends all these messages to EP-2 so that they may be incorporated into the *trace*. The trace is a verbatim description of the interaction, including user advice. EP-2 processes the trace (either incrementally or all at once) to create a *model*. A user who wants to correct an error can edit the trace. When the user edits the trace, the current model is deleted and a new model is constructed from the edited (and presumably correct) trace by reprocessing the trace. An interpretable version of the model is then stored as a program (or "agent") in a *library* under the name provided by the user. (The trace is also stored.) When the user calls an agent, EP-2 goes into execute mode; it locates and reads the model from the library and then interprets it in a manner similar to executing an ordered production system.

The model is a data structure that represents the algorithm the user had in mind to perform the actions shown in the trace. The model is represented as a graph structure of nodes and arcs. The nodes represent states. The arcs have two components: conditions and actions. Several arcs may originate from each node (state). During execution, EP-2 tests the conditions on all the arcs emanating from a particular node. The arc whose condition is true (there should be at most one) is the branch to be taken. The arc's action is executed and the state of the agent is set to the succeeding node.

8.3.2 ■ Applications of EP-2

We briefly describe two prototypical applications of EP-2 to illustrate the kinds of agents that have been constructed by example. (The reader is referred to Faught et al., (1980) for more detailed discussions and examples.)

The first application is a network access task. An agent is created to retrieve a file from a remote system, print it on a local printer, and delete the extra copy from the local system. The agent call is "print <filename> from <remote system name>." The user demonstrates the protocol using operating system and file transfer commands. A trace of this protocol is shown in Appendix A.

The second application is a database retrieval task using the LADDER system (Sacerdoti, 1977; Hendrix et al., 1978) operating on a naval database. This application uses several subagents, all constructed by example. The global agent's call is "<ship type> within <distance> miles." The global agent then calls the subagents in turn. The first subagent logs into a remote system using the ARPANET and starts the LADDER system. The second subagent writes several definitions in the LADDER system's language. The third subagent types a specification to LADDER using the global agent's parameters. The fourth subagent logs out of the LADDER system. Finally, the fifth subagent edits a transcript of the LADDER session and appends the transcript to a log of LADDER sessions. The advantages of the database application are that the user does not have to remember a complicated protocol and is freed from a time-consuming, laborious task. See Appendix B for an example of an EP-2 LADDER scenario.

EP-2 is also useful for constructing tutorial agents that demonstrate the use of some applications programs, such as a message system, and then allow the user to try it. Subagents can even be created to demonstrate various system commands. This capability of EP can be used to provide a general facility for creating tutorial programs on any user-interactive system.

8.3.3 ■ Evaluation of EP-2

EP-2 has been successful at helping users produce simple interactive software by example. It allows agent creation, editing by example to correct errors, agent storing in a library that catalogs and indexes the agents, and agent execution on request. The computer operating systems and database retrieval systems domains used to test EP-2 cover a large set of interesting, repetitive, time-consuming tasks appropriate for exemplary programming.

However, EP-2 does have its drawbacks. The EP-2 system is limited to creating agents with straight-line code and simple loops, which severely restricts the usefulness of the resulting agent. Biermann (1976) developed algorithms for synthesizing flowcharts that could be applied to EP. The main problem is limiting the search space of possible flowcharts. A semantic knowledge base (see Section 8.4) is needed to help limit this space. EP-2 relies primarily on simple syntactic information, such as system prompts, and does not contain semantic knowledge of the user-system interaction. EP-2 needs knowledge bases containing both domain and programming constructs. For example, a database of typical programming constructs, such as "for" loops or sequential file reading, could greatly simplify understanding the branch conditions and data flow in user protocols. Tables of system input and output could be used to help select candidate global-agent variables and track data flows through the agent. Finally, flowcharts of system programs could list the possible system responses at each point and help EP-2 identify potential branches in the agent.

8.4 Design Goals for an Advanced Exemplary Programming System

As a result of our experience with EP-2 we are now able to formulate some basic design goals for the next-generation EP system, EP-3. This section discusses four basic goals to be used to guide the design of the EP-3 system.

The first basic goal is *example-generalization,* that is, mapping specific examples of user interactions into a general procedure applicable in other situations. The example-generalization ability of EP-2 is somewhat superficial; it does not represent deep learning in the sense of producing analogous behavior in new contexts. The second goal involves the *acquisition and application of domain knowledge.* In EP-2, little domain knowledge is built in and no accommodations are made for acquiring new knowledge of this type automatically. The third goal is *induction of program structure.* This involves recognizing regularities in the trace and mapping them into appropriate program constructs, such as loops and branches. Because EP-2 is not able to handle this problem, it is severely limited in its scope of application. The final goal is *human engineering.* Although significant effort is put into making EP-2 helpful and easy to use, there is much room for improvement. For each area, we consider several feasible approaches for an advanced exemplary programming system and attempt to reach realistic design goals for EP-3.

8.4.1 ■ Superficial vs. Deep Learning

The task of the EP system is to observe a user's behavior and acquire the ability to produce analogous behavior in the future. The problem is defining what we mean by *analogous.*

On the one hand, we would certainly not want to equate *analogous* with *identical;* a system capable of creating only *verbatim* agents would be of little use. On the other hand, it is unreasonable to define analogous as "achieving the user's main goal by any means available," since this implies unlimited problem-solving abilities on the part of EP. EP's capabilities should lie somewhere between these two extremes.

In defining EP's ability to analogize, two components can be discerned: (1) how we define the class of behaviors that EP can *recognize,* and (2) once recognized, to what extent these behaviors can be *operationalized* or instantiated in new contexts. The most realistic approach to the first component is to provide EP with an extensible set of schemata and some rules for recognizing instances of a schema or relatively simple combinations of schemata. Since the second component potentially involves the ability to synthesize arbitrary programs, a realistic approach would be to provide EP with a repertoire of specialized techniques guaranteed to operationalize those schematic actions it can recognize.

The EP system can still exhibit a good deal of flexibility in learning even when schemata are provided in advance. For instance, a schema may be only partially specified, with the remaining parts to be extracted from the trace. The complexity of the resulting structures may be considerable and, in a sense, may blur the distinction between recognition and learning.

8.4.2 ■ Domain-specific Knowledge

The EP system will require domain-specific knowledge to be effective in helping users perform useful tasks. For example, to create an agent to help the user logon to a variety of machines, EP must know the appropriate logon sequence for each machine and must recognize that this is the agent the user wants. By observing the user complete a logon sequence on a familiar machine, EP might infer that certain basic steps are necessary in a logon agent.

A more complicated task is creating an agent capable of executing an analysis program on a text file and printing the result, given the name and directory location of the program and file. If the example trace illustrates this process for a program and data residing in the local machine, a basic problem is determining the kind of knowledge EP needs to generalize to the case of arbitrary machines accessed over a network. EP would have to know how a program's input dataset is defined under different operating systems. EP would also have to know what operating system was running on a particular machine. These facts could be learned by observation of the user on other occasions (given that EP can recognize specific operating systems), or they could be built-in knowledge. EP would also have to know how to logon to remote systems and transfer files. Some of this knowledge is obviously general and should be built in. Nonetheless, many details (e.g., specific logon sequences) could be learned from repeated observations or from user advice.

One promising approach is to build into EP numerous descriptions of commonplace activities that require domain knowledge. This should be done in a way that allows EP to fill in details later through observation and advice. Thus EP will learn not only what the user does, but also relatively permanent domain knowledge.

8.4.3 ■ Learning Algorithmic Structures

Much of EP's effort will be spent determining the desired internal structure of the agent it is to construct. It tries to answer such questions as: Are these three user commands that look so similar really instances of a single command being executed repeatedly in a loop, or are the similarities coincidental? Why did the user put the results of a certain operation in a certain file? Which file should be used in general?

To answer questions like these, EP needs more than just domain knowledge. It must know what kinds of things users typically do, and how they do them. This knowledge should be at various levels of abstraction. For instance, EP should be able to interpret a segment of a user-typed string from multiple viewpoints: a string, the name of a file, an argument of a certain operator, and so on. Furthermore, EP should contain heuristics for identifying common control structures using all the syntactic and semantic cues at its disposal.

8.4.4 ■ Human Engineering

Looking at the intended users of EP and the anticipated characteristic applications, it becomes clear why the success of EP is so dependent on effective human engineering. EP is for use by both novices and experts. It helps them use computers by letting them do things they don't know how to do themselves, and by doing things faster and more conveniently. A poorly designed system that frustrates the user would defeat the purpose of EP.

The design should explicitly take into account the various classes of users EP will serve: ARPAnet users, application programmers, editors, novices using special subsystems, and so on. Each type of user has different needs, approaches to programming, and levels of understanding. For example, it may be convenient to allow an experienced programmer to give EP advice with standard notions such as variable, parameter, and so on. Yet a nonprogrammer who uses the computer just to send and receive messages should not have to confront these concepts when using EP.

The general characteristics we seek are reliability, clarity, and ease of use. EP should make it easy to correct errors, make small modifications to existing agents, and retrieve agents by name and by a description of their purpose. The user should be able to give EP advice, when appropriate, in a natural and concise way. These considerations play a role in the design of both the user interface and the agents themselves.

8.4.5 ■ General Considerations

Since this knowledge is likely to be diverse, incomplete, and often fragmented, it is essential that EP's basic design take these characteristics into consideration. A design well suited to handling information of this type is one based on *cooperating specialists*. For EP, each specialist would offer a partial characterization of the trace from its own point of view (e.g., file command specialist, common loop recognizer). Synthesis specialists would integrate these views, thus producing the final agent. An important advantage of this approach is the ability to control the allocation of processing resources directly by intelligent scheduling of specialists. This is especially important for EP, given the large space of alternative interpretations of a trace and the amount of unnecessary information (e.g., the exact contents of a file being displayed but not used in any other way).

8.5 Architectural Considerations for EP-3

In this section, we explore the architectural alternatives for the EP-3 system. Drawing from our research discussions and experience, as well as from implementations of related ideas, we delineate the specific EP-3 architectures that satisfy the design goals of Section 8.4 and are most likely to achieve high performance using current technology.

Recall that the problem for our new system is to

1. Construct a structure that accounts for the sequence of user actions (the trace) in some general sense;
2. Acquire and apply domain-specific knowledge to the problem of recognizing user intentions;
3. Learn the algorithmic structure of complex agents; and
4. Provide a helpful interface for both new and sophisticated users.

A good model for what we expect this structure to be can be found in the interaction between an experienced computer terminal user and a novice. "Now, compile the programs, leaving the source code in the SOURCE directory and the object code in the RUN directory," is a typical high-level instruction from the experienced teacher. It specifies a goal-oriented task, omitting such details as the implicit loop when more than one program exists and the syntactic distinctions that must be made between source and object code names in the machine. Like the novice, our EP-3 must be capable of storing the general and specific knowledge about user activities and using that knowledge to understand the trace at various levels of abstraction.

At the foundation of many of the architectures we have considered is the *generate-and-test* problem-solving paradigm. EP-3 will operate by proposing explanations of the trace and correlating them with what is actually present. One possibility is to make EP-3 a *model-directed* system, proceeding from the more abstract to the specific by initially assuming a particular user activity, deducing the required specifics, and checking them against the trace. Another is to make EP-3 a *data-directed* system, using specific trace sequences to suggest the more abstract concepts. EP-3 could apply both of these approaches, combining the best of both worlds. These approaches are detailed and evaluated here.

A common framework for this discussion can be found in the Hearsay-II speech-understanding system (Erman & Lessor, 1975; Lessor & Erman, 1977). A somewhat modified form of its terminology will be used here, as the following synopsis of its structure and operation suggests: A common data structure, the *blackboard*, is shared among many *knowledge source* (KS) modules. Each KS, an expert at what it does, is responsible for a specific subpart of the problem. The KSs share their information by writing *hypotheses* on the blackboard. A hypothesis may be an explanation of some part of the data stream, or it may be a prediction that some datum should be present. KSs *support* and *reject* the hypotheses posed by other KSs. When a set of mutually supportive hypotheses emerges beyond some threshold level, or the computational resources are exhausted, the program stops and the hypotheses are its solution. This short description of the Hearsay-II architecture should suffice for our purposes. We will, of course, be introducing other concepts and terms and redefining the preceding ones for our purposes, but their basic meanings remain.

8.5.1 ■ Model-directed Inference

Consider first a goal-directed technique — hypothesize first and confirm later. We call this technique *model-directed inference*, because the system is assumed initially to possess models of the computer systems to be used, the tasks to be performed, and possibly the user. Such a system operates by inferring the meaning of the trace from these models, as well as by using the trace to extend the models.

Turning to the novice user for illustration, assume that EP-3 could somehow represent the concepts necessary for temporal sequencing as well as more primitive ones such as compiling, file transfer, and directory. It could thus have models to represent expected user activities at various levels of detail and generality encoded in these concepts. The syntax, expected output, and reasons for issuing a compile monitor command would be included in system models, and more specific information such as the fact that this user typically renames the compiler output files according to some convention before storing them away would be part of a user model. Using these concepts, EP-3 could make predictions about what it should see in the trace. The selection of specific components of models to represent hypotheses about segments of user activity could be activated by many clues, from the compile statement in the trace to a user directive stating, "I'm going to do some compiling now." When activated, these components automatically establish a complex context that simplifies EP-3's understanding of the lower-level actions appearing in the trace.

We will call the action sequences that represent a unified higher-level activity *scripts* because they resemble drama scripts by specifying contexts and sequences of actions to be performed (Schank & Abelson, 1977). Our scripts are more general than those of the playwright because they allow choice points and alternative behaviors. A compile script for our imaginary user might look like this:

1. Locate the source code to be compiled, for example, <source>
2. Issue the monitor command "Compile <source>"
3. Then do any of the following:
   Edit and recompile if errors; or
   Test-run the object code; or
   Rename the object code; or
   Do nothing here.
4. Save the object code.

Scripts might exist at various *levels of abstraction*. The preceding script, for instance, could be part of a larger *program construction* script composed of many lower-level scripts that further specify its own abstractions (e.g., there might be a "locate source code" script for the first action in the preceding script).

We envision the hypothesizing of user activities to begin at the highest level. Thus, for example, there will be scripts that specify a typical user's daily activities, such as logging in, checking and reading mail, deleting old or unused files, and editing some files. There will also be scripts for different types of users, such as system maintainers, editors, application programmers, and ARPAnet users. Thus, the EP-3 system would initially have some idea of what a user typically accomplishes in a computer session.

These models of potential user activities will generate expectations about what the user is doing and is going to do. We anticipate that they will not be used in a purely top-down manner, but rather will guide the pattern-matching inherent in both model-directed and pattern-directed inference. Particular items in the trace might suggest that a specific script is being used, and the expectations generated by that script can then be matched against the actual trace data and the script instantiated or rejected in favor of another. Once a particular script has been validated as what the user did, it provides a high-level representation of that behavior and can be reinstantiated to replicate it. When a script includes alternative means of accomplishing a goal, the reinstantiation might perform the task more efficiently than the original user keystrokes, thereby realizing true expertise by helping the user perform a task better than before.

In summary, we see four main uses for our proposed scripts:

- *Recognizers.* Scripts recognize that certain activities are being performed by a user;
- *Predictors.* Scripts predict subsequent commands and activities in the trace; the confirmation of such predictions will improve the credibility of the proposed scripts;
- *Evaluators.* Scripts can support or refute existing hypotheses about user actions; and
- *Generators.* Scripts can generate agents by being instantiated within a particular computer environment.

Note that the use of scripts as generators enables an EP-3 agent to be specified at a high, abstract level. Executing an agent would involve the instantiation of the specified scripts relative to the current computer environment. Thus, for example, an agent can be created on one machine and then executed on another machine. The data independence of these high-level scripts is a necessary requirement for transferring agents between system environments.

8.5.2 ■ Pattern-directed Inference

At the other end of the spectrum of understanding programs lie those whose activities are almost purely data directed. Many *pattern-directed inference* systems are of this character (Waterman and Hayes-Roth, 1978a). They possess little control structure; instead, the incoming data stream fires recognition rules that perform actions upon that stream and other internal data.

Applied to the domain of exemplary programming, such a system would proceed in a bottom-up fashion, drawing inferences from what the user did at the lowest level—the primitive trace actions—to determine what higher-level goals the user was trying to accomplish. Encoded within a production system framework (Davis and King, 1976), the knowledge sources for EP-3 might be of the following sort:

Rule "Look for a compile call":
  IF there is a "Compile <source>" monitor call anywhere in the trace
  THEN generate the hypothesis "Compiling <source> at trace location x"

Rule "Look for a save call":
  IF there is a "Save <program>" monitor call anywhere in the trace
  THEN generate the hypothesis "Saving <program> at trace location y"

Rule "Look for a compile sequence":
  IF there is a hypothesis "Compiling <source> at trace location x"
  & there is a hypothesis "Saving <program> at trace location y"
  & <program> is the object version of <source>
  & location x is just before location y
  THEN generate the hypothesis "Compile sequence between x and y"

An EP-3 with perhaps hundreds of these rules would successively generate more and more abstract hypotheses directly from the trace. As with most data-directed behavior, this approach might achieve impressive levels of accomplishment if there are enough constraints and redundancies in the data. Care must be taken, however, to avoid pursuit of long search paths obviously at odds with the overall solution being generated.

8.5.3 ■ Suggested Architecture

The most promising architecture appears to be one that combines the model-directed and pattern-directed approaches (cf. Nii and Feigenbaum, 1978). Working top-down when a script is being checked out and bottom-up to generate the script hypotheses, this architecture would use each approach when appropriate. Control, and therefore search, would proceed opportunistically, much as humans are said to do (Hayes-Roth and Hayes-Roth, 1978). Although there would be a knowledge source to provide overall focus when required, for the most part, each knowledge source would be free to operate in a manner most amenable to its particular specialty. Some would, for example, examine the data and propose explanations (pattern-directed), and others would try to instantiate high-level scripts (model-directed).

The architecture proposed here follows this theme. We have tried to be specific when possible, making the design choices necessary to achieve opportunistic analysis along the lines of a Hearsay-II type of structure. The executive, for example, is not specified, but clearly needs to contain a scheduler to resolve duplicate KS firings. This architecture results from our efforts to produce an EP-3 design that will achieve the highest level of performance possible with current technology.

The data structure chosen is the first instance of a change to the Hearsay-II structure. As others have done (e.g., Englemore and Nii, 1977), we divide the blackboard into several levels. The example we present here concerns the transfer of a set of files from one machine to another. An initial specification of blackboard levels and examples relative to transferring files includes:

1. Scripts:

   Top-level knowledge about typical activities users are likely to do and how they do them; for example,

   STORE-FILES script:
       copy {fileset} from <from-machine> to <to-machine>

2. Abstract procedures:

   The steps needed to execute a script specified at an abstract level; for example,

   for STORE-FILES script:
       logon to <from-machine>
       determine set of files to transfer—{fileset}
       execute <file-transfer-program> (<to-machine>)
       logon to <to-machine>
       foreach <file> in {fileset} do
           copy <file> from <from-machine> to <to-machine>

   These abstract procedures become concrete when they are instantiated according to a particular computer environment.

3. Specific procedures:

   Instantiations of the preceding steps in a formalized language. For example, the "foreach" statement represented as a specific procedure:

   ENVIRONMENT:
       <FROM-MACHINE>: unix
       <TO-MACHINE>: ecl
       <FILE-TRANSFER-PROGRAM>: ftp

```
VARS:
     fileset: SET OF unix-FILE;
     from-filename: unix-FILE;
     to-filename: ecl-FILE;
WHILE NOT NULL(fileset) DO
BEGIN
     from-filename <- NEXT-ELEMENT(fileset);
     USER-SEND (CONCAT("store",from-filename,to-filename);
     note: to-filename is bound to anything
            fitting type descr.
IF NOT (SYS-SEND(...,"250...",...,"252...",">"))
THEN ERROR("bad file transfer," etc.)
END.
```

4. Abstract trace:

   A generalization of the actual trace, with specific commands and their parameters replaced by typed variables. For example, the last part of the STORE-FILES script:

```
Sys:  Connect...                   LOGON
Sys:  300 USC-ECL..                  variables:
Sys:  >                                to-machine
Usr:  USER WATERMAN                      TYPE:    op-sys
Sys:  330...                             VALUE:   ecl
Sys:  >                                environment
Usr:  PASS ABC              =>           TYPE:    program
Sys:  230...                             VALUE:   ftp
Sys:  >                                user-sent
Usr:  ACCT 701                           TYPE:    Boolean
Sys:  200...                           VALUE:   true
                                       password-sent
                                         TYPE:    Boolean
                                         VALUE:   true
                                       acct-sent
                                         TYPE:    Boolean
                                         VALUE:   True
Sys:  >                            STORE
Usr:  store...                       variables:
Sys:  200...                           from-filename
Sys:  255...                =>           TYPE:    <from-machine>file
Sys:  250...                           VALUE:    code.ep
Sys:  252...                           to-filename
   .                                     TYPE:    <to-machine>file
   .                                     VALUE:   code.ep
   .                                   successful-transfer
   .                                     TYPE:    Boolean
   .                                     VALUE:   True
```

5. Actual trace

   Obvious; see for example the left preceding column.

We will then have the KSs operating between the levels, generating, evaluating, and deleting hypotheses. Some of the KSs might look like:

ENVIRONMENT-SCANNER (level 5 -> level 4)
Task: Scans the actual trace to instantiate the environment variables at the abstract-trace level.
Knowledge: Operating systems, application programs.

TRACE-GENERALIZER (level 5 -> level 4)
Task: Scans the actual trace trying to recognize trace segments that it can hypothesize on the abstract trace level.
Knowledge: Operating systems, application programs.

HYPOTHESIZE (levels 2, 3, 4 -> level 1)
Task: At any time, sufficient information may be present in the lower levels to make a very good guess about what the user is doing. Once a script hypothesis has been made, the system can operate top-down to instantiate its holes. In this domain, particularly, it may be possible to make an accurate guess at the correct script early on.
Knowledge: User goals, script descriptions.

SPECIFY-PROCEDURES (levels 2 -> level 3)
Task: Instantiate the abstract procedures at level 2 by hypothesizing specific procedures at level 3.
Knowledge: User goals, operating systems, application programs.

REALIZE-SCRIPT (level 1 -> levels 2, 3)
Task: Once a script has been hypothesized, generate all hypotheses spawned by it at level 2. A lot of user-specific knowledge might be incorporated here, for example, "User X usually lists files before doing a transfer" might signify a step at level 2, or "User X usually lists files using 'ls -l'" might appear at level 3.
Knowledge: Script description, user goals.

DATA-VALIDATION (levels 4, 5 -> level 3)
Task: By looking at the trace, some information may be found to validate hypotheses at level 3.
Knowledge: Operating systems, application programs, programming constructs.

DATA-FLOW (levels 4, 5 -> level 3)
Task: By looking at the trace, some information may be hypothesized at level 3.
Knowledge: Operating systems, application programs, programming constructs.

ADVICE-TAKER (level 5 -> all other levels)
Task: Advice is used to interpret the trace and make hypotheses at all other levels. Trying to figure out

what someone is doing without specific knowledge of the person's intentions is extremely difficult. Allowing EP-3 to take even the simplest advice may be the avenue to large increases in performance. Information from the user on the trace ("now I'm doing ...") can be applied at almost every level to limit the number of alternative hypotheses being considered.

Knowledge: Advice grammar, user goals, operating systems, application programs.

STATE-DETERMINER (levels 4, 5 -> levels 1, 2, 3)

Task: Determining the relevance of trace information. The upper levels will need to know whether certain "spurious" trace information affected their hypotheses. For example, if the user does:

```
% dir
...system lists user files
% pwd
...prints working directory
% ftp ecl
...executes file transfer program
```

the KS hypothesizing a "STORE-FILES" script needs to know if "pwd" is important. This KS should know about such things.

Knowledge: User goals, operating systems, application programs

SYMBOLIC-EXECUTOR (level 3 <-> level 4)

Task: When a specific program has been hypothesized enough to execute it symbolically, this KS does so and compares the results to the trace information at level 4.

Knowledge: Programming constructs.

A novel feature of this particular representation comes as a side-effect of the recognition process. When the entire trace has been "explained" as a particular instance of some script, what falls out is a rather formal program, complete with state and environment variables, loops, and so on. The program can then be used to tackle EP-3's "generational" problem—performing the same tasks itself. Operationally, this model is similar to the opportunistic planner since it generates its plan as a data-driven side-effect of the more direct answer to the question: How do we get from START to GOAL (or FINISH)?

Once such a plan (program) has been generated, with suitable KSs available, EP-3 can proceed to apply it to new tasks:

1. Directly, by substituting new values for variables where requested and defaulting to the stored ones when necessary; or
2. Even more intelligently, by using the script information and some evaluation KSs to generate alternate, more efficient ways to accomplish the same thing.

As previously noted, the realization of this scheme requires that EP possess a great deal of domain-specific knowledge—in this example, various ways of doing a file transfer.

8.6 Conclusions

The EP methodology has the potential to make a significant impact on the computing community because it cuts across task domains, system requirements, and user types. It is most appropriate for repetitive tasks involving extensive human-machine dialogue. The program created by the EP system acts as a repository of information about how to perform the task and as an autonomous agent capable of performing that task. As shown by the discussion of EP-2 applications, the EP paradigm is also useful for tasks composed of many similar subtasks. The user performs a few of the subtasks while the EP system watches, and the user then tells the system to do the rest itself. Not only is an agent created to perform the task, the user is relieved of providing the EP system with a repetitious example.

An essential part of the design of an advanced EP system is a pattern interpretation component. We have described a multilevel framework for this component based on the Hearsay-II architecture that combines a model-directed top-down approach to program synthesis with a pattern-directed bottom-up approach.

The model-directed approach, based on scripts, provides a concise way to represent contiguous, context-dependent knowledge. It merges nicely with the learning-by-example paradigm, suggesting more sophisticated future extensions such as automatic script acquisition by example. The mechanism suggested for the advanced EP system contains most of the machinery needed for monitoring, analyzing, reformulating, and storing examples as new scripts. Thus, this approach lends itself to the problem of learning permanent domain knowledge.

The pattern-directed approach, based on data-directed evocation of rules, is a useful way to represent the knowledge sources that map knowledge from one level to another. It facilitates both recognizing behavior in a trace and putting that behavior into operation in new contexts. Maintaining these specialized KS experts not only gives us the modularity and clarity needed to promote good human engineering but also allows us as system designers to incorporate as much high-level expertise as is needed in the individual modules. Thus KSs involved in particularly difficult tasks such as recognizing regularities in the trace and mapping them into conventional programming constructs can be easily expanded and augmented until they contain enough expertise to perform as desired.

A fundamental problem related to the use of exemplary programming for program construction is the handling of unexpected or novel tasks that are demonstrated by example. In this situation the model-directed approach may be of little help, since existing scripts will tend not to match the example in a consistent manner. Furthermore, the data-directed approach may lead to false interpretations of the user's intent, since without sufficiently primed knowledge sources, the example could appear ambiguous. To handle this difficult type of situation, the EP approach may have to be used in conjunction with other program synthesis techniques, such as summarizing the task in a high-level language or describing the algorithm used.

References

1. Anderson, R. H., and J. J. Gillogly, "The Rand Intelligent Terminal Agent (RITA) as a Network Access Aid," *AFIPS Proceedings,* Vol. 45, 1976(a), pp. 501–509.
2. Anderson, R. H., and J. J. Gillogly, *Rand Intelligent Terminal Agent (RITA): Design Philosophy,* The Rand Corporation, R-1809-ARPA, February 1976(b).
3. Anderson, R. H., M. Gallegos, J. J. Gillogly, R. Greenberg, and R. Villanueva, *RITA Reference Manual,* The Rand Corporation, R-1808-ARPA, September 1977.
4. Balzer, R., N. Goldman, and D. Wile, "Informality in Program Specifications," *IEEE Transactions on Software Engineering,* March 1978.
5. Bauer, M. A., "Programming by Examples," *Artificial Intelligence,* Vol. 12, No. 1, 1979.
6. Biermann, A. W., *Regular LISP Programs and Their Automatic Synthesis from Examples,* Computer Science Department Report CS-1976-12, Duke University, 1976.
7. Biermann, A. W., R. I. Baum, and R. E. Petry, "Speeding up the Synthesis of Programs from Traces," *IEEE Transactions on Computers,* Vol. C-24, No. 2, 1975.
8. Biermann, A. W., and R. Krishnaswamy, "Constructing Programs from Example Computations," *IEEE Transactions on Software Engineering,* Vol. SE-2, No. 3, 1976.

9. Buchanan, J. R., *A Study in Automatic Programming,* Computer Science Report, Carnegie-Mellon University, 1974.
10. Davis, R., *Applications of Meta Level Knowledge to the Construction, Maintenance and Use of Large Knowledge Bases,* AI Memo AIM-283, Stanford University, 1976.
11. Davis, R., and J. King, "An Overview of Production Systems," in *Machine Intelligence* (E. W. Elcock and D. Michie, eds.), Wiley, New York, 1976, pp. 300–332.
12. Englemore, R. S., and H. P. Nii, *A Knowledge-based System for the Interpretation of Protein X-ray Crystallographic Data,* STAN-CS-77-589, Stanford University, 1977.
13. Erman, L. D., and V. R. Lesser, "A Multi-level Organization for Problem Solving Using Many Diverse Cooperating Sources of Knowledge," *Proceedings of the Fourth International Joint Conference on Artificial Intelligence,* 1975, pp. 483–490.
14. Faught, W. S., D. A. Waterman, P. Klahr, S. J. Rosenschein, D. M. Gorlin, and S. J. Tepper, *EP-2: An Exemplary Programming System,* The Rand Corporation, R-2411-ARPA, 1980.
15. Girdonsky, M., and R. Neudecker, "Making the Computer Easier to Use," *IBM Research Highlights,* November 1976.
16. Green, C., "The Design of the PSI Program Synthesis System," *Proceedings of the Second International Conference on Software Engineering,* San Francisco, California, 1976, pp. 4–18.
17. Green, C., "A Summary of the PSI Program Synthesis System," *Proceedings of the Fifth International Joint Conference on Artificial Intelligence,* 1977.
18. Hayes-Roth, B., and F. Hayes-Roth, "Concept Learning and the Recognition and Classification of Exemplars," *Journal of Verbal Learning and Verbal Behavior,*, Vol. 16, 1977, pp. 321–338.
19. Hayes-Roth, B., and F. Hayes-Roth, *Cognitive Processes in Planning,* The Rand Corporation, R-2366-ONR, December 1978.
20. Hayes-Roth, F., "A Structural Approach to Pattern Learning and the Acquisition of Classificatory Power," *Proceedings of the First International Joint Conference on Pattern Recognition,* I.E.E.E., New York, 1973.
21. Hayes-Roth, F., "Patterns of Induction and Associated Knowledge Acquisition Algorithms," in *Pattern Recognition and Artificial Intelligence* (C. H. Chen, ed.), Academic Press, New York, 1976(a).
22. Hayes-Roth, F., "Uniform Representations of Structured Patterns and an Algorithm for the Induction of Contingency-Re-

sponse Rules," *Information and Control,* Vol. 33, 1976(b), pp. 87–116.

23. Hayes-Roth, F., "Learning by Example," in *Cognitive Psychology and Instruction* (A. M. Lesgold et al., eds.), Plenum, New York, 1978.
24. Hayes-Roth, F., and J. McDermott, "Learning Structured Patterns from Examples," *Proceedings of the Third International Joint Conference on Pattern Recognition*, Coronado, California, 1976.
25. Hayes-Roth, F., and J. McDermott, "Knowledge Acquisition from Structural Descriptions," *Communications of the ACM*, May 1978.
26. Hayes-Roth, F., D. A. Waterman, and D. Lenat, "Principles of Pattern-Directed Inference Systems," in *Pattern-Directed Inference Systems* (D. A. Waterman and F. Hayes-Roth, eds.), Academic Press, New York, 1978.
27. Heidorn, G. E., "Automatic Programming Through Natural Language Dialogue: A Survey," *Journal of Research and Development*, Vol. 20, No. 4, 1976.
28. Hendrix, G. G, E. D. Sacerdoti, D. Sagalowicz, and J. Slocum, "Developing a Natural Language Interface to Complex Data," *ACM Transactions on Database Systems,* Vol. 3, No. 2, June 1978, pp. 105–147.
29. Hunt, E. B., *Concept Formation: An Information Processing Problem*, Wiley, New York, 1962.
30. Lenat, D., "AM: An Artificial Intelligence Approach to Discovery in Mathematics as Heuristic Search," SAIL AIM-286, Artificial Intelligence Laboratory, Stanford University, 1976.
31. Lenat, D., "Automated Theory Formation in Mathematics," *Proceedings of the Fifth International Joint Conference on Artificial Intelligence*, 1977, pp. 833–842.
32. Lenat, D., and G. Harris, "Designing a Rule System that Searches for Scientific Discoveries," in *Pattern-Directed Inference Systems* (D. A. Waterman and F. Hayes-Roth, eds.), Academic Press, New York, 1978.
33. Lesser, V. R., and L. D. Erman, "A Retrospective View of the Hearsay-II Architecture," *Proceedings of the Fifth International Joint Conference on Artificial Intelligence*, MIT, 1977, pp. 790–800.
34. Manna, Z., and R. Waldinger, "The DEDuctive ALgorithm Ur-Synthesizer," *AFIPS-NCC Conference Proceedings*, 1978.
35. Nii, H. P., and E. A. Feigenbaum, "Rule-Based Understanding of Signals," in *Pattern-Directed Inference Systems* (D. A. Water-

man and F. Hayes-Roth, eds.), Academic Press, New York, 1978.

36. Sacerdoti, E., "Language Access to Distributed Data with Error Recovery," *Proceedings of the Fifth International Conference on Artificial Intelligence*, 1977.

37. Schank, R. C., and R. P. Abelson, *Scripts, Plans, Goals, and Understanding*, Lawrence Erlbaum Associates, New Jersey, 1977.

38. Shortliffe, E. H., *Computer-Based Medical Consultations: MYCIN*, American Elsevier, New York, 1976.

39. Siklossy, L., and D. A. Sykes, "Automatic Program Synthesis From Example," *Proceedings of the Fourth International Joint Conference on Artificial Intelligence*, 1975, pp. 268–273.

40. Simon, H. A., and K. Kotovsky, "Human Acquisition of Concepts for Sequential Patterns," *Psychological Review*, Vol. 70, 1963, pp. 534–546.

41. Vere, S. A., "Inductive Learning of Relational Productions," in *Pattern-Directed Inference Systems* (D. A. Waterman and F. Hayes-Roth, eds.), Academic Press, New York, 1978.

42. Waterman, D. A., "Adaptive Production Systems," *Proceedings of the Fourth International Joint Conference on Artificial Intelligence*, 1975, pp. 296–303.

43. Waterman, D. A., "Serial Pattern Acquisition: A Production System Approach," in *Pattern Recognition and Artificial Intelligence* (C. H. Chen, ed.), Academic Press, New York, 1976.

44. Waterman, D. A., *Rule-Directed Interactive Transaction Agents: An Approach to Knowledge Acquisition*, The Rand Corporation, R-2171-ARPA, 1978(a).

45. Waterman, D. A., *A Rule-Based Approach to Knowledge Acquisition for Man-Machine Interface Programs*, The Rand Coporation, P-5823, 1978(b).

46. Waterman, D. A., "Exemplary Programming in RITA," in *Pattern-Directed Inference Systems* (D. A. Waterman and F. Hayes-Roth, eds.), Academic Press, New York, 1978(c).

47. Waterman, D. A., W. S. Faught, P. Klahr, S. J. Rosenschein, and R. Wesson, *Design Issues for Exemplary Programming*, The Rand Corporation, N-1484-RC, 1980.

48. Waterman, D. A., and F. Hayes-Roth, *Pattern-Directed Inference Systems*, Academic Press, New York, 1978(a).

49. Waterman, D. A., and F. Hayes-Roth, "An Overview of Pattern-Directed Inference Systems," in *Pattern-Directed Inference*

Systems (D. A. Waterman and F. Hayes-Roth, eds.), Academic Press, New York, 1978(b).

50. Winston, P. H., "Learning Structural Descriptions from Examples," in *The Psychology of Computer Vision* (P. H. Winston, ed.), McGraw-Hill, New York, 1975.

Appendix A

Example of an EP-2 Scenario

The following is a scenario of the EP-2 system in operation. The user interacts with the UNIX operating system to create a program to print locally a file that he or she has on a remote system. To do this, the program must retrieve the file from the remote system using FTP (file transfer program), print it, and delete it.

In this protocol, the Unix prompt is "%". The user-system interaction is at the left margin. The EP-user interaction is indented. User input is shown in italics, and agent input in boldface type. Annotation is in braces at the right.

% *ep*
Telnetting... logging in... starting EP...

{The user starts the EP system.}

%

The GOTO button is control-P
For help, type GOTO and "help<carriage return>".

%

{EP displays a standard "help" message.
To get EP's attention, the user types
types a special character, <control-P>.}

[EP]: *create*

{The user tells EP to create an agent.}

Name of agent: *print do.doc from ecl*

{EP responds by asking for the name of
the agent.}

Variables in agent call: *do.doc*

{EP then asks the user what variables are
in the agent call.}

Making new var: VAR1, with value: do.doc

{EP makes variables for later instantiation.}

Describe agent...
Text: *This agent retrieves the file do.doc*
Text: *from ecl and prints it locally.*
Text:

{The user can give a description of the agent as a form of documentation.}

EP is watching
-EP waiting-

{EP has finished acquiring the initial information about the agent, and now watches the user interact with the system.}

% *ftp ecl*

{The user starts up FTP, and logs on to the remote server.}

Connections established.
300 USC-ECL FTP Server 1.44.11.0 - at WED 12-JUL-78 14:12-PDT
> *user faught*
330 User name accepted. Password, please.
> *pass*
Password:
230 Login completed.
> *retr do.doc*

{The user tells FTP what remote file to retrieve. EP recognizes the file name as being a variable in the agent call. EP creates an action in the model to evaluate the variable at run time.}

localfile: *temp.bak*

{The user selects a temporary filename as the local destination.}

255 SOCK 3276867075
250 ASCII retrieve of <FAUGHT>DO.DOC;2 started.
252 Transfer completed.
> *bye*
231 BYE command received.
% *print temp.bak*

{The user prints and deletes the local file.}

% *del temp.bak*
temp.bak
%

[EP]: *end*

{The user tells EP that he or she is done with the task.}

End agent called: print do.doc from ecl
End agent construction

```
      Agent stored in library
      Trace stored in library
        -EP dormant-
%
            {The agent is now available for use. The
             user calls it on a different file.}
        [EP]: print pattern from ecl
        -Calling: print pattern from ecl
%
      [This agent retrieves the file pattern
      from ecl and prints it locally.]
            {The agent starts running by first printing
             the description of its task.}
% ftp ecl
            {The agent types to the system, just as
             the user did.}
Connections established.
300 USC-ECL FTP Server 1.44.11.0 - at WED 12-JUL-78 14:15-PDT
> user faught
330 User name accepted. Password, please.
> pass
Password:
230 Login completed.
> retr pattern
            {The agent tells FTP which remote file is
             to be retrieved. The file "pattern" is
             instantiated from the agent call.}
localfile: temp.bak
255 SOCK 3276867075
250 ASCII retrieve of <FAUGHT>PATTERN.;1 started.
252 Transfer completed.
> bye
231 BYE command received.
% print temp.bak
            {The agent prints and deletes the local file.}
% del temp.bak
temp.bak
%
        -Ending agent: print pattern from ecl
        -EP dormant-
%
```

Appendix B

Example of an EP-2 LADDER Scenario

The following is an example of a database retrieval task using the LADDER database system. The agent uses the LADDER system to print the status of all ships within 200 miles of the default location (currently NORFOLK). The agent calls five subagents in sequence to perform the following operations:

1. Log into a remote system (SRI-KL) and start up the LADDER system;
2. Define the term *opstatus* in LADDER, referring to the current position, fuel status, state of readiness, and commanding officer of a ship;
3. Type the specific retrieval request for ships within 200 miles;
4. Exit from the LADDER system; and
5. Format, print, and save the transcript.

In this protocol, the Unix prompt is "% ". The only user input is the call to EP and the agent call "ship status 200 miles." Agent input is shown in boldface. Agent descriptive statements are in brackets; they are printed by the agent itself.

```
% ep
Telnetting... logging in... starting EP...
%
        The GOTO button is control-P
        For help, type GOTO and "help<carriage return>".
        [EP]: ships status 200 miles
        -Calling: ships status 200 miles
%
      [This agent uses the LADDER system to print the status of all
      ships within 200 miles of the default location (currently
      NORFOLK). Types of ships recognized by LADDER are: ships
      submarines carriers cruisers.]
%
      [PHASE 1: Start the LADDER system.]
%
        -Calling: ladder
%
```

```
    [This starts the LADDER system at SRI-KL.]
%
    [Telnet to SRI with a TEE for saving results of this session.
% tn sri|tee ladder. temp
Open

SRI-KL, TOPS-20 Monitor 101B(116)
System shutdown scheduled for Mon 18-Sept-78 00:01:00,
Up again at Tue 19-Sept-78 04:00:00
There are 43+8 jobs and the load av. is 3.94
@
    [Login as a LADDER user.]
@login
(user) fhollister
(password)
(account)
 Job 84 on TTY251 14-Sep-78 17:09
 Previous login: 13-Sep-78 14:46 from host RAND-UNIX
 [There are 3 other jobs in group DA]
@
    [Logged in; now start LADDER.]
@ladder
    Language Access to Distributed Data with Error Recovery
                                   —SRI International—

Please type in your name: epdemo
    [User's name (for repeated requests).]
When you are finished, please type DONE.
This will close the Datacomputer files.
Do you want instructions? (type FIRST LETTER of response) No
    [Bypass the instructions.]
Do you want to use 2 Data Computers? No
    [Use only 1 Data Comuter.]
Do you want to specify a current location (default = Norfolk)? No
    [Use the default location (for this user).]
Do you wish distance/direction calculations to default to Great Circle
or RHUMB LINE? (you can override by specifying in the query)
  Great Circle
    [Use the Great Circle calculation.]
1_
    [Suppress the Data Computer Specification.]
1_set verbosity to be -1
        PARSED!
-1
2_
    [LADDER is now waiting for English input.]
2_
      -Ending agent: ladder
2_
```

[PHASE 2: Define special terms.]
2_
-Calling: ladstatus
2_
[This defines opstatus in LADDER.]
2_**define (what is the opstatus of jfk)**
like (what is the current position, fuel status, state of readiness, and commanding officer of jfk)
PARSED!

WHAT IS THE CURRENT POSITION FUEL STATUS STATE OF READINESS AND COMMANDING OFFICER OF JFK
PARSED!

For SHIP equal to KENNEDY JF, give the POSITION and DATE and PCFUEL and READY and RANK and NAME.

May LIFER assume that "CURRENT POSITION FUEL STATUS STATE OF READINESS AND COMMANDING OFFICER" may always be used in place of "OPSTATUS"?

Yes

<RELN> => OPSTATUS
(OPSTATUS)
3_
["Opstatus" is now defined.]
3_
-Ending agent: ladstatus
3_
[PHASE 3: Type the specific retrieval request.]
3_
[LADDER processes the request by interacting with the Data Computer.]
3_**what is the opstatus of all ships within 200 miles**
FROM NORFOLK
PARSED!

For great circle distance to 37-00N, 76-00W less than or equal to 200, give the POSITION and DATE and PCFUEL and READY and RANK and NAME and SHIP.

Connecting to Datacomputer at CCA:
>> ;0031 78091501150 IONETI: CONNECTED TO SRI-KL-30700010
>> ;J150 780915001151 FCRUN; V='DC-5/01.00.13' J=7
DT='THURSDAY, SEPTEMBER 14, 1978 20:11:51-EDT' S='CCA'
>> ;J200 780915001151 RHRUN: READY FOR REQUEST
*> Set parameters
*< Exit
*> Set parameters
*< V Verbosity (-1 to 5): −1. . . . . .

POSITION DATE	PCFUEL	READY	RANK		NAME	SHIP
37-00N, 076-00W 17Jan76,	1200	0	C5	CAPT	HALSEY W	AMERICA
37-00N, 076-00W 17Jan76,	1200	100	C1	CAPT	BROWN A	SARATOGA
37-00N, 076-00W 17Jan76,	1200	100	C1	CDR	SMITH R	STURGEON
37-00N, 076-00W 17Jan76,	1200	100	C1	CDR	COHEN X	WHALE
37-00N, 076-00W 17Jan76,	1200	100	C1	CDR	HIGH J	TAUTOG
37-00N, 076-00W 17Jan76,	1200	100	C1	CDR	DAUGHERTY R	GRAYLING

4_
        -Calling: beep
4_
    [This beeps the user's terminal.]
4_
        -Ending agent: beep
4_
        -Ending agent: ships status 200 miles
            -EP dormant-
4_
        [EP]: ladexit
        -Calling: ladexit
4_
    [Exiting LADDER, back to unix. . .]
4_
    [PHASE 4: Exit from the LADDER system.]
4_**done**
    PARSED!
Thank you
@**k**
[Confirm]
System shutdown scheduled for Mon 18-Sept-78 00:01:00,
Up again at Tue 19-Sep-78 04:00:00
Logout Job 84, User FHOLLISTER, Account DA, TTY 251, at 14-Sep-78
    17:14:02
    Used 0:0:12 in 0:4:56
%
    [PHASE 5: Formant, print, and save the transcript.]
%
        -Calling: ladsave
%
    [This saves the results of each LADDER run by appending them
    on the file LADDER.RESULTS and printing them on the computer.]
%
    [Delete cr's and DEL's.]
% **tr -d"/015/177" < ladder.temp > ladder. temp1**
%
    [Use the ED editor to delete unwanted parts of the LADDER
    protocol.]
% **ed ladder. temp1**

```
        {Edit deletes occur here, but are not shown.}
q
%
    [Append the results to the archive file.]
% cat ladder.temp1>>ladder.results
%
    Print a hard copy of today's results.]
% print ladder.temp1
%
    [Remove the temporary files.]
% del ladder.temp ladder.temp1
ladder.temp
ladder.temp1
%
        -Ending agent: ladsave
%
    [You are now talking to unix.]
%
        -Ending agent: ladexit
         -EP dormant-
```

Chapter 9

Knowledge Acquisition, Knowledge Programming, and Knowledge Refinement

Frederick Hayes-Roth, Philip Klahr, and David J. Mostow

9.1 Background: Machine-aided Knowledge Acquisition in Perspective

In this century, the growth of behavioral and information sciences has stimulated various forms of basic and applied research about learning. Behavioral psychology, for example, has made impressive gains in developing practical procedures for improved training of people and animals. This type of work focuses primarily on the nature and the appropriate timing of contingent reinforcements. The essential finding has been that a reward received soon after some desirable behavior occurs increases the chance that the behavior will recur. Cognitive psychology, on the other hand, emphasizes the ideas and concepts governing ordinary thought. For example, researchers in this field attempt to ex-

This chapter originally appeared as R-2540-NSF, The Rand Corporation, May 1980.

plain how people induce common category concepts such as *dog* or *criminal* from examples. Researchers in the relatively new field of artificial intelligence (AI) have addressed both of these kinds of learning problems. However, their emphasis on machine learning imposes demanding constraints on potential theories. For AI purposes, a theory of learning must lead to a computer program that exhibits improved performance over time.

This chapter describes only one of many approaches to machine learning. We first briefly review the related AI research that forms the scientific context. The several approaches that have developed over time have emphasized, in order, adaptively adjusting feature weights; generalizing examples of categories, transformations, and more general procedures; using heuristics to synthesize new concepts; and directly transferring human knowledge to computers.

Early AI work studies adaptive learning schemes that could adjust control parameters to correlate the machine's output with a desired standard. In this sense, the early learning devices acted somewhat like adaptive control devices. The Perceptron (Minsky and Papert, 1969), for example, was a pattern-recognition device that classified test patterns by computing weighted sums of feature-detector output. When the sum exceeded some threshold, the response indicated corresponding class membership; if the sum fell below the threshold, the pattern was rejected from the class. When an incorrect decision occurred, a learning algorithm prescribed how to adjust the feature weights. Because the machine adjusted its weighting factors to accommodate its training experiences, this kind of learning might be considered the first of many subsequent paradigms for learning by example. A different application of a similar technique addressed tactics in the game of checkers (Samuel, 1963).

Over time, AI researchers moved increasingly toward a belief that intelligent behavior requires substantial world knowledge. Most intelligent tasks require specific feature detectors, complex descriptions of patterns and structures, and correspondingly complicated procedures for comparing one description with another. Without these, very few human capabilities could be simulated. Soon after the development of behavioral learning theories and devices like the Perceptron, scientists began to point out the need for these more complex mechanisms. Work in machine-vision programs, for example, established the need for specialized detectors for edges, corners, and intersections, and sophisticated procedures for following and interpreting their connections in scenes. These kinds of internal structures lay outside the scope of the earlier learning frameworks.

A number of AI researchers then developed improved methods for learning by example that could generalize rules from arbitrarily complex structural descriptions (Buchanan et al., 1969; Buchanan and Mitchell, 1978; Hayes-Roth, 1974; Hayes-Roth, 1976a; Hayes-Roth, 1976b; Hayes-Roth, 1977; Hayes-Roth, 1978b; Hayes-Roth and Burge, 1976; Hayes-Roth and McDermott, 1976; Hayes-Roth and McDermott, 1978; Mitchell, 1977; Soloway and Riseman, 1977; Vere, 1978a; Vere, 1978b; Winston, 1975). These procedures use initially provided feature detectors as well as *structural* or *relational* connections to describe each example of a given class. Then by partial-matching the descriptions of many examples, common subdescriptions emerge as candidate general rules (Hayes-Roth, 1978a). This methodology has supported machine induction of transformational grammar rules (Hayes-Roth and McDermott, 1978), chemical reaction rules (Buchanan et al., 1969; Buchanan and Mitchell, 1978), and simple robot plans (Vere, 1978a), among others.

The basic limitation of this more recent work, derives from its *subtractive* approach to learning. The learning programs devised under this approach produce new rules by detecting which of the currently known features and relations appear jointly in each example. By assumption, each example reflects required features as well as some irrelevant features peculiar to the specific example. Learning by example, in this context, simply requires subtracting the irrelevant features in each case. Although this approach can be very useful for practical problems in pattern recognition and data interpretation, it provides little insight into the discovery of new features or new functions for performing a task.

Two recent research projects have shed some light on such discovery problems. Exemplary-programming research at Rand (Waterman, 1978b; Faught et al., 1980) has investigated the problem of inferring programs capable of recreating the interactions between a person and a machine engaged in a task (see also Biermann and Krishnaswamy, 1976). The creation of a program from a human/machine dialogue requires methods that are more constructive or *synthetic* than other learning-by-example tasks. The two chief problems concern interpretation of the example behaviors and the subsequent regeneration of corresponding behavior in new contexts. Interpreting an arbitrary human/machine interaction appears to require a variety of sources of knowledge, including sources for explaining: (1) the meaning of special typed symbols; (2) the state of various systems employed during the session; (3) the semantics of computer system output; (4) the goal of the person performing the task; and (5) the problem-solving procedure that person apparently applied. Each of these types of knowledge contributes to understanding both why and how the person and the machine cooperated to solve the task. To construct a generalized program that can replace the person in such tasks, we must convert this passive understanding of the task's purpose and solution methods into effective procedures. These procedures, if truly general, must accomplish the same effects, although various situational characteristics will differ from the data initially observed. This requires several types of knowledge in addition to that previously noted: knowledge concerning system control and interactions; knowledge of planning and problem solving; and knowledge of programming methods.

Another recent project that illuminates the synthetic nature of learning attempted to simulate the discovery process in mathematics (Lenat, 1976; Lenat, 1977a; Lenat, 1977b; Lenat and Harris, 1978). This project employed two types of knowledge to induce new concepts of elementary set theory. The first type of knowledge consisted of a variety of mathematical concepts, such as sets, lists, equalities, and functions. Over time, the program's conceptual knowledge grew as new concepts were created from existing ones. The methods for discovering new concepts constituted the second type of knowledge. A few hundred rules called *discovery heuristics* modified existing concepts to produce new ones. For example, several heuristics formulated new concepts by generalizing old ones. Although the program knew at the outset the concepts of a *list* (defined as "an ordered collection of elements") and *length,* it conjectured for itself a new concept that generalized these notions to produce the concept of "length of a list of identical elements." In this way, it produced the concept of *unary numbers,* that is, a list of n tick marks meaning the number n. Other rules formed new concepts by specializing existing concepts, by searching for examples of newly conjectured concepts, or by forming new mathematical functions with arbitrary attributes (e.g., by restricting binary functions that applied only when the first and second arguments were equal). In this way, several insightful and interesting developments of mathematical history were retraced in a few hours of computer time.

The last type of machine learning we must mention might be called *transfer of expertise* (Anderson, 1977; Balzer et al., 1977; Davis et al., 1977; Davis, 1977; Davis, 1978; Hayes-Roth et al., 1978; Heidorn, 1976; Heidorn, 1974; Mostow and Hayes-Roth, 1979a; Mostow and Hayes-Roth, 1979b; Samuel, 1963; Waterman, 1978a; Waterman et al., 1979; Barr et al., 1979). Work in this area has aimed toward constructing intelligent systems according to heuristic techniques prescribed by human experts (Feigenbaum, 1977). The major obstacle to implementing intelligent programs described in this way arises from the need to translate human knowledge into computable formalisms. Several research projects have demonstrated the viability of using English-like, rule-based languages (Anderson and Gillogly, 1976; Davis and King, 1976; Shortliffe, 1976; Waterman and Hayes-Roth, 1978; Waterman et al., 1979) that enable people to express their knowledge in rules of the form, "If there is a drilling site whose iron content exceeds 12 ppm and whose location is within 12 miles of an oil field, then the probability of a moderate iron deposit is high." Although this particular rule is fanciful, a number of expert systems have been created for problems as diverse as infectious blood-disease therapy (Shortliffe, 1976), artificial respirator maintenance (Fagan, 1978), internal medicine (Pople, 1975, 1977), and geological prospecting (Duda et al., 1978). The major lines of continuing effort in this context aim to develop improved high-level languages for such rule-based programming (Waterman and Hayes-Roth, 1978; Waterman et al., 1979) and assist in the construction and maintenance of large sets of rules by developing meta-knowledge—knowledge about the likely and appropriate kinds of knowledge that should enter the data-base (Davis, 1978; Davis, 1979; Stefik, 1979).

The principal concepts of previous learning research that we have discussed are summarized in Table 9.1. The table also gives rough definitions of these terms and brief descriptions of the mechanisms AI researchers have proposed for accomplishing various types of learning.

Our current research attempts to integrate and extend the best aspects of these alternative approaches to machine learning and knowledge acquisition. Specifically, we believe the following contributory factors to learning can and should be accommodated in a single system:

1. *Contingent reinforcement.* When behavior produces undesirable consequences, the knowledge responsible should be altered, and tendencies that produce desirable outcomes should be strengthened.
2. *Learning by example.* Systems should benefit from and generalize their experiences.
3. *Knowledge as the source of power.* A learning system should acquire, manipulate, and apply knowledge in the pursuit of increased capabilities.
4. *The understanding of goals and the capability for planning to achieve them.*
5. *Acceptance of human advice and knowledge about the task.*

Integrating these five capabilities into a system will require significant effort, and only a small proportion of the necessary programs have been implemented to date. On the other hand, we now clearly understand many of the residual problems. Section 9.2 explains our formulation of and approach to the problem of understanding and assimilating knowledge about an arbitrary task. The concepts and mechanisms that characterize our approach are summarized in Table 9.2. Knowledge is acquired from people, used to develop plans for achiev-

TABLE 9.1 Previous Learning Concepts and Mechanisms.

Concept	*Traditional Meaning*	*Mechanism*
Learning	Changing behavior to improve performance	Rote memorization and conditioning to contingent reinforcement.
Adaptive learning procedures	Changing behavior output to more closely approximate desired standard.	Use positive/negative feedback to adjust the association weights that connect stimulus features to output.
Learning by example	Inferring a general classification rule from training sets.	Propose any boolean combination of features consistent with the examples as the classifying rule.
Exemplary programming	Inferring a general procedure from sample human/machine dialogue	Infer the person's purpose that motivates the dialogue, interpret the dependencies between machine and human input, then create a program to mimic the person.
Concept discovery	Inferring the existence and definition of a general class.	Detect that several distinct things or events share some features, find a common description, and propose it as a concept definition; or heuristically modify a prior concept definition, conjecture the concept's validity, and find examples of it.
Transfer of expertise	Supplying human problem-solving knowledge to a machine.	Program corresponding procedures directly; or express the knowledge within a narrow formalism suitable for machine interpretation; or express the knowledge in a high-level problem-solving language (e.g., a rule-based system).
Knowledge acquisition	Incremental addition of knowledge to an intelligent system.	Formulate a representation for a type of knowledge the system uses, use any mechanism to identify new units of knowledge, and add these to the knowledge base.

TABLE 9.2 Learning Concepts and Mechanisms in the Current Approach.

Concept	*Meaning*	*Mechanism*
Human/machine cooperation	Person and machine cooperate to build intelligent systems and improve them over time.	A person provides initial advice on task knowledge and problem-solving methods; the person helps to convert the advice into working programs and to diagnose and refine knowledge.
Advice taking	People define domain concepts, specify behavioral constraints, and suggest problem-solving methods.	Develop a knowledge representation, express the knowledge in this form, and integrate it into a working program semiautomatically.
Goal-directed planning	Development of a plan for achieving the expressed goals that uses suggested methods and satisfies expressed constraints.	Work backward from goals to sufficient conditions and actions by deductively pursuing logical, heuristic, and instrumental transformations. These transformations symbolically manipulate domain concepts, constraints, and problem-solving methods to produce an effective procedure. The planning process etablishes assumptions and expectations about plan-related situations and effects.
Contingent reinforcement	Stengthening of rewarded behavioral tendencies and weakening of others.	Reinforce knowledge contributing to favorable outcomes; diagnose and refine knowledge causing failures.
Learning by example	Use of actual situations and results to trigger learning.	Compare expected outcomes to actual outcomes, and assumed conditions to observed conditions in order to diagnose fallacious planning knowledge and to suggest knowledge refinements.
Knowledge refinement	Amendment or extension of knowledge in response to behavioral feedback.	Adjust the conditions assumed necessary or sufficient for an action to produce an effect; generalize or further specify the expectations associated with an action.

ing goals, and finally converted into executable programs. Section 9.3 discusses an iterative cycle of planning, acting, and evaluating that relates initial knowledge to specific behaviors and finally to new or modified concepts. After relating observed effects to specific problematic components of plans and, in turn, attributing these to erroneous elements of domain knowledge, the system diagnoses deficiencies and conjectures new knowledge elements. Such knowledge refinements engender a new cycle of plans, acts, observed effects, and inductions. Learning, in this paradigm, is equivalent to the iterative improvement of performance arising from discoveries made while implementing and refining knowledge.

9.2 Advice-taking and Knowledge Programming

9.2.1 ■ Two Paradigms for Developing Expert Systems

Many of the recent successful applications of AI have shown the power of implementing, more or less directly, the heuristic rules of human experts. In tasks requiring only one or two types of inferential procedure, such as interpreting symptoms and test results in medical diagnosis (Shortliffe, 1976), nearly all domain knowledge can conform to a few generic forms or representations. Many applications of this type have adopted an *if-then* rule format for expressing the casual and inferential relationships (Feigenbaum et al., 1971; Waterman et al., 1979). To derive implications of known facts, the system applies the rules to any data that satisfy the rule antecedents (the *if* component), and the corresponding rule consequents become derived facts. The system infers likely causes of observed symptoms by reasoning deductively from observations to plausible causes. When the situation data match rule consequents (the *then* components), the system hypothesizes that the associated antecedent conditions may also be true. In this way, the system reasons backward from effects to likely causes.

These systems succeed, in part, because they use constrained rule formalisms and perform only one or two specialized kinds of inference. These constraints enable program designers to provide naturalistic languages in which nonprogrammers can conveniently express their knowledge. Such English-like languages make it easy for experts in various domains to create large and powerful rulesets by communicating directly with the computer. Because of their specialization, these systems can also help check the consistency and completeness of the human rulesets.

The simplicity of these systems means, of course, that they lack the capabilities needed for solving most types of problems. Although many domains have problems similar to the medical diagnosis problem, most intelligent systems, in terms of their underlying causes, need to perform a wider variety of actions than interpreting symptoms. If we consider such interpretation tasks as a special kind of perceptual process, we can easily see that intelligent behavior involves more than interpretation. Usually, we think of perception, planning, adaptive control, and knowledge acquisition as essential components of intelligence. We are presently unable to formulate all of these activities in terms of one uniform type of representation that requires only a small number of related inference methods.

Thus, although a human expert may know exactly what intelligent behavior requires in some new domain of interest, the current state of the art requires that a human programmer design and implement a unique system for most new tasks. Weeks or months after the initial transfer of knowledge from the expert to the programmer, a program is ready to run. Figure 9.1 illustrates this typical process.

Of course, when the program finally runs, it typically produces a variety of unexpected results. At this point, both the expert and the programmer discover that the original knowledge apparently underspecified the program, because a variety of situations produce unanticipated effects. Four types of problems explain most of the behavioral deficiencies:

1. The expert neglected to express rules to cover all of the special cases that arise;
2. The expert's rules did not produce correct conclusions because they made erroneous assumptions;
3. Although the programmer's implementation decisions were consistent with ambiguities in the original specifications, they generated undesirable behaviors; or
4. The programmer overlooked or incorrectly implemented some of the expert's advice.

Observations of undesirable behaviors motivate a variety of discoveries and changes: new knowledge arises from efforts to handle additional special cases; the expert modifies initial knowledge to correct the errors in it; the expert refines initial rules to resolve problematic ambiguities; the programmer modifies inference methods or associated program code so that the program behaves as it should. Unfortunately, all of these changes require programmer intervention, and most of them take significant time and effort.

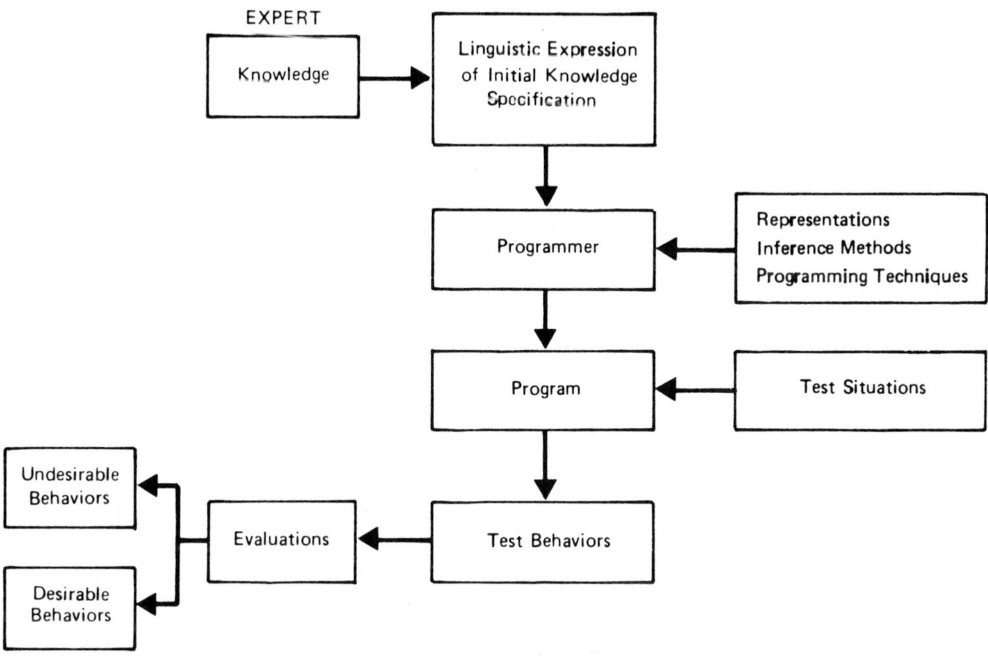

FIGURE 9.1 Expert System Development and Testing.

Iterative refinements generally cause programs to become progressively more obtuse in their knowledge representations and control structures. This, in turn, makes it increasingly difficult for the expert to manage or comprehend a knowledge-based system. Ordinarily, the costs of programming and refinement are onerous; few programs ever satisfy their designers because design goals continually evolve as experience reveals additional system shortcomings.

This analysis suggests an alternative paradigm for the programming and iterative refinement of intelligent systems. The principal components of this paradigm are shown in Fig. 9.2.

This paradigm views the programming problem primarily as one of translating expert advice into an operational program, and the iterative improvement problem as one of diagnosing program behavior to modify those elements of knowledge that produce undesired behaviors. This proposed scheme emphasizes the problems of understanding high-level advice, converting it into effective behavior, and, inevitably, changing the knowledge and reiterating the cycle. These problems are referred to as *knowledge acquisition*, *knowledge programming*, and *knowl-*

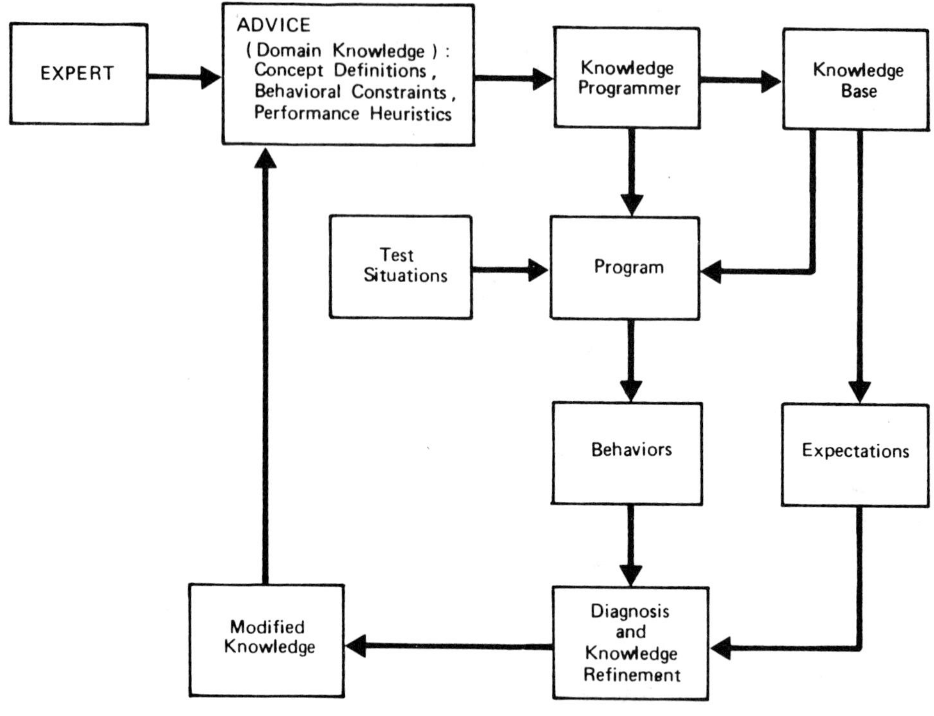

FIGURE 9.2 Knowledge Programming and Knowledge Refinement.

edge refinement, respectively.[1] For some time to come, all of these processes will require some human participation. Thus, throughout this report we describe semiautomatic procedures for performing these functions.[2]

In the remainder of this section, we explain the primary problems

[1] Knowledge acquisition, in our paradigm, refers to the transfer of expertise from a human expert to a machine. The machine *acquires* a person's knowledge in the form of concepts and heuristics. When the machine extends its initial knowledge by various learning methods, we refer to this as *knowledge refinement*. Different researchers might apply the term *knowledge acquisition* to varying aspects of these processes.

[2] We do not know if machine learning techniques will ever achieve sufficient levels of success to obviate the role of people in such efforts. Thus, we see machines more as calculating aids than as stand-alone investigators of complex domains. For the foreseeable future, at least, people will play a major role in guiding deductive processes that the machines execute more rapidly and systematically than would otherwise be possible.

and proposed methods for the first two processes, that is, acquiring the expert's knowledge by understanding advice and converting this advice into executable programs. These are the tasks of the *knowledge programmer*. In the process of knowledge programming, the knowledge programmer develops plans and procedures used by the resulting program. These plans create expectations about the way the program should behave. Contrasts between observed and expected behavior stimulate highly constrained searches for underlying deficiencies in the knowledge base. These deficiencies, in turn, suggest knowledge refinements. The refinement processes of diagnosis and knowledge modification are described in Section 9.3.

9.2.2 ■ Converting Knowledge into an Executable Program

We believe that a very large class of intelligent systems can be specified quite easily. A behavioral description would include constraints on permissible actions as well as prescriptive methods for attacking problems in the domain. Our approach rests on the central idea of expressing these behavioral constraints and heuristics in terms of natural domain concepts. A description of mathematical discovery methods, for instance, should employ terms familiar to a mathematician. When we ask mathematicians for advice about their problems, such as *what to do* or *when and how to do it*, we should allow them to talk in their own terms. Asking them to express their knowledge in terms familiar to computer programmers forces them to translate mathematics into programming. On the other hand, asking programmers to bridge the gap between the mathematician and the computer requires them to translate between cultures—they must first comprehend much of the field of mathematics and then map its concepts and methods into their own repertoire of computer capabilities.

To avoid the need for cross-cultural translation, we are developing systems that will accept an expert's advice expressed in familiar domain concepts. To understand the advice, we need to know the meaning of each constituent concept, and we must transform higher-level advice into actual procedures that the computer can perform. Our approach aims to assimilate individual concepts as terms with formally defined properties. Then, we attempt to understand advice (e.g., constraints among elements, or heuristic rules for goal-directed actions) as specific compositions of the constituent terms. At present, much of this overall process is understood, and some of it has actually been accomplished by our computer programs. We sketch the primary features of this approach in the following paragraphs. (Detailed technical descriptions are given in Hayes-Roth et al., 1978; Mostow and Hayes-Roth, 1979a; Mostow and Hayes-Roth, 1979b.)

From the general perspective, *knowledge programming converts advice expressed in some naturalistic syntax into actions in the task environment.* This requires several processes: *parsing* the advice into syntactic structures; *interpreting* these structures by converting them to meaningful semantic representations; *operationalizing* the meaning structures by converting them into effective, executable expressions; *integrating* multiple pieces of advice into a coherent set of procedures; and, finally, *applying* these procedures in actual situations to generate actions.[3] These operations use a knowledge base that stores individual domain concepts and their interrelationships (see Fig. 9.3). Assimilating each new piece of advice requires the knowledge programmer to appreciate how the advice relates to other elements of the knowledge base. Thus, the knowledge base both feeds the assimilation processes and represents the incremental additions they produce.

Several different tasks we have explored in this paradigm have exhibited remarkably similar properties. Each task employs a small set of domain-specific concepts, a few constraints or rules, and an open-ended set of prescriptive heuristic methods. Such problem domains include music composition, legal reasoning, tactical planning, and game playing. We have found that a familiar card game, hearts, provides a good basis for illustrating the major points of this research (see also Balzer, 1966). The problem represented by the game of hearts is discussed in the following subsection.

9.2.3 ■ Examples of Operationalization

What does it take to design a program that will simply play hearts in accordance with the rules?[4] The rules of the game define mandatory behavioral constraints. A program that behaves in accordance with

[3] Although all five of these subtasks are difficult, we have focused our efforts on the problem of operationalization. Parsing and interpretation are fairly well understood as a result of the attention they have received in natural-language-understanding projects. Operationalization is a new topic of study. In the new paradigm, emphasizing rapid implementation of expert knowledge and rapid reimplementation of modified knowledge, operationalization plays a crucial role. Integration is also a very important and difficult problem. Unfortunately, we have not addressed this problem in a substantial way during the course of this research project. A neat solution to the integration problem would yield a single, comprehensive program that could be applied simply, as if it were a typical computer procedure.

[4] The reader who is concerned with the concept rather than the technical details of this problem can skim the technical material that follows without seriously affecting the continuity of the discussion.

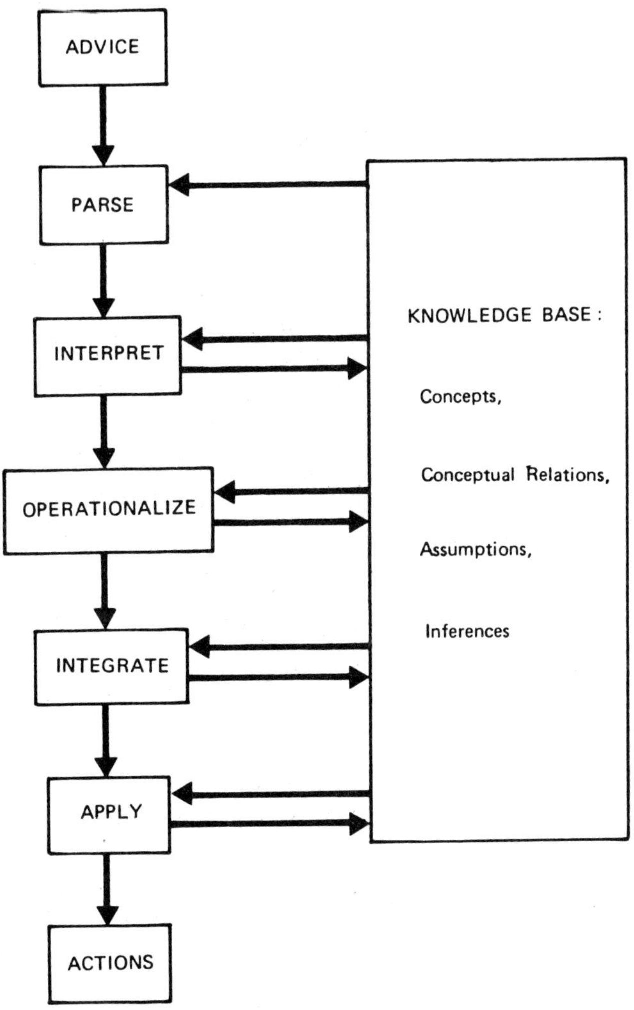

FIGURE 9.3 Information Flow in Knowledge Programming.

these rules will play a legal, albeit poor, game. A few simple rules illustrate the nature of this advice-taking problem.

> PLAYERS RULE: The game is played by four players.[5]
>
> PLAYERS SEQUENCE RULE: During a trick, players play in clockwise order around the table.

[5] For simplicity, we ignore variations on this rule (for example, one variation allows a three-player game).

TRICK RULE: A trick is a sequence in which each player plays one card.
TRICK LEADER RULE: The first person to play in the first trick is the one who has the two of clubs. The first player plays the two of clubs. In other tricks, the winner of the preceding trick plays first.
FOLLOW SUITE RULE: Each player, if possible, must play a card in the suite of the first card played in the trick.
WIN TRICK RULE: In each trick, the player who plays the highest card in the suite led wins the trick.

The processes of parsing and interpreting these rules would generate knowledge-base elements of the following sorts:[6]

Players rule.
Players = {*p*1, *p*2, *p*3, *p*4}.

Players sequence rule.
If *p*1 has just played in a trick and *p*2 has not played in the same trick then *p*2 plays next;
If *p*2 has just played in a trick and *p*3 has not played in the same trick then *p*3 plays next;
If *p*3 has just played in a trick and *p*4 has not played in the same trick then *p*4 plays next;
If *p*4 has just played in a trick and *p*1 has not played in the same trick then *p*1 plays next.

Trick rule.
If *t* is a trick
then *q*1 plays *c*1 during *t*
followed by *q*2 plays *c*2 during *t*
followed by *q*3 plays *c*3 during *t*
followed by *q*4 plays *c*4 during *t*
and {*q*1,*q*2,*q*3,*q*4} = players
and *c*1, *c*2, *c*3, *c*4 are elements of cards.

Trick leader rule.
If and only if player *p* has card two of clubs
then player *p* plays first in the first trick
and player *p* plays the card two of clubs in the first trick.

If and only if player *p* wins a trick *t*
then player *p* plays first in the trick *t*' following *t*.

Follow suit rule.
If the first card *c* played in a trick *t* is of suit *s*
and player *p* before playing in trick *t* has some cards in suit *s*
then player *p* plays some card *d* in suit *s* during trick *t*.

[6] To avoid unnecessary formality and technicality, we have expressed propositions and conceptual statements in terms of simple English equivalents. Readers interested in our LISP-based representations may refer to the technical reports cited previously.

Win trick rule.
If and only if
the card *c* is the first card played in trick *t*
and the suit of card *c* is *s*
and the cards played in trick *t* are called *C*
and *C'* is the subset of *C* whose suit is *s*
and the highest valued element of *C'* is card *d*
and card *d* was played by player *p*
then player *p* wins trick *t*.

The concept definitions supporting such interpretations are of two sorts. The first are domain-dependent definitions, such as *card, game, hand,* and *play*. For example, play would be defined as an action by a player that changes the location of a card from the hand of the player to the pot. The possible locations of cards include a player's hand, a player's pile, and the pot. In our work, we use a form of the lambda calculus (Church, 1941; Allen, 1978) for encoding these definitions. The second type of definition is used for representing domain-independent concepts, such as *set, subset, some, exists, sequence, if, then,* and *and*.

Let us suppose for the current example that only the preceding rules were specified, along with a minimal additional set prescribing how players receive their initial hands and how the winner of each trick takes the cards in the pot. Could we directly apply the knowledge to produce behavior? The answer is no, because the constraints recognize acceptable behavior without telling us how to generate it. That is, the constraints partially define *what* to do without explaining *how*. Discovering how to achieve such desired behavior requires us to *operationalize* the advice. In effect, we need to convert the advice concerning *what* into executable *methods*.

Even in this simple case, the search for effective methods to achieve the desired goal requires planning and problem solving, which incidentally produce additional insights into the domain.

The general methods we have employed for operationalization may be summarized as goal-directed planning. We begin with a statement of desired behavior, which, in this example, might be "player *p* plays a card *c* in the current trick *t*." The problem is to convert this goal expression into a procedure that achieves the goal and satisfies the constraints. Because this statement does not tell us how we may choose a satisfactory card, we regard it as an *ineffective expression*. We then attempt to transform this expression into a composite of individual subexpressions in which each component represents an *effective expression*; that is, each corresponds to either a known value or an executable procedure that can produce a value. Several different problems need to be solved, and we use a variety of different methods.

In this simple example, we might attempt to transform the expression by adapting a general-purpose AI problem-solving method to this task. For example, we might attempt to adapt the general method of *generate-and-test* (Newell, 1969; Newell and Simon, 1972). To exploit this method, we need only find some generator that suggests each possible action and then apply some effective procedure for verifying that the suggested action satisfies the constraints. This approach would lead us to an operationalization such as the following:

Plan 1:

> Consider each card *c* in turn;
> assume you were to play *c*;
> if you can prove that *c* would satisfy the constraints,
> then play *c*.

This plan has two interesting aspects that reflect some deep and recurring issues. First, formulating a plan of action without having the actual situation data in hand requires very general and abstract reasoning. When we do not know exactly which cards have been played and which cards are in a player's hand, for example, we have difficulty formulating any specific action. In an actual situation, however, we might find a similar judgment straightforward. For example, we could easily prove that playing the three of clubs is legal when the two of clubs has just been played. These alternative tasks—forming general plans before situations unfold vs. planning on the spot—we distinguish as ordinary operationalization vs. *dynamic operationalization*. The first point then is that in most circumstances, dynamic operationalization seems both easier and more effective. Its primary disadvantage arises from the need to postpone planning until actions are required. This means that, at each point, the system cannot act until it has thought through the issues.

The second point concerns the *degree of effectiveness* we demand from an operationalization. The general plan proposed previously may or may not be effective. It presupposes two capabilities: generating each possible card in turn, and proving that the card satisfies the constraints. Although in simple cases like the hearts task we can achieve the first capability, we can rarely establish valid proofs of such abstract propositions as in the second. The difficulty arises from the complete generality of the assertion to be proved, that is, "c would satisfy the constraints." To certify Plan 1 as *effective*, we need a procedure that we know can prove such assertions. Thus, we might simply assume the use of a general theorem-proving procedure to perform this subtask. This procedure, in turn, may or may not be assuredly effective. The overall degree of effectiveness of Plan 1 would then depend on the theorem prover's own effectiveness and the eventual success or failure of its theorem-proving efforts.

The point we want to make in this context concerns the degree of effectiveness we ascribe to an operationalization. Two kinds of uncertainties ordinarily preclude developing assuredly effective plans. First, most real-world tasks address inherently uncertain environments. In these tasks, the constraints and behavioral heuristics may not be strictly provable. Worse yet, in tasks that require both reward-seeking and risk-avoidance behaviors (e.g., playing hearts), knowledge usually prescribes simultaneously opposing, hence inconsistent, objectives. Second, plans themselves introduce a different type of uncertainty. This uncertainty, considered previously, arises from the residual ineffectiveness or incompleteness of the operationalization. We have found that both kinds of uncertainties require heuristic solutions. That is, intelligent systems can reason informally to control uncertainty partially, but they cannot eliminate it completely. Much of our research revolves around the nature of the heuristics both human experts and knowledge programmers can employ to control such uncertainty efficiently.

Because Plan 1 represents quite a weak or unspecific operationalization, we might reasonably seek a stronger, more detailed solution. A more interesting plan for playing a card can be derived by adopting another general AI problem-solving approach. In this case, we view the problem from the perspective of the general *heuristic search method*. This method specifies that to reach a goal state G from an initial situation S, we should choose actions from some set A that successively change attributes of S until they satisfy G. To apply this general method to the problem at hand requires matching aspects of the given problem to components of the general approach. What elements of the current problem correspond to G, S, and A? The initial statement corresponds to G: Reach a state in which player p plays a card c that satisfies all of the constraints. Situation S corresponds to a set of quite general assertions about what is known, such as that player p has cards C. The set of possible operations A is not immediately apparent.

To transform an initial state S into a goal state G, we employ three different kinds of transformations: logical, heuristic, and instrumental. Logical transformations convert an initial expression into a logically equivalent one. One common kind of logical transformation is a symbolic type of case analysis. To analyze an expression, we reexpress it as a set of alternatives, each of which rests on an additional, distinctive assumption characterizing that particular case. For example, we might reexpress the assertion that p plays card c as a disjunction of two cases: (1) p plays first in the trick and plays card c; or (2) some other player p' plays first in the trick, and later in the trick p plays card c. This transformation preserves the truth value of the initial expression, but, more important, it suggests one promising way to divide and conquer the initial problem.

Case analyses break a single general problem into separable subproblems and at the same time further characterize aspects of the task situation that bear directly upon constraint satisfaction. In Case 2, in which *p* is assumed to play after the trick has begun, *p* must choose a card in the same suit as the first card played. In this example, the Case 2 assumption can key the knowledge programmer to apply the *follow suit* rule in subsequent operationalization of this path.

Heuristic transformations make plausible, if not necessarily valid, substitutions in expressions. For example, in developing a plan of play with attention to likely effects, we might transform the initial expression "after the trick is opened, *p* plays card *c*" into the two following cases: (3) "after the trick is opened, *p* plays card *c*, and *c* is the trick-winning card," or (4) "after the trick is opened, *p* plays a card whose suit is different from the suit of the first card played." Although these cases are verifiably exclusive, they do not exhaust the possible situations that might arise. Hence, a transformation of this sort might be plausible, but does not preserve equivalence. We have found many practical situations which such heuristic transformations can lead to clever, if somewhat incomplete, plans. In this illustration, for example, Case 3 leads to application of the *win trick* rule, further specifying the suit and value of card *c*. Case 4, on the other hand, suggests an operationalization that confronts the *follow suit* rule. The prerequisites for that rule in turn become additional conditions on this line of reasoning.

The third type of transformation to expressions is modeled after the result of instrumental action in the task environment. In the initial problem of generating a legal play, the only actions known to the system would be dealing, playing, leading, and winning a trick. Each of these corresponds to a transformation that will affect the description of any supposed game situation. In the preceding analysis of Case 3, in addition to inferring requisite properties of the winning card *c*, we can also deduce that *p* moves cards from the pot to his or her pile. In this simple example, the only instrumental action that sheds much light on operationalizing the initial expression is the primitive action of playing a card, that is, moving a card from a player's hand to the pot. Later, however, the actions of winning a trick and moving cards from the pot to players' piles play significant roles in operationalizing behavioral heuristics suggested by experts.

The knowledge programmer represents a variety of general reasoning methods as transformations, and applies them to convert high-level objectives into corresponding, effective procedures. The reasoning used includes case analysis, partial-matching between an expression and the description of a general method to guide attempts at adapting the general method to the specific problem, simplification of complex expressions, approximation of uncertain or combinatorial alternatives, and reformulation of an expression in terms of other known concepts. Each specific operationalization task requires some or all of these methods. For example, if the knowledge programmer adapted the heuristic search method to the task of playing a legal card, one resulting operational expression for "*p* plays card *c* and satisfied the constraints" would correspond to the following:

Plan 2:

If *p* plays first
  and this is the first trick
  and *p* has the two of clubs
then *p* plays the two of clubs,
else if *p* plays first in the trick
  and *p* has a card *c* whose suit is *s*
then *p* plays *c*,
else if card *c'* was the first card played in the trick
  and the suit of *c'* is *s*
  and *p* has a card whose suit is *s*
then *p* plays *c*,
else if *p* has a card *c*
then *p* plays *c*.

Of course, because we have thus far considered only the mandatory constraints on behavior, no expertise has been included in this initial set of advice. In addition to necessary conditions on behavior, the kinds of heuristics we want to acquire directly from experts tell the program how it *should* behave. This goes beyond the notion of behavioral *acceptability* to the concept of *desirability*. As anyone familiar with law, music, hearts, and most other difficult tasks realizes, the bulk of human knowledge in these domains directly concerns such prescriptive heuristics.

9.2.4 ■ Operationalizing Strategies, Tactics, and Procedures

In a game like hearts, in which the objective is to minimize winning tricks that contain point cards, expert advice concerns strategies, tactics, and procedures that can help reach this objective. The rules of the game reward some kinds of risk aversion and some kinds of risk-seeking behaviors. For example, a player can improve his or her (relative) score by either taking fewer points than the opponents or taking all the points in a round. Thus, a very simple type of heuristic advice might be to *avoid taking points*. We will consider this example briefly to convey the nature of the knowledge-programming problem it exemplifies. (A detailed technical discussion of this particular example appears in Mostow and Hayes-Roth, 1979b.)

Before proceeding with the example, however, we need to postulate a few more bits of knowledge. We will assume the knowledge programmer has assimilated the following facts: Any card that is in the suit of hearts has a point value of 1, and the queen of spades has a point value of 13. We also assume that the concept *take* has been defined to mean that a player winning a trick *t* takes all cards played in that trick, that is, the cards played in the trick are moved from the pot to the player's pile. The concept *avoid an event x* is defined to mean *prevent event x* or *achieve not* [*x*]. Using such basic definitions, our program has transformed the initial ineffective advice to *avoid taking points* into an effective procedure. It generates a plan that recreates the typical high-level steps most people apparently follow, although it works through many more and lower-level steps than people consciously make.

Given the rules of the game and the advice to *avoid taking points,* people reason roughly as follows: taking points means taking cards with point values; the only way to take cards is to win a trick; *avoid taking points* means not winning a trick; this in turn means playing a card that is not the highest one; and this suggests playing the lowest card in your hand.[7]

For the sake of brevity, we summarize the actual machine-aided derivation at the same high level as the introspective human analysis. First, the program logically transforms *avoid taking points* by substituting for the term *avoid* its literal definition. This produces an expression such as *establish not* [*player p takes points*]. Although the objects of *take* actions are cards and cards can have points, it is impossible to *take* points directly. The program reasons heuristically that *taking points* seems equivalent to *taking cards that have points.* From this, the program notices that a sufficient condition for taking points is winning a trick in which some of the cards have points. To preclude this from happening, it reasons that negating any of the necessary conditions should do. It then produces a new expression that corresponds to *do not win a trick.* It uses the constraints on trick winning to infer that the player wins only if he or she plays the highest card in the same suit as the card first played. Finally, it reasons instrumentally that this condition would not occur if the player played a card of lower value. This type of plan leads directly to a corresponding procedure for applying the advice.

[7] After a little thought, people often notice ways to improve this plan, but we reconsider those kinds of insights later when we discuss the role of plan evaluation as a source of knowledge refinement.

In a similar way, the program has been used with human assistance to produce plans for other kinds of advice in this game. For example, one useful heuristic for new players is to *flush the queen of spades,* that is, force another player to play it. The kind of reasoning the program uses to develop its plan is as follows: By substituting the definition of *flush,* it infers that it needs to establish the condition "some player *p* must play the queen of spades." It uses its concept of *must* and the *follow suit* rule to infer that this objective requires that *p* have only one legal card to play—the queen of spades. This in turn means that either *p* has only the queen of spades, or player *q* leads a spade, and *p*'s only spade is the queen. It focuses on the second case and then develops a plan for how player *q* could force such a situation. In brief, it develops a plan for *q* to win a trick to take the lead. Then as long as *q* retains the lead, *q* continues to lead spades. As players familiar with the game will realize, this is an effective method for flushing the queen.[8]

9.2.5 ■ Integration

We have done little thus far to address the question of integrating a variety of separate pieces of advice. This type of problem lends itself to two approaches. The first aims at an overall consistent integration, and the second presumes no such comprehensive integration is feasible. As in the preceding examples, operationalizing a single piece of advice often requires simultaneously satisfying numerous constraints. Such an approach to comprehensive integration fits the overall framework we illustrate throughout this section. In the second type of approach, we presumably do not know the ways in which several pieces of advice interact or, worse yet, the ways in which independent pieces may contradict one another. This type of situation arises when we advise, for example, both *avoid taking points* and *take all the points* or *take at least one point if no one else has.*

Our approach to integrating multiple pieces of advice takes two basic forms. First, we try to formulate independent recommendations that themselves may become the objects of *meta-heuristics.* That is, we want to accept advice about when, how, and why to combine or favor one heuristic over another. Second, we want to infer these dependencies by understanding why some heuristics produce undesirable results in actual situations. In such cases, we want to eliminate the ambiguity

[8] Readers may also develop variations of this plan that seem superior. Such variations are discussed in more detail in Section 9.3.

by refining the initial heuristic to restrict its application to appropriate situations. This kind of refinement is discussed in Section 9.3.

In summary, we have presented our paradigm for knowledge programming and iterative reprogramming of intelligence systems. This section has focused on knowledge-programming processes, which are pertinent to both initial programming and recurrent reprogramming. (The next section motivates and explains the reprogramming problem in more detail.) We have briefly explained the kinds of advice we expect our systems to assimilate and a variety of methods for converting the advice into operational programs. In this process, we see that the knowledge programmer formulates plans that develop its initially vague concepts into effective procedures for accomplishing goals. These plans also play a major role in identifying weaknesses in knowledge that stimulate learning.

9.3 Plan Evaluation and Knowledge Refinement

9.3.1 ■ Bugs Revealed in Program Execution

To convert constraints and heuristics into action, the knowledge programmer develops a plan that integrates task-environment actions and logical or heuristic inferences. In planning, the knowledge programmer reasons about the effects of the various transformations it employs. Some of its transformations preserve logical equivalence, and others introduce approximate or plausible reasoning. These latter kinds of transformations may introduce undesirable effects, or *bugs.* The second phase of intelligent system development is concerned with the *identification, diagnosis,* and *elimination* of such bugs.

We have developed a list of bugs that arise in knowledge programming. Some of these bugs, which are summarized in Table 9.3, arise from omissions, errors, or ambiguity in the initial knowledge, and others are introduced by the knowledge-programming process. (Other AI researchers have considered bugs in problem-solving procedures, but these have little in common with those under consideration here; see, for example, Davis, 1978; Davis, 1979; Miller and Goldstein, 1976; Sussman, 1975; Sussman and Stallman, 1975; Brown and Burton, 1975.)

The nine problems listed in Table 9.3 span a large set of potential weaknesses in intelligent programs. For the sake of brevity, we con-

TABLE 9.3 Bugs Arising from Knowledge Programming.

Type of Problem	*Source of Problem*	*Manifestation*
1. Excess generality	Special cases overlooked.	Good rule occasionally produces bad effects.
2. Excess specificity	Generality undetected.	Rules fail to cover enough cases.
3. Concept poverty	Useful relationship not detected and exploited.	Limited power and capability of system.
4. Invalid knowledge	Misstatement of facts or approximations.	Expert's expectations violated.
5. Ambiguous knowledge	Implicit dependencies not adequately articulated.	Conflicts arise in some situations about what is best to do.
6. Invalid reasoning	Programmer incorrectly transforms knowledge.	Knowledge programmer's expectations violated.
7. Inadequate integration	Dependencies among multiple pieces of advice incompletely integrated.	Rejected action alternatives actually satisfy more criteria than selected action does.
8. Limited horizon	Consequences of recent past or probable future events not exploited.	Judgmental logic seems static, not sensitive to changing or foreseeable situations.
9. Egocentricity	Little attention paid to probable meaning of others' actions.	No apparent adaptation of one's behavior to exploit knowledge of other's plans.

sider in detail only one of these bugs as an illustration of knowledge-refinement techniques. We have chosen invalid reasoning because it illustrates many of the ideas that recur in knowledge refinement. After we explain our approach to debugging reasoning problems, we briefly characterize the approaches taken for the other kinds of problems.

9.3.2 ■ Diagnosing and Fixing a Reasoning Error

We address here only a limited class of reasoning errors, namely those that manifest themselves as discrepancies between the observed and the expected of executing a plan. Here we are focusing on the expectations that knowledge programmers generate as by-products of their operationalizations and integrations. Knowledge programmers act as if they believe the transformations used to convert ineffective statements to specific procedures will produce results that satisfy the original objectives. This belief applies, in turn, to each successive transformation applied during the planning process. The transformations may, however, yield procedures that do not always satisfy these expectations.

The approach we take to knowledge refinement in this type of problem begins with an attempt to analyze an unexpected event. Thus expectations motivate and trigger the knowledge-refinement process, as shown in Table 9.4. By analyzing the violated expectation, we identify both what went wrong and why. Then, we propose changes to the underlying knowledge to remedy the problem. The success of this method often depends on isolating missing, extraneous, or imprecise predicates used to restrict the time at which some action occurs. (This approach parallels that discussed in Lakatos, 1976.) This becomes clearer in the context of a concrete illustration.

TABLE 9.4 Knowledge-refinement Approach.

Step	*Source of Mechanism*
1. Establish expectations	During knowledge programming, planning establishes plausible antecedents and consequences of actions; these beliefs represent expectations.
2. Trigger analysis	When an actual event violates an expectation, the reasoning behind the expectation is reanalyzed in light of observable data.
3. Locate faulty rules	A set of diagnostic rules debugs the planning logic by contrasting the *a priori* beliefs with actual data. If a heuristic rule used by the plan assumes a false premise or entails a false conclusion, it is faulty.
4. Modify faulty rules	A set of learning rules suggests plausible fixes to the erroneous heuristic rule. These might alter its preconditions, assumptions, or expectations to keep it from producing the same faulty result in a subsequent situation.
5. Reimplement and test	Incorporate a modified heuristic rule into a new system by reinvoking the knowledge programmer. Verify that the rule eliminates the previous problem and test it in new situations.

As one example of the act-evaluate-refine process, consider what happens when the machine attempts to execute the previously developed plan to flush the queen of spades. The plan was, roughly, to take the lead, then lead spades until a player is forced to play the queen. Suppose that this plan worked well in several games, but during one game a sequence such as the following unexpectedly occurred: The machine player wins a trick. It then leads the jack of spades, and the other players follow suit. The queen is still held by one of the players. On the next trick, the machine chooses another spade to lead. This time, it has only two spades left, the four and the king, and it chooses arbitrarily to play the king. The next player plays the five, the one after plays the queen, and the last plays the ten. The machine has just won a trick according to its plan, and it has even flushed the queen. Unfortunately, it has also taken 13 points, presumably a very undesirable outcome.

What might a person in the machine's situation do at this point? With apparently little effort, a person would recognize that the plan was buggy because it achieved an undesirable result that was unexpected. Implicit in the plan was the notion that the player with the queen would be coerced into playing it and, presumably, winning the spade trick with it. In response to this insight, a human player would amend the plan appropriately. The fix in the case would require that when trying to flush the queen, a player must lead only spades below the queen.

Our learning methods capture the general logic behind this type of analysis. There are many chains of reasoning that might lead to the same proposed refinement as our hypothetical human produced. We explain one type of argument that appears programmable.

Let us suppose that the machine (unlike a person) has no precise expectation regarding the queen-flushing plan. However, since it followed supposedly expert advice, it has a general expectation that bad consequences should not result. When, as in this case, undesirable results occur, the program tries to understand why it suffered such an outcome and how it could have prevented it.

The machine analyzes the last trick to infer cause-effect relations, based on its current knowledge. To take 13 points in the trick, it had to win the trick during which the queen was played. So it conjectures for itself some refined advice: Flush the queen of spades but do not win a trick in which the queen is played. Because this refined advice surpasses the original advice in quality, the machine has already improved its knowledge. On the other hand, this high-level advice requires operationalization if it is to be useful. However, our current knowledge programmer does correctly operationalize this advice by producing a plan corresponding to the following: Take the lead, then continue leading spades below the queen. Thus, this type of bug is eliminated by formulating a refinement directly in terms of a new high-level prescriptive heuristic. The refined heuristic, in turn, is implemented by the same knowledge-programming methods previously used for accepting advice from humans. (In some cases, as in this example, the refined heuristic can also be implemented simply by modifying the previous plan, as opposed to starting over from scratch.)

To continue our illustration, let us suppose that the machine begins to apply its refined plan. Because it knows that the plan has been refined to prevent it from taking the queen of spades itself, it notes this specific expectation in the knowledge base as a predicted consequence of the plan. In a new game, however, suppose it has the ten, jack, and king of spades. It wins a trick, then leads the ten. All players follow suit with lower cards, so the machine leads again with the jack. Again it wins the trick. At this point, its revised plan proscribes leading spades, so it plays a diamond. Another player wins the trick, and continues to lead spades. The machine is forced to play the king, and the player after it follows suit with the queen of spades. Again, contrary to its specific expectation, it wins the trick and takes 13 points. Now it attempts to discover why its expectation was violated. It constructs a cause-effect model of the events leading to the disaster. In this model, it notes that at the time it played the king, it had no other choices. Apparently by that time only by keeping the other player from leading spades could it have prevented the disaster. Alternatively, it reviews events prior to that trick to see what, if anything, it did that contributed to creating a situation in which no options existed. It notes that playing the ten and jack of spades earlier produced the state in which it had only the king of spades. It notes that these actions were taken with the express intention of preventing it from taking the queen, but apparently they contributed directly to just that outcome.

It now proposes to itself another refinement. It should prevent a recurrence of this type of situation in the future. Its proposed advice: Do not lead low spades if you can be forced to play a spade higher than the queen.[9] This, in turn, leads to an operationalization that re-

[9] This example has not actually been performed by a machine implementation. Before it could be implemented, several difficult issues would arise. Foremost among these, the diagnostic system would need to conjecture several alternative problems and solutions. Each of these proposed solutions would require, in turn, experimental testing through additional play. For example, the program might have hypothesized the remedy, do not begin to flush the queen of spades if you cannot retain the lead. This heuristic seems beneficial, but we cannot be certain. Empirical validation of alternative heuristics seems unavoidable.

quires an estimation of the probable distributions of spades among players. Although we have developed some methods for handling such probability functions, we have not yet implemented those needed for this particular problem. However, as people who know hearts will note, the proposed concept of a card that is *safe* vis-a-vis the opposing distributions is quite sophisticated. In fact, generalizations of this *safe spade* concept, such as *safe in suit x* or *safe with respect to all suits,* play major roles in expert strategies.

As another example of knowledge refinement, consider again the plan developed in Section 9.2 to avoid taking points. That plan proposed playing the lowest possible card. Using this plan, the machine expects it will avoid taking points, but there are numerous ways that the plan leads to violated expectations, each of which reflects characteristics similar to those in the queen-flushing examples. For example, it may play its lowest card (a five, for example) and still win a trick with points. This causes it to weaken its expectations (i.e., to associate some uncertainty with this predicted outcome). Pursuant to such a play, it may take another trick with its current lowest card (a ten, for example), again with points. However, if it had played the ten before the five, it might have avoided winning the second trick, because in the second trick the five might have been lower than another player's card. Each of these problems gives rise to new attempts to refine both the expectations and the plan, in a manner similar to that previously described. Our general knowledge-refinement strategy can be characterized simply, as shown in Fig. 9.4.

The contrast between expectations and actual outcomes focuses the learning system directly on specific problems. The system then attempts to find the flaws in its original causal model in light of the new data at hand. This in turn suggests additional conditions or new goals for knowledge programming.

The overall approach we have taken to this problem uses three basic elements: proofs, diagnostic rules, and learning rules. Although these steps have not actually been implemented on a computer, we have hand-simulated all of them. The knowledge programmer associates with each plan and its expectations a *proof* (or an informal rationale). The proof of a plan links assumed conditions to expectations by following paths representing the equivalence of logical transformations, the plausible sufficiency of heuristic transformations, or the antecedent-consequent relations of instrumental acts. At each point, a transformation links premises to expectations, and these expectations may become a part of the premises for a later inference. In short, a proof maps a general model of cause-effect relations into a specific derivation of the expected consequences of the planned actions.

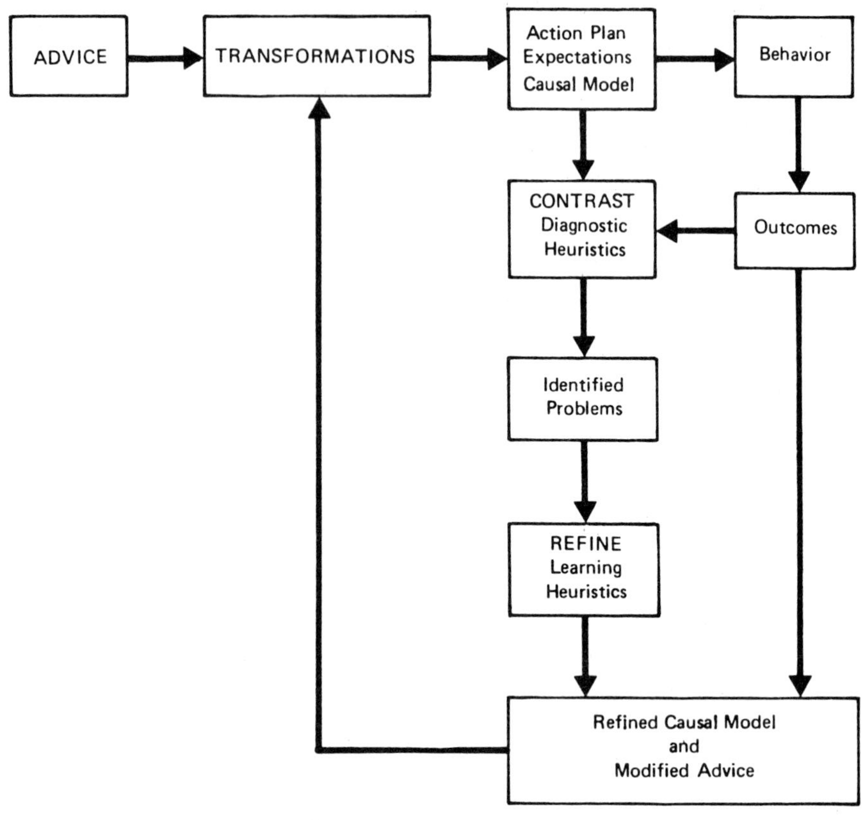

FIGURE 9.4 Knowledge-refinement Strategy.

Diagnostic rules examine the proof in light of the evidence and identify hypothetical deficiencies in the knowledge base. A typical diagnostic rule is as follows:

> INVALID PREMISE DIAGNOSTIC RULE: If an expectation is violated, find a premise in the proof of the expectation that is falsified by the data. If the false premise follows from some inference rule whose own antecedent premises (necessary conditions) are true, declare that rule faulty.

Learning rules, on the other hand, specify ways to modify heuristics to correct deficiencies. We have generated a large set of such rules to date. Two examples of learning rules are given here:

REQUIRE IMPLICITLY ASSUMED PREMISE EXPLICITLY: If an implicit assumption of a rule is falsified during proof analysis, add the premise to the required conditions of the rule and delete any other premises that it implies.

GUARANTEE ASSUMED CONDITIONS: If an assumed premise is falsified during proof analysis, identify sufficient conditions for its validity and make these required conditions for the associated plan component.

We demonstrate here how these diagnostic and learning rules are used to refine the original flush-the-queen-of-spades plan as discussed previously. This also exemplifies the knowledge-refinement approach outlined in Fig. 9.4.

Plan.
Flush queen of spades:

If	player *P* takes the lead
and	*P* doesn't have the queen of spades
then	*P* continues leading spades.

Expectation. *P* doesn't take the queen of spades.

Proof of Expectation:

1.	Player *P* takes the lead.	Premise (condition of plan)
2.	*P* doesn't have the queen of spades.	Premise (condition of plan)
3.	*P* continues leading spades.	Premise (action of play)
4.	If player *P* takes the lead and *P* doesn't have the queen of spades then opponent will play queen of spades.	Heuristic rule
5.	Opponent will play queen of spades.	Derived premise from 1,2,3,4
6.	If an opponent plays queen of spades then the opponent wins the trick and opponent takes the queen of spades.	Heuristic rule
7.	Opponent takes the queen of spades.	Derived premise from 5,6
8.	If opponent takes the queen of spades then player *P* doesn't take queen of spades.	Heuristic rule
9.	Player *P* doesn't take queen of spades.	Derived premise from 7,8

Behavior in actual play. *P* leads king of spades;
Opponent plays queen of spades.

Outcome. *P* wins the trick; *P* takes the queen of spades.

Expectation of flush-queen-of-spades plan is violated.

Apply diagnostic rules to identify problems:

Using the Invalid Premise diagnostic rule, the derived premise in Statement 7 is falsified by the data. The inference rule used to derive this false premise is the rule specified in Statement 6. Its premise is true, but its conclusion is false. Declare this rule faulty.

Apply Learning Rules to modify plans and heuristics.

Using the Guarantee Assumed Conditions learning rule, the system looks for other rules in the knowledge base that identify conditions for inferring Statement 7. It may find, for example, the inference rule:

If	opponent player plays a high card *C*
and	player P plays below *C*
then	opponent wins trick and takes *C*.

In our current example, *C* is the queen of spades.
This rule now replaces the faulty rule in Statement 6 with
the new premise:

Player *P* plays below the queen of spades

added as a premise to the plan and the proof. The resultant plan is

If	player *P* takes the lead
and	*P* doesn't have the queen of spades
then	*P* continues leading spades below the queen of spades.

We have thus found many ways to evaluate a plan against observable outcomes to identify weaknesses, conjecture refinements, and evaluate these refinements experimentally. Very little of this work has been implemented because of the vast number of possible learning strategies (see Table 9.5) and the wide variety of specific possible applications. Any efforts to implement these concepts in a realistically complex task will encounter considerable combinatorial difficulties. Each error may suggest several hypothetical bugs and fixes. Each of these will require independent empirical (or formal) validation, usually accomplished best by experimental testing. The need for testing hypothetical concepts and rules will lead to alternative knowledge bases and associated operational programs. Multiple systems of this sort are, of course, difficult to manage even in limited software-development environments.

9.3.3 ■ Summary

Once a plan is executed, much can be learned from a retrospective analysis. When advice is provided initially, two important things are missing that later support evaluation and discovery. The first new source of information is the actual situation description. The details of the actual situation in which the plan executes reveal and implicitly

TABLE 9.5 Knowledge-refinement Strategies.

Type of Problem	*Refinement Strategy*
1. Excess generality	Specialize the rules, using case analysis, proof analysis, and concept hierarchy specializations.
2. Excess specificity	Generalize the rules, using equivalence of cases, proof analysis, and concept hierarchy generalizations.
3. Concept poverty	Create new concepts by characterizing a particular problem, adding its definition, consequences, and proposed solution to knowledge base (e.g., "sacrifice," "safe" distribution).
4. Invalid knowledge	Correct faulty advice, using proof analysis, diagnosis, and refinement.
5. Ambiguous knowledge	Explore alternative interpretations; prune those that produce least desirable effects.
6. Invalid reasoning	Correct faulty operationalizations, using proof analysis, diagnosis, and refinement.
7. Inadequate integration	Develop comprehensive operationalizations that satisfy multiple pieces of advice simultaneously; sequentially order separable criteria to satisfy most important considerations first.
8. Limited horizon	Elaborate plans to incorporate contingencies and predict, monitor, and remember their outcomes; when possible, prefer dynamic operationalizations to static ones.
9. Egocentricity	During planning, consider what others are likely to do; use your own plans to model what you would do in their places; then monitor their behavior to assess its consistency with your model.

define important special cases that the general operationalization overlooks. Second, having acted, we can see the true effects of our behavior on the environment. This provides sources of confirmation or disconfirmation of parts of our plans, which then stimulate focused efforts at diagnosis and knowledge refinement. These provide numerous opportunities for concept formulation, and each, in turn, initiates a new cycle of knowledge acquisition, knowledge programming, and knowledge refinement.

9.4 Conclusions and Recommendations

9.4.1 ■ Findings

In today's environments, major advances in AI arise primarily in conjunction with knowledge-engineering research. In this area, the power of intelligent systems derives primarily from the knowledge of human experts. The primary bottlenecks in the construction of intelligent systems are formulating knowledge for programmers, converting the knowledge into effective procedures, and iteratively evaluating a program's behavior, modifying the knowledge, and reimplementing the corresponding program code.

We have formulated a framework for exploring solutions to these problems. The framework provides a basis for experts to express domain knowledge in terms of natural domain-specific concepts. This requires a formal knowledge-representation scheme and a substantial set of built-in primitive concepts from which the specific domain concepts are constructed. Once the concepts are defined, the expert can express two kinds of advice about the behavior of the program. Constraints specify restrictions on allowable behavior, whereas heuristics prescribe desirable modes of behavior. These may be ambiguous, incomplete, or even inconsistent.

This advice is converted into a working program through a process of operationalization, which transforms constraints and heuristics into effective procedures. In this process, the current program uses the expert's supplied knowledge along with about 300 transformation rules. Some of these reformulate expressions in equivalent terms, for example, by substituting a definition for some specific term. Some of the rules prescribe sufficient or approximately sufficient means of achieving ends. Finally, the operationalization process uses instrumental reasoning to predict effects of potential actions or to reason backwards from desired effects to sufficient conditions and actions.

In the process of operationalizing advice, a plan that prescribes a sequence of actions required to accomplish the goals and satisfy the constraints is developed. To do so, the knowledge programmer uses a casual model to establish a proof of the plan's expected effects. When the plan is executed, new data about the situation and the effects are obtained. By contrasting observations with expectations and premises in the proof, diagnosis rules indicate faulty components of the plan. These in turn lead to plausible refinements to the plan and corresponding changes to the knowledge base. These refinements, in turn, reinitiate the cycle of operationalization, execution, and evaluation.

We have found this paradigm quite valuable as a source of new ideas and methods for knowledge acquisition and refinement. We have implemented only the operationalization component and have experimented with several knowledge representations in different tasks to develop diagnostic and learning rules. We have not yet converged on a small set of rules for any aspect of this paradigm. We have approximately 300 rules of operationalization for two tasks (hearts and a simple music composition task), and fewer than 100 diagnostic and learning rules. However, we foresee these number increasing to as many as a few thousand. For example, many of Lenat's proposed general concept-discovery methods (e.g., generalization and specialization heuristics) seem to apply to behavioral tasks as well as to mathematics (Lenat, 1976; Lenat, 1977b). Our current ceilings have been imposed by funding and personnel limitations: We have found many more interesting and productive lines of investigation than we have had resources to pursue.

9.4.2 ■ Recommendations

We recommend that the proposed research paradigm be adopted widely. It focuses on a set of learning problems that are considerably different from those addressed in most previous learning research in AI and cognitive psychology. Much previous research (our own included) addressed isolated concept, pattern, and rule-learning problems—tasks that seem fundamentally tied to limited applications. Although the number of potential applications for pattern- or rule-induction systems is large, most learning problems will arise in the context of more fully integrated intelligent systems. These systems will require capabilities for recognizing patterns, gathering information, assessing uncertainties, trading off between multiple goals, satisfying a variety of constraints, and dynamically applying general principles to specific situations. These capabilities in turn create demands for both rapid knowledge programming and rapid refinements.

We also recommend that learning issues be approached within the broader context of purposive behavior. In this context, the value of knowledge derives from its contributions to attaining goals. Goal-oriented planning provides a basis for contrasting the expected with the actual effects of knowledge. This in turn dictates what new knowledge must be produced and how to integrate it into an existing knowledge base. This type of teleological orientation strongly motivates and guides knowledge acquisition and refinement.[10]

Finally, we suggest an increased emphasis on the core research problems standing between our current state of technology and the capability of automatic knowledge programming and refinement discussed in this paper. The primary research problems include (1) representations for concepts, constraints, and heuristics amenable to machine interpretation and semantic analysis; (2) translators for mapping natural domain descriptions into these knowledge representations; (3) operationalization and planning; (4) plan evaluation and proof analysis; and (5) knowledge-refinement and concept-discovery heuristics.

Acknowledgments

We gratefully acknowledge the substantive contributions of our Rand, Stanford, and Carnegie-Mellon colleagues to this work. John Burge collaborated with us on learning heuristics. Stanley Rosenschein made frequent contributions to our efforts on knowledge representation. Douglas Lenat assisted in the development of knowledge representations, heuristics, and procedures for cognitive economy. As advisors to Jack Mostow, both Allen Newell and Jaime Carbonell contributed to our understanding of operationalization. The paper represents only the authors' attitudes, however, and not the opinions of others with whom we have collaborated.

References

1. Allen, J., *Anatomy of LISP*, McGraw-Hill book Company, New York, 1978.
2. Anderson, R. H., "The Use of Production Systems in RITA to Construct Personal Computer 'Agents'," *SIGART Newsletter 63*, 1977, 23–28.

[10] A corollary to this recommendation argues that when constructing or modifying AI programs, we should try to analyze the reasoning involved. One step in this direction is to identify operators for transforming specifications into working code. (See Balzer et al., 1977; Barstow, 1977; Mostow & Hayes-Roth, 1979a.)

3. Anderson, R. H., and J. J. Gillogly, *Rand Intelligent Terminal Agent (RITA): Design Philosophy*, The Rand Corporation, R-1809-ARPA, February 1976.

4. Balzer, R., "A Mathematical Model for Performing a Complex Task in a Card Game," *Behavioral Sciences*, 2, 1966, 219–236.

5. Balzer, R., N. Goldman, and D. Wile, "Informality in Program Specifications," *Proceedings of the Fifth International Joint Conference on Artificial Intelligence*, Cambridge, Massachusetts, 1977, 389–397.

6. Barr, A., J. Bennett, and W. Clancey, *Transfer of Expertise: A Theme for AI Research*, Technical Report HPP-79-11, Stanford University, March 1979.

7. Barstow, D., "A Knowledge-Based System for Automatic Program Construction," *Proceedings of the Fifth International Joint Conference on Artificial Intelligence*, Cambridge, Massachusetts, 1977, 382–388.

8. Biermann, A. W., and R. Krishnaswamy, "Constructing Programs from Example," *IEEE Transactions on Software Engineering*, SE-2, 3, 1976.

9. Brown, J. S., and R. R. Burton, "Multiple Representations of Knowledge for Tutorial Reasoning," in *Representation and Meaning* (D. Bobrow and A. Collins, eds.), Academic Press, New York, 1975, 311–349.

10. Buchanan, B. G., and T. Mitchell, "Model-Directed Learning of Production Rules," in *Pattern-Directed Inference Systems* (D. A. Waterman and F. Hayes-Roth, eds.), Academic Press, New York, 1978, 297–312.

11. Buchanan, B. G., G. Sutherland, and E. A. Feigenbaum, "Heuristic Dendral: A Program for Generating Explanatory Hypotheses in Organic Chemistry," in *Machine Intelligence 4* (B. Meltzer and D. Michie, eds.), American Elsevier, New York, 1969, 209–254.

12. Church, A., *The Calculus of Lambda-Conversion*, Princeton University Press, Princeton, 1941.

13. Davis, R., "Interactive Transfer of Expertise: Acquisition of New Inference Rules," *Artificial Intelligence*, 12, 1979, 121–158.

14. Davis, R., "Knowledge Acquisition in Rule-Based Systems—Knowledge About Representations as a Basis for System Construction and Maintenance," in *Pattern-Directed Inference Systems* (D. A. Waterman and F. Hayes-Roth, eds.), Academic Press, New York, 1978, 99–134.

15. Davis, R., B. Buchanan, and E. H. Shortliffe, "Production Rules as Representation for a Knowledge-Based Consultation System," *Artificial Intelligence*, 8, 1977, 15–45.
16. Davis, R., and J. King, "An Overview of Production Systems," in *Machine Intelligence 8* (E. W. Elcock and D. Michie, eds.), John Wiley & Sons, New York, 1976, 300–332.
17. Duda, R. O., P. E. Hart, N. J. Nilsson, and G. L. Sutherland, "Semantic Network Representations in Rule-Based Inference Systems," in *Pattern-Directed Inference Systems* (D. A. Waterman and F. Hayes-Roth, eds.), Academic Press, New York, 1978, 203–221.
18. Fagan, L., *Ventilator Manager: A Program to Provide On-Line Consultative Advice in the Intensive Care Unit*, Technical Memo HPP-78-16, Computer Science Department, Stanford University, 1978.
19. Faught, W., D. A. Waterman, P. Klahr, S. J. Rosenschein, D. Gorlin, and S. J. Tepper, *EP-2: An Exemplary Programming System*, The Rand Corporation, R-2411-ARPA, February 1980.
20. Feigenbaum, E. A., "The Art of Artificial Intelligence: Themes and Case Studies of Knowledge Engineering," *Proceedings of the Fifth International Joint Conference on Artificial Intelligence*, Cambridge, Massachusetts, 1977, 1014–1029.
21. Feigenbaum, E. A., B. G. Buchanan, and J. Lederberg, "On Generality and Problem Solving: A Case Study Using the Dendral Program," in *Machine Intelligence 6* (B. Meltzer and D. Michie, eds.), American Elsevier, New York, 1971, 165–190.
22. Hayes-Roth, F., "Schematic Classification Problems and Their Solution," *Pattern Recognition*, 6, 1974, 105–113.
23. Hayes-Roth, F., "Patterns of Induction and Associated Knowledge Acquisition Algorithms," in *Pattern Recognition and Artificial Intelligence* (C. H. Chen, ed.), Academic Press, New York, 1976(a).
24. Hayes-Roth, F., "Representation of Structured Events and Efficient Procedures for Their Recognition," *Pattern Recognition*, 8, 1976(b), 141–150.
25. Hayes-Roth, F., "Uniform Representations of Structured Patterns and an Algorithm for the Induction of Contingency-Response Rules," *Information and Control*, 33, 1977, 87–116.
26. Hayes-Roth, F., "The Role of Partial and Best Matches in Knowledge Systems," in *Pattern-Directed Inference Systems*

(D. A. Waterman and F. Hayes-Roth, eds.), Academic Press, New York, 1978(a), 557–574.

27. Hayes-Roth, F., "Learning By Example," in *Cognitive Psychology and Instruction* (A. M. Lesgold et al., eds.), Plenum, New York, 1978(b).

28. Hayes-Roth, F., and J. Burge, "Characterizing Syllables as Sequences of Machine-Generated Labelled Segments of Connected Speech: A Study in Symbolic Pattern Learning Using a Conjunctive Feature Learning and Classification System," *Proceedings of the Third International Joint Conference on Pattern Recognition*, Coronado, California, 1976, 431–435.

29. Hayes-Roth, F., P. Klahr, J. Burge, and D. J. Mostow, *Machine Methods for Acquiring, Learning, and Applying Knowledge*, The Rand Corporation, P-6241, October 1978.

30. Hayes-Roth, F., and J. McDermott, "Learning Structured Patterns from Examples," *Proceedings of the Third International Joint Conference on Pattern Recognition*, Coronado, California, 1976, 419–423.

31. Hayes-Roth, F., and J. McDermott, "An Interference Matching Technique for Inducing Abstractions," *Communications of the ACM*, 21, 1978, 401–410.

32. Heidorn, G. E., "Automatic Programming Through Natural Language Dialog: A Survey," *IBM J. Research and Development*, 20, 1976, 302–313.

33. Heidorn, G. E., "English as a Very High Level Language for Simulation Programming," *ACM SIGPLAN Symposium on Very High Level Languages*, Santa Monica, California, 1974, 91–100.

34. Lakatos, I., *Proofs and Refutations*, Cambridge University Press, Cambridge, 1976.

35. Lenat, D., *AM: An Artificial Intelligence Approach to Discovery in Mathematics as Heuristic Search*, SAIL AIM-286, Stanford Artificial Intelligence Laboratory, Stanford, California, 1976. Jointly issued as Computer Science Department Report No. STAN-CS-76-570.

36. Lenat, D., "Automated Theory Formation in Mathematics," *Proceedings of the Fifth International Joint Conference on Artificial Intelligence*, Cambridge, Massachusetts, 1977(a), 833–842.

37. Lenat, D., "The Ubiquity of Discovery: 1977 Computers and Thought Lecture," *Proceedings of the Fifth International Joint Conference on Artificial Intelligence*, Cambridge, Massachusetts, 1977(b), 1093–1105.

38. Lenat, D. B., and G. Harris, "Designing a Rule System that Searches for Scientific Discoveries," in *Pattern-Directed Inference Systems* (D. A. Waterman and F. Hayes-Roth, eds.), Academic Press, New York, 1978, 25–51.
39. Lenat, D. B., F. Hayes-Roth, and P. Klahr, *Cognitive Economy*, The Rand Corporation, N-1185-NSF, June 1979(a).
40. Lenat, D. B., F. Hayes-Roth, and P. Klahr, "Cognitive Economy in AI Systems," *Proceedings of the Sixth International Joint Conference on Artificial Intelligence*, Tokyo, 1979(b), 531–536.
41. Miller, M. L., and I. P. Goldstein, *SPADE: A Grammar Based Editor for Planning and Debugging Programs*, AI Memo 386, MIT Artificial Intelligence Laboratory, December 1976.
42. Minsky, M. L., and S. Papert, *Perceptrons: An Introduction to Computational Geometry*, MIT Press, Cambridge, 1969.
43. Mitchell, T. M., "Version Spaces: A Candidate Elimination Approach to Rule Learning," *Proceedings of the Fifth International Joint Conference on Artificial Intelligence*, Cambridge, Massachusetts, 1977, 305–310.
44. Mostow, D. J., and F. Hayes-Roth, *Machine-Aided Heuristic Programming: A Paradigm for Knowledge Engineering*, The Rand Corporation, N-1007-NSF, February 1979(a).
45. Mostow, D. J., and F. Hayes-Roth, "Operationalizing Heuristics: Some AI Methods for Assisting AI Programming," *Proceedings of the Sixth International Joint Conference on Artificial Intelligence*, Tokyo, 1979(b), 601–609.
46. Newell, A., "Heuristic Programming: Ill-Structured Problems," in *Progress in Operations Research* (J. Aronofsky, ed.), John Wiley & Sons, New York, 1969, 363–414.
47. Newell, A., and H. A. Simon, *Human Problem Solving*, Prentice-Hall, Englewood Cliffs, New Jersey, 1972.
48. Pople, H. E., "The Formation of Composite Hypotheses in Diagnostic Problem Solving: An Exercise in Hypothetical Reasoning," *Proceedings of the Fifth International Joint Conference on Artificial Intelligence*, Cambridge, Massachusetts, 1977, 1030–1037.
49. Pople, H. E., J. D. Myers, and R. A. Miller, "The DIALOG Model of Diagnostic Logic and its Use in Internal Medicine," *Proceedings of the Fourth International Joint Conference on Artificial Intelligence*, USSR, 1975, 848–855.
50. Samuel, A. L., "Some Studies of Machine Learning Using the Game of Checkers," in *Computers and Thought* (E. A. Feigenbaum and J. Feldman, eds.), McGraw-Hill Book Company, New York, 1963, 71–105.

51. Shortliffe, E. H., *Computer-Based Medical Consultations: MYCIN*, American Elsevier, New York, 1976.

52. Soloway, E. M., and E. M. Riseman, "Knowledge-Directed Learning," *Proceedings of the Workshop Pattern-Directed Inference Systems*, SIGART Newsletter 63, 1977, 49–55.

53. Stefik, M., "An Examination of a Frame-Structured Representation System," *Proceedings of the Sixth International Joint Conference on Artificial Intelligence*, Tokyo, 1979, 845–852.

54. Sussman, G. J., *A Computational Model of Skill Acquisition*, American Elsevier, New York, 1975.

55. Sussman, G. J., and R. Stallman, *Heuristic Techniques in Computer Aided Circuit Analysis*, Memo 328, MIT Artificial Intelligence Laboratory, Cambridge, Massachusetts, 1975.

56. Vere, S. A., "Inductive Learning of Relational Productions," in *Pattern-Directed Inference Systems* (D. A. Waterman and F. Hayes-Roth, eds.), Academic Press, New York 1978(a), 281–295.

57. Vere, S. A., *Multilevel Counterfactuals for Generalizations of Relational Concepts and Productions*, Technical Report, University of Illinois, Chicago Circle, 1978(b).

58. Waterman, D. A., *Rule-Directed Interactive Transaction Agents: An Approach to Knowledge Acquisition*, The Rand Corporation, R-2171-ARPA, February 1978(a).

59. Waterman, D. A., "Exemplary Programming in RITA," in *Pattern-Directed Inference Systems* (D. A. Waterman and F. Hayes-Roth, eds.), Academic Press, New York, 1978(b), 261–279.

60. Waterman, D. A., and F. Hayes-Roth (eds.), *Pattern-Directed Inference Systems*, Academic Press, New York, 1978.

61. Waterman, D. A., R. H. Anderson, F. Hayes-Roth, P. Klahr, G. Martins, and S. J. Rosenschein, *Design of a Rule-Oriented System for Implementing Expertise*, The Rand Corporation, N-1158-1-ARPA, May 1979.

62. Winston, P. H., "Learning Structural Descriptions from Examples," in *The Psychology of Computer Vision* (P. H. Winston, ed.), McGraw-Hill Book Company, New York, 1975.

Chapter 10

INFERNO: A Cautious Approach to Uncertain Inference

J. Ross Quinlan

10.1 Introduction

The central postulate of knowledge engineering is that systems achieve expert performance from rich, diverse knowledge bases rather than from clever algorithms. The process of solving a problem in some application area is seen as the task of combining domain knowledge and information specific to the problem so that appropriate conclusions can be drawn. As attention continues to shift to real-world problems of practical importance, however, it has become apparent that the corresponding domain and problem knowledge is usually less than certain. Feigenbaum states, "Experience has shown us that [expert] knowledge is largely heuristic knowledge—mostly 'good guesses' and 'good practice' in lieu of facts and rigor" [Feigenbaum, 1979, p. 7]. On the other

This chapter originally appeared as N-1898-RC, The Rand Corporation, September 1982. It also appeared in *The Computer Journal,* vol. 26, no. 3, August 1983, 255–269.

hand, traditional methods of forming inferences are derived from logic and use techniques such as the Resolution Method [Robinson, 1965] that deal only with categorical information. This chapter is concerned with how uncertain knowledge can be used to find inferences that are well-founded even if they are not categorical.

We start with a collection of *propositions* consisting of facts, expectations, and hypotheses relevant to some problem domain. Subgroups of the propositions are bound by logical, causal, or other mechanisms, so that knowing something about one proposition may have consequences for others. The information available about the propositions is not clear-cut, but vague, uncertain, or probabilistic. The task of inference under uncertainty is then to maintain an integrated world view represented by the sum of deduced and given information about the propositions as more data are gathered or alternative hypotheses are postulated. Early examples of problem domains analyzed in this way include medical diagnosis and therapy [Shortliffe and Buchanan, 1975], in which propositions are symptoms, diseases, and treatments; and geological analysis [Duda, Hart, Nilsson, Reboh, Slocum, and Sutherland, 1977], with propositions about levels of geological structure, geography, and exploitable mineral.

A useful model of this type of problem is the *inference network*, [Duda, Gaschnig, and Hart, 1979; Gaschnig, 1981; Hayes-Roth, Waterman, and Lenat, 1978], in which propositions are represented as nodes, each with some measure of validity in the light of information gathered to date. Interdependencies among propositions become links among combinations of nodes. When information is injected at some point in the system, the links allow it to be propagated to all nodes to which it is directly or indirectly relevant and enable the validity measure of these nodes to be altered in the process. When all the propagation ripples have subsided, the new state of the network represents what is known directly about the propositions or can be deduced from their relationships to other propositions.

Section 10.2 explores some key ideas relevant to current inference network systems. These lead to the conclusion that another approach is warranted, and Section 10.3 introduces a new system called INFERNO. The two major contributions of INFERNO are the guaranteed validity of any inferences that it makes, and its concern for, and assistance in establishing, the consistency of the information about the problem and its domain. Section 10.4 illustrates the use of INFERNO and compares it with one of the more powerful Bayesian systems in common use. Section 10.5 summarizes and evaluates INFERNO's contribution to inference under uncertainty and suggests directions for further work.

10.2 Key Ideas in Inference Network Systems

Figure 10.1 shows a simple inference network adapted from the AL/X model of Reiter (1980) for diagnosing faults that arise on oil-drilling rigs. In addition to providing a good example of many of the important concepts, this particular network is used for a comparative study in Section 10.4. The propositions or nodes are represented by boxes, with relationships given by directed links. The numbers that appear on top of the boxes are the validity measures for the propositions, in the form of probabilities that the proposition is true; their initial values are the respective prior probabilities. There are two kinds of links. The first kind corresponds to antecedent-consequent implications and have two values associated with them. If the antecedent proposition is found to hold, the odds of the consequent proposition are multiplied by the first value; if the antecedent is found to be false, the odds of the consequent are multiplied by the second value; and if the antecedent is found to have some intermediate probability p, the odds of the consequent proposition are multiplied by an interpolated value determined by p, the prior probability of the antecedent, and the two values. The second type of link has no values and is used to produce propositions that are Boolean combinations of other propositions. The probability of these nodes is determined by the probabilities of their constituent propositions.

The information in this network is general domain knowledge, in that it is not restricted to the problem of diagnosing a single fault occurrence. Typically, most knowledge codified in an inference network is applicable to a range of problems in the domain and usually includes the relationships among all propositions of interest. This information is often tedious to set up and debug, but it can then be used repeatedly. To use the network on a particular problem, the general or domain information is augmented with specific observations, hypotheses, and so forth, such as "V01SDHP has occurred with probability 0.95." The two bodies of information, specific and general, jointly allow inferences to be drawn for the particular case.

As this example illustrates, the information in an inference network is divided between the part, relevant to propositions, that is associated with nodes, and the part, relevant to relations, that resides on the links among nodes. The distinction is important in practice because typically only the values associated with propositions can be altered as a result of inference. With a few exceptions, such as PI [Friedman, 1981], systems do not allow us to deduce the existence of a connection between nodes.[1] Most systems do not even permit parameters characterizing a relation (such as the values of an antecedent-consequent link) to be modified. This is presumably because the specification of interdependencies belongs to the general information relevant to the domain and so is not expected to change from case to case. The example also shows the two forms of interrelationship that seem to be standard in all systems: expressing one proposition as a Boolean function of other propositions, and a kind of attenuated implication of the form "if *A*, then (to extent *E*) conclude *B*".

In other respects, inference network systems show considerable dissimilarity. The principal differences can be reduced to four areas of special functional significance: (1) the way in which uncertain information about propositions is represented; (2) the assumptions that form the basis for propagating information; (3) the control structure used for this propagation; and (4) the treatment of inconsistent information. The following discusses alternative approaches in these areas as exemplified in several systems. To avoid continual repetition of references, the principal models used here are Prospector [Duda, Hart, and Nilsson, 1976; Gaschnig, 1980, 1981]; PI [Friedman, 1981]; the system described in Garvey, Lowrance, and Fischler (1981); WAND [Hayes-Roth, unpublished]; SPERIL [Ishizuka and Yao, 1981]; Konolige's information-based approach [Konolige, 1982; Duda, Hart, Konolige, and Reboh, 1979]; AL/X [Reiter, 1980, 1981]; MYCIN [Shortliffe, 1975]; and EMYCIN [van Melle, 1979, 1980]. The widely known work of Zadeh (1979) has been excluded from this list because his possibilistic approach using linguistic quantification is so different from the other systems that comparison is difficult.

10.2.1 ■ Uncertain Knowledge about Propositions

There are three common ways to represent uncertain information about propositions. The most straightforward approach (employed in Prospector and AL/X and used in the sample network) provides a subjective probability for each proposition.[2] In other words, if *E* is the sum

[1] If it can be deduced that the proposition *AvB* is true, this is equivalent to deducing that the relation "~*A* implies *B*" holds. However, many systems use a form of one-directional inference (discussed later) that precludes conclusions about *A* or *B* being drawn from Boolean combinations such as *AvB*, with the result that the consequences of this sort of ersatz relation are not discovered.

[2] The adjective *subjective* means that the probability does not have to come from ideas of relative frequency in the limit but can reflect fair odds on the proposition being true.

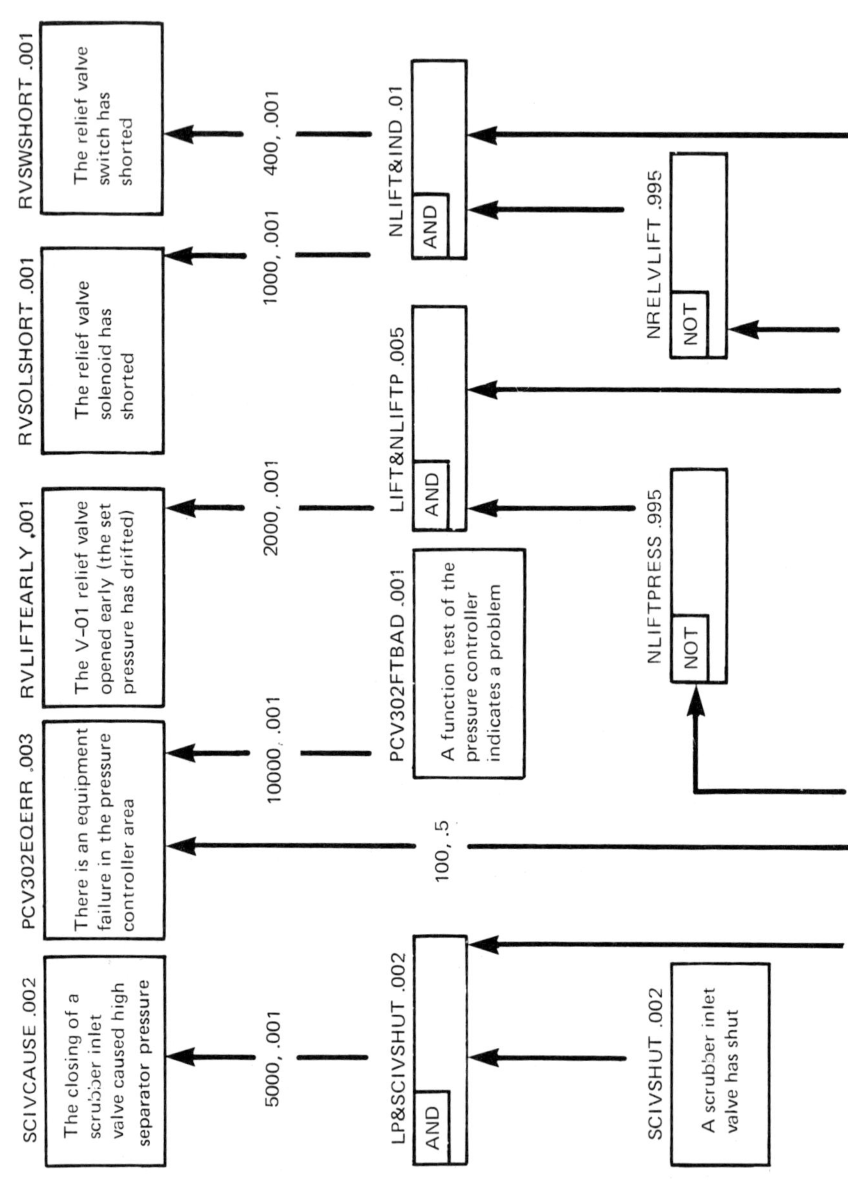

RVSWSHORT .001
The relief valve switch has shorted
RVSOLSHORT .001
The relief valve solenoid has shorted
RVLIFTEARLY .001
The V–01 relief valve opened early (the set pressure has drifted)
PCV302EQERR .003
There is an equipment failure in the pressure controller area
SCIVCAUSE .002
The closing of a scrubber inlet valve caused high separator pressure
400, .001
1000, .001
2000, .001
10000, .001
100, .5
5000, .001
NLIFT&IND .01
AND
LIFT&NLIFTP .005
AND
PCV302FTBAD .001
A function test of the pressure controller indicates a problem
LP&SCIVSHUT .002
AND
NRELVLIFT .995
NOT
NLIFTPRESS .995
NOT
SCIVSHUT .002
A scrubber inlet valve has shut

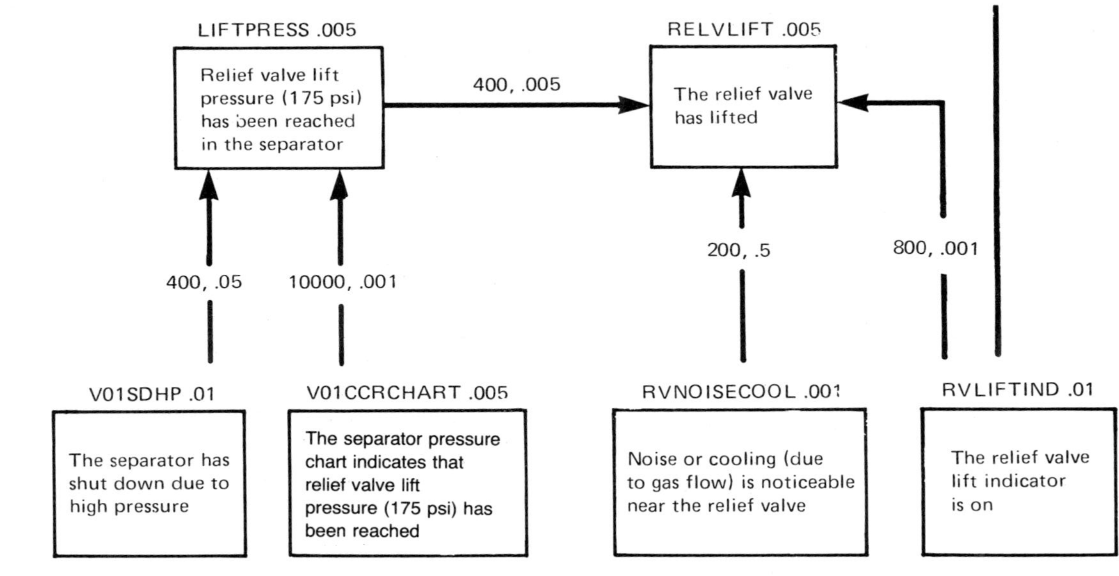

FIGURE 10.1 An AL/X Inference Network.

of all information available to the system, each proposition A has associated with it a value representing the probability $P(A|E)$ that A holds in the light of E, derived under some regimen such as Bayesian inference. The main point here is not how this value is derived, but the fact that what we know or have inferred about a proposition is represented by a single value.

Two criticisms have been advanced concerning this approach. The first is that the single value tells us nothing about its precision, which may be very low when the value is derived from uncertain evidence. To say that $P(A|E)$ is 0.5 might mean either 0.5 plus or minus 0.001, or 0.5 plus or minus 0.3, two very different pieces of information. Barnett writes, "There is trouble representing what we actually know without being forced to overcommit when we are ignorant" [Barnett, 1981]. Garvey et al. note, "A likelihood represented by a point probability value is usually an overstatement of what is actually known" [Garvey et al., 1981]. The second criticism is that the single value combines the evidence for and against A without indicating how much there is of each. Intuitively, the probability of A in the light of E might have the same value when no evidence in E is relevant to A as when E contains strong but counterbalancing arguments for A and against A.

MYCIN uses an alternative approach in which there are two separate values for the validity of each proposition. $MB[A,E]$ is a probability-like measure of belief in A given E, and $MD[A,E]$ is a similar value for disbelief in A given E. If E could be partitioned into two parts, $E+$ favoring A and $E-$ opposing A, $MB[A,E]$ corresponds in intent with $P(A|E+)$ and $MD[A,E]$ with $P(\sim A|E-)$. However, the belief and disbelief measures are independent and so cannot be probabilities, although they have the same interpretation at their extremes; if $MB[A,E]$ is 1, E provides incontrovertible evidence that A is true. The two measures are combined into a single assessment of A in the light of E, called the certainty factor $CF[A,E]$ and defined as $MB[A,E] - MD[A,E]$.

The two-value approach is also subject to the criticism about precision, since both of the belief measures are point values. It does, however, overcome the second objection because the interplay of evidence pro and con is manifest. This separation can be nullified if the belief and disbelief measures are used not as distinct entities but only as an amalgamated certainty (as is the case in MYCIN's successor, EMYCIN), because the amalgamation restores what is essentially the original single-value system. The scheme suffers from a new disability, however, in that there is no foundation of theory underpinning and justifying the interpretation and weighing of separate belief and disbelief measures.

The third approach is used in systems with different pedigrees, including those that employ the Dempster-Shafer theory of evidence (such as Garvey et al., 1981; Barnett, 1981) and others (SPERIL, WAND). Instead of representing the probability of a proposition A by a point value, this approach bounds the probability to a subinterval $[s(A),p(A)]$ of $[0,1]$. The exact probability $P(A)$ of A may be unknown but bounded by $s(A) \leq P(A) \leq p(A)$. The precision of our knowledge about A is immediately plain, with our uncertainty characterized by the difference $p(A) - s(A)$. If this is small, our knowledge about A is relatively precise; if it is large, we know correspondingly little. If $p(A)$ equals $s(A)$, our knowledge about A is exact and reverts to the point probability of the first approach. Note that the preceding inequality can be recast as two assertions: (1) that the probability of A is at least $s(A)$; and (2) that the probability of $\sim A$ is at least $1 - p(A)$. Thus this representation also addresses the second criticism, because it keeps what amount to separate measures of belief and disbelief in A derived from the available evidence. Finally, as with the first scheme, there is the solid ground of probability theory on which to base the interpretation of the values $s(A)$ and $p(A)$.

10.2.2 ■ Assumptions

We now turn to some of the assumptions underlying the ways in which information is propagated in the network. Recent findings have cast doubts on the appropriateness of many of these assumptions, and thus indirectly on the methods of propagation that use them. The position from which these assumptions are assessed is a conservative one: rather than rely on questionable assumptions, it is preferable to accept the penalty of less definitive inferences.

The systems that use Bayes' theorem provide a good starting point. A seminal paper of Duda, Hart and Nilsson (1976) is meticulous in explicitly setting out the basis for the propagation scheme used in Prospector and subsequently in AL/X. One trouble arises when two distinct pieces of evidence $E1$ and $E2$ are relevant to a proposition A. To update our assessment of A we need to compute $P(A|E1\&E2)$, but knowing how to update A separately for each of $E1$ and $E2$, such as by knowing each of $P(E1)$, $P(E2)$, $P(A\&E1)$, and $P(A\&E2)$, is not sufficient to determine this. The general case would require propagation parameters (such as the upper and lower values on links in the earlier example) for every subset of inputs to a proposition or, equivalently, the complete joint distribution of all propositions.

In many large inference networks, asking system designers to specify separate values for each possible combination of evidence relevant to a proposition would tax their knowledge and presumably their patience, although some systems such as PIP [Szolovits and Pauker,

1978] do require just this. Prospector and AL/X sidestep this problem by making the conditional independence assumptions

$$P(E1\&E2|A) = P(E1|A) \times P(E2|A)$$
$$P(E1\&E2|{\sim}A) = P(E1|{\sim}A) \times P(E2|{\sim}A)$$

$P(A|E1\&E2)$ can now be determined under these constraints. Although they seem reasonable at first sight, Szolovits and Pauker report that "The assumption of conditional independence is usually false" [Szolovits et al., 1978, p. 121]. Pednault, Zucker, and Muresan go further still [Pednault et al., 1981]. In consultation systems, the case-specific information can often be regarded as evidence on which "to distinguish among competing hypotheses" [Duda et al., 1976, p. 1], where the hypotheses are a subset of the propositions. In particular, if there are three or more mutually exclusive and exhaustive propositions to which the evidence is apparently relevant, Pednault et al. prove that conditional independence implies strict independence. They then cite a theorem proving that conditional independence plus strict independence is sufficient to establish that the evidence is really irrelevant to the propositions! Since this is a preposterous conclusion, assuming the network builders knew their work, the contradiction shows that the conditional independence assumption must have been false.[3]

Systems of the MYCIN family and those based on the Dempster-Shafer theory of evidence make similar assumptions for the purpose of combining evidence. The former use formulas that mirror the calculation of probabilities of independent events; for example,

$$MB[A,E1\&E2] = MB[A,E1] + MB[A,E2] - MB[A,E1] \times MB[A,E2]$$

which seems to indicate that $MB[A,E1]$ and $MB[A,E2]$ are taken to be independent. The latter uses a combination rule called the *orthogonal sum* that assumes the evidence being combined is independent even if it is imprecise [Barnett, 1981]. But we observe in general that unless the inference network resembles a tree, there will be one or more cases in which $E1$ and $E2$ are relevant to A but the sets of propositions indirectly relevant to $E1$ and $E2$ are not disjoint. Diagrammatically, this is

[3] A recent paper [Pearl, 1982] shows how this difficulty can be circumvented if propositions can be generalized to multivalued variables. If A, B, and C are mutually exclusive and complete propositions, they can be replaced by a single proposition H with values A, B, and C. The corresponding conditional independence assumption is thereby weakened, and independence of the pieces of evidence relevant to H is no longer implied.

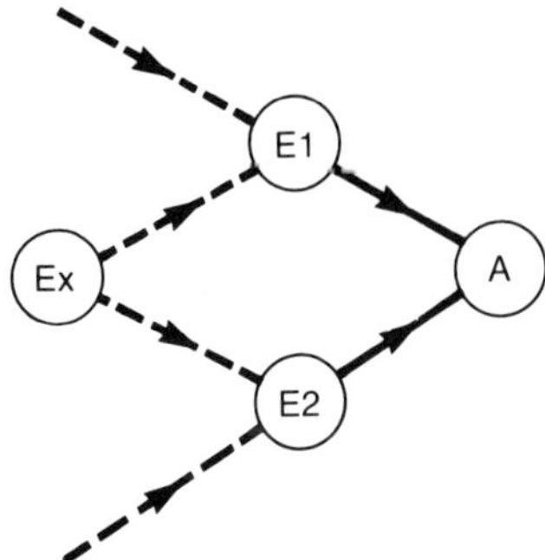

Situations such as this are the rule rather than the exception in practical inference networks (see, for example, those given by Gaschnig, 1980), and in such cases, *E*1 and *E*2 are clearly not independent. Since once again the propagation schemes depend on an assumption that is at least questionable, the inferences reached via such propagation also contain seeds of doubt.

Konolige has developed a novel approach to Bayesian inference that does not require the conditional independence assumption. Imagine a system with only three propositions, *A*, *B*, and *C*. The joint distribution of these propositions is the set of eight elementary probabilities $P(A\&B\&C)$, $P(A\&B\&\sim C)$, $P(A\&\sim B\&C)$, ... $P(\sim A\&\sim B\&\sim C)$. The usual sorts of information specified in inference nets, such as prior and conditional probabilities $P(A)$ and $P(A|B)$, can be mapped into corresponding linear constraints on these elementary probabilities. In the absence of assumptions such as conditional independence, the joint distribution is underconstrained, and we will let $\{Z\}$ denote the set of distributions satisfying the constraints. The choice of different joint distributions from $\{Z\}$ will in general assign different posterior probabilities to the propositions. Konolige argues that the best choice of a single distribution from the candidates in $\{Z\}$ is the one that contains the least additional information about dependencies among the propositions, and he shows that this is equivalent to selecting the candidate with maximum entropy.

This approach is clearly a powerful and interesting one, but difficulties remain. First, the best choice of a candidate distribution may still happen to be incorrect and thereby misleading, especially if the range of candidates in $\{Z\}$ is large. Second, the results can be sensitive to the way in which propositions are formulated. As a trivial illustration, a single unconstrained proposition will be assigned a probability of 0.5, but if it is expressed as the conjunction of two unconstrained propositions, its probability will be taken as 0.25. Third, the necessary computations are feasible only if the problem can be decomposed into small overlapping groups of propositions and if all constraints on the joint distribution are linear (e.g., propositions cannot be asserted to be independent).

Another type of assumption concerns the way Boolean combinations of propositions are handled. Prospector, AL/X, and many others use the "fuzzy" formulas for conjunction and disjunction:

$$P(AvB|E) = \max(\ P(A|E),\ P(B|E)\ )$$
$$P(A\&B|E) = \min(\ P(A|E),\ P(B|E)\ )$$

This gives the most pessimistic estimate possible for the probability of the disjunction, but the most optimistic estimate for the probability of the conjunction. It is unclear why a consistent approach should not be taken, by using for example, the corresponding optimistic estimate for disjunction:

$$P(AvB|E) = \min(\ 1,\ P(A|E) + P(B|E)\ )$$

The MYCIN and PI computations of belief and disbelief for conjunctions and disjunctions take a similar form to the fuzzy formulas, so the same criticism applies.

Finally, there is the question of how to update a consequence of proposition *A* when *A* is known with less than certainty. The approach taken in both the MYCIN and Prospector families is to interpolate from the case in which *A* is true.[4] Several interpolation schemes are discussed by Duda et al. (1976) and more recently by Paterson (1981). The choice of a particular scheme seems to be a matter of taste, and it is unclear in practice what effects the different schemes have on the conclusions reached through chains of inferences.

In summary, current systems typically depend on assumptions of one form or another. If these assumptions turn out to be unjustified in a particular application, then the inferences drawn in that case are erroneous to some degree. On the other hand, no system as yet seems to allow the user to provide information about the independence of subsets of the propositions *when that independence is known.* For example, if propositions *A* and *B* are known to be independent, it would seem beneficial to be able to assert (as opposed to assume) this information; the probability of *A&B* could be then computed accurately rather than derived from either optimistic or pessimistic estimates.

[4] Konolige's approach manages to avoid this difficulty also.

10.2.3 ■ Control Structure for Propagating Information

Many inference network systems were designed to operate in a consulting environment. They therefore draw a clear distinction between nodes representing propositions about which the system must be informed and those hypotheses that depend on other propositions. Such consultation systems do not allow information in a case to be volunteered about a hypothesis; the user can provide input concerning only those propositions that cannot be inferred from others. The distinction is significant because the flow of inference is constrained to a single direction, from the propositions that constitute the raw evidence to the furthest removed propositions (often called *goals*). The AL/X example of Fig. 10.1 illustrates this approach. Data can be given concerning only the six propositions that have no input from other propositions, and the inferences from this information follow the directions of the links. Thus, like most systems, AL/X does not allow a hypothesis to be posited for the purpose of drawing conclusions about the pattern of evidence that might be expected to support it.

The distinction is carried one step further in Garvey et al. (1981), in which the raw evidence is regarded as coming from sensors. Internal nodes whose only input comes from sensor nodes are treated differently from other nodes, as illustrated here:

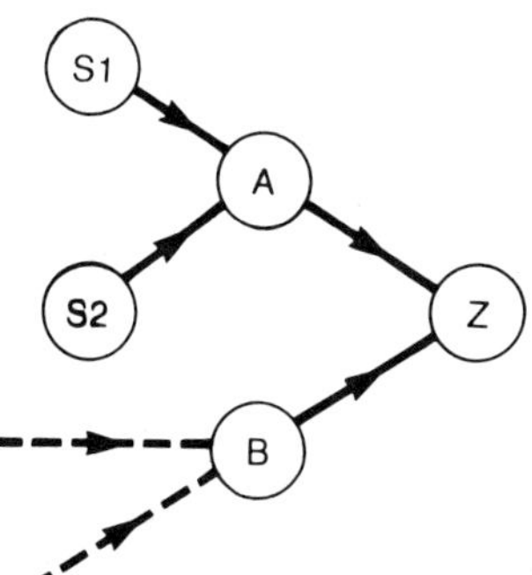

When two or more sensor nodes provide evidence supporting hypothesis *A*, this evidence is combined using Dempster's orthogonal sum mentioned previously; *S*1 and *S*2 are taken as independent. But when two internal nodes such as *A* and *B* provide (inferred) evidence supporting *Z*, no such assumption is made, and all but the strongest evidence is ignored.

10.2.4 ■ Inconsistent Information

The idea of evidence for and against a proposition was introduced in the discussion of how information is represented. One particular case arises when both sets of evidence are fairly convincing, that is, when the given information supports powerful arguments that proposition *A* is true but also counterarguments that show that *A* is false. Since both the arguments and counterarguments are derived from the same given information, the conflict is implicit in the information itself, and the information can well be labeled inconsistent. Situations of this kind arise frequently in expert domains—after all, most specialist areas exhibit well-known controversies—so they should also be anticipated in expert systems for such domains. Yet an examination of current inference network systems reveals significant deficiencies in detecting inconsistency and in treating it appropriately.

The conflict of evidence pro and con cannot even be detected in the straightforward Bayesian approach typified by Prospector and AL/X. As is illustrated in Fig. 10.1, the input for a particular problem consists of certainties or probabilities for some or all of the input propositions. These certainties are used to determine multipliers for the odds of higher hypothesis-type propositions, and thus information propagates. Any combination of values for the input certainties is as acceptable as any other as far as the propagation machinery is concerned; the only effect is to change some or all of the computed certainties for the hypotheses. As a result, the concept of conflicting problem information does not exist in this formalism. The position regarding the domain information, however, is not so simple. Specifying the prior probability of each proposition and two odds multipliers for each inferential link represents an overconstraint of the system [Duda et al., 1976], so there would seem to be a mechanism for detecting conflict. The trouble is that inconsistency of this type (produced by overconstraint) is almost inevitable, so consistency is not an achievable goal. In fact, the piecewise linear interpolation function used by Prospector can be regarded as a way of living with inconsistency. The case is clearer still when we turn to Konolige's modified system, discussed previously. Here, any nondegenerate system is guaranteed to be underconstrained, so inconsistency of problem or domain information is simply not possible.

Recall that MYCIN keeps separate measures of belief $MB[A,E]$ and disbelief $MD[A,E]$ for every proposition A in the light of evidence E. On the surface, this offers the possibility of detecting inconsistency, but since MYCIN's measures are not probabilities, there is no indication of when these values are irreconcilable. For example, can the measures be said to be in conflict when they both have a value of 0.6? Only when both measures are 1 is there a proven contradiction, and in this unlikely event, MYCIN would accept only the first finding and would ignore evidence implying the second. MYCIN's descendent EMYCIN has abandoned the two-valued approach, so it is be unable to detect any contradiction.

It is only in systems using a two-valued approach in which the values are probabilities that there is a firm basis for detecting general inconsistency. If the probability of proposition A lies in the interval $[s(A),p(A)]$ and $s(A)$ is greater that $p(A)$, the lines of reasoning leading to these bounds clearly make use of inconsistent information in the form of relations among propositions and/or assertions about the probability of propositions. Inconsistency can be detected at different stages. For example, Barnett (1981) and Garvey et al. (1981) set out conditions that must be satisfied if two pieces of evidence relevant to a hypothesis are consistent. WAND accepts information incrementally and detects that a datum is inconsistent with previous input when it would lead to unsatisfiable bounds of the type previously described.

Even more important than detecting inconsistency is the question of what to do about it when it occurs. No system for uncertain inference seems to have arrived at a satisfactory answer. For example, the Dempster-Shafer systems previously cited do not appear to address the question, and in fact the orthogonal sum operation that they use to combine evidence breaks down if the evidence is inconsistent. Again, WAND will simply refuse to accept a datum found to contradict previous data, even though the previous information may be the cause of the problem.

10.3 INFERNO

There were several motivations for producing a new system, all of which are apparent from the previous section:

1. An inference system should not depend on any assumptions about the probability distributions of the propositions;
2. Conversely, it should be possible to assert common relationships between propositions (such as independence) when the relationships are indeed known;
3. There should be no distinction between propositions; it should be possible to posit information about any set of propositions and observe the consequences for the system as a whole; and
4. If the information provided to the system is inconsistent, this

fact should be made evident along with some notion of alternative ways that the information could be made consistent.

The first point is obvious enough: if no assumptions are made, no errors will be generated (and propagated) by the process of deriving inferences. This does not prevent the drawing of erroneous conclusions from faulty information, but it does guarantee that any errors that arise will be attributable to the data and not to the system. In the absence of assumptions, the inferences that are made may be weak, and requirement (2) enables them to be strengthened when it is safe to do so. Requirement (3) concerns the ways that the system might be used. It should be possible both to reason backward from hypothetical situations and to reason forward from observations to conclusions using the same proposition relationships. Consequently, it must be possible to propagate information in all directions from a node, not just towards a goal. As a simple example, from knowing A and B, the system must be able to deduce $A\&B$; from knowing AvB and $\sim A$, the system must be able to deduce B. The final requirement is that the system must be aware of the presence of inconsistent information but be able to accept and propagate it nonetheless. INFERNO flags propositions about which inconsistent inferences can be drawn and incorporates a mechanism akin to dependency-directed backtracking [Stallman and Sussman, 1977] for suggesting changes to the data that are sufficient to remove all inconsistencies.

10.3.1 ■ Representation

The decision that no assumptions are to be used when propagating information immediately rules out using point probabilities in the general case. INFERNO uses a two-value scheme similar in intent to the interval approach $[s(A),p(A)]$ discussed previously. It turns out that INFERNO can more easily be described if the two values characterizing a proposition A are $t(A)$ and $f(A)$, where

$$P(A) \geq t(A) \text{ and } P(\sim A) \geq f(A)$$

i.e., $t(A)$ is a lower bound on the probability of A derived from the evidence for A, and $f(A)$ is a lower bound on $\sim A$ derived from the evidence against A. Evidence is for A if it allows the inference that $P(A) \geq X$ and against A if it gives $P(A) \leq X$. We define (the information about) proposition A to be consistent as long as

$$t(A) + f(A) \leq 1$$

in which case, $s(A) = t(A)$ and $p(A) = 1 - f(A)$.

INFERNO uses relations among propositions that are patterned on

TABLE 10.1 INFERNO Relations and Their Interpretation.

Relation	*Interpretation*
A enables S with strength X	$P(S\|A) \geq X$
A inhibits S with strength X	$P(\sim S\|A) \geq X$
A requires S with strength X	$P(\sim A\|\sim S) \geq X$
A unless S with strength X	$P(A\|\sim S) \geq X$
A negates S	$A \equiv \sim S$
A conjoins $\{S_1, S_2, \ldots, S_n\}$	$A \equiv \&_i S_i$
A conjoins-independent $\{S_1, S_2, \ldots, S_n\}$	$A \equiv \&_i S_i$; and for all $i \neq j$, $P(S_i \& S_j) = P(S_i) \times P(S_j)$
A disjoins $\{S_1, S_2, \ldots, S_n\}$	$A \equiv V_i S_i$
A disjoins-independent $\{S_1, S_2, \ldots, S_n\}$	$A \equiv V_i S_i$; and for all $i \neq j$, $P(S_i \& S_j) = P(S_i) \times P(S_j)$
A disjoins-exclusive $\{S_1, S_2, \ldots, S_n\}$	$A \equiv V_i S_i$; and for all $i \neq j$, $P(S_i \& S_j) = 0$
$\{S_1, S_2, \ldots, S_n\}$ mutually exclusive	For all $i \neq j$, $P(S_i \& S_j) = 0$)

and extend those in WAND, although the interpretation of these relations and the ways in which they are used in propagation differ from those in WAND. The relations themselves and their interpretation are given in Table 10.1; despite their somewhat arbitrary appearance, they seem sufficient to express common interdependencies. In addition to variants of weak implication and Boolean combinations of propositions, the relations permit assertions that sets of propositions are independent or mutually exclusive as in requirement (2) although INFERNO currently uses this information only in the context of the relation in which it appears. Note that *inhibits, requires,* and *unless* can be defined in terms of *enables* and *negates*; the discussion of propagation and rectification will be simplified by lumping the four of them together as *enables-type* relations.

10.3.2 ■ Propagation

Each proposition A initially has the trivial bounds $t(A) = 0$ and $f(A) = 0$. These bounds may be changed by explicit information from the case being studied or by inferences from other bounds through the relations connecting A with other propositions. As more information is provided or inferred, the range within which the probability $P(A)$ of proposition A is known to lie can become only smaller. This is reflected in larger values for one or both of $f(A)$ and $t(A)$.

Suppose that we have just computed a higher value for one of the bounds of a proposition. This new information is propagated by checking all relations in which the proposition is involved and perhaps increasing the bounds of other propositions to ensure that relevant *propagation constraints* are satisfied. These constraints are summarized relation by relation in Table 10.2 and are formally derived in Appendix A. They make no assumptions about the probability distributions of any propositions and follow mainly from the universal inequality

$$\max P(S_i) \leq P(S_1 v S_2 v \ldots v S_n) \leq \Sigma_i P(S_i)$$

TABLE 10.2 INFERNO Propagation Constraints.

A enables S with strength X:	
$t(S) \geq t(A) \times X$	(1.1)
$f(A) \geq 1 - (1 - f(S)) / X$	(1.2)
A negates S:	
$t(A) = f(S)$	(2.1)
$f(A) = t(S)$	(2.2)
A conjoins $\{S_1, S_2, \ldots, S_n\}$:	
$t(A) \geq 1 - \Sigma_i(1-t(S_i))$	(3.1.1)
$f(A) \geq f(S_i)$	(3.1.2)
$t(S_i) \geq t(A)$	(3.1.3)
$f(S_i) \geq f(A) - \Sigma_{j \neq i} (1 - t(S_j))$	(3.1.4)
A conjoins-independent $\{S_1, S_1, \ldots, S_n\}$:	
$t(A) \geq ¶_i t(S_i)$	(3.2.1)
$f(A) \geq 1 - ¶_i(1 - f(S_i))$	(3.2.2)
$t(S_i) \geq t(A) / ¶_{j \neq i}(1 - f(S_j))$	(3.2.3)
$f(S_i) \geq 1 - (1 - f(A)) / ¶_{j \neq i} t(S_j)$	(3.2.4)
A disjoins $\{S_1, S_1, \ldots, S_n\}$:	
$t(A) \geq t(S_i)$	(4.1.1)
$f(A) \geq 1 - \Sigma_i(1 - f(S_i))$	(4.1.2)
$t(S_i) \geq t(A) - \Sigma_{j \neq i}(1 - f(S_j))$	(4.1.3)
$f(S_i) \geq f(A)$	(4.1.4)
A disjoins-independent $\{S_1, S_1, \ldots, S_n\}$:	
$t(A) \geq 1 - ¶_i(1 - t(S_i))$	(4.2.1)
$f(A) \geq ¶_i f(S_i)$	(4.2.2)
$t(S_i) \geq 1 - (1 - t(A)) / ¶_{j \neq i} f(S_j)$	(4.2.3)
$f(S_i) \geq f(A) / ¶_{j \neq i}(1 - t(S_j))$	(4.2.4)
A disjoins-exclusive $\{S_1, S_1, \ldots, S_n\}$:	
$t(A) \geq \Sigma_i t(S_i)$	(4.3.1)
$f(A) \geq 1 - \Sigma_i(1 - f(S_i))$	(4.3.2)
$t(S_i) \geq t(A) - \Sigma_{j \neq i}(1 - f(S_j))$	(4.3.3)
$f(S_i) \geq f(A) + \Sigma_{j \neq i} t(S_j)$	(4.3.4)
$\{S_1, S_1, \ldots, S_n\}$ mutually exclusive:	
$f(S_i) \geq \Sigma_{j \neq i} t(S_j)$	(5.1)

in various guises. Each inequality asserts that some bound is greater than or equal to some expression involving other bounds, and is interpreted as a form of production rule:

if the previous value of the bound on the left side
is less than the value of the right side
then the bound is increased to this new value.

Each constraint is activated when any bound mentioned in its right side is changed. As an illustration, consider the hypothetical relation "*A* conjoins $\{Q,R\}$." From constraints (3.1.1) through (3.1.4) in Table 10.2,

- $t(A)$ must be checked when $t(Q)$ or $t(R)$ is increased;
- $f(A)$ must be checked when $f(Q)$ or $f(R)$ is increased;
- $t(Q)$ and $t(R)$ must be checked when $t(A)$ is increased; and
- $f(Q)$ must be checked when $f(A)$ or $t(R)$ is increased, and likewise $f(R)$ for $f(A)$ or $t(Q)$.

If one of these bounds is increased in line with the constraints, that increase must be propagated in turn. If the current value of a bound satisfies the constraint, then of course no change need take place and no propagation is involved.

There are two detrimental comments that must be made about this propagation mechanism. First, while the constraints can be derived from the interpretations of Table 10.1, the converse is not true; the constraints are weaker than the interpretations. Consider, for example,[5] the two relations

A enables *B* with strength *X*
C conjoins-independent $\{A,B\}$

whose interpretation from Table 10.1 consists of the assertions

$$P(B|A) \geq X$$
$$C \equiv A\&B$$
$$P(A\&B) = P(A) \times P(B)$$

From the latter, one can deduce (inter alia) that $P(B) \geq X$. The constraints in Table 10.2 do not allow this inference because knowledge of the independence of *A* and *B* is confined to the single relation that asserts it. The values of the bounds inferred by the propagation mechanism will always be correct, but in some cases may be weaker than those that can be derived using the interpretations rather than the constraints.

[5] This example is from Norman Shapiro.

The second point concerns the termination of propagation. It turns out that if the information about propositions is not consistent, a propagation chain with ever-increasing bounds can arise. Consider the relation "A conjoins-independent $\{Q,R\}$" and suppose the bound $t(Q)$ is increased to a value, for example, X. By propagation constraint (3.2.1), $t(A)$ must be increased to $X \times t(R)$, and by substituting this value in constraint (3.2.3),

$$t(Q) \geq X \times t(R) \,/\, (1 - f(R))$$

If $t(R) + f(R) > 1$, this would require $t(Q)$ to be greater than X, so there is a positive feedback loop. Shapiro provided an elegant demonstration that the same problem can arise even when the data are consistent. It is possible to construct a set of relations whose corresponding constraints are satisfied only by a unique assignment of irrational values to the bounds. But since the bounds are initially zero and the propagation constraints compute only rational functions of the set of bounds, this unique solution cannot be found by a finite number of such computations. In practice, however, inference network systems usually prohibit changes that propagate back to the source of the original disturbance.[6] With this prohibition, propagation will always terminate, even when one or more propositions have inconsistent bounds. The result again is that the bounds computed by INFERNO are correct consequences of the data, but may not be the tightest bounds that can be inferred from the data.

The propagation mechanism can be illustrated with the small network shown in Fig. 10.2. There are five propositions labeled A through E and three relations among them: C is the conjunction of A and B, where nothing is known about the joint distribution of A and B; E is the disjunction of C and D and these are known to be independent; and B directly suggests E with $P(E|B)$ at least 0.8. Suppose that in some case $P(C)$ is found to lie in the interval [0.55,0.65], that is, $t(C) = 0.55$ and $f(C) = 0.35$. The relation "C conjoins $\{A,B\}$," constraint (3.1.3), and $t(C)$ combine to give the inference that $t(A)$ and $t(B)$ must be at least 0.55. Since $t(D)$ and $f(D)$ are initially zero, the relation E disjoins-independent $\{C,D\}$ and $t(C)$ give $t(E) = 0.55$ by constraint (4.2.1). If it is now learned that the probability of B is 0.9 (i.e., $t(B) = 0.9$ and $f(B) = 0.1$), the following inferences can be made:

$f(A) = 0.25$ from constraint (3.1.4), $f(C)$, and $t(B)$
$t(E) = 0.72$ from constraint (1.1) and $t(B)$
$t(D) = 0.2$ from constraint (4.2.3), $t(E)$, and $f(C)$

[6] Friedman (1981), for example, describes this prohibition as "an axiom of plausible inference." An undesirable side effect of the prohibition is that any relaxation-style computation of values is precluded, leading to bounds that are weaker than the relations would otherwise support.

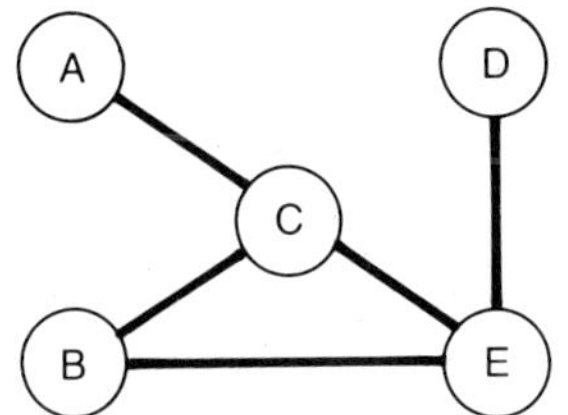

C conjoins {A,B}

E disjoins-independent {C,D}

B enables E with strength 0.8

FIGURE 10.2 A Small Inference Network.

The sum of our knowledge of the propositions, both given and inferred, is shown in the fragment of INFERNO output in Fig. 10.3. Note that a justification is given for each nontrivial lower bound (LB) or upper bound (UB) on the probability of a proposition. This justification is either by assumption when the information was supplied to INFERNO, or another bound and a relation that together triggered the inference.

10.3.3 ■ Consistency and Rectification

When $t(A) + f(A) > 1$ for some proposition A, the information about A is inconsistent and one or both of the bounds must be incorrect. Since the propagation constraints are provably correct, this inconsistency can arise only from contradictions implicit in the information given to the system, that is, the interdependencies among the propositions expressed by the relations or the explicit bounds on the probabilities of propositions. When INFERNO detects that a proposition is

FIGURE 10.3 INFERNO Output.

"A": range 0.55 - 0.75
LB from *Pr*(*"C"*) ≥ 0.55, by conjoins
UB from *Pr*(*"B"*) ≥ 0.9, by conjoins

"B": range 0.9 - 0.9
LB by assumption
UB by assumption

"C": range 0.55 - 0.65
LB by assumption
UB by assumption

"D": range 0.2 - 1
LB from *Pr*(*"E"*) ≥ 0.72, by disjoins-independent

"E": range 0.72 - 1
LB from *Pr*(*"B"*) ≥ 0.9, by enables

inconsistent, it places a flag ** in front of it. In addition, those constraints whose derivation requires the consistency axiom are weakened by using looser bounds $t'(A)$ and $f'(A)$; $t'(A)$ is the smaller of $t(A)$ and $1 - f(A)$, and $f'(A)$ is defined similarly.

In the example of Fig. 10.3, it is inferred that $P(E)$ lay in the interval [0.72,1]. What would happen if the system were explicitly informed that $P(E) \leq 0.5$? The INFERNO output in Fig. 10.4 shows the consequences of this additional assertion. Taking proposition B as an example, we are told that $t(B) = 0.9$. We can infer from $f(E)$ and constraint (1.2) that $f(B)$ is at least 0.375. These bounds on the probability of B are clearly incompatible.

INFERNO can be asked to suggest combinations of changes that will make all the information consistent. Each change takes the form of lowering the value of an externally specified bound or reducing the strength of an enables-type relation. A combination of changes that is sufficient to make the bounds on all propositions consistent is called a *rectification*.

The first step is to examine each inconsistent proposition A in turn, to see how its bounds could be made consistent. This can be achieved by lowering $t(A)$ to $1 - f(A)$, lowering $f(A)$ to $1 - t(A)$, or changing both bounds to intermediate values; INFERNO currently considers only the first two alternatives. Suppose that we are trying to lower some bound to a value V. There are two possibilities:

1. The bound was supplied explicitly as input to the system. In

FIGURE 10.4 Output with Inconsistencies.

	"A":	range 0.55 - 0.6
		LB from Pr("C") ≥ 0.55, by conjoins
		UB from Pr("C") ≤ 0.5, by conjoins
**	"B":	range 0.9 - 0.625
		LB by assumption
		UB from Pr("E") ≤ 0.5, by enables-inverse
**	"C":	range 0.55 - 0.5
		LB by assumption
		UB from Pr("E") ≤ 0.5, by disjoins-independent
**	"D":	range 0.2 - 0
		LB from Pr("E") ≥ 0.72, by disjoins-independent
		UB from Pr("C") ≤ 0.5, by disjoins-independent
**	"E":	range 0.72 - 0.5
		LB from Pr("B") ≥ 0.9, by enables
		UB by assumption

this case, it can clearly be changed only with the consent of the user.

2. The bound was inferred from a propagation constraint and the values of one or more antecedent bounds. Once more there are two cases:
   a) If the propagation constraint came from an enables-type relation, then the relation itself can be weakened. INFERNO calculates the reduced strength of the relation that would have produced the desired value V.
   b) Whatever the nature of the relation, the inferred value is a function of the antecedent bounds. INFERNO looks for lower values of these bounds that would have allowed the lower value V to be inferred.

In the last case, the lower values of the antecedent bounds must then be analyzed in a similar fashion, so that finding changes is a lot like propagation in reverse. The backing-up constraints are similar, but not identical, to the propagation constraints. Appendix B lists them without proof, since their derivation parallels that of the propagation constraints.

The process of finding changes is not exact in the current implementation of INFERNO. First, the system considers only single changes that will make a proposition consistent; trying to reduce the value of $t(AvB)$, for example, can present a problem. Second, it does not verify that there are no relations, other than the one referenced in its justification, that also constrain the value of the bound to something greater than V. There is no fundamental difficulty (other than program complexity) in removing these limitations.

The second step involves assembling the changes discovered by this process into rectifications. Each rectification contains one change from each of the inconsistent propositions, so the conjunction of the changes is sufficient to fix the entire collection of propositions (subject to the preceding caveat). Some of the inconsistent propositions may have matching or compatible changes associated with them, so there are often fewer changes in a rectification than there are inconsistent propositions.

The third step is to rank the rectifications in order of potential utility. The rule of thumb used here is that small adjustments of values do less violence to the input information than gross alterations and are therefore more likely to be acceptable to the user. As a simple model, we define the *reluctance* of (the user to accept) a change to be the magnitude of the modification that it entails, either the numeric reduction in strength of an enables-type relation or the difference in the old and new values of a bound. The reluctance of a rectification is similarly taken as the sum of the reluctances of the changes it contains. Alternative rectifications are presented in order of increasing reluctance, so that those suggested first are more likely to be reasonable.

If there are many inconsistent propositions, each with many alternative changes, the process of finding and ranking all possible rectifications is combinatorially explosive, and there would be too many rectifications to display to the user anyway. This problem is circumvented by establishing a parameter (*R*, for example) so that only the *R* best rectifications are ever displayed. The processes of generation and ranking are then combined; if a partial rectification has a reluctance greater than that of all the *R* best rectifications found so far, then no rectification containing the partial rectification need ever be generated. With this technique the time taken to assemble the best *R* rectifications from the changes found in the first step appears to be practically independent of the number of inconsistent propositions and so is feasible even for large networks.

The INFERNO output in Fig. 10.5 shows these processes applied to our continuing example. We look first at proposition *B*. Since $t(B)$ was supplied explicitly, *B* could be made consistent if the given value of $t(B)$ were reduced to 1 - $f(B)$, that is, to 0.625. Alternatively, we could reduce $f(B)$ to 1 - $t(B)$ or 0.1. But $f(B)$ was inferred from the given value of $f(E)$ and the relation "*B* enables *E* with strength 0.8" via constraint (1.2). If either $f(E)$ were 0.28 or the strength of the relation were 0.556, $f(B)$ would have been 0.1 and B would have been consistent. By this reasoning, there are three changes, any one of which would make the bounds on *B* consistent:

- Reducing $t(B)$ from 0.9 to 0.625;
- Reducing $f(E)$ from 0.5 to 0.28; or
- Reducing the strength of "*B* enables *E*" from 0.8 to 0.556.

with reluctances 0.275, 0.22, and 0.244, respectively. After changes have been found for all contradictory propositions, INFERNO shows the various rectifications that can be constructed. Note that reducing $f(E)$ to 0.28 satisfies all sets of changes and so is a rectification in its own right. This is comforting because the system became inconsistent only when $f(E)$ was increased beyond 0.28! Again, partially weakening $f(E)$ to 0.45 will fix proposition *C*, whereas reducing the strength of "*B* enables *E*" will fix the other inconsistent propositions, so this pair of changes is also a rectification.

The rectifications constructed by this algorithm are sufficient rather than necessary to make all propositions consistent and so may be ex-

"*B*" can be resolved by changing:
Pr("*B*") from 0.9 to 0.625
Pr("*E*") from 0.5 to 0.72
["*B*" enables "*E*" with strength 0.8] to 0.556

"*C*" can be resolved by changing:
Pr("*C*") from 0.55 to 0.5
Pr("*E*") from 0.5 to 0.55

"*D*" can be resolved by changing:
Pr("*E*") from 0.5 to 0.6
Pr("*C*") from 0.55 to 0.375
Pr("*B*") from 0.9 to 0.688
["*B*" enables "*E*" with strength 0.8] to 0.611

"*E*" can be resolved by changing:
Pr("*E*") from 0.5 to 0.72
Pr("*B*") from 0.9 to 0.625
["*B*" enables "*E*" with strength 0.8] to 0.556

Alternative rectifications:

Pr("*E*") from 0.5 to 0.72
Total reluctance 0.22

["*B*" enables "*E*" with strength 0.8] to 0.556
Pr("*E*") from 0.5 to 0.55
Total reluctance 0.29

["*B*" enables "*E*" with strength 0.8] to 0.556
Pr("*C*") from 0.55 to 0.5
Total reluctance 0.29

Pr("*B*") from 0.9 to 0.625
Pr("*E*") from 0.5 to 0.55
Total reluctance 0.32

Pr("*B*") from 0.9 to 0.625
Pr("*C*") from 0.55 to 0.5
Total reluctance 0.32

FIGURE 10.5 Changes and Rectifications.

cessive when possible relationships between the changes are taken into account. In the second preceding rectification, the reduced strength of 0.556 for the enables relation was computed on the basis of $f(E)$ being 0.5. Since we also reduced the value of $f(E)$ to 0.45, the change in strength is slightly more than it need be. Of course, changes can be made one at a time and the residual rectifications recomputed after each change; this would give a new strength of 0.611 for the relation "*B* enables *E*".

10.4 A Complete Example

This section returns to the AL/X inference network of Fig. 10.1 that is discussed in Section 10.2, recasts it as INFERNO relations, and runs the network on a case given by Reiter (1981). The purpose of this exercise is to highlight the differences between the Bayesian inferencing employed by AL/X (using the conditional independence assumptions mentioned earlier) and INFERNO's conservative approach with no assumptions.

The comparison of these systems immediately runs into a problem because they are based on different world models. The Bayesian approach requires that the prior probability of each proposition A be known and computes the posterior probability of A given all evidence E. Inferential links between propositions A and B are defined in terms of the conditional probabilities $P(B|A)$ and $P(B|{\sim}A)$ that again refer back to the prior probability distributions. In contrast, INFERNO makes no reference to a prior distribution, but represents by $P(A)$ what is known about the proposition A so far. The acquisition of evidence is viewed as a means for further constraining $P(A)$. This may appear to be a fine distinction, but consider, for example, the inequality $P(B|A) \geq X$. In a Bayesian system, this constrains only the prior distribution, and if $P(A|E)$ turns out to be 1, it does not follow that $P(B|E)$ is at least X. INFERNO would interpret the inequality as a constraint that must be satisfied by any assignment of probability intervals in any particular example, and the addition of further evidence could not weaken this constraint. Thus the findings that $P(A) = 1$ while $P(B) \leq X$ would be regarded as inconsistent with the earlier inequality. This difference significantly qualifies the following comparison.

The Boolean relations employed by AL/X are transferable immediately to INFERNO. Let the prior probability of proposition B be prior(B), that is, the prior odds of B are given by

$$\text{odds}(B) = \text{prior}(B) \,/\, (1 - \text{prior}(B))$$

Consider an inferential link from A to B with odds multipliers 1s (if A is found to be true) and 1n (if A is found to be false), respectively. If A is found to be true, in the absence of other evidence the posterior probability of B is given by

$$\text{odds}(B|A) = 1s \times \text{odds}(B)$$

and the posterior probability of B is then

posterior($B|A$) = odds($B|A$) / (odds($B|A$) + 1)

If A is false, we get a corresponding probability by replacing 1s with 1n in the odds formula. This link thus becomes a pair of INFERNO relations:

A enables B with strength posterior($B|A$)
B requires A with strength (1 - posterior($B|{\sim}A$))

Each link is translated here in isolation, but this should be an accurate translation if the network designer assigned the values of 1s and 1n in isolation (as advised in Reiter (1980), p. 10) and when A is known with certainty. Differences will arise when A is known with less than certainty and when multiple inferential links relate to the same proposition, because AL/X then makes use of assumptions that have no counterpart in INFERNO.

The case to be analyzed is defined by probability assignments to the propositions that represent raw evidence. AL/X uses quantities called certainty factors (not to be confused with MYCIN's use of the term) in which -5 means false, 5 means true, and 0 means that no information is available. Values in the range 0 to 5 are interpolated linearly between the prior probability of the proposition and 1, with a similar interpolation in the negative range. For the case being analyzed, the certainty factors and probabilities are shown in Table 10.3. The certainty factor of 0 for proposition RVNOISECOOL presents a minor problem. It could be interpreted as implying the probability shown, but AL/X takes it to mean that the information is either unavailable or is conflicting and makes no use of it. This is more accurately reflected in INFERNO as the absence of any statement about the probability, which is the policy followed in this example.

TABLE 10.3 AL/X Case for Analysis.

Proposition	*Certainty Factor*	*Equialent Probability*
RVLIFTIND	5	1
V01CCRCHART	4.5	0.9
RVNOISECOOL	0	0.001
V01SDHP	5	1
PCV302FTBAD	-4	0.0002*
SCIVSHUT	5	1

* This value is below INFERNO's minimum probability and is treated as 0.

TABLE 10.4 Comparison of Findings by AL/X and INFERNO.

Proposition	*AL/X*	*INFERNO*
SCIVCAUSE	0.909	0.802 - 0.883
PCV302EQERR	0.057	0.204
RVLIFTEARLY	false	0.000 - 0.118
RVSOLSHORT	false	0.059 - 0.199
RVSWSHORT	false	0.033 - 0.199

An annotated transcript of the presentation of this case to INFERNO appears as Appendix C. In INFERNO's world view, the information concerning probabilities and relations is inconsistent. PCV302FTBAD is false, for example; thus, LIFTPRESS and V01SDHP are also false, directly contradicting another piece of evidence. INFERNO is asked to find alternative rectifications and prints the best ten of them. The first rectification is simply to adjust the probability of PCV302FTBAD to 0.204, and this seems plausible—the information about this proposition was indefinite on the certainty scale and only its very low prior probability of 0.001 caused -4 to be mapped to a near-definite 0.0002 on the probability scale. If this rectification is made, the information becomes consistent, and the findings of AL/X and INFERNO regarding the goal propositions can be compared in Table 10.4. The results obtained by both systems agree well in general tendency, but AL/X's lie outside the probability limits derived by INFERNO; this is not altogether surprising, since one of the input probabilities had to be altered to achieve consistency. INFERNO's bounds also give a good measure of the uncertainty of the various conclusions—note that SCIVCAUSE is more tightly bound than is RVSWSHORT.

10.5 Conclusion

The study reported here was undertaken to develop a useful mechanism for plausible reasoning in the context of uncertain knowledge and culminated in the specification and implementation[7] of INFERNO. A detailed description of the system's attributes is given in Section 10.3, but a brief reiteration is appropriate here. INFERNO is cautious because it does not depend on assumptions about joint probability distributions of propositions, so its conclusions about the probability bounds of propositions are provably correct consequences of the given information. The absence of assumptions would be expected to lead to weaker conclusions, but this tendency is partially offset because sets of propositions that are mutually exclusive or independent can be identified, with the result that probability bounds can be tightened in some cases. The system does not distinguish between hypotheses and evidence and thus can be used for forward (data-driven) inference, backward (hypothesis-driven) inference, or any mixture of these two modes. Finally, INFERNO incorporates a strong notion of the consistency of the information presented to it, and by reasoning backward about conclusions, it can provide approximate but informative suggestions for remedying any inconsistencies.

As illustrated in the previous section, conventional inference networks can be recast to equivalent INFERNO formalisms subject to the qualification of an underlying non-Bayesian world model. In the oil-rig example, AL/X and INFERNO reached conclusions that were certainly not identical, but both would support the same diagnosis of the problem. The main advantages of the approach embodied in INFERNO are (1) it requires less information, since it does not need anything corresponding to the prior probability of a hypothesis; (2) it brings out the conflicts that may be implicit in the evidence; and (3) its probability bounds give a measure of the potential error in the conclusions, a feature that has no direct counterpart in Bayesian systems such as AL/X.

INFERNO has also been applied to several more demanding test domains, including a diagnosis network for carburetor malfunctions (also taken from AL/X), several of the published Prospector submodels, transportation planning via a network of unreliable routes, resource allocation among competing but interdependent projects, and assessment of an opponent's poker hand, using clues from his or her bidding and draw. The last case was the only one in which the system proved to be relatively weak. Some prior probabilities in this domain can be calculated, so a Bayesian approach would potentially be more powerful. However, systems such as AL/X do not have any mechanism for enforcing the mutual exclusivity of propositions or for computing accurately the probability of conjunctions or disjunctions of propositions,

[7] INFERNO has been implemented in a mixture of Pascal and C for a VAX 11/780 minicomputer and should be relatively portable among UNIX systems. It is quite economical to run: the entire output in Appendix C, including finding the alternative rectifications, requires about 3 seconds of CPU time.

so the poker domain would probably be a difficult one for them also.

Perhaps the most novel features of INFERNO are its concern for consistency and its rectification-constructing mechanisms. This approach provides a valuable tool to help the user debug the knowledge or adapt general rules for a particular problem. In addition, it has a somewhat unexpected application in planning whereby the user deliberately introduces contradictions! Consider, for example, a transportation planning domain in which the goal is to move some combination of loads to their appropriate destinations. One inference from the available information might be that achieving this goal has a probability strictly less than 1. If the goal is also asserted to be satisfied, the information will thus become inconsistent, but the possible rectifications suggested by the system will include combinations of changes sufficient to guarantee achievement of the goal. Thus INFERNO can be used to isolate those characteristics of the domain that bear most significantly on the accomplishment of the planning objective.

In summary, INFERNO is a powerful and flexible tool for dealing with uncertain knowledge as long as the knowledge can be cast in the form of a fixed set of propositions and relations among them. Nevertheless, several areas for possible improvement suggest themselves. First, it would be handy to be able to incorporate Bayesian submodels where the required information is available and the necessary assumptions are found to be valid. Second, real-world tasks often entail budgetary and other numeric but nonprobabilistic constraints, and some formalism is needed for marrying numeric and probability-bounding constraints. Finally, INFERNO is essentially a zeroth-order system in which propositions and relations concern individuals. A quantified relation such as "$A(x)$ enables $B(x)$ for every x" can be represented only as a collection of zeroth-order relations obtained by instantiating over every individual x, an unsatisfactory approach if there are many such individuals. We are investigating ways in which an INFERNO-like approach can be moved to a first-order environment.

Acknowledgments

INFERNO grew out of a study of Frederick Hayes-Roth's WAND, and it incorporates many ideas developed in that system. I gratefully acknowledge the importance of the insights provided by Norman Shapiro and Donald Waterman of Rand, Donald Michie and Tim Niblett of Edinburgh University, and John Reiter and Peter Cheeseman of SRI International.

References

1. Barnett, J. A., "Computational Methods for a Mathematical Theory of Evidence," *Proceedings of the Seventh International Joint Conference on Artificial Intelligence,* Vancouver, 1981, pp. 868–875.
2. Duda, R. O., P. E. Hart, and N. J. Nilsson, *Subjective Bayesian Methods for Rule-Based Inference Systems,* Technical Note 124, Artificial Intelligence Center, SRI International, 1976.
3. Duda, R. O., P. E. Hart, N. J. Nilsson, R. Reboh, J. Slocum, and G. L. Sutherland, *Development of a Computer-Based Consultant for Mineral Exploration,* SRI International, 1977.
4. Duda, R. O., J. Gaschnig, and P. E. Hart, "Model Design in the Prospector Consultant System for Mineral Exploration," in *Expert Systems in the Micro Electronic Age* (D. Michie, ed.), Edinburgh University Press, 1979.
5. Duda, R. O., P. E. Hart, K. Konolige, and R. Reboh, *A Computer-Based Consultant for Mineral Exploration,* SRI International, 1979.
6. Feigenbaum, E. A., "Themes and Case Studies of Knowledge Engineering," in *Expert Systems in the Micro Electronic Age* (D. Michie, ed.), Edinburgh University Press, 1979.
7. Friedman, L., "Extended Plausible Inference," *Proceedings of the Seventh International Joint Conference on Artificial Intelligence,* Vancouver, 1981, pp. 487–495.
8. Garvey, T. D., J. D. Lowrance, and M. A. Fischler, "An Inference Technique for Integrating Knowledge from Disparate Sources," *Proceedings of the Seventh International Joint Conference on Artificial Intelligence,* Vancouver, 1981, pp. 319–325.
9. Gaschnig, J., *Development of Uranium Exploration Models for the Prospector Consultant System,* SRI International, 1980.
10. Gaschnig, J., "Prospector: An Expert System for Mineral Exploration," in *State of the Art Report on Machine Intelligence* (A. Bond, ed.), Pergamon Infotech, London, 1981.
11. Hayes-Roth, F., "Probabilistic Dependencies in a System for Truth Maintenance and Belief Revision," unpublished working paper, The Rand Corporation.
12. Hayes-Roth, F., D. A. Waterman, and D. B. Lenat, "Principles of Pattern-Directed Inference Systems", in *Pattern-Directed In-*

ference Systems (D. A. Waterman and F. Hayes-Roth, eds.), Academic Press, New York, 1978.

13. Ishizuka, M., and J. T. P. Yao, "Inexact Inference for Rule-Based Damage Assessment of Existing Structures," *Proceedings of the Seventh International Joint Conference on Artificial Intelligence*, Vancouver, 1981, pp. 837–842.
14. Konolige, K., "An Information-Theoretic Approach to Subjective Bayesian Inference in Rule-Based Systems," unpublished draft, SRI International.
15. Paterson, A., *AL/X User Manual*, Intelligent Terminals Ltd., Oxford, 1981.
16. Pearl, J., *Distributed Bayesian Processing for Belief Maintenance in Hierarchical Inference Systems*, Cognitive Systems Laboratory, UCLA, Report UCLA-ENG-CSL-82-11, 1982.
17. Pednault, E. D. P., S. W. Zucker, and L. V. Muresan, "On the Independence Assumption Underlying Subjective Bayesian Inference," *Artificial Intelligence*, Vol. 16, 1981, pp. 213–222.
18. Reiter, J., *AL/X: An Expert System using Plausible Inference*, Intelligent Terminals Ltd., Oxford, 1980.
19. Reiter, J., *AL/X: An Inference System for Probabilistic Reasoning*, M.Sc. Thesis, Department of Computer Science, University of Illinois at Urbana-Champaign, 1981.
20. Robinson, J. A., "A Machine Oriented Logic Based on the Resolution Principle," *Journal of the Association for Computing Machinery*, Vol. 12, 1965, pp. 23–41.
21. Shortliffe, E. H., and B. G. Buchanan, "A Model of Inexact Reasoning in Medicine," *Mathematical Biosciences*, Vol. 23, 1975, pp. 351–379.
22. Stallman, R. M., and G. J. Sussman, "Forward Reasoning and Dependency-Directed Backtracking in a System for Computer-Aided Circuit Analysis," *Artificial Intelligence*, Vol. 9, 1977, pp. 135–196.
23. Szolovits, P. S., and S. G. Pauker, "Categorical and Probabilistic Reasoning in Medical Diagnosis," *Artificial Intelligence*, Vol. 11, 1978, pp. 115–144.
24. van Melle, W., "A Domain-Independent Production Rule System for Consultation Programs," *Proceedings of the Sixth International Joint Conference on Artificial Intelligence*, Tokyo, 1979.
25. van Melle, W., *A Domain-Independent System that Aids in Con-*

structing Knowledge-Based Consultation Programs, Department of Computer Science, Stanford University, Report STAN-CS-80-820, 1980.

26. Zadeh, L. A., "A Theory of Approximate Reasoning," in *Machine Intelligence 9* (J. E. Hayes, D. Michie, and L. I. Mikulich, eds.), Ellis Horwood, London, 1979.

Appendix A

Derivation of Propagation Constraints

The following derivations are straightforward manipulations of a few relations, using the identities

$$P(Z) + P(\sim Z) = 1$$
$$t(Z) \leq P(Z) \leq 1 - f(Z)$$

for any proposition Z. Note that the second presumes the consistency of information about Z.

1. *A* enables *S* with strength *X*

   The interpretation of this relation gives

$$P(S) \geq P(S\&A) = P(A) \times P(S|A) \geq P(A) \times X$$

so

$$P(S) \geq t(A) \times X \qquad (1.1)$$

By inverting the earlier relation,

$$P(A) \leq P(S) / X$$

and thus

$$P(\sim A) = 1 - P(A) \geq 1 - (1 - f(S)) / X \qquad (1.2)$$

2. *A* negates *S*

The constraints are immediate consequences of the preceding identities.

3. Conjunction

If A is the conjunction of $\{S_1, S_2, \dots, S_n\}$, then $\sim A$ is the disjunction of $\{\sim S_1, \sim S_2, \dots, \sim S_n)$. Thus the derivations for the various conjunction constraints are mirror images of those for disjunction, interchanging both signs and the bounds t and f throughout.

4.1. A disjoins $\{S_1, S_2, \dots, S_n\}$

The basic relation used here is

$$\max_i P(S_i) \leq P(A) \leq \Sigma_i P(S_i)$$

The left-side inequality gives the two constraints

$$P(A) \geq P(S_i) \geq t(S_i) \qquad (4.1.1)$$
$$P(\sim S_i) \geq P(\sim A) \geq f(A) \qquad (4.1.4)$$

The right-side inequality gives

$$P(\sim A) \geq 1 - \Sigma_i(1 - f(S_i)) \qquad (4.1.2)$$

and by rewriting it in the form $P(S_i) \geq P(A) - \Sigma_{j \neq i} P(S_j)$

we get the constraint

$$P(S_i) \geq t(A) - \Sigma_{j \neq i}(1 - f(S_j)) \qquad (4.1.3)$$

4.2. A disjoins-independent $\{S_1, S_2, \dots, S_n\}$

The rule for combining the probabilities of independent events is

$$P(\sim A) = \P_i P(\sim S_i)$$

giving

$$P(A) = 1 - P(\sim A) \geq 1 - \P_i(1 - t(S_i)) \qquad (4.2.1)$$
$$P(\sim A) \geq \P_i f(S_i) \qquad (4.2.2)$$

Rewriting the preceding rule as

$$P(\sim S_i) = P(\sim A) / \P_{j \neq i} P(\sim S_j)$$

gives

$$P(\sim S_i) \geq f(A) / \P_{j \neq i}(1 - t(S_j)) \qquad (4.2.4)$$
$$P(S_i) = 1 - P(\sim S_i) \geq 1 - (1 - t(A)) / \P_{j \neq i} f(S_j) \qquad (4.2.3)$$

4.3 A disjoins-exclusive $\{S_1, S_2, \dots, S_n\}$

The rule in this case is

$$P(A) = \Sigma_i P(S_i)$$

hence

$$P(A) \geq \Sigma_i t(S_i) \tag{4.3.1}$$
$$P(\sim A) = 1 - P(A) \geq 1 - \Sigma_i(1 - f(S_i)) \tag{4.3.2}$$

Rearranging the rule,

$$P(S_i) = P(A) - \Sigma_{j \neq i} P(S_j)$$

which gives

$$P(S_i) \geq t(A) - \Sigma_{j \neq i}(1 - f(S_j)) \tag{4.3.3}$$
$$P(\sim S_i) = 1 - P(S_i) \geq f(A) + \Sigma_{j \neq i} t(S_j) \tag{4.3.4}$$

5. $\{S_1, S_2, \ldots, S_n\}$ mutually exclusive
   The rule is

$$\Sigma_i P(S_i) \leq 1$$

or

$$P(S_i) \leq 1 - \Sigma_{j \neq i} P(S_j)$$

Thus

$$P(\sim S_i) = 1 - P(S_i) \geq \Sigma_{j \neq i} t(S_j) \tag{5.1}$$

Appendix B

Constraints for Backing Up Inconsistencies

A enables *S* with strength *XG*

$$t(A) \leq t(S) / X$$
$$f(S) \leq 1 - (1 - f(A)) \times X$$

A negates *S*:

$$t(A) = f(S)$$
$$f(A) = t(S)$$

A disjoins $\{S_1, S_1, \ldots, S_n\}$:

$$t(A) \leq t(S_i) + \Sigma_{j \neq i}(1 - f(S_j))$$
$$f(A) \leq f(S_i)$$
$$t(S_i) \leq t(A)$$

$$f(S_i) \leq t(S_j) + \Sigma_{k \neq i,j}(1 - f(S_k)) + 1 - t(A)$$
$$f(S_i) \leq f(A) + \Sigma_{j \neq i}(1 - f(S_j))$$

A disjoins-independent $\{S_1, S_1, \ldots, S_n\}$:

$$t(A) \leq 1 - (1 - t(S_i)) \times \P_{j \neq i} f(S_j)$$
$$f(A) \leq f(S_i) \times \P_{j \neq i}(1 - t(S_j))$$
$$t(S_i) \leq \mathrm{x} - (1 - t(A)) / \P_{j \neq i}(1 - t(S_j))$$
$$t(S_i) \leq 1 - f(A) / (f(S_j) \times \P_{k \neq i,j}(1 - t(S_k)))$$
$$f(S_i) \leq f(A) / \P_{j \neq i} f(S_j)$$
$$f(S_i) \leq (1 - t(A)) / ((1 - t(S_j)) \times \P_{k \neq i,j} f(S_k))$$

A disjoins-exclusive $\{S_1, S_1, \ldots, S_n\}$:

$$t(A) \leq t(S_i) + \Sigma_{j \neq i}(1 - f(S_j))$$
$$f(A) \leq f(S_i) - \Sigma_{j \neq i} t(S_j)$$
$$t(S_i) \leq t(A) - \Sigma_{j \neq i} t(S_j)$$
$$t(S_i) \leq f(S_j) - \Sigma_{k \neq i,j} t(S_k) - f(A)$$
$$f(S_i) \leq f(A) + \Sigma_{j \neq i}(1 - f(S_j))$$
$$f(S_i) \leq t(S_j) + \Sigma_{k \neq i,j}(1 - f(S_k)) + 1 - t(A)$$

$\{S_1, S_1, \ldots, S_n\}$ mutually exclusive:

$$t(S_i) \leq f(S_j) - \Sigma_{k \neq i,j} t(S_k)$$

Appendix C

INFERNO Run with AL/X Example

Define the various relations corresponding to AL/X links.

"V01SDHP" enables "LIFTPRESS" with strength 0.668;
"LIFTPRESS" requires "V01SDHP" with strength 1.000;

"V01CCRCHART" enables "LIFTPRESS" with strength 0.980;
"LIFTPRESS" requires "V01CCRCHART" with strength 1.000;

"LP&SCIVSHUT" conjoins {"LIFTPRESS","SCIVSHUT"};

"LP&SCIVSHUT" enables "SCIVCAUSE" with strength 0.909;
"SCIVCAUSE" requires "LP&SCIVSHUT" with strength 1.000;

"PCV302FTBAD" enables "PCV302EQERR" with strength 0.968;

```
"PCV302EQERR" requires "PCV302FTBAD" with strength 1.000;
"LIFTPRESS" enables "PCV302EQERR" with strength 0.231;
"PCV302EQERR" requires "LIFTPRESS" with strength 0.998;
"LIFTPRESS" enables "RELVLIFT" with strength 0.668;
"RELVLIFT" requires "LIFTPRESS" with strength 1.000;
"RVNOISECOOL" enables "RELVLIFT" with strength 0.501;
"RELVLIFT" requires "RVNOISECOOL" with strength 0.997;
"RVLIFTIND" enables "RELVLIFT" with strength 0.801;
"RELVLIFT" requires "RVLIFTIND" with strength 1.000;
"NLIFTPRESS" negates "LIFTPRESS";
"LIFT&NLIFTP" conjoins {"RELVLIFT","NLIFTPRESS"};
"LIFT&NLIFTP" enables "RVLIFTEARLY" with strength 0.667;
"RVLIFTEARLY" requires "LIFT&NLIFTP" with strength 1.000;
"NRELVLIFT" negates "RELVLIFT";
"NLIFT&IND" conjoins {"RVLIFTIND","NRELVLIFT"};
"NLIFT&IND" enables "RVSOLSHORT" with strength 0.500;
"RVSOLSHORT" requires "NLIFT&IND" with strength 1.000;
"NLIFT&IND" enables "RVSWSHORT" with strength 0.286;
"RVSWSHORT" requires "NLIFT&IND" with strength 1.000;
```

Enter the probabilities defining this particular case.

```
assume "RVLIFTIND";
assume "V01CCRCHART" with probability 0.9;
assume "V01SDHP";
assume "PCV302FTBAD" false;
assume "SCIVSHUT";
show events;
** "V01SDHP": range 1 - 0
        LB by assumption
        UB from "LIFTPRESS" being false, by enables-inverse
** "LIFTPRESS": range 0.882 - 0
        LB from Pr("V01CCRCHART") ≥ 0.9, by enables
        UB from "PCV302EQERR" being false, by enables-inverse
** "V01CCRCHART": range 0.9 - 0
        LB by assumption
        UB from "LIFTPRESS" being false, by enables-inverse
   "LP&SCIVSHUT": false
        UB from "LIFTPRESS" being false, by conjoins
   "SCIVSHUT": true
        LB by assumption
```

```
   "SCIVCAUSE": false
        UB from "LP&SCIVSHUT" being false, by requires
** "PCV302FTBAD": range 0.204 - 0
        LB from Pr("PCV302EQERR") ≥ 0.204, by requires-inverse
        UB by assumption
** "PCV302EQERR": range 0.204 - 0
        LB from Pr("LIFTPRESS") ≥ 0.882, by enables
        UB from "PCV302FTBAD" being false, by requires
** "RELVLIFT": range 0.801 - 0
        LB from "RVLIFTIND" being true, by enables
        UB from "LIFTPRESS" being false, by requires
** "RVNOISECOOL": range 0.8 - 0
        LB from Pr("RELVLIFT") ≥ 0.801, by requires-inverse
        UB from "RELVLIFT" being false, by enables-inverse
** "RVLIFTIND": range 1 - 0
        LB by assumption
        UB from "RELVLIFT" being false, by enables-inverse
** "NLIFTPRESS": range 1 - 0.118
        LB from "LIFTPRESS" being false, by negates
        UB from Pr("LIFTPRESS") ≥ 0.882, by negates
   "LIFT&NLIFTP": false
        UB from "RELVLIFT" being false, by conjoins
   "RVLIFTEARLY": false
        UB from "LIFT&NLIFTP" being false, by requires
** "NRELVLIFT": range 1 - 0.199
        LB from "RELVLIFT" being false, by negates
        UB from Pr("RELVLIFT") ≥ 0.801, by negates
** "NLIFT&IND": range 0.1 - 0
        LB from "NRELVLIFT" being true, by conjoins
        UB from "RVLIFTIND" being false, by conjoins
** "RVSOLSHORT": range 0.05 - 0
        LB from Pr("NLIFT&IND") ≥ 0.1, by enables
        UB from "NLIFT&IND" being false, by requires
** "RVSWSHORT": range 0.029 - 0
        LB from Pr("NLIFT&IND") ≥ 0.1, by enables
        UB from "NLIFT&IND" being false, by requires
```

Find ways of making the information consistent.

```
show rectifications;
"V01SDHP" can be resolved by changing:
     Pr("V01SDHP") from 1 to 0
```

["V01SDHP" enables "LIFTPRESS" with strength 0.668] to 0
["LIFTPRESS" enables "PCV302EQERR" with strength 0.231] to 0
Pr("PCV302FTBAD") from 0 to 0.154

"LIFTPRESS" can be resolved by changing:
["LIFTPRESS" enables "PCV302EQERR" with strength 0.231] to 0
Pr("V01CCRCHART") from 0.9 to 0
["V01CCRCHART" enables "LIFTPRESS" with strength 0.98] to 0
Pr("PCV302FTBAD") from 0 to 0.204

"V01CCRCHART" can be resolved by changing:
Pr("V01CCRCHART") from 0.9 to 0
["V01CCRCHART" enables "LIFTPRESS" with strength 0.98] to 0
["LIFTPRESS" enables "PCV302EQERR" with strength 0.231] to 0
Pr("PCV302FTBAD") from 0 to 0.204

"PCV302FTBAD" can be resolved by changing:
Pr("PCV302FTBAD") from 0 to 0.204
["LIFTPRESS" enables "PCV302EQERR" with strength 0.231] to 0
Pr("V01CCRCHART") from 0.9 to 0
["V01CCRCHART" enables "LIFTPRESS" with strength 0.98] to 0

"PCV302EQERR" can be resolved by changing:
Pr("PCV302FTBAD") from 0 to 0.204
["LIFTPRESS" enables "PCV302EQERR" with strength 0.231] to 0
Pr("V01CCRCHART") from 0.9 to 0
["V01CCRCHART" enables "LIFTPRESS" with strength 0.98] to 0

"RELVLIFT" can be resolved by changing:
Pr("RVLIFTIND") from 1 to 0
["RVLIFTIND" enables "RELVLIFT" with strength 0.801] to 0
["LIFTPRESS" enables "PCV302EQERR" with strength 0.231] to 0
Pr("PCV302FTBAD") from 0 to 0.185

"RVNOISECOOL" can be resolved by changing:
["RVNOISECOOL" enables "RELVLIFT" with strength 0.501] to 0
["RELVLIFT" requires "RVNOISECOOL" with strength 0.997] to 0.199
Pr("RVLIFTIND") from 1 to 0.004
["RVLIFTIND" enables "RELVLIFT" with strength 0.801] to 0.003
["LIFTPRESS" enables "PCV302EQERR" with strength 0.231] to 0
Pr("PCV302FTBAD") from 0 to 0.093

"RVLIFTIND" can be resolved by changing:
Pr("RVLIFTIND") from 1 to 0
["RVLIFTIND" enables "RELVLIFT" with strength 0.801] to 0
["LIFTPRESS" enables "PCV302EQERR" with strength 0.231] to 0
Pr("PCV302FTBAD") from 0 to 0.185

"NLIFTPRESS" can be resolved by changing:
["LIFTPRESS" enables "PCV302EQERR" with strength 0.231] to 0
Pr("V01CCRCHART") from 0.9 to 0
["V01CCRCHART" enables "LIFTPRESS" with strength 0.98] to 0
Pr("PCV302FTBAD") from 0 to 0.204

"NRELVLIFT" can be resolved by changing:
Pr("RVLIFTIND") from 1 to 0
["RVLIFTIND" enables "RELVLIFT" with strength 0.801] to 0
["LIFTPRESS" enables "PCV302EQERR" with strength 0.231] to 0
Pr("PCV302FTBAD") from 0 to 0.185

"NLIFT&IND" can be resolved by changing:
Pr("RVLIFTIND") from 1 to 0
["RVLIFTIND" enables "RELVLIFT" with strength 0.801] to 0
["LIFTPRESS" enables "PCV302EQERR" with strength 0.231] to 0
Pr("PCV302FTBAD") from 0 to 0.018

"RVSOLSHORT" can be resolved by changing:
["NLIFT&IND" enables "RVSOLSHORT" with strength 0.5] to 0
Pr("RVLIFTIND") from 1 to 0
["RVLIFTIND" enables "RELVLIFT" with strength 0.801] to 0
["LIFTPRESS" enables "PCV302EQERR" with strength 0.231] to 0
Pr("PCV302FTBAD") from 0 to 0.009

"RVSWSHORT" can be resolved by changing:
["NLIFT&IND" enables "RVSWSHORT" with strength 0.286] to 0
Pr("RVLIFTIND") from 1 to 0
["RVLIFTIND" enables "RELVLIFT" with strength 0.801] to 0
["LIFTPRESS" enables "PCV302EQERR" with strength 0.231] to 0
Pr("PCV302FTBAD") from 0 to 0.005

Alternative rectifications:

Pr("PCV302FTBAD") from 0 to 0.204
Total reluctance 0.20
["LIFTPRESS" enables "PCV302EQERR" with strength 0.231] to 0
Total reluctance 0.23

Pr("PCV302FTBAD") from 0 to 0.185
Pr("V01CCRCHART") from 0.9 to 0
Total reluctance 1.09

Pr("PCV302FTBAD") from 0 to 0.185
["V01CCRCHART" enables "LIFTPRESS" with strength 0.98] to 0
Total reluctance 1.17

Pr("PCV302FTBAD") from 0 to 0.154
Pr("V01CCRCHART") from 0.9 to 0
["RVLIFTIND" enables "RELVLIFT" with strength 0.801] to 0
Total reluctance 1.86

Pr("PCV302FTBAD") from 0 to 0.154
["V01CCRCHART" enables "LIFTPRESS" with strength 0.98] to 0
["RVLIFTIND" enables "RELVLIFT" with strength 0.801] to 0
Total reluctance 1.94

Pr("PCV302FTBAD") from 0 to 0.154
Pr("V01CCRCHART") from 0.9 to 0
Pr("RVLIFTIND") from 1 to 0
Total reluctance 2.05

Pr("PCV302FTBAD") from 0 to 0.154
["V01CCRCHART" enables "LIFTPRESS" with strength 0.98] to 0
Pr("RVLIFTIND") from 1 to 0
Total reluctance 2.13

["V01SDHP" enables "LIFTPRESS" with strength 0.668] to 0
Pr("V01CCRCHART") from 0.9 to 0
["RVLIFTIND" enables "RELVLIFT" with strength 0.801] to 0
Total reluctance 2.37

["V01SDHP" enables "LIFTPRESS" with strength 0.668] to 0
["V01CCRCHART" enables "LIFTPRESS" with strength 0.98] to 0
["RVLIFTIND" enables "RELVLIFT" with strength 0.801] to 0
Total reluctance 2.45

Adopt the first rectification given previously.

assume "PCV302FTBAD" with probability 0.204;
show events;

"V01SDHP": true
LB by assumption

"LIFTPRESS": range 0.882 - 0.883
LB from Pr("V01CCRCHART") ≥ 0.9, by enables
UB from Pr("PCV302EQERR") ≤ 0.204, by enables-inverse

"V01CCRCHART": range 0.9 - 0.901
LB by assumption
UB from Pr("LIFTPRESS") ≤ 0.883, by enables-inverse

"LP&SCIVSHUT": range 0.882 - 0.883
LB from Pr("LIFTPRESS") ≥ 0.882, by conjoins
UB from Pr("LIFTPRESS") ≤ 0.883, by conjoins

"SCIVSHUT": true
LB by assumption

"SCIVCAUSE": range 0.802 - 0.883
LB from Pr("LP&SCIVSHUT") ≥ 0.882, by enables
UB from Pr("LP&SCIVSHUT") ≤ 0.883, by requires

"PCV302FTBAD": range 0.204 - 0.204
LB by assumption
UB by assumption

"PCV302EQERR": range 0.204 - 0.204
LB from Pr("LIFTPRESS") ≥ 0.882, by enables
UB from Pr("PCV302FTBAD") ≤ 0.204, by requires

"RELVLIFT": range 0.801 - 0.883
LB from "RVLIFTIND" being true, by enables
UB from Pr("LIFTPRESS") ≤ 0.883, by requires

"RVNOISECOOL": range 0.8 - 1
  LB from Pr("RELVLIFT") ≥ 0.801, by requires-inverse

"RVLIFTIND": true
  LB by assumption

"NLIFTPRESS": range 0.117 - 0.118
  LB from Pr("LIFTPRESS") ≤ 0.883, by negates
  UB from Pr("LIFTPRESS") ≥ 0.882, by negates

"LIFT&NLIFTP": range 0 - 0.118
  UB from Pr("NLIFTPRESS") ≤ 0.118, by conjoins

"RVLIFTEARLY": range 0 - 0.118
  UB from Pr("LIFT&NLIFTP") ≤ 0.118, by requires

"NRELVLIFT": range 0.117 - 0.199
  LB from Pr("RELVLIFT") ≤ 0.883, by negates
  UB from Pr("RELVLIFT") ≥ 0.801, by negates

"NLIFT&IND": range 0.117 - 0.199
  LB from Pr("NRELVLIFT") ≥ 0.117, by conjoins
  UB from Pr("NRELVLIFT") ≤ 0.199, by conjoins

"RVSOLSHORT": range 0.059 - 0.199
  LB from Pr("NLIFT&IND") ≥ 0.117, by enables
  UB from Pr("NLIFT&IND") ≤ 0.199, by requires

"RVSWSHORT": range 0.033 - 0.199
  LB from Pr("NLIFT&IND") ≥ 0.117, by enables
  UB from Pr("NLIFT&IND") ≤ 0.199, by requires

Chapter 11

Distributed Problem Solving for Air Fleet Control: Framework and Implementation

Randall Steeb, David J. McArthur, Stephanie J. Cammarata, Sanjai Narain, and William D. Giarla

11.1 Introduction

Distributed problem solving, or multiple-agent problem solving, refers to the process by which several agents interact to achieve goals. The intent of a theory of distributed problem solving is to develop an information-processing account of effective group problem-solving performance. As part of our attempt to learn how groups can cooperate effectively, we describe in formal, computational terms the actions of each agent as the group achieves a collective goal.

This chapter originally appeared as N-2139-ARPA, The Rand Corporation, April 1984.

Previous work in cognitive science helps little in achieving this understanding. Few studies have focused on group problem solving. Over the past twenty years, beginning with the pioneering work of Newell and Simon, cognitive scientists have learned much about the information processing that underlies the problem solving of individuals. Cognitive psychologists have, for example, carefully studied the way in which people play games, solve mathematical problems and program computers. In a similar way, workers in artificial intelligence have developed computational models of how single agents might do medical diagnosis, and plan genetics experiments and so forth. These efforts have resulted in the development of a variety of techniques for modeling the environment, planning under uncertainty, and executing complex sequences of actions. Unfortunately, recent work suggests that the representations of knowledge (Konolige, 1981; Appelt, 1982) and planning expertise (McArthur and Klahr, 1982) required of agents in distributed or group problem-solving situations are quite different than those required for single-agent problem solvers. Organizational psychologists have explicitly studied group performance (Dalkey, 1977), but because of the difficulties of representing multiple disparate world views and specifying sequences of activities within and between agents, their theories are usually expressed informally. Also, the theories are typically stated in aggregate terms, not in terms of the information processing of individual agents. The related area of distributed processing has more formal underpinnings but is also of limited applicability. In distributed processing, multiple computers interact in a relatively simple fashion through the sharing of data. In distributed problem solving, agents must not only share data, but they must also *share the problem solving*.

In this chapter, we present a model of distributed problem-solving processes. Our approach has been first to study carefully the competences or capabilities of agents in groups, then develop a computational model of how these capabilities might be achieved. Then we proceed to implement the computational theory and develop and test specific distributed problem-solving systems. Section 11.2 discusses the difficulties and opportunities facing multiple-agent problem solvers in many domains and contrasts these domains with more frequently studied single-agent problem-solving environments. Section 11.3 uses this analysis to infer a set of requirements on the cooperative strategies of group problem-solving agents. In Section 11.4, we discuss the computational theory that follows from our analysis of competences. The remaining sections are devoted to descriptions of several specific systems we have implemented in the domains of distributed air-traffic control and distributed remotely piloted vehicle (RPV) coordination.

11.2

Distributed and Single-agent Problem Solving

To understand the capabilities of agents that solve problems in a distributed fashion, and to understand how they differ from single-agent problem solvers, we begin by examining some important characteristics of distributed problems.

11.2.1 ■ Characterization of Distributed Problem Solving

Several general characteristics of distributed problem-solving situations are particularly important for our purposes:

- Most situations consist of a collection of agents, each with various *skills*, including sensing, communication (often over limited-bandwidth channels), planning, and acting.
- The group as a whole has a set of assigned *tasks*. As in single-agent problem-solving situations, these tasks may need to be decomposed into subtasks, not all of which may be logically independent. The group must somehow assign subtasks to appropriate agents.
- Each agent typically has only *limited knowledge*. An agent may be subject to several kinds of limitations: limited knowledge of the environment (e.g., because of restricted sensing horizons), limited knowledge of the tasks of the group, or limited knowledge of the intentions of other agents.
- There are often limited shared *resources* that each agent can apply to tasks. For example, if the agents are in a blocks-world environment, the shared resources are the blocks out of which their constructions must be made.
- Agents typically have a different degree of *appropriateness* for a given task. The appropriateness of a particular agent for a task is a function of how well the agent's skills match the expertise required to do the task, the extent to which its limited knowledge is adequate for the task, its current processing resources, and the quality of its communication links with other agents.

11.2.2 ■ Difficulties in Distributed Problem Solving

When solving problems in a distributed fashion, several difficulties that are not significant in most single-agent problem-solving situations can arise. First, in single-agent problem solving, the agent is typically *given* its task as part of the problem definition (Sacerdoti, 1974; Fahlman, 1974), whereas in distributed situations, the *assignment* of tasks to the agents is part of the group problem-solving activity. This assignment can be challenging. Many mappings of tasks to agents are possible, but because agents typically have different available expertise for a given task, only a few agents will be acceptable for each task. Thus in many distributed problems, it is crucial for agents to adopt the right *role*. It would not be reasonable to assign the role of inventing a new chip to a lawyer, or the role of writing the patent to an engineer. In addition to ensuring that each task is assigned to an acceptable agent, the group has to ensure *task coverage*. Specifically, this means that all tasks should be assigned to some agent (complete role assignment) and that extra or redundant agents should not be assigned tasks (*consistent role assignment*). For example, in air-traffic control, if the task is to solve a possible spatial conflict, it may be critical to ensure that only one aircraft detours; if two or more adopt that role, they may possibly create a new collision situation.

Compounding the difficulty of finding an optimal task assignment is the limited knowledge of the agents. In most single-agent problem solvers, the agent has a complete world model, which usually remains complete for two reasons: all changes in the environment are made by the agent, and thus it can always update its world model; and a single agent does not have to worry about unknown intentions of other agents. The incomplete or incorrect world models of distributed agents may degrade the effectiveness of task assignment because either agents that know the breakdown of tasks may not know which agents have the most appropriate available expertise, or, conversely, the agents with the best expertise may not know about appropriate tasks for them. Similarly, the incomplete knowledge of agents may prevent consistent and complete role assignment because there may be no one agent that has a global knowledge of all the roles or subtasks that need to be assigned. In a single-agent problem solving situation, this issue does not arise. The agent knows how it has decomposed a task into subtasks, and it knows exactly which subtasks it has to do—all of them.

Once tasks or roles have been assigned, distributed problem solvers face severe difficulties in *coordinating task execution*. Like single-agent tasks or subtasks, group tasks may not be independent. Temporal or logical dependencies may exist. For example, if the group problem is to build a new chip, the designer's role must be completed prior to the initiation of the manufacturer's role. In addition, tasks that are not logically connected may interact through shared resources. For example, if two blocks-world agents are each to build towers, one agent's plan will negatively interact with another's if both intend to use the same block (Davis, 1981). The interaction is negative because the first agent is satisfying its task at the cost of preventing the second agent from doing the same. In contrast, the plans might interact positively, for example if, one agent's plan entails using (hence picking up) a block that currently lies on top of the block another agent intends to use. The interaction is positive in the sense that the first agent is not only satisfying its task, it is also helping the second agent satisfy its task.

Single-agent problem solvers have difficulties handling interdependent tasks or subgoals (Sussman, 1975), but these difficulties multiply for distributed problem solvers because of limited knowledge. If two agents have only local knowledge—for example, if they know only the local environment and their own tasks and intentions—they will not be able to prevent negative interactions between goals or roles. If the chip designer does not know about the chip manufacturer, there is no basis for coordinating their subtasks; if one blocks-world agent doesn't know the intentions of another, there is no basis for ensuring that their projected uses of resources will not conflict. Similarly, without some knowledge of others' tasks and intentions, positive interactions, which are the essence of effective group problem solving, cannot be encouraged.

In summary, the main challenge in distributed problem solving is to make the solutions a distributed agent produces not only locally acceptable, achieving the assigned tasks, but also interfaced correctly with the actions of other agents solving dependent tasks. The solutions must be not only reasonable with respect to the local task, but also *globally coherent*, and this global coherence must be achieved by *local computation alone*. Global coherence is less difficult to achieve for a single-agent problem solver, simply because its computation and knowledge are themselves as global as the task requires.

11.3 Strategies for Cooperation

How can global coherence be achieved in distributed problem-solving groups in the face of limited knowledge and the requirement that all computation be local? Intuition says that it can be achieved, since there are cases in which groups act synergistically, solving problems *better* than any individual could. Broadly, the key for coherent distributed problem solving lies in the fact that although distributed agents have greater difficulties solving a given task, they have potentially more options as well. A single-agent problem solver must gather all information itself; distributed agents work singly as well, but they may also ask others to help. A single-agent problem solver must perform all planning itself; a distributed agent may plan or act, but it may also request others to do so, which results in speed through parallelism. In short, much of the power of distributed problem solving comes through cooperation and communication.

We have come to believe that there are no general algorithms to dictate optimal cooperation. Methods that yield good distributed performance under one set of conditions fail under others. Although communication between agents provides the basis for effective cooperative problem solving, it is just another problem-solving tool that may be used either poorly or effectively. If the tool is used poorly, then group problem-solving performance may be worse than individual problem-solving performance.

It requires considerable expertise to use communication effectively. This expertise seems to take the form of a broad range of heuristic rules. We refer to such expertise collectively as *cooperative strategies*. Our main theoretical and empirical goals have been to understand such strategies. In a theoretical vein, we have attempted to analyze the components of cooperative strategies and the range of alternative strategies that may be adopted. More empirically, we have attempted to determine the performance characteristics of such strategies and the conditions under which each will perform poorly or effectively. We have classified these heuristic cooperation strategies under two headings: *organizational policies* and *information distribution policies*.

In the following sections, we briefly discuss some theoretical aspects of cooperation. Subsequently, we present some empirical tests of several specific policies we have implemented in a distributed problem solver for air-traffic control. We finish by describing some further implementations in RPV coordination.

11.3.1 ■ Organizational Policies

Organizational policies dictate how a larger task should be decomposed into smaller subtasks that can be assigned to individual agents. Typically, a given organizational policy assigns specific roles to each of the agents in a group. Such a policy is useful if for some tasks the resulting division of labor enables agents to work independently. For example, the corporate hierarchy is an organizational policy that can be particularly effective if the corporate task can be decomposed in such a way that an agent at one level can work independently of others at that level, reporting results only to its immediate superior, who takes care of any necessary interfacing.

Organizational policies not only define task decomposition, but they also prescribe communication paths among agents. They turn a random collection of agents into a network that is fixed, at least for a given task. In the corporate hierarchy, again, the arcs between agents usually indicate which pairs are permitted to talk to one another, and, in addition, they determine the nature of the messages that are allowed. Such communication restrictions are beneficial if they encourage only those agents who should communicate to do so—in particular, agents who have dependent tasks or who may share resources. In general, organizational policies strongly direct and constrain the behavior of distributed agents. If those constraints are appropriate to the task at hand, then the organization is effective; otherwise, its performance may be suboptimal.

Agents must know not only which policy is appropriate to the current circumstances, but also the *techniques by which a group can implement the chosen policy in a distributed fashion.* How is the assignment of roles that is specified by the policy made to agents? How is the agent that is most appropriate for a given task found?

Briefly, any distributed method of implementing an organizational policy must answer a variety of questions, including:

- Are agents externally directed or data-directed (Lesser, 1981)? That is, does an agent arrive at its roles by being told them, or is information relayed, allowing the agent to assign the roles itself?
- When an agent is requested by another agent to conform to a role or to take on another subtask, does the first agent have the right to negotiate?
- How does an agent weigh the value of competing tasks?

Smith (1978) has proposed the contract net as a formalism for implementing certain organizational policies in a distributed fashion. Other possible distributed policies can be derived from the blackboard scheduling techniques of HEARSAY-III (Erman, 1981) and AGE (Nii, 1979), and from hierarchical control structures used in production systems (see, for example, the goal-oriented control in OPS5, Forgy, 1981). In Section 11.4, we discuss a somewhat different organizational policy that uses our framework.

11.3.2 ■ Information-distribution Policies

An information-distribution policy addresses the nature of communication between cooperating agents. Decisions about how agents communicate with each other are, first of all, constrained by the choice of organizational policy, since that policy decides the network of permissible communicators. However, within these constraints, a great number of lower-level decisions must be made about how and when communications should occur:

- *Broadcast or selective communication.* Are agents discriminating about those to whom they talk? If so, what criteria are used to select recipients?
- *Unsolicited or on-demand communication.* Assuming an agent knows with whom it wants to communicate, does it do so only if information is requested, or does it infer the informational needs of other agents and transmit data accordingly? What form of information (data, constraints, commands, goals) should it send?
- *Acknowledged or unacknowledged communication.* Does an agent indicate that it has received information?
- *Single-transmission or repeated-transmission communication.* Is a piece of information sent only once, or can it be repeated? How frequently? Lesser (1981) refers to a repeated-transmission policy as *murmuring*.

Poor decisions at this level result, at best, in the highly inefficient use of limited-bandwidth channels. At worst, such choices endanger global coherence by preventing communication between agents whose tasks may interact. The goal of information-distribution policies is to minimize these possibilities. As with organizational policies, the choice of communication policies depends on current conditions. These include the bandwidth of the communication channel, the reliability of the channel, the load of the channel, the maximum acceptable information turn-around time, and the relative cost (and time) of computation versus communication. Effective communications management also requires accurate modeling of other agents' knowledge.

11.4 A Framework for Distributed Problem Solving

The previous sections give an analysis of distributed problem-solving situations, as compared with single-agent problem-solving environments, and informally describe the special competence that multiple-agent problem solvers must possess. In the following sections, we attempt to develop a computational theory of these cooperative capabilities. Our goal here is to explain how organizational policies and information-distribution policies can be computed, and then to describe specific implementations of such policies.

11.4.1 ■ Reasoning About Tasks

What sorts of computations are involved when groups successfully use a cooperative strategy? Abstractly, such successful cooperative actions require each agent to make decisions about:

- Which of planning, execution, evaluation, and so on, it should do.;
- When it should do them;
- How it should do them;
- To whom it should talk;
- When it should communicate; and
- What it should say.

In short, each agent needs to make decisions about its preference among tasks, their timing relative to one another, and their content. It needs to *reason about possible tasks.*

Reasoning about possible tasks plays a much less significant role in single-agent problem-solving situations than in distributed problem solving. Many theories of individual problem solving (Fahlman, 1974; Sacerdoti, 1974) suggest that a problem solver's activities are decomposed into separate, strictly ordered phases of information gathering, planning, and execution. Because this task ordering is so trivial, there is little need to reason explicitly about it. Almost all reasoning goes on *within the planning task*. Unless the problem solver must maintain multiple lines of reasoning or deal with time-varying data, there is little or no meta-level reasoning *about planning*—whether it should be done, or how it should be done in relation to a variety of other tasks that comprise the problem-solving process. However, the kinds of competence we described earlier indicate that a simple, fixed ordering of tasks is not possible for multiple-agent problem solvers. The ordering of tasks is not simple because there are many tasks to manage, and they are frequently interdependent (e.g., the agent must receive and send communications as well as plan and execute). The ordering of tasks cannot be fixed but must be *dynamically changed* because agents will be accruing information about the environment and the activities of the other agents and will need to alter their task preferences on the basis of this new information.

11.4.2 ■ The Framework: Tenets

To achieve a computational understanding of distributed problem solving, we therefore need a vocabulary that enables us to represent task entities formally, and to express formally those rules that reason about the represented tasks. We have developed a framework that meets these needs. Briefly, the main tenets of the framework are:

1. Each agent has several distinct kinds of *generic tasks,* such as information gathering (sensing and input-communication), information distribution (output-communication), plan generation, plan evaluation, plan fixing, and plan execution.
2. Each kind of generic task invocation (or *task instance*) is a process: It can be suspended and resumed; hence tasks can be interwoven without losing *continuity.*
3. Each agent has a knowledge base that represents its beliefs about other agents and their intentions, as well as information about the static environment and its own intentions.
4. Within an individual agent, the knowledge base is shared by all task instances, like a HEARSAY blackboard (Erman, 1981). Any change in the knowledge base made by a task (e.g., information gathering) while another task is suspended (e.g., planning) will be visible to the latter when it resumes. Thus tasks such as planning exhibit *currency* as well as continuity; they do not base computations on an outdated world-model.
5. Task instances are both data-driven and event-driven. Instances of generic tasks are triggered in two ways: by sets of well-defined knowledge-base states, or by well-defined events that result in changes to the knowledge base. Tasks that are created do not immediately get executed but are enabled and may compete for processing resources.
6. Each enabled task has a limited amount of self-knowledge, including explicit intentions and validity conditions. This information can be used to determine if a task is justified in continuing as conditions change. Thus tasks will exhibit *relevance.*
7. Enabled tasks are not invoked in a fixed order, as in single-agent problem solvers. Rather, the agent acts as a scheduler, reasoning about the ordering of task instances. More specifically, the agent uses a set of *heuristic reasoning rules* to prioritize processes that represent enabled tasks.
8. A task selected by the agent for execution is not necessarily allowed to run to completion. It is given an upper limit of pro-

cessing resources (time). The extent of this limit is also controlled by the agent.

9. During the execution of a task or process, (a) the task may complete, in which case it is eliminated from the set competing for resources; (b) new tasks may be created because of knowledge-base changes or events affected by the running task; or (c) the changes may cause existing tasks to lose their justification.
10. After a task has consumed its allocated supply of resources (time), the agent reorders the priority of enabled tasks and, in light of the conditions in the altered knowledge base, selects a new one to run. It also eliminates unjustified tasks (if the tasks have not eliminated themselves).
11. This procedure iterates until there are no more enabled tasks worth running.

Generally, then, we view the agent in a group problem-solving situation as a kind of knowledge-based operating system. The view is not a model of an agent in a specific distributed domain, but rather represents a theoretical framework for describing distributed agents or a set of guidelines for constructing a specific model. The framework is similar to that used in blackboard systems (Erman, 1981), but is more dynamic, in that tasks can be interrupted at any point. Adhering to the framework, the user still needs to provide several sorts of domain-specific expertise, including the procedures that comprise each generic task, the triggering conditions under which a task instance is to be created, the validity conditions under which it is permitted to continue, and the heuristic rules that order the priority of enabled tasks in light of the current state of knowledge.

11.4.3 ■ The Framework: Implementation

To facilitate the development of our specific distributed problem solvers, we have used a simple task language to implement the framework. The task language is a set of Interlisp functions with a convenient vocabulary stating the required domain-specific expertise. Once stated, the task language takes care of all the specifics of task management. It ensures that an appropriate task instance is enabled when the triggering conditions of a user-defined generic task are met. The task language also takes care of the low-level implementation of tasks as resumable coroutines, and it guarantees that these processes suspend after the appropriate amount of time is consumed. Finally, it handles the details of scheduling the next task to run; the user needs only to state the reasoning rules of the scheduler that its application requires.[1] By attending to the details of task creation and management, the task language frees the user to focus on the theoretically more interesting issues of designing (and debugging) rules that achieve the appropriate interweaving of tasks.

Our task language can be compared with the several specialized artificial intelligence languages built on top of LISP. Such languages were developed to provide a special set of primitives for building programs in a limited domain. For example, EMYCIN (van Melle, 1979) facilitates the development of diagnostic systems such as MYCIN (Shortliffe, 1976) and PUFF (Kunz et al., 1978)—although it may not help in constructing fundamentally different systems—by providing expert-systems concepts as primitives. To the extent that the primitives provided actually suit the intended domain of application, they simplify the programmer's design and implementation problems. In the next section we test out the primitives of our task language by using the language to implement several distributed air-traffic-control problem solvers. Concrete examples show how agents, tasks, and rules for reasoning about tasks are represented.

11.5 Air-traffic Control as a Distributed Problem

Problem solving in air-traffic control (ATC) may be distributed in several ways. In Steeb et al. (1981), we discuss a variety of architectures of distribution. Our present systems are all *object-centered,* with an agent associated with each aircraft. That is, each aircraft has its own onboard planning, control, and communication systems. In our ATC task, aircraft enter a rectangular (14 by 23 miles) airspace at any time, either at one of 10 infixes (entry points) on the borders of the airspace or from one of two airports. Figure 11.1, taken from our ATC task simulation, shows the airspace in a relatively congested state. The main goal of an agent is to navigate its associated aircraft through the airspace to an assigned destination—either a boundary outfix or an airport. Each aircraft has only a limited sensory horizon, hence its knowledge of the world is never complete, and it must continually gather information as it moves through the airspace. Information may be accumulated by either sensing or communication. Agents are allowed to

[1] For more details on the capabilities of task language, see McArthur et al., 1982.

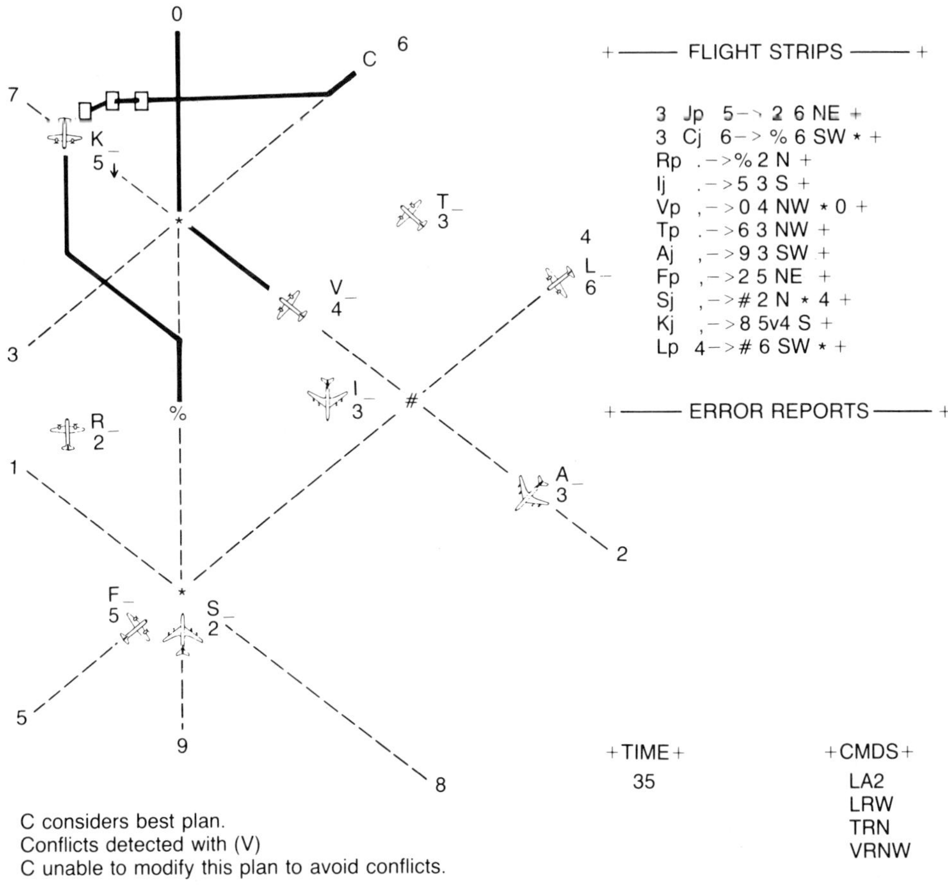

FIGURE 11.1 Air-traffic Control Task Simulation.

communicate over a limited-bandwidth channel to other aircraft for purposes of exchanging information and instructions.

Distributed ATC is a group problem not only because agents may help one another gather information, but also because the goals of one agent may interact with those of another. Goal interactions come in the form of shared interaircraft conflicts. A conflict among two or more agents arises when, according to their current plans, the agents will violate minimum separation requirements at some point in the future. When shared conflicts arise, agents must negotiate to solve them. In a crowded airspace, such goal conflicts can become particularly complex and may involve several aircraft, necessitating a high degree of group cooperation.

In terms of the vocabulary developed in Section 11.2, the detection and resolution of conflicts are the main distributed problem-solving *tasks*. These tasks may be decomposed into several *subtasks*, or distinct *roles*. Agents may gather information about a shared conflict, evaluate or interpret the information, develop a plan to avoid a projected conflict, or execute such a plan. Agents may be more or less *appropriate* for such roles, depending on their current processing load (Are they currently involved in helping resolve other conflicts?), their state of knowledge (Do they know a lot about the intentions of other agents in the conflict?), and their spatial constraints (Can they locate many nearby aircraft through sensing and do they have much excess fuel?).

The issue of *optimal task assignment* arises because a group of aircraft may fail to assign the most appropriate agent to each role in a conflict task if some of the aircraft do not know about a shared conflict. In addition, care must be taken to assign a complete and consistent set of roles. Some role inconsistencies can be fatal. For example, two agents would be adopting inconsistent roles if one decided to move left to avoid a head-on collision with the second, while the second decided to move in the same direction. Severe *task coordination problems* may also arise in distributed ATC. The action of moving to avoid one conflict may create or worsen other conflicts (negative task interactions), or it may lessen other conflicts (positive task interactions). Both forms of interaction are caused by the fact that although agents may be dealing with different conflict tasks, they are nevertheless exploiting shared, limited spatial resources.

11.6 Four Distributed Problem Solvers for Air-traffic Control

We outline in this section the implementation of four distinct air-traffic control (ATC) systems, concentrating particularly on the organizational and information-distribution policies embedded in each. All four systems are implemented in our framework for constructing distributed agents. This in turn is implemented in Interlisp-D, running on Xerox 1100 computers. Before discussing the implementation of cooperative strategies, we turn first to a general description of the tasks that must be reasoned about by a distributed ATC (DATC) agent.

11.6.1 ■ Tasks in Air-traffic Control

To define our system within the framework of the task language, we must identify the tasks that comprise each agent and specify the expertise associated with each task. The top-level generic tasks of each DATC agent currently include:

- Sensing (gathering information about positions and types of other aircraft);
- Input-communication (gathering information about routes, plans, and requests of other aircraft);
- Output-communication (distributing information about the agent's routes, plans, and requests to others);
- Initial plan generation (computing a reasonable path through the airspace to one's outfix);
- Plan evaluation (finding conflicts between the agent's plan and the plans it believes others are following; and reviewing new information for consistency with beliefs about others' plans);
- Plan fixing (using existing plans and evaluations to create new plans that avoid conflicts with others); and
- Plan execution (performing the time-tagged actions called out in the plan).

Defining ATC Generic Tasks and Conditions of Invocation

A major part of defining a generic task is stipulating the conditions under which an instance of that task should be created. Consider plan evaluation: We want to define the ATC agent so that an evaluation task is created when

1. The agent has a plan and, via some information-gathering task, learns the plan of some other aircraft;
2. The agent changes its own plan; or
3. The agent believes it knows the plan of another aircraft and senses a new position for that aircraft that is inconsistent with the plan.

In the first two cases, the kind of evaluation needed is *conflict detection;* in the third, it is *consistency checking*. Using the task language, the conflict detection case is implemented as follows:

```
(1)  (CREATE-SUBTASK-TYPE 'Evaluation 'Scheduler)
(2)  (CREATE-SUBTASK-TYPE 'DetectConflict)
```

```
(3)  (SET-TASK-FUNCALL 'DetectConflict
                       '(COMPUTE-CONFLICTS Aircraft OtherAircraft))
(4)  (DEFINE-TASK-TRIGGER 'DetectConflict 'Evaluation
        '(SET-AIRCRAFT-PLAN OtherAircraft y)
        '(Check new plan of OtherAircraft for conflicts against yours)
        '(AND (AIRCRAFT-PLAN OtherAircraft)
            (EQUAL y (AIRCRAFT-PLAN OtherAircraft))))
```

Line (1) establishes the generic task of plan evaluation. *Evaluation* can be thought of as a class object in the SMALLTALK sense (Goldberg and Kay, 1976). Instances of *Evaluation* represent specific plan evaluation tasks that might be created. The second argument in line (1) says that when a plan evaluation task is created, it is to be a subtask of the current instance of *Scheduler,* the top-level generic task of the ATC agent. Only one instance of *Scheduler* is ever created for each agent, and its role is to select the next enabled top-level task to execute (e.g., sensing, planning, input-communication, etc.).

Line (2) establishes a generic subtask of plan evaluation. When triggering conditions of *DetectConflict* are met and an instance of it is created, the instance becomes a subtask of the current *Evaluation* task of the agent. Thus whereas the agent's *Scheduler* task chooses from among enabled tasks that are instances of generics such as *Evaluation* and *Sensing,* an *Evaluation* instance itself is a scheduler that chooses from among instances of *CheckConsistency* and *DetectConflict.*

Line (3) associates a function call with *DetectConflict.* When an instance of a generic task becomes enabled, it may be selected to execute by the *Evaluation* task. If the task has previously executed and suspended, *Evaluation* knows where to resume; if this is the first time the task has been allocated processing resources, *Evaluation* needs to have a way to initiate the task. It does this by evaluating the function call. Line (3) assumes that COMPUTE-CONFLICTS has been defined by the user and encodes the appropriate expertise.

Line (4) stipulates the conditions under which task instances of *DetectConflict* will be created and will become a subtask of *Evaluation.* The interpretation of DEFINE-TASK-TRIGGER is:

```
(DEFINE-TASK-TRIGGER
    "create an instance of this type of generic task"
    "let the scheduler of the new instance be the current instance
     of this generic"
    "create the instance when a form of this type is evaluated"
    "let this be the intention of the created task instance"
    "this form must always be true for the instance to be justified")
```

Thus line (4), for example, says, "Any time you believe you know some other aircraft's plan, it is reasonable to create a *DetectConflict* task, as a subtask of the current *Evaluation* task, to see if your current plan conflicts with its new one. This task is justified as long as you still believe you know the aircraft's plan and it is the new one."

Defining Reasoning Rules that Interweave ATC Task Instances

Declarations such as line (4) in the conflict-detection example show how task creation is data-driven, how tasks ensure that they are relevant as conditions change, and how tasks may be suspended and resumed. But to be able to reason about intelligently interweaving tasks such as plan evaluation, information gathering, and so forth, to permit the DATC agent to perform intelligently, we still need to define heuristic rules that will reason about the priority of enabled tasks. Two reasoning rules currently used are:

```
(1)  (DEFINE-SCHEDULING-RULE 'Scheduler
       (if (TASK-TYPE Subproc) = 'PlanFixing
         and (SUBTASK-OF-TYPE Process 'Evaluation)
       then (SET-TASK-PRIORITY Subproc 0)))
(2)  (DEFINE-SCHEDULING-RULE 'Scheduler
       (if (TASK-TYPE Subproc) = 'SendReplanRequest
         and (SUBTASK-OF-TYPE Process 'PlanFixing)
         and (GREATERP (TASK-TOTAL-TIME
                             (SUBTASK-OF-TYPE Process 'PlanFixing))
             5000)
         and (NOT (IN-IMMINENT-DANGER Aircraft))
       then (SET-TASK-PRIORITY (SUBTASK-OF-TYPE Process
                                                    'PlanFixing)
                                              0)
           (SET-TASK-PRIORITY Subproc 200)))
```

Rule (1) defines a choice of the DATC agent's scheduler; thus it helps the agent decide which of the enabled top-level tasks to execute next. The rule says that if *PlanFixing* is enabled (because an aircraft's plan has a conflict in it), then it is a good idea not to allocate further resources to this task if there is some evidence that the conflict status of the plan should be reevaluated. The rationale is that the *Evaluation* task may have been enabled by receipt of a new plan for the aircraft that is causing the conflict, and this plan may avoid the conflict.

Rule (2) also defines a top-level reasoning process for the DATC agent. Details aside, its role is to decide when a given agent (aircraft) has tried hard enough to solve a conflict shared with another aircraft. Note that "hard enough" has a natural definition in terms of the processing resources (time) that have already been devoted to attempts at *PlanFixing*. If this criterion is met, the agent will use its other option to solve a shared conflict: It will ask the other conflictee to try to resolve it (by invoking the *SendReplanRequest* task) instead of expending more effort to try to resolve the conflict itself.

Rules such as (1) and (2) are the key to the DATC agent's ability to interweave its several enabled tasks in a way that is sensitive to changing conditions. Many of the rules the DATC problem solver currently employs are devoted to ordering tasks that are purely internal to the agent. These tasks, which include sensing, evaluation, plan fixing, and plan execution, often must be interwoven because of the existence of external, unpredictable, agents. The tasks are affected by and do not directly involve those agents. On the other hand, rules like (2) reason about tasks that involve interaction (communication) with others, in the service of either one's own goal or others' goals. The resulting group interactions tend to be much like the dynamics of constraint propagation (Stefik, 1981), or least-commitment planning (Sacerdoti, 1977). An agent pursues a planning option until it is unable to satisfy all constraints or until its alloted time runs out. It then suspends its planning, requests another agent to replan, and sends its own partial plan as a constraint. The process continues without backtracking. In the following section, we discuss the implementation of such strategies in four different ATC problem solvers.

11.6.2 ■ Organizational Policies in ATC

Four organizational policies for dictating task decomposition and role assignment are discussed in this subsection. The organizational policy embedded in three of the four systems may be characterized as *task centralization*; the fourth system adheres to a policy of *task sharing*. Under *task centralization*, the agents involved in any given conflict task will choose one of their number to play most of the roles. In effect, one agent will perform the evaluation role (do all the evaluation of the potential conflicts between aircraft), the plan-fixing role (attempt to devise a plan-fix to dissolve the entire conflict), and the actor role (act on the new plan). The selected agent is required to modify only its plan to resolve the conflict; thus the remaining agents perform no planning or actions. Instead, having agreed on the choice of a replanner, they adopt passive information-distribution roles, merely sending their intentions (plan) to the selected agent. As mentioned earlier, if the selected agent is unable to resolve the entire conflict, it requests another agent to replan. This process continues until all conflicts are resolved or a solution cannot be found. The policy of task centralization, whatever its shortcomings, is worth considering because it has many of the advantages of the centralized, single-agent problem solving that it is meant to mimic. Specifically, by centralizing most task roles in a single agent, the group has to worry less about negative task interactions such as the threat of two aircraft acting in an inconsistent fashion, noted previously.

Although three of our four systems embed a task centralization policy, they differ in how they measure and choose the agent that is most appropriate for the several centralized roles. Also, these schemes represent forms of distributed problem solving in spite of being termed centralized, because many conflicts may be resolved simultaneously by different aircraft over the airspace. The term *centralized* applies only within a given instance of a conflict.

Selection by Shared Convention. In selection by shared convention, each aircraft uses only directly sensed information about the other aircraft (position, heading, and speed) to decide which should plan and which should transmit its current route. The aircraft silently use a common set of conventions for this decision, minimizing communications. Figure 11.2 shows a prototypical sequence of tasks, including communication tasks, between two aircraft, *A* and *B*, under this policy. Each entry in the time line for an aircraft represents the execution of a task instance, using task triggers and scheduler reasoning rules such as the ones presented previously. Because of the limited criteria used, the aircraft selected as the replanner is not likely to be the most appropriate. This version mainly serves as a benchmark against which to judge the utility of more intelligent methods of selection, which are also more costly in terms of computation and communication.

FIGURE 11.2 Prototypical Task Sequence under the Shared-convention Policy (time lines are for tasks executed by aircraft *A* and *B*; solid lines indicate communications).

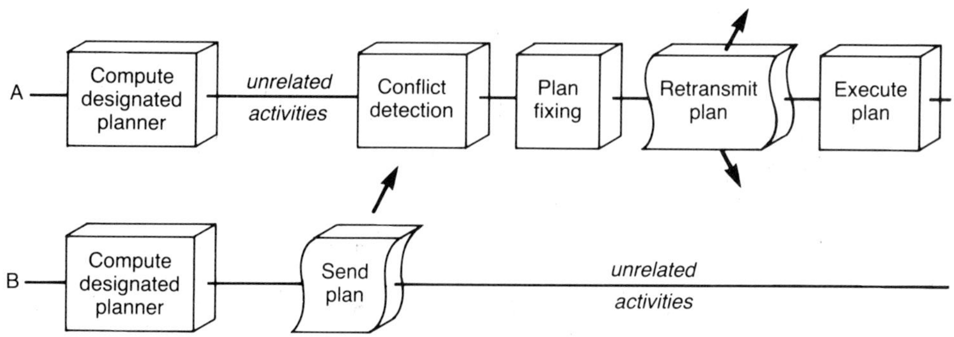

Selection of the Least Spatially Constrained Agent. With this selection method, each aircraft in a potential conflict computes and transmits its *role factor* to the other aircraft. The role factor is an estimate of the appropriateness of an aircraft for the planning role; it results from the constraints under which an aircraft is operating. It is an aggregation of such considerations as the number of other nearby aircraft, fuel remaining, distance from destination, and message load. Figure 11.3 shows the standard sequence of tasks and communications under this policy. This method of selection maintains that the most appropriate agent is the one with the most degrees of freedom for modifying its plan. It is a more complex process than the *shared convention* and should result in more effective replanner choices, although at some additional cost in initial communications.

Selection of the Most Knowledgeable, Least Committed Agent. As in the preceding selection scheme, aircraft share *role factors*, but here they are computed differently. This method of selection maintains that the best replanning agent is the one that knows the most about other agents' intentions because, in replanning, a well-informed agent can explicitly take account of possible interactions between its intentions and those of other agents. More globally coherent plan-fixes should therefore result. In addition, this method says that agents whose intentions are known by others should not replan. If such an agent does modify its plan, it will have violated the expectations of cooperating agents, making their knowledge incorrect and in turn making cooperation difficult. Thus, this policy implements a common adage of cooperation: Don't do the unexpected.

FIGURE 11.3 Prototypical Task Sequence under the Least Spatially Constrained Policy.

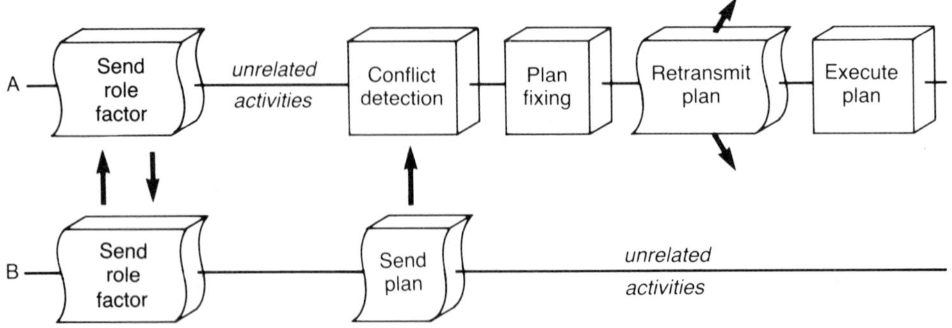

In spite of their simplicity, task-centralization policies are often ineffective. Although the agent selected to perform the centralized roles may be the best *overall*, that agent is rarely the best for *each* of the centralized roles. For example, we still might want to assign the actor role to the agent in a conflict set that is least constrained in the sense defined previously. However, that agent might not be the best in the set for fixing its plan—for making a modification to the plan and evaluating the implications of such a change. Presumably the best agent for this role is the (possibly distinct) member of the conflict set that knows most about the environment and the intentions of aircraft near the one whose plan is to be fixed. This aircraft is in the best position to determine whether any changed plan is not only locally reasonable (solving the conflict), but also globally reasonable (not creating new conflicts with other aircraft).

Task Sharing. The *task-sharing* policy attempts to avoid such problems by evaluating agents' qualifications with respect to each of the roles associated with a conflict. Whereas in centralized policies a single negotiation determines an overall replanner, in the task-sharing policy two rounds of negotiation are necessary, one to determine the plan-fixer and one to determine the actor. Figure 11.4 presents a prototypical sequence of tasks and communications that show how such a policy is implemented in a distributed fashion. The performance of groups working under a task-sharing policy is potentially superior to that of groups working under a task-centralization policy, because in the former the group attempts to optimize in each role. However, in practice this policy has several possible drawbacks. It is communication-intensive and may be inappropriate when communication channels are un-

FIGURE 11.4 Prototypical Task Sequence under Task Sharing Policy.

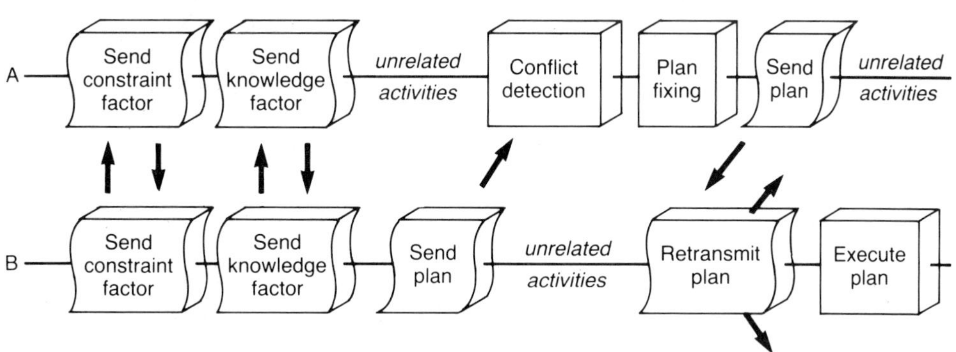

reliable or costly. Moreover, it risks potential negative interactions because several agents have to coordinate intimately to achieve a solution.

11.6.3 ■ Information-distribution Policies in ATC

Much of the information-distribution behavior in the four systems is set by the choice of organizational policy (who to contact, what to send, when to send it). We assume in all cases that information should be sent to other aircraft selectively (no broadcasting), without waiting for a request, without expecting an acknowledgment, and without repeating the information a second time. These choices are reasonable, since we assume in all systems that communication is error-free. When we add noise to the communication channel, we envision adopting a policy that injects some needed redundancy or safety into communication, for example, a policy that includes murmuring (Lesser, 1981). We also assume a constant effective communication bandwidth for all four systems. Each aircraft is allowed to send a maximum of five messages per 15 seconds of time.

11.7 Experimental Studies in Air-traffic Control

We conducted a series of rudimentary experimental studies on the four policies outlined previously. We focus here on results pertaining to the three task-centralization policies; our studies on the task-sharing policy were performed later and were limited in scope. The task-centralization variants were tested on eight distributed scenarios. Each scenario stipulated (1) how many aircraft would enter the airspace in the session; (2) when and where they would enter; and (3) where they would exit. This control over the parameters of distributed problem-solving situations allowed us to isolate situation features that uncovered the strengths and weaknesses of our policies in performance. We varied the scenarios considerably in task density, time stress, and task difficulty. The primary factor affecting these conditions was the number of aircraft in simultaneous conflict.

We examined three performance indices when comparing the systems: communication load, processing time, and task effectiveness. Task effectiveness was indicated by two distinct factors: separation errors (more important) and fuel usage (less important). A summary of the main results is given in Table 11.1.

We found that the *shared-convention* policy, relying on essentially arbitrary assignment of planning responsibility, performed well only in low-complexity, low-difficulty tasks. It minimized communications and response times compared with the other policies, but it quickly foundered in three- and four-body conflicts.

Of the three task-centralization strategies, the *least constrained* policy performed best. It did particularly well on high-complexity, high-difficulty tasks. In such cases, the planning aircraft tended to be located at the edge of the fray, able to find more viable solutions than the aircraft in the interior. The policy is time- and communication-intensive, however, largely because of the high number of messages needed to determine the replanner cooperatively and to maintain consistency after replanning. In any of the three task-centralization systems, when a replanner is successful it must send *data retransmission messages* to all aircraft to which it had previously sent its intentions. The number of data retransmissions was especially high under the *least constrained* policy.

The *most knowledgeable* policy was intermediate in performance. It performed best in tasks of low complexity and high difficulty, that is, tasks with primarily two- and three-body interactions and few potential solutions. In complex multiaircraft situations, when the wrong aircraft was chosen for planning, the result was often catastrophic because the aircraft that then received replan requests tended to have little knowledge of the routes of other aircraft. By design of the policy, this knowl-

TABLE 11.1 Performance Measures of Three Organizational Policies (statistics averaged across eight scenarios).

Item	*Shared convention*	*Least constrained*	*Most knowledgeable*
Communication load[1]	10.9	28.6	28.2
Processing time[2]	1265	1726	1651
Separation errors[3]	4.3	1.4	2.3
Fuel usage[4]	96	108	101

[1]Mean messages sent per aircraft while flying from infix to outfix.

[2]Mean Xerox 1100 cpu seconds per aircraft while flying.

[3]Mean number of near misses or collisions for all aircraft in a scenario.

[4]Mean number of fuel units used for all aircraft.

edge was typically concentrated in the initially selected planner. That planner normally continued to be the most knowledgeable in later interactions.

When successful, the *most knowledgeable* policy's performance was in some ways better than that of the *least constrained* policy. In particular, when an agent found a solution to a local conflict task under the *most knowledgeable* policy, that solution was likely to be more globally coherent than solutions found under other policies, since the replanning agent was selected partially because of its wide knowledge of the plans of the other aircraft. This knowledge allowed it to replan more effectively without incurring new conflicts. In addition, a successful replanning agent generally needed to issue fewer data retransmission messages under a *most knowledgeable* policy than under the other policies, since it was selected partially because its intentions were known to fewer others (i.e., it was the least committed agent).

We had initially anticipated that minimizing data retransmissions would be very important for guaranteeing globally coherent performance. We envisioned situations in which one retransmission would cause the receiving agent to reevaluate, possibly finding new conflicts, causing more replanning, further data retransmissions, and so on, in a vicious propagation of changes. This did not happen as often as we had expected under the *least constrained* policy, although a few instances were observed.

Another erroneous expectation was that there would be a wide variation in processing times among the aircraft under the *most knowledgeable* policy. This policy should tend to bias replanning in favor of a few agents. If an agent is the replanner once, it gains new knowledge of others' plans, making it an even better choice as replanner for later conflict tasks. We anticipated that this concentration would skew the processing times, compared to a more uniform distribution of responsibilities under the other policies. This would have been a disadvantage in a truly distributed system, as some agents would be quiescent much of the time. The expected variation in times did not exhibit itself, however, except in the relatively easy scenarios.

Although limited in scope, the data collected from our fourth policy, *task sharing*, indicated some interesting trends. This policy, a composite of the best of the *least constrained* and *most knowledgeable* policies, had the advantage of choosing one agent to act, and another with more knowledge of the situation to compute the first agent's plan. This policy was often effective when subtasks are easily separable and an explicit selection of the agent with the best available expertise could be made for each subtask individually, rather than for the conflict task as a whole.

11.8 Remotely Piloted Vehicle Fleet Control

We next moved to a richer and more difficult domain: surveillance RPV (remotely piloted vehicle) fleet control. Coordination of groups of military RPVs is a much more demanding application of distributed problem solving than is air-traffic control because of unreliable communications, distinct roles for each aircraft, needs for coordinated actions, and frequent attrition from the hostile environment. In this section, we describe a new RPV fleet-control implementation that embodies many of these problem aspects. We discuss some of our preliminary findings relating to role assignment, data fusion, communication management, and cooperative planning.

11.8.1 ■ Tasks in RPV Fleet Coordination

One of the principal goals of RPV development today is to realize greater vehicle autonomy. Current RPV technology—represented by Israel's Mastiff (Smith, 1983) and the Lockheed Acquila (Hyman, 1981)—relies on the use of close in-the-loop control by skilled remote human operators. Each operator controls a single RPV through a continuous and vulnerable communication link. Operations during radio silence or jamming are usually confined to a few preprogrammed actions (such as spiraling up to regain contact, continuing on the same path, and self-destructing). The few attempts at multiple RPV control, such as IBM's large-scale experimental system (Gray et al., 1982), have relied entirely on a vulnerable centralized airborne or ground center to perform all control operations. We hope to extend this technology by developing techniques for onboard autonomous or semi-autonomous planning and control. Such capabilities should provide enhanced performance using only local communication and computation, including:

- *Autonomous patterned flight.* In many surveillance tasks, the RPVs must fly in formation to ensure complete coverage, maintain interaircraft distance, or present minimal radar return. This involves negotiating over task responsibilities, establishing communication protocols among the group members, and defining procedures for transitions between formations or flight patterns in response to threats.
- *Data fusion among vehicles.* The different RPVs may be responsible for different portions of the intelligence-gathering process. This

requires some means of representing hypotheses and confidence estimates, integrating new data, and deciding what information to send to others. Like Hearsay-II (Erman et al., 1981), the on-board systems will have to access multiple knowledge sources and maintain multiple lines of reasoning.

- *Cooperative planning and replanning.* The RPV fleet must react to contacts, altering the group's flight path to locate defenses and targets. The fleet members must also avoid dangerous terrain and weather and respond to threats. Such dynamic planning may be performed in a centralized manner by one member of the group (a leader), or it may be done by multiple group members, acting asynchronously and cooperatively. In either case, the planning will require the generation of maneuver options, simulation of the resulting trajectories (using any available data), and evaluation of the projected partial solutions (Stefik et al., 1983).
- *Reconstitution after losses.* When RPVs are shot down or otherwise lost, the surviving vehicles must close ranks and determine new roles. Also, the vehicles must frequently reconstitute communication networks disrupted by jamming, noise, or damage. This requires polling group members, determining connection tables and capabilities, computing effective communication routings, and specifying new task assignments.

We produced a series of demonstration systems, described in the following subsections, that exhibited many of these capabilities. We did not pursue formal experiments with these systems, but we did examine many implementation options. In terms of the vocabulary introduced in Section 11.2, the main distributed problem-solving tasks were formation keeping, data fusion, and communications management. Conflict avoidance, the central task of ATC, was not of major importance here.

11.8.2 ■ Initial RPV Demonstration System: Patterned Flight

We began our series of demonstration systems with the simplest problem: patterned flight over a benign environment. As shown in Fig. 11.5, this simulation involves three aircraft flying over a region without hostile defenses. The aircraft change coverage pattern (racetrack or figure eight), formation geometry (wave, vee, or stream), and spacing (close or wide) in response to command input. The coordination process involves several steps. The aircraft first determine if a change in leadership is necessary, and if so, they select a new leader by using a negotiation procedure much like that in our ATC implementation.

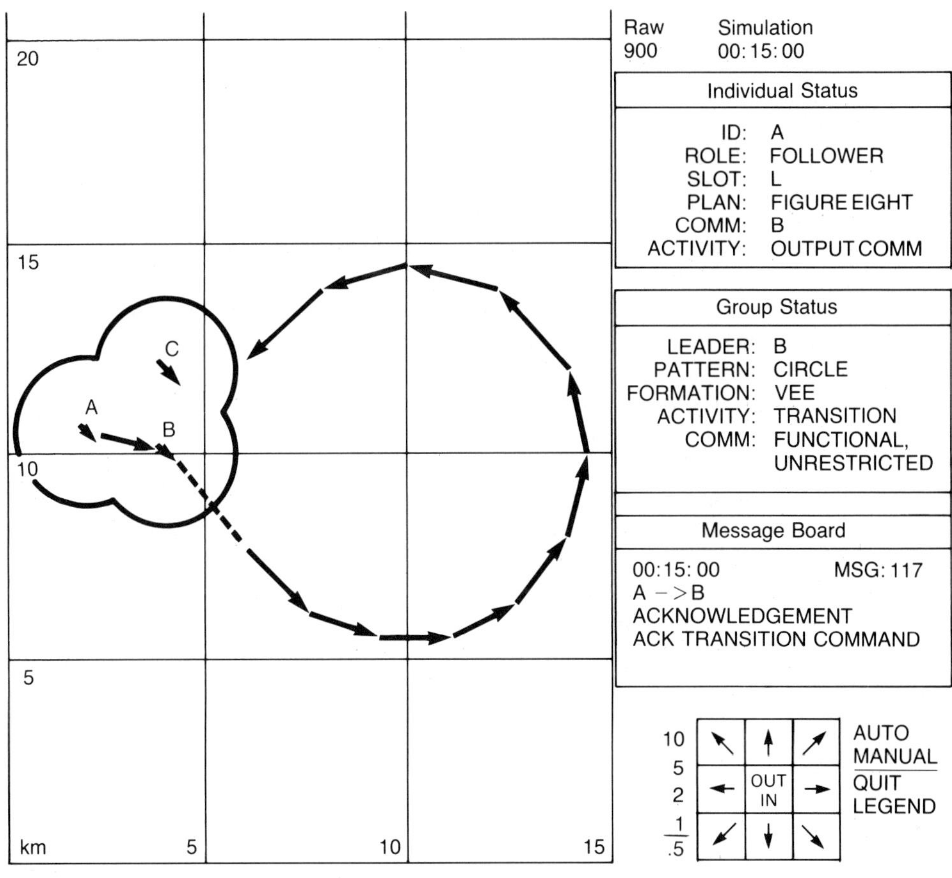

FIGURE 11.5 Initial Simulation of Surveillance RPV Coordination.

Coordination is achieved by having the lead aircraft determine its own trajectory and then send messages detailing its course and desired spacing to the other aircraft, who plan collision-free, minimum-time paths to match up with the leader. All messages in this initial system are error-free and have a free format structure. A typical message might be:

Message #112
sender: RPV1
recipient: RPV3
content: vee formation, wide spacing
type: point-to-point
time-stamp: 0400

The actual process of formation keeping can be accomplished in two ways: by maintaining a physical relationship with respect to the leader, or by following a trajectory that should maintain group spacing. The first method requires frequent sensing or communication of the leader position and execution of error-correcting responses. This tracking approach is appropriate if sensing and communication are reliable, course changes are frequent, or onboard navigation is difficult. The second option, relying on accurate trajectory following, should require only occasional updates of the leader position for confirmation of group spacing. In fact, if the aircraft can plan and follow their own path trajectories, they should be able to split off the group in response to threats or opportunities and rejoin later. This technique appears most appropriate in wide formations with few course changes or in situations with frequent threats and jamming. We implemented a combination of the two approaches in an object-oriented simulation. (The characteristics of the simulation are described in Section 11.8.5.) The follower RPVs used sensing and adjustment when possible, but maintained their own trajectory plans.

Overall, this first demonstration system exhibited a rudimentary level of distribution. The several RPVs negotiated over roles, and each planned its own trajectory. We focused on leader-based behavior (in which the follower aircraft reacted to the leader's commands and keyed on its position) because this structure provided the simplest and most direct interactions. The alternative, an anarchic structure in which each aircraft can command any other, adds many complications, including deadlock and looping. In our scheme, a single leader was present, and leadership changed from aircraft to aircraft according to the circumstances. The leader assumed the bulk of planning responsibility, receiving information from and sending commands to the other aircraft. Each of our succeeding implementations relaxed the degree of centralization.

11.8.3 ■ Second Demonstration System: Uncertainty Representation

We next expanded the system to explore the problems of unreliable sensing and communication. As shown in Fig. 11.6, the aircraft fly over an environment with active defenses—command centers, ground control intercept (GCI) radar installations, and surface-to-air missile (SAM) sites. When necessary, the RPVs poll each other regarding status, sensing capabilities, and communication links. Each vehicle builds up its own uncertain model of the environment and fleet status, taking into account confidence degradations due to inaccurate sensing, communi-

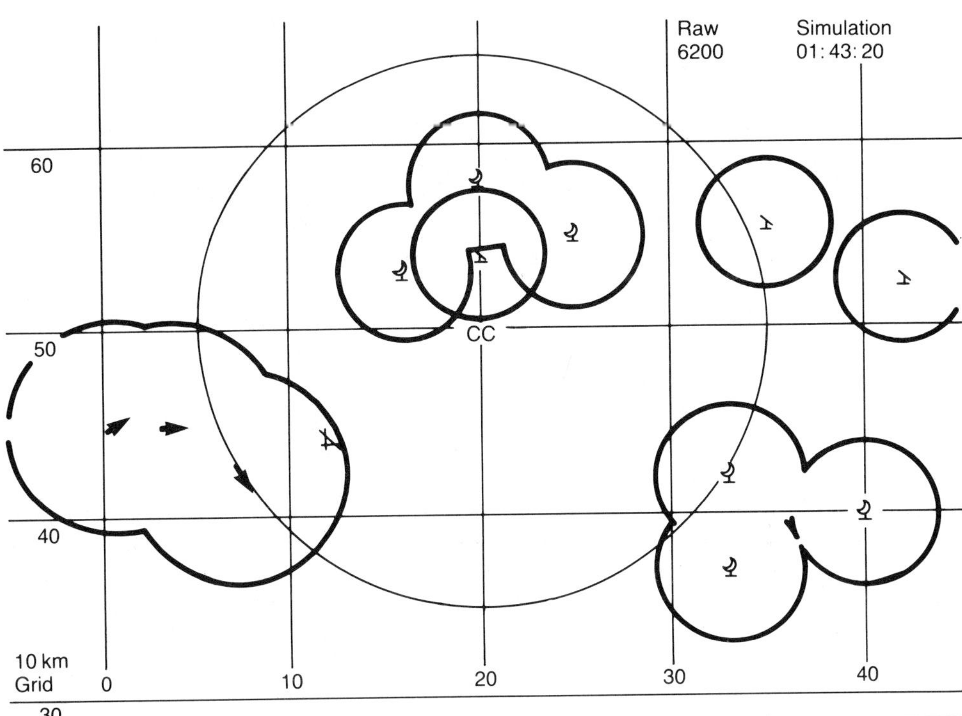

Individual Status	Group Status	Message Board
ID: ROLE: SLOT: PLAN: COMM: ACTIVITY:	LEADER: (RPV3) PATTERN: CIRCULAR FORMATION: STREAM	

FIGURE 11.6 Second Implementation of Surveillance RPV Task Simulation, with Active Defenses.

cation noise, and incorrect intelligence. Database entries for defenses take the form of property lists with confidence factors, such as:

```
GCI site #4
    location: (45,34)
    status: active
    jammed: no
    confidence factor: 0.8
```

We used the uncertainty representation form of MYCIN (Shortliffe, 1976) to update each RPV's estimates of belief and disbelief in hypotheses about the defenses. This approach does not require the many prior and posterior probability estimates required by Bayesian analysis (Duda et al., 1979) or the many range estimates demanded by the Dempster-Shafer calculus (Garvey et al., 1981) or INFERNO (Quinlan, 1982). Although the MYCIN approach has many limitations, primarily with respect to independence assumptions, we felt that the simplicity of form and ease of rule writing outweighed the possible errors. Such errors should be of minor significance in these early demonstration systems because of the low frequency of updating and the coarseness of the behavioral responses.

The dynamics required for simulating sensing and detection are relatively straightforward. As shown in Fig. 11.6, the SAM and GCI sites have circular regions in which they can detect RPVs, and the RPVs have somewhat larger regions of defense sensing (they can passively sense radar emissions and therefore do not require a long reflection path). Sensing and detection in these regions are probabilistic, representing the effects of terrain, weather, ECM, and other factors. Updating is a sequential process—confidence in a hypothesis should increase if further contacts are made.

We introduced these effects in the simulation by adding false defenses, incorporating probabilistic sampling in the sensing/detection process, and corrupting some percentage of the communication messages. Figure 11.7 shows the sequence of events possible at each simulation update.

The sensing/detection cycle works in the following manner. At the beginning of an update, the system checks to see if any real or false defenses are within an RPV's sensing range. If a defense is within range, it has a $P1$ likelihood of being real, and if real, a $P2$ likelihood of being sensed. False objects have a $P3$ chance of being sensed. If an RPV does sense a defense, the likelihood of that defense being real is

$$(P1 * P2) / ((P1 * P2) + ((1 - P1) * P3)) \quad [1]$$

The next layer in the event tree assumes the RPV is within detection range of a defensive site. If within range, the RPV believes it has a $P4$ probability of being detected. A randomization process uses the same $P4$ probability to send a message to the defense, if so indicated.

When an RPV senses a defense, it incorporates that information into its world-model. The sensing itself results in a measure of belief (MB) equal to the probability in Eq. [1]. The RPV checks to see if it already has an entry for the sensed defense type and location. If not, the RPV enters the MB directly into its database and sets the confi-

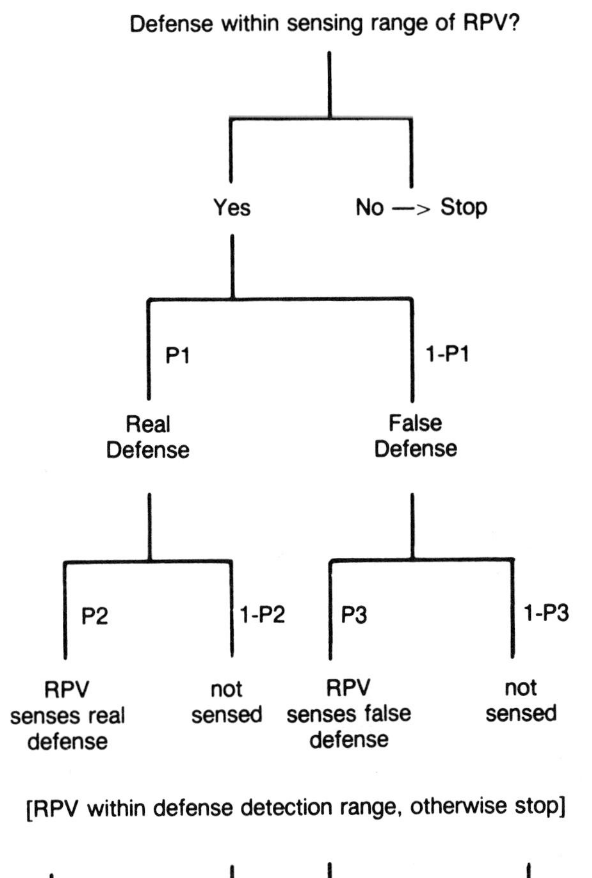

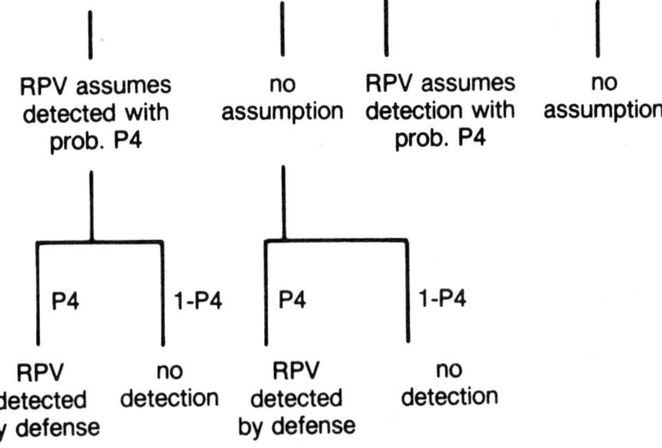

FIGURE 11.7 Event Tree for Sensing and Detection.

dence factor (CF) equal to it. If such an entry already exists, the RPV revises the measure of belief according to the following rule:

$$MB = MB1 + ((1 - MB1) * MB2) \qquad [2]$$

where MB1 is the original entry and MB2 results from the current sensing.

There also may be disbelief present, represented as MD. The confidence factor CF equals the difference between MB and MD. An MD can arise if a previously sensed defense is not again sensed (this indicates that the original contact may have been false). If this occurs, the probability of the defense being false is roughly

$$MD = (1 - P1) / ((1 - P1) + (P1 * (1 - P2))) \qquad [3]$$

Communications further add to the uncertainty present by introducing a noise factor. The receiving RPV adjusts the original data confidence by the probability of message corruption and updates its database entry in the same manner as in sensing.

With the introduction of degraded communications and unreliable sensing, we found that the role-negotiation process became more complex and the maneuver choices more important. The criteria used during leader negotiation expanded to include task knowledge (environment data and plans of others), current role, sensing region, communication-link strengths, and physical position. The RPVs also used these criteria to negotiate over data-fusion tasks—specifically, responsibility for GCIs and SAMs, command centers, and airfields.

The many formation, pattern, and spacing choices open to the group also had much more influence on task performance in this scenario than they did in the earlier perfect sensing and communication scenarios. For example, the wave formation with wide spacing provides the greatest coverage area but is most vulnerable to detection. The vee formation gives the shortest overall communication links but results in some penalty in coverage. The stream formation provides minimal radar return and easy following of the leader and, because of its narrow sensing area, is effective only for avoidance and strong secondary sensing confirmation. The following two rules illustrate some of the formation changes invoked by the leader in response to environmental conditions:

If group is in stream or vee formation, and 20 seconds have passed without a contact or threat, change to wide wave formation.

If group is in wave or vee formation, and leader senses a SAM site with CF > 0.5, designate follower on opposite side to defense as leader and change to stream formation (this way the group may vector around the defense).

We also found that as the distributed problem-solving task became more complex, it became necessary to prioritize the functions of sensing, communication, planning, and control. We implemented a scheme similar to that developed in our ATC work. The following list shows the nomimal ordering of activities:

1. Input user message;
2. Input command message;
3. Plan trajectory in response to leader command;
4. Execute action (if follower);
5. Perform sensing;
6. Input data message;
7. Announce leader;
8. Input role-negotiation message;
9. Send role-negotiation message;
10. Plan formation change;
11. Send commands;
12. Send acknowledgment; and
13. Input acknowledgment.

We attempted with this ordering to perform all information gathering activities prior to planning. In this way, the time-consuming leader planning operation would be assured of up-to-date information.

11.8.4 ■ Third Demonstration System: General Surveillance

Our final implementation represented a general surveillance task in a hostile environment, with the RPVs avoiding defenses, sustaining losses, and regrouping. Here, communications are highly constrained because of the likelihood of detection and loss. The primary problems we encountered involve communication management, the user interface, and forms of logical inference.

One question that arises in communications management is information volunteering vs. information demanding. We examined these two options in the context of leader negotiation and communication-table updating. Information volunteering (in which the sender transmits data it expects the recipient needs) appears to result in fewer transmissions than does a demand protocol, provided the sender has an accurate model of the recipient's needs. A comparison of volunteer and demand messages for a role-negotiation interaction is summarized in Fig. 11.8. In this example, we assume N RPVs are present. The min-

	Messages
Demand:	
1. Follower encounters problem, messages leader;	(1)
2. Current leader sends messages to followers requesting role factors;	$(N - 1)$
3. Followers send role factors to leader;	$(N - 1)$
4. Leader compares responses (unless incomplete) and sends messages announcing new leader.	$(N - 1)$
Total:	$3N - 2$
Volunteer:	
1. Follower encounters problem, messages others with own role factor;	$(N - 1)$
2. Other send role factors (except to initiator);	$(N)(N - 1) / 2$
3. First to have all role factors announces leader.	$(N - 1)$
Total:	$(N^2 + 3N - 4) / 2$

FIGURE 11.8 Comparison of Demand and Volunteer Protocols for Communication.

imum number of messages for each step is shown in parentheses at the right of the table. The demand form requires fewer messages (order N) than does the volunteer form (order N^2), but tends to be time consuming (at least one extra stage) and vulnerable to loss of the central agent.

Communications management problems also appeared when we changed from three to five RPVs. In a larger fleet, the aircraft frequently do not have a direct transmission path to other aircraft. They have to route messages by the most-direct and least-loaded path, much like a packet radio system (Kahn et al., 1978). We considered three methods of routing: communication tables, route set-up packets, and spreading activation. Communication tables are built up by each RPV by listing which aircraft can communicate with which others. This requires the RPVs to indicate any changes in their links when they send a message, and to update their tables when they receive such an indication. The second method uses route set-up packets, special short-length messages sent prior to a multihop communication. When acknowledged, they provide a means for comparing the speed and noise of each possible path, but they tend to burden the channel. The third method, spreading activation, means that copies of a multihop message are sent along each possible pathway. This increases redundancy, virtually assures receipt, and requires no table-management overhead, but it can severely tax the channel capacity. We chose the communication table method in our work because of the limited number of available agents and the high costs of communication.

11.8.5 ■ RPV Fleet-control Implementation

We implemented the RPV simulation routines, the planning and problem-solving procedures, and some of the graphics facilities for the three demonstration systems in ROSS, an object-oriented programming language developed at Rand and written in Franz Lisp (McArthur and Klahr, 1982). Programs written in object-oriented languages consist of a set of objects that interact with each other via the transmission of messages. Each object has a set of attributes describing itself and a set of message templates and associated behaviors. A behavior is invoked when an object receives a message that matches the corresponding message template. A behavior is itself typically a set of message transmissions to other actors. In this fashion, ROSS and other object-oriented programming languages enforce a *message-passing* style of programming.

The ROSS programming style is well suited to simulation in domains that consist of autonomous interacting objects. The style aids the understanding and modeling of distributed problem-solving systems because objects can control their own activities through individual behaviors and maintain their own models of the world via their local databases. For example, data about sensed defenses are represented in the vehicle's database, and reactions to the defenses result from behaviors triggered by the receipt of messages. Our distributed fleet-control implementation can be thought of as consisting of three distinct types of processing: behaviors for simulating the scenario, behaviors for cooperative planning and control by the RPVs, and graphics behaviors for user display and interaction.

The simulation behaviors define aspects of the scenario and capabilities of the objects. Among these behaviors are defining trajectories, specifying time increments, calling randomization programs, sensing objects, and communicating messages. Special objects were defined for some of these functions. These processes were considered operational requirements rather than problem-solving activities.

The second type of processing consists of behaviors for distributed planning, coordination, and problem solving. Most of the activities described in the three demonstration sections fall into this category. Reasoning about role assignments, making decisions about coverage pattern, formation geometry, and vehicle spacing, and performing trajectory planning are included. Here we show the English and ROSS versions of a behavior for avoiding a sensed defense:

```
If the group is in a stream formation, and the leader estimates
its probability of detection by a SAM is greater than .6, then
change to another coverage pattern.
(if    (and
       (eq (~your formation) 'stream)
       (~you are leader))
       (greaterp (~your probability-of-detection of
                  (~your sensed >SAM)) .6)
then
       (~you change coverage-pattern))
```

This example only hints at the fact that code in a ROSS simulation can be highly intelligible, modular, and modifiable. Most of the actions in the RPV simulation can be viewed as responses to messages and therefore are expressed naturally in this paradigm.

The graphics environment for our demonstration systems was programmed in a combination ROSS and C-based subsystem. Communication with the simulation objects was performed in ROSS, and device-dependent operations were implemented in C. The graphics subsystem was responsible for displaying task conditions, individual aircraft views, and rule firings. We found that these graphics capabilities, which are substantially more involved than those used in our ATC work, highlighted the user-interface problems of portraying concurrent activities in a distributed system.

In some ways, the situation dynamics that had to be portrayed were more similar to those of a Time Warp mechanism (Jefferson and Sowizral, 1982) than to those of a conventional distributed simulation, in which all objects step forward at the same rate. Each RPV tries to plan its route for some distance into the future, and it is often at a different look-ahead time than its cohorts. If an RPV receives a message describing another RPV's plan, it checks for conflicts or constraints and, if necessary, backtracks to an earlier simulation time and replans. (This goes beyond Time Warps, as some actions are not virtual and cannot be rescinded.) The RPV then sends messages of its new plan to other affected RPVs. Tracking down chains of interactions can thus be quite involved. The user, who is already one frame behind in the animation, must trace backward and forward through all pertinent messages and resulting actions until the root cause is located.

The problem of simulating the maintenance and coordination of several independent databases also led us to consider implementing some of the functions using logic programming forms (specifically,

Prolog). Prolog can be particularly effective for database management because it unifies the notions of data, rules, and queries (Kowalski, 1979). It derives answers to queries, using a very efficient inference procedure, and its basis in logic suggests its application for such inferential tasks as constraint satisfaction and data fusion.

Prolog clauses are of the form "*A* if *B*1 and *B*2 and ... *Bk*", where each of *A*, *B1* ... *Bk* are conditions. The rule has an IF-THEN reading. If the right-side of a rule is empty, *A* may be regarded as unconditionally true and hence as a piece of data. Thus, if RPV1 has the following current state:

```
position        (30.0 40.0)
leader          rpv2
velocity        (600.0 0.0)
detected__by    radar1
```

RPV1 may represent this information by the following set of unconditional clauses:

```
position(rpv1,[30.0,40.0]) if ( )
leader(rpv1,rpv3) if ( )
velocity(rpv1,[600.0,0.0]) if ( )
detected__by(rpv1,radar1) if ( )
```

and RPV1 may use the same representation to express what it knows about its leader (RPV3):

```
position(rpv3,[20.0,25.0]) if ( )
velocity(rpv3,[550.0,100.0]) if ( )
detected__by(rpv3, radar3) if ( )
```

Rules are then easily added. If RPV1 is always constrained to keep a distance greater than 15 units from another RPV, it would have a rule of the following form:

```
properly__spaced(Vehicle1,Vehicle2)<-position(Vehicle1,P1) and
                        position(Vehicle2,P2) and
                        distance(P1,P2,D) and
                        D>15.
```

If RPV1 wants to determine whether it is properly spaced with respect to its leader, it would execute the query,

```
leader(rpv1,L) and properlyspaced(rpv1,L).
```

In this case, it will execute successfully, since the distance between RPV1 and RPV3 is approximately 18.

Prolog's inferencing capabilities are expected to be useful for such query answering, for verifying consequences of actions, and for reducing communications. Consequence verification may be performed by checking whether each consequence (desirable or undesirable) is logically implied by its present model of the world and the contemplated action. Communications may be reduced in a similar way. An RPV would attempt to infer whether another RPV knows a certain piece of information before transmitting it. Conversely, an RPV would attempt to infer a piece of information from its own database before explicitly querying another RPV.

The advantage of using Prolog for database management (and, more generally, for inferencing) instead of LISP is that Prolog provides a simple, unified framework for representing data, rules, and inferencing. We implemented a Prolog based in LISP, so that the Prolog programs could easily interface with our existing programs. We found that the existence of logic programming primitives in the ROSS system will considerably increase ROSS's expressive power.

11.9 Conclusions and Future Work

Our approach to distributed problem solving is primarily an empirical one in which we use several forms of simulation to explore key aspects of agent interaction—task negotiation, communication management, cooperative planning, and reorganization. Our initial work in air-traffic control, for example, showed the importance of being able to interrupt, suspend, and resume activities within each agent. The ATC work also points out the sensitivity of system behavior and performance to changes in organization and information-distribution policies, particularly with respect to leadership decisions. Our subsequent simulation of surveillance RPV fleet control demonstrates the effectiveness of object-oriented programming for simulating and displaying behaviors of multiple interacting objects with common goals. The system was able to illustrate the flow of data and the evolution of responsibility as conditions changed. The system also lent itself well to the problem of local uncertainty representation in a highly probabilistic environment, and we were able to augment the ROSS object-oriented system with activity prioritization and logical-inference functions.

The ATC and RPV work concentrated on functions that involve cooperation among *autonomous* vehicles, principally collision avoidance, patterned flight, and surveillance of a hostile environment. We plan to extend these functions in the near future to involve *shared con-*

trol, in which a human operator acts in a supervisory role or takes over direct control of one of the aircraft. We also plan to widen the scope of actions to include defense suppression, decoy operations, special attack maneuvers, and damage assessment. Invoking these added options, the RPV fleet would make frequent transitions between organizational forms, altering its communication networks and "regrowing" connections that follow each operational phase. Protocols for such transitions are expected to be much more complex than those developed for the basic functions of formation keeping, data fusion, and avoidance responses.

Another major goal is to demonstrate a fully distributed system in which the agents take actions in a heterarchic, asynchronous fashion. Such a cooperative structure might involve frequent negotiation over tasks, burst communications when possible to minimize database disparities, and plan backtracking in response to commands and constraints sent by the other group members. We expect that such a heterarchical organization will primarily be useful in situations of extreme duress—radio silence, heavy jamming, and high attrition. Our next step will be to modify the simulation to examine the performance of such an organization.

One of our more pervasive problems is that of the user interface in a distributed system—producing a window on the workings of the many separate agents. We noted that certain displays appeared to be essential: textual displays of activities being performed by each agent, graphic displays of situation assessments (with interaircraft disparities highlighted), and animated graphic displays that show how each aircraft's plans and assumptions play out over time and space. At the same time, the user needs the control over such conventional functions as pan, zoom, time stepping, and level of detail. Development of an appropriate user environment for observing or participating in the distributed problem-solving process should occupy researchers well after the mechanics of interagent communication and planning are solved.

References

1. Appelt, D. E., *Planning Natural-Language Utterances to Satisfy Multiple Goals,* Technical Note 259, SRI International, 1982.
2. Dalkey, N. C., *Group Decision Making,* Report UCLA-ENG-7749, School of Applied Science, University of California, Los Angeles, July 1977.

3. Davis, R., "A Model for Planning in a Multi-agent Environment: Steps Toward Principles for Teamwork," Working Paper, MIT Artificial Intelligence Laboratory, Cambridge, 1981.

4. Davis, R. and R. G. Smith, *Negotiation as a Metaphor for Distributed Problem Solving*, Memo 624, MIT Artificial Intelligence Laboratory, Cambridge, 1981.

5. Duda, R. O., J. G. Gaschnig, and P. E. Hart, "Model Design in the PROSPECTOR Consultant System for Mineral Exploration," in *Expert Systems in the Micro-electronic Age* (D. Michie, ed.), Edinburgh University Press, Edinburgh, 1979, pp. 153–167.

6. Erman, L. D., P. E. London, and S. F. Fikas, "The Design and an Example Use of HEARSAY-III," *IJCAI*, Vol. 7, 1981, pp. 409–415.

7. Fahlman, S., "A Planning System for Robot Construction Tasks," *Artificial Intelligence*, 5(1), 1974, pp. 1–49.

8. Fikes, R. E., and N. J. Nilsson, "Strips: A New Approach to the Application of Theorem Proving to Problem Solving," *Artificial Intelligence*, 2(2), 1971, pp. 189–208.

9. Forgy, C. L., *The OPS5 Users Manual*, Technical Report, CMU-CS-79-132, Computer Science Dept., Carnegie-Mellon University, Pittsburgh, 1981.

10. Garvey, T., J. Lowrance, and M. Fischler, "An Inference Technique for Integrating Knowledge from Disparate Sources," *IJCAI*, Vol. 7, 1981, pp. 319–325.

11. Goldberg, A., and A. Kay, *Smalltalk-72 Instruction Manual*, Report SSL 76-6, Xerox PARC, Palo Alto, 1976.

12. Gray, C. M., K. D. Rehm, and D. R. Woods, "The Drone Formation Control System," *Military Science*, 1982, pp. 11–26.

13. Hyman, A., "Where are the RPVs?" *Aerospace International*, 17(3), July–August 1981, pp. 40–44.

14. Jefferson, D., and H. Sowizral, *Fast Concurrent Simulation Using the Time Warp Mechanism, Part I: Local Control*, The Rand Corporation, N-1906-AF, December 1982.

15. Kahn, R., S. Gronemeyer, J. Burchfiel, and R. Kunzelman, "Advances in Packet Radio Technology," *Proceedings of the IEEE*, 66(11), November 1978, pp. 1468–1496.

16. Konolige, K., "A First Order Formalization of Knowledge and Action for a Multi-agent Planning System," *Machine Intelligence 10*, 1981.

17. Kowalski, R., "Algorithm =Logic + Control," *Communications of the ACM*, 22(7), July 1979.

18. Kunz, J. C., R. J. Fallat, D. H. McClung, J. J. Osborne, R. A. Votteri, H. P. Nii, J. S. Aikins, L. M. Fagan, and E. A. Feigenbaum, *A Physiological Rule-based System for Interpreting Pulmonary Function Test Results*, Report HPP-78-19, Heuristic Programming Project, Computer Science Dept., Stanford University, 1978.

19. Lesser, V. R., S. Reed, and J. Pavlin, "Quantifying and Simulating the Behavior of Knowledge-based Interpretation Systems," *Proceedings of the First Annual National Conference on Artificial Intelligence*, Stanford University, 1980, pp. 111–115.

20. Lesser, V., *A High-level Simulation Testbed for Cooperative Problem Solving*, COINS Technical Report 81-16, University of Massachusetts, Amherst, 1981.

21. McArthur, D. A., and P. Klahr, *The ROSS Language Manual*, The Rand Corporation, N-1854-AF, September 1982.

22. McArthur, D. A., R. Steeb, and S. Cammarata, "A Framework for Distributed Problem Solving," *Proceedings of the National Conference on Artificial Intelligence*, Pittsburgh, 1982, pp. 181–184.

23. Newell, A., and H. Simon, "GPS—A Program that Simulates Human Thought," in *Computers and Thought* (E. Feigenbaum and J. Feldman, eds.), McGraw-Hill, New York, 1963.

24. Newell, A., and H. Simon, *Human Problem Solving*, Prentice-Hall, New York, 1972.

25. Nii, H. P., and N. Aiello, "AGE (Attempt to Generalize): A Knowledge-based Program for Building Knowledge-based Programs," *IJCAI*, Vol. 6, 1979, pp. 645–655.

26. Quinlan, R., *INFERNO: A Cautious Approach to Uncertain Inference*, The Rand Corporation, N-1898-RC, September 1982.

27. Sacerdoti, E., "Planning in a Hierarchy of Abstraction Spaces," *Artificial Intelligence*, 5(2), 1974, pp. 115–135.

28. Sacerdoti, E., *A Structure for Plans and Behavior*, Elsevier North-Holland, New York, 1977.

29. Shortliffe, E. H., *Computer-based Medical Consultation: MYCIN*, American Elsevier, New York, 1976.

30. Smith, B. A., "Israeli Use Bolsters Interest in Mini-RPVs," *Aviation Week and Space Technology*, July 18, 1983, pp. 67–71.

31. Smith, R. G., *A Framework for Problem Solving in a Distributed*

Processing Environment, STAN-CS-78-700, Stanford University, 1978.

32. Steeb, R., S. Cammarata, F. A. Hayes-Roth, P. W. Thorndyke, and R. B. Wesson, *Distributed Intelligence for Air Fleet Control*, The Rand Corporation, R-2728-ARPA, 1981.
33. Stefik, M., " Planning with Constraints (MOLGEN: Part 2)," *Artificial Intelligence*, Vol. 16, 1981, pp. 141–169.
34. Stefik, M., J. Aikins, R. Balzer, J. Benoit, L. Birnbaum, F. Hayes-Roth, and E. Sacerdoti, "The Architecture of Expert Systems," in *Building Expert Systems* (F. Hayes-Roth, D. Waterman, and D. Lenat, eds.), Addison-Wesley, Reading, Pa., 1983.
35. Sussman, G., *A Computational Model of Skill Acquisition*, American Elsevier, New York, 1975.
36. van Melle, W., "A Domain-independent Production-rule System for Consultation Programs," *IJCAI*, Vol. 6, 1979, pp. 923–925.

Index

Selected Rand Books

Aumann, R. J., and L. S. Shapley. *Values of Non-Atomic Games,* Princeton, N.J.: Princeton University Press, 1974.

Bagdikian, B. H. *The Information Machines: Their Impact on Men and the Media,* New York: Harper & Row, 1971.

Bellman, R. *Adaptive Control Processes: A Guided Tour,* Princeton, N.J.: Princeton University Press, 1962.

Bellman, R. E. *Dynamic Programming,* Princeton, N.J.: Princeton University Press, 1957.

Bellman, R., and S. E. Dreyfus. *Applied Dynamic Programming,* Princeton, N.J.: Princeton University Press, 1962.

Brelsford, W. M., and D. A. Relles. *STATLIB: A Statistical Computing Library,* Englewood Cliffs, N.J.: Prentice-Hall, Inc., 1981.

Dantzig, G. B. *Linear Programming and Extensions,* Princeton, N.J.: Princeton University Press, 1963.

Dresher, M. *The Mathematics of Games of Strategy: Theory and Applications,* New York: Dover Publications, Inc., 1981. Original edition, entitled *Games of Strategy: Theory and Application,* published by Prentice-Hall, Inc. in 1961.

Dreyfus, S. E. *Dynamic Programming and the Calculus of Variations,* New York: Academic Press, 1965.

Ford, L. R., Jr., and D. R. Fulkerson. *Flows in Networks,* Princeton, N.J.: Princeton University Press, 1962.

Glaseman, S. *Comparative Studies in Software Acquisition,* Lexington, Mass.: Lexington Books, D.C. Heath and Company, 1982.

Gruenberger, F. and G. Jaffray. *Problems for Computer Solution,* New York: John Wiley & Sons, Inc., 1965.

Hastings, C., Jr. *Approximations for Digital Computers,* Princeton, N.J.: Princeton University Press, 1955.

Morris, C. N., and J. E. Rolph. *Introduction to Data Analysis and Statistical Inference.* Englewood Cliffs, N.J.: Prentice-Hall, Inc., 1981.

Sharpe, W. F. *The Economics of Computers,* New York: Columbia University Press, 1969.

Williams, J. D. *The Compleat Strategyst,* New York: Dover Publications, Inc., 1986. (Originally published by McGraw-Hill Book Company, Inc. in 1954.)